MANUAL FOR PRACTICAL EXAM PREPARATION

MANUAL FOR PRACTICAL EXAM PREPARATION

Pratik D. Patil MBBS

Intern at
Seth GS Medical College and KEM Hospital
Mumbai

Samarth A. Thakkar MBBS

Intern at
Seth GS Medical College and KEM Hospital
Mumbai

BHALANI PUBLISHING HOUSE

Mumbai | New Delhi | Pune

INDIA

Reprint : Aug. 2025, Feb. 2024, Jan. 2019
First Edition: 2018

ISBN 978 93 81496 45 9

Published by

Bhalani Publishing House

11 Mavawala Building

Opp. Seth G.S. Medical College & K.E.M. Hospital

Parel

Mumbai 400012

India

E-mail: publishing@bhalani.com

Web: www.bhalani.com

eBook: www.bhalanidigital.com

Printed and Bound in India

Dedicated to

Our parents and siblings

for their unconditional support and love

Preface

This book contains 4 sections - History Taking and General Examination, Medicine, Pediatrics and Surgery. Each section is a compilation of multiple clinics, lectures and books pertaining to practical cases as required for a final year MBBS student.

History taking includes systematic proforma covering common points of every subject. It further includes definitions, concepts, brownie points and FAQs. With experience, we have noticed that general examination is often abridged in most of the books. The fundamental concepts of general examination, which hold a key position in successfully clearing the practical examination, have been thoroughly discussed. A system based approach is followed in the Medicine section. Each system (CVS, GIT, RS, and CNS) is discussed in depth starting from specific points on general examination followed by a detailed proforma on systemic examination. Case based approach has not been adopted to ensure a holistic understanding of the system and not just case relevant content. In view of uniqueness of Pediatric History Taking and General Examination, special emphasis has been laid on topics such as Birth History, Developmental History, Dietary history and Anthropometry. Unlike Medicine and Pediatrics, a case based approach has been adopted for Surgery. Each topic is discussed under six headings: history, general examination, local examination, diagnosis, discussion, and management. Only additional points on history taking and general examination pertaining to that case have been mentioned. Local examination is discussed in depth. Discussion part contains basic concepts and details pertaining to that topic. Management part includes 'management protocol' for algorithmic understanding by the readers. Further management in depth has also been discussed here.

Best attempts have been made to simplify controversies and ensure that the text is up to date. Keeping in mind the ever changing literature, it is advised to be open to additional/alternate facts. Readers kindly note that this book is not a complete guide but is a manual that lays out all the essentials to help sail through exams. At the same time it covers brownie points required to ace the exams.

When to read the book: Prior clinical exposure and reading of standard books is a must before approaching this book. Thus it will help to consolidate concepts and organize data for quick revision. As a pre-final year student, one can use this book after clinics to obtain complete understanding of each topic. We strongly advice final year students to use this book in their preparatory leave in sync with case taking.

We welcome suggestions or advice from readers regarding the text. Please contact us.

Pratik D. Patil
Samarth A. Thakkar

mpepbook@gmail.com

Acknowledgements

If I have seen farther than others,
it is by standing upon the shoulders of giants

— Sir Isaac Newton

Our sincere thanks to the staff of Department of Medicine, Department of General Surgery, and Department of Pediatrics, Seth GS Medical College and KEM Hospital, Mumbai.

- We specially acknowledge the expert assistance and advice of Dr. Amrit Nasta, M.S. (General Surgery), D.N.B. (General Surgery), F.M.A.S. (MUHS), Fellowship in Bariatric Surgery (Belgium), presently at Wockhardt Hospital

- We also acknowledge the contribution by:
  - Dr. Saneya Pandrowala, M.S. (General Surgery), KEM Hospital
  - Dr. Smrati Bajpai, M.D. (Medicine), KEM Hospital
  - Dr. R. Anusha, M.D. (Pediatrics), KEM Hospital

- We appreciate the contribution of all our dear colleagues of Seth GSMC and KEMH for their constant support in early gestation of this book, in particular:
  - Dr. Yashendu Sarda (Intern, Seth GSMC and KEMH)
  - Dr. Tanmay Boob (Intern, Seth GSMC and KEMH)
  - Dr. Anwesh Chaudhari (Intern, Seth GSMC and KEMH)
  - Dr. Vaibhav Nagpal (Intern, Seth GSMC and KEMH)
  - Dr. Prarthna Shah (Intern, Seth GSMC and KEMH)
  - Dr. Devashree Sane (Intern, Seth GSMC and KEMH)

- We thank Miss. Charmie Shah, graphic designer, for her artistic help
- We thank Mr. Hemant S. Bhalani and his son Himanshu H. Bhalani (Bhalani Publishing House) for their full support and cooperation

Pratik D. Patil

Samarth A. Thakkar

Contents

Section I

HISTORY TAKING AND GENERAL EXAMINATION

History Taking includes systematic proforma covering common points of every subject. It further includes definitions, concepts, brownie points and FAQs.

General Examination Chapter begins with a systematic proforma. Each and every point in the proforma is laid out exhaustively ensuring no stone is left unturned. Remember general examination holds a key position in successfully clearing the practical examination.

1

History Taking

- Proforma: (go in the same order)
    1. Personal profile (PP)
    2. Chief complaints (CC)
    3. History of present illness (HOPI)
    4. Past history
    5. Personal history
    6. Family history
    7. Menstrual and obstetric history
    8. Summary of history with differential diagnosis and provisional diagnosis

- Personal profile: Name, age, sex, occupation, address, hailing from, religion, handedness (central nervous system case), informant (pediatric case), consanguinity (pediatric case)

❖ Name: Significance of knowing the name of patient:
1. Identification of patient
2. To build rapport
3. Indicates religion

❖ Age: According to individual case

❖ Sex:
- X-linked recessive (XLR): Color blindness, hemophilia, Duchenne and Becker muscular dystrophy, G6PD
- X-linked dominant (XLD): Vitamin D deficiency rickets (VDDR), familial hypophosphatemic rickets
- Females are more commonly affected by autoimmune diseases and thyroid disorders

❖ Occupation:
- Commercial sex worker (CSW): HIV, syphilis, sexually transmitted diseases

- Sedentary: Diabetes mellitus (DM), obesity, metabolic syndrome, deep vein thrombosis
- Farmer: Snake bite, injury, heatstroke, mycetoma
- Health care professionals: Blood borne diseases
- Veterinary, animal handlers: Zoonosis
- Dye industry workers: Aniline, benzene, naphthalene (bladder cancer)
- Factory workers: Asbestosis (mesothelioma) and other pneumoconiosis
- Painter, firework industry: Lead poisoning

❖ Religion:

- Parsi: Consanguineous marriages
- Muslim: Circumcision (only if done in childhood) leads to reduced rates of penile cancer
- Agarwal community: Hemoglobinopathies
- Gujarati, Sindhi, Lohia: Thalassemia

Autosomal recessive (AR)	Autosomal dominant (AD)
Thalassemia Sickle cell disease Cystic fibrosis Congenital adrenal hyperplasia Polycystic kidney disease (AR form) Phenylketonuria Wilson's disease Galactosemia Homocystinuria	Hereditary spherocytosis Polycystic kidney disease (AD form) Marfan's syndrome Ehler - Danlos syndrome Familial hypercholesterolemia

❖ Address/hailing from:

- South: Peptic ulcer, iodine deficiency (SOUTH > NORTH)
- West: Kidney stones
- East: Gall bladder diseases, Japanese encephalitis, kala-azar
- North: Iodine deficiency
- UP, Bihar: Kala-azar
- Vidarbha: Hemoglobinopathies
- Ratnagiri, Satpura, and Vindhya ranges: Iodine deficiency

- Chief complaints:

  (Mention these in chronological sequence. Also mention the time since onset of each complaint.)

  Say "patient presents with chief complaints of yellowish discoloration of sclera since 3 months and pain in abdomen since 5 days"

- HOPI:

  (Say "Patient was apparently asymptomatic since ___")

  (Some teachers accept the term "apparently alright")

  - ODP of chief complaints
  - On enquiry/positive history:
    1. Of symptoms
    2. Of etiology
    3. Of complications

    (Any positive/relevant history from past/personal history should be added here. For example, history of alcohol, smoking if etiologically significant.)
  - Negative history:
    1. Of symptoms
    2. Of etiology
    3. Of complications

    (Mention only relevant data)
  - Treatment history (significant procedures, e.g. ascitic tap)

- Past history: [Always ask these 5 points]
  - TB, TB contact (explained below)
  - Hypertension
  - DM
  - Asthma
  - Any medical or surgical history

- Personal history:
  - Bowel
  - Bladder
  - Sleep
  - Addiction: Smoking, alcohol, chewable tobacco
  - Appetite (include dietary history if relevant)

  - Known allergy
  - Travel history (if relevant)

- Family history:
  - Of similar illness
  - Multifactorial diseases like DM and hypertension which have familial predisposition should be enquired for in relevant cases

- Menstrual and obstetric history (to be taken in brief for ALL female patients)

- After a complete history, student should note down following points:
  - Summary
  - Differential diagnosis
  - Provisional diagnosis

  (Say these only when asked by examiner)

FAQs

❖ TB contact: Living within 4 walls with an active case of pulmonary TB for ≥6 hours/day for >2 weeks within last 2 years

❖ Constipation: Rome III criteria: ≥2 criteria present for ≥12 weeks with onset ≥6 months

1. <3 defecations/week
2. Straining for ≥25% of defecations
3. Sensation of incomplete evacuation for ≥25% of defecations
4. Digital evacuation for ≥25% of defecations

❖ Diarrhea:

WHO definition: ≥3 loose or liquid stools/day OR More stools than normal for that person (Consistency is more important than frequency)

❖ Alcohol:

1. Quality
2. Quantity
3. Duration
4. Dependency

- Quality:

  (in decreasing order of concentration)

  (10 g = 1 alcohol equivalent)

Type	Volume of it containing 10 g alcohol	Percentage
Vodka	25 ml	40%
Whisky	30 ml	33%
Country liquor	45 ml	22% (highly variable)
Wine	100 ml	10%
Beer	250 ml	4%

- Quantity:

  1 quarter - 180 ml

  1 small peg - 30 ml

  1 large peg - 60 ml

- Dependency:

  CAGE questionnaire: **C**ut down, **A**nnoyed on criticism, **G**uilty, **E**ye opener

  1 'yes' indicates strong suspicion and ≥2 'yes' indicate dependence

- Chronic alcoholism:

  60 to 80 g/day for 8 to 10 years (male)

  40 to 60 g/day for 8 to 10 years (female)

Permissible limit for driving: 30 mg % blood alcohol level

Healthy limit of alcohol consumption:

Males: Up to 30 g/day or 210 g/week with at least 2 alcohol-free days per week

Females: Up to 20 g/day or 140 g/week with at least 2 alcohol-free days per week

- Stages of alcohol intoxication:

Stage	Blood alcohol concentration
Stage of excitement	50 - 150 mg%
Stage of incoordination	150 - 250 mg%
Stage of coma	> 300 mg%

- Danger dose:

Effect	Dose in male	Dose in female
Hepatitis	80 g/day for 10 years	1/4th of the male dose
Cirrhosis	80 g/day for 20 years 160 g/day for 10 years	

- Smoking:
    1. Quality - cigarette, bidi, cigar, pipe
    2. Quantity - in pack year index
    3. Duration

    - 1 pack of cigarettes is 20 cigarettes; 1 pack of bidis is 20 to 30 bidis (variable in each pack)
      (Most reliable source for number of bidis/cigarettes in each pack is the patient himself)
    - Smoking index (SI): Number of cigarettes per day × number of years of smoking (unit of SI is cigarettes)
    - Pack year index (PYI): Number of packets of cigarettes per day × number of years of smoking (units of PYI is packs, not pack years)
    - Health effects of chronic smoking:

Parameter	Effect
PYI >20	High risk for chronic obstructive pulmonary disease
PYI >40	High risk for bronchogenic carcinoma
PYI >40	High risk for PVD
SI >300	High risk for PVD

In a chronic smoker, risk reduction for lung cancer occurs only after 10 years of quitting smoking.

- If there is h/o weight loss (loosening of clothes) but not measured by the patient, say "H/O weight loss but unmeasured (or undocumented)."

- Diet:
    - Say "Diet is mixed/vegetarian/vegan of adequate/less/excess quantity with average daily caloric intake of __ kcal, protein intake of __ g and a deficit/excess of ___ kcal and ___ g"
    - Recommended daily allowance (RDA):

      For proteins: 1 g/kg/day (in pregnancy, it is 1.5 g/kg/day)

      For calories:

Work	RDA in male	RDA in female	
Heavy	3,500	2,800	+350 kcal in pregnancy
Moderate	2,800	2,300	+600 kcal in lactation (upto 6 months)
Sedentary	2,300	1,900	+520 kcal in lactation (from 6 to 12 months)

[These values are not exact, and have been rounded off for ease of remembrance.]

- List providing calories and protein value of common food items:

Food	Calorie (in kcal)	Protein (in gram)
Chapatti	100	2
Bhaji	150	
Dal	100	10
Rice	150	2
Bread (2 slices)	150	
Biscuit	25	0.5
Tea	75	1.5
Milk	75 (per 100 ml)	3
Egg	100	6
Fruit	100	

[These values are not exact, and have been rounded off for ease of remembrance.]

- Sample diets of male and female which provide adequate calorie content have been described below:

Gender	Time	Diet	Total
Females	Breakfast	tea + 2 bread slices + egg/fruits/milk	2300 kcal and 50 - 60 g
	Lunch	3 chapattis + 1 bhaji + dal + rice	
	Snacks	tea + 2 bread slices + egg/fruits/milk	
	Dinner	3 chapattis + 1 bhaji + dal + rice	
Males		+ 1 chapatti at lunch + rice at dinner	2700 kcal and 60 - 70 g

[Readers should note that this is an ideal balanced diet which provides adequate nutrition for adult males and females. Most of the patients in government hospitals consume inadequate diet. Hence students can use this sample diet to quickly assess adequacy of diet. This will also help students obtain an accurate diet history without wasting time.]

LIST OF SYMPTOMS OF EACH SYSTEM

[It is not necessary to enquire in the given order]

- CVS (5 cardinal symptoms of CVS):
  1. Chest pain
  2. Dyspnea

3. Palpitation
4. Syncope
5. Edema

- RS (5 cardinal symptoms of RS):
    1. Chest pain
    2. Dyspnea
    3. Cough
    4. Expectoration
    5. Hemoptysis
    6. Wheezing [some authorities consider it as the 6th cardinal symptom]

- GIT:
    1. Anorexia, nausea, vomiting
    2. Abdominal pain
    3. Hematemesis, malena, hematochezia
    4. Altered bowel habits (diarrhea, constipation)
    5. Abdominal distension
    6. Jaundice
    7. Dyspepsia (BBBEF): **B**loating, **B**elching (air + food), **B**urping (air), **E**pigastric discomfort, **F**latulence

- CNS:
    1. Motor symptoms (weakness, incoordination, abnormal movements)
    2. Sensory symptoms (positive or negative)
    3. Autonomic symptoms (bladder, bowel, sweating)
    4. Higher functions (altered consciousness, speech, convulsion)
    5. Cranial nerve symptoms

2

General Examination

- Proforma: (say in this order only)
  1. Conscious, cooperative, coherent (CCC)
  2. Well oriented to time, place, person (TPP)
  3. Averagely built and nourished + body mass index (BMI)
  4. Decubitus
  5. Temperature (T), pulse (P), respiration (R), blood pressure (BP)
  6. Jugular venous pressure (JVP)
  7. P O L I C e

     (**P**allor, **O**edema, **L**ymphadenopathy, **I**cterus, **C**yanosis, **C**lubbing)
  8. Skull, skin, spine
  9. Gait
  10. Others:
      - Signs of vitamin deficiency
      - Stigmata of TB
      - Stigma of syphilis
      - Signs of liver cell failure
      - Signs of HIV
      - Facies
      - Signs of atherosclerosis
  11. Treatment:
      - Intravenous (IV) line, central line
      - Ryle's tube
      - Foley's catheter
      - ICD
      - Drain
      - Diagnostic tap mark

12. Tattoo mark

> Importance of tattoo mark:
> 1. HBV, HCV, HIV
> 2. Infective endocarditis
> 3. Identity of individual
> 4. Idea about religion (religious tattoos)

CONSCIOUSNESS

- Say "Patient is conscious, co-operative, coherent, well oriented to time, place, person"
- Definition: State of awareness of one's self and one's environment
- Grades of altered consciousness - 4
    1. Somnolence (drowsy)
    2. Stupor
    3. Semi-coma
    4. Coma

❖ Somnolence:
- Pathological state that resembles normal sleep
- Patient can be aroused by external stimulus but reverts back to drowsy state on withdrawal of stimulus
- Difference from normal sleep:
    - i. Sleep can wake up spontaneously
    - ii. Maintains arousal even after withdrawal from stimulus

❖ Stupor: Pathological state that resembles sleep but patient can be aroused only by vigorous (painful) stimulation (pinching or supra-orbital pressure)

❖ Semi-coma: Not defined in any standard books

❖ Coma: Deepest level of unconsciousness with no response to any kind internal or external stimulus (plantar response is extensor)

> Controversy with respect to stupor:
>
> Psychiatry references say that:
>
> Sopor: Is a quantitative impairment of consciousness where patient reverts back to sleepy state when stimulus is withdrawn
>
> Stupor: Is a qualitative impairment of consciousness where though the patient appears conscious, is unresponsive to environment, mute and immobile

- Causes:
    1. Conditions affecting circadian rhythm (shifts)
    2. Endocrine: Hypothyroidism, diabetes mellitus, hyponatremia, hypercalcemia
    3. Central Nervous System: Head injury, meningitis, concussion, brain tumor
    4. Mood disorder: Depression, anxiety, stress
    5. Drugs: Antidepressants, antiepileptics, antipsychotics, tranquilizers
- Scales to assess level of consciousness:
    1. GCS - **G**lasgow **C**oma **S**cale
    2. AVPU - **A**lert, response to **V**oice, response to **P**ain, **U**nresponsive
    3. ACDU - **A**lert, **C**onfused, **D**rowsy, **U**nresponsive
    4. RASS - **R**ichmond **A**gitation **S**edation **S**cale
- GCS:
    - Glasgow Coma Scale
    - Components: EVM: 4, 5, 6

E - eye opening		**V - Verbal**		**M - Motor**	
1	None	1	No response	1	None
2	To pain	2	Incomprehensible words	2	Abnormal extension
3	To speech	3	Inappropriate words	3	Abnormal flexion
4	Spontaneous	4	Confused, disoriented	4	Withdrawal on pain
		5	Oriented	5	Localizes pain
				6	Obeys commands
NOTE THE BEST RESPONSE					

- Maximum score is 15 (max score for intubated patient is 10, since no verbal response)
- Minimum score is 3

- Impairment of consciousness as per GCS:
  - i. Mild ≥ 13
  - ii. Moderate 8-12
  - iii. Severe <8 (it is an INDICATION OF INTUBATION)
- Original GCS constituted 14 points, as it did not have abnormal flexion
- If score is >11, patient has 85% chance of recovery
- If score is 3 or 4, patient has 85% chance of dying
- Uses:
  - i. Monitoring course of disease
  - ii. Intubation if score <8
  - iii. Prognosis

Presentation	Posturing	Cause	Site of lesion
Abnormal flexion	Decorticate rigidity	Preservation of rubrospinal tract	Above red nucleus
Abnormal extension	Decerebrate rigidity	Loss of rubrospinal tract	Below red nucleus

(Rubrospinal tract causes flexion of upper limb.)

❖ Good to know:

1. Confusion: Inability of the patient to think with customary speed and clarity
2. Locked-in syndrome: Patient is aware and awake but cannot move or communicate verbally due to complete paralysis of nearly all voluntary muscles in the body except for vertical eye movements and blinking
3. Vegetative state: Signifies awake but unresponsive state in a patient who has regained from coma
4. Brain death:
   - Irreversible loss of all brain functions involving brain-stem
   - Indication of organ transplant
   - Diagnosed by:
     - i. Coma (tested by GCS)
     - ii. Apnea test positive
     - iii. Absence of brainstem reflexes

Brain stem reflexes:
- Light reflex
- Dolls eye movement (absent vestibulo-ocular reflex - VOR)
- Caloric test
- Pharyngeal reflex

Apnea test:
Remove ventilator for 8 min and give only 100% O_2 and monitor SpO_2. Lack of spontaneous chest movements and drop in SpO_2 indicates positive test.

COHERENCE

To be coherent is to be logical + consistent

ORIENTATION

- Definition: Function of mind involving awareness of three dimensions (time, place, and person)
- Order of loss: Time is earliest to be lost, followed by place, and last to be lost is person
- Recovery: In opposite order i.e. earliest to recover is person, last to recover is time

BUILD AND NOURISHMENT

- Say "Averagely built and well nourished"
- Build:
  - It is the skeletal framework of a person in relation to his or her age and sex compared to normal person
  - Types:
    - i. Short stature: <3rd percentile
    - ii. Average
    - iii. Tall stature: >97th percentile
- Nourishment:
  - Definition: It is the soft tissue mass (including muscle of the person)
  - Assessment:
    1. Subcutaneous fat:
       - i. Clinical method: Pinch skin between thumbs
       - ii. Gold standard method: By callipers (Harpenden or Schofield)
       - iii. Most common site: Mid-triceps
       - iv. Other sites: Biceps, infrascapular, suprailiac

2. Muscle mass:
    i. Mid-arm or mid-thigh circumference
    ii. Decrease in muscle mass: sarcopenia
3. Signs of vitamins, minerals, nutrient deficiency

- Average triceps skin fold thickness is 12.5 mm in males and 16.5 mm in females
- Average MAC is 25.5 cm in males and 23 cm in females
- Classification:
    i. Underweight
    ii. Normal
    iii. Overweight
    iv. Obesity
- Cachexia is anorexia + anemia + emaciation
- Calorie deficit of 1000 kcal/day = loss of 1 kg/week

Loss of 4.5 kg or >5% of body weight over 6-12 months : Harrison 19th edition

- Indicators of nutritional depletion:

Anthropometry	Chemical	Others
1. Weight loss >10%	1. Albumin <3.5 g/dL	1. Skin anergy
2. MAC (M < 23, F < 22)	2. S. transferrin <0.2 g/dL	2. Lymphocytopenia
3. Triceps skin fold thickness (M < 10, F < 13)		

- Obesity:
    - Definition: Abnormal growth of adipose tissue due to increase in fat cell size or number or combination of both
    - Clinical classification:
        1. Android: Waist (men)
        2. Gynoid: Hip or thigh (women)

3. Truncal: Face, neck, upper trunk (cushing's syndrome)
4. Abdominal obesity (visceral obesity): In viscera and omentum (apple-shaped obesity)

- BMI/Quetelet index: Formula $= \frac{\text{Wt (Kg)}}{\text{Ht}^2\,(\text{m}^2)}$
- Classification of obesity according to BMI:
  1. Underweight: <18.5
  2. Normal: 18.5-24.99
  3. Overweight:

     Preobese: 25-29.99

     Obese class I: 30-34.99

     Obese class II: 35-39.99

     Obese class III: ≥40

     (Note that obesity is BMI ≥ 30)
- Morbid obesity: BMI > 40 or BMI > 35 with comorbidity
- Super obesity: BMI > 50
- Disadvantage:
  1. Does not differentiate muscle mass from adipose tissue
  2. Less reliable in children
- Abdominal obesity: Clinically measured by waist - hip ratio (WHR)

  (Truncal obesity, central obesity)

$$\text{WHR} = \frac{\text{Waist circumference (cm)}}{\text{Hip circumference (cm)}}$$

  (Waist circumference is taken midway between iliac crest and costal margin. Hip circumference is taken at one-third distance between ASIS and patella or at level of greater trochanter.)
- Other criteria for obesity:
  1. Body weight of >2 SD
  2. Ponderal index
  3. Brocca index = height – 100 (in kg)
  4. Lorentz formula
  5. Corpulence index
  6. Skin-fold thickness: Take at four sites - mid triceps, biceps, subscapular, suprailiac
  7. WHR

DECUBITUS

- Definition: Posture a patient adopts when lying in bed.
- Types:
  1. Normal decubitus: Normal supine
  2. Rigid dorsal decubitus:
     - Supine with minimal movement, to minimize pain
     - Seen in peritonitis, polyarthritis, hip - joint disease
  3. Opisthotonus:
     - Arched back with extension of spine
     - Seen in meningeal irritation or extreme pyramidal rigidity: Meningitis, tetanus, encephalitis, pontine hemorrhage, strychnine
  4. Emprosthotonus:
     - Arched back with spine flexion
     - Same causes as point 3
  5. Pleurosthotonus:
     - Lateral arching of back
     - Same causes as point 3
  6. Lateral decubitus (right or left):
     - RS: Dry pleurisy, pleural effusion, cavitation, abscess, empyema, bronchiectasis
     - CVS: Causes which have massive enlargement of heart
     - CNS: Meningitis, cerebral irritation, sciatica
     - Abdomen: Appendicular abscess, amoebic liver abscess
     - Dry pleurisy: Can lie on either side
     - Other conditions: Lies on affected side because there is increased expansion of normal lung in doing so
     - Amoebic liver abscess: In left lateral position to reduce pain which is caused by widening of right intercostal spaces
  7. Coiled up decubitus (jack knife position):
     - Lateral decubitus with body curled up (legs and trunks approximated)
     - Abdominal colic, meningeal irritation
  8. Orthopneic posture:
     - Propped up or sitting
     - Seen in:
       i. CVS: LVF, effusion, COPD

ii. RS: Pneumonia

iii. GI: Large ascites

iv. Kidney: Uremia

9. Squatting posture (knee chest posture): Cyanotic spell in TOF
10. Prone position: TB spine, gastroenteritis
11. Decubital restlessness: Tossing about in bed, seen in any acute painful condition
12. Decubitus of PVD: Legs hanging down
13. Decubitus of varicose veins: Legs hanging up
14. Hemiplegia:
    i. Arms are flexed, adducted, semipronated
    ii. Legs are extended, adducted, plantar flexed
15. Decerebrate rigidity: Extended elbow + extended wrist + arms pronated + extension and plantar flexion of lower limbs + head retraction + jaw clenching
16. Decorticate rigidity: Flexed elbow and wrist with arm supinated + extension of lower limbs
17. Meningitis: Head turned away from light due to photophobia

TEMPERATURE

- Normal temperature: 36.5°C - 37.5°C (97.7°F - 99.5°F)
- $T_{(°F)} = T_{(°C)} \times 9/5 + 32$ (every 1° rise in Celsius = 1.8° rise in Fahrenheit)
- Mean oral temperature: 36.8 ± 0.4°C with lowest levels at 6 a.m. and highest levels at 4-6 p.m.
- Normal daily temperature variation: 0.5°C (maintained even during fever)
- Fever:
  - Definition: a.m. temperature of >37.2°C or p.m. temperature of >37.7°C with an increase in hypothalamic set point
  - Types (according to severity):

Mild:	37.2 - 37.8
Moderate:	37.8 - 39.4
Severe:	39.4 - 40.5
Hyperpyrexia:	>41.5
Subnormal:	<36.7
Hypothermia:	<35

Causes of hyperpyrexia:

- Malaria
- Septicemia
- Encephalitis
- Thyroid storm
- Pneumonia
- Serotonin syndrome

Causes of hypothermia:

- Myxedema coma
- Peripheral circulatory failure
- Hypoglycemia
- Near drowning
- Panhypopituitarism
- Prolonged exposure to cold

- Temperature to be measured by dorsum of middle phalanx as they are most sensitive due to maximum heat receptors
- Sites:
  1. Oral
  2. Axilla
  3. Groin
  4. Rectal
  5. Esophagus
  6. Tympanic membrane
  7. Vaginal

Rectal temperature is taken by special low reading thermometer which is stouter with rounded bulb graduated up to 90°F.

Rectal > oral by 0.4°C > axillary by 1°C.

- Temperature rises by 0.6°C after ovulation
- Difference between fever and hyperthermia:

Fever	Hyperthermia
Increase in hypothalamic set point	No change in set point
Responds to antipyretics	No response to antipyretics

- Pyrogens(PG E_2) → Central effect: raise the hypothalamic set point
  → Peripheral effect: nonspecific myalgias and arthralgia

  For every 1° rise in temperature, O_2 consumption increases by 13%

- Causes of fever:
  1. Infectious
  2. Neoplasm: RCC, hepatoma, lymphoid malignancy, bone cancer, etc.
  3. Vascular: Pontine hemorrhage (3Ps - pyrexia, pinpoint pupils, paralysis), stroke in hypothalamus, MI, pulmonary embolism
  4. Autoimmune: RA, SLE, collagen vascular disease, serum sickness, allergy, sarcoidosis
  5. Endocrine: Thyrotoxicosis, Addison's disease
  6. Physical: Heatstroke, radiation sickness

> Fever with chills and rigors:
>
> Malaria, Kala-azar, filariasis, pneumonia, cholangitis, pyelonephritis and UTI, SABE, abscess (anywhere), septicemia

Chills	Rigor
Feeling of cold	Shivering
Disappear on putting blanket	Does not

- Types:
  1. According to intensity
     - High grade
     - Low grade
       - Does not exceed 37.8°C
       - TB, SLE, collagen vascular diseases

2. According to pattern

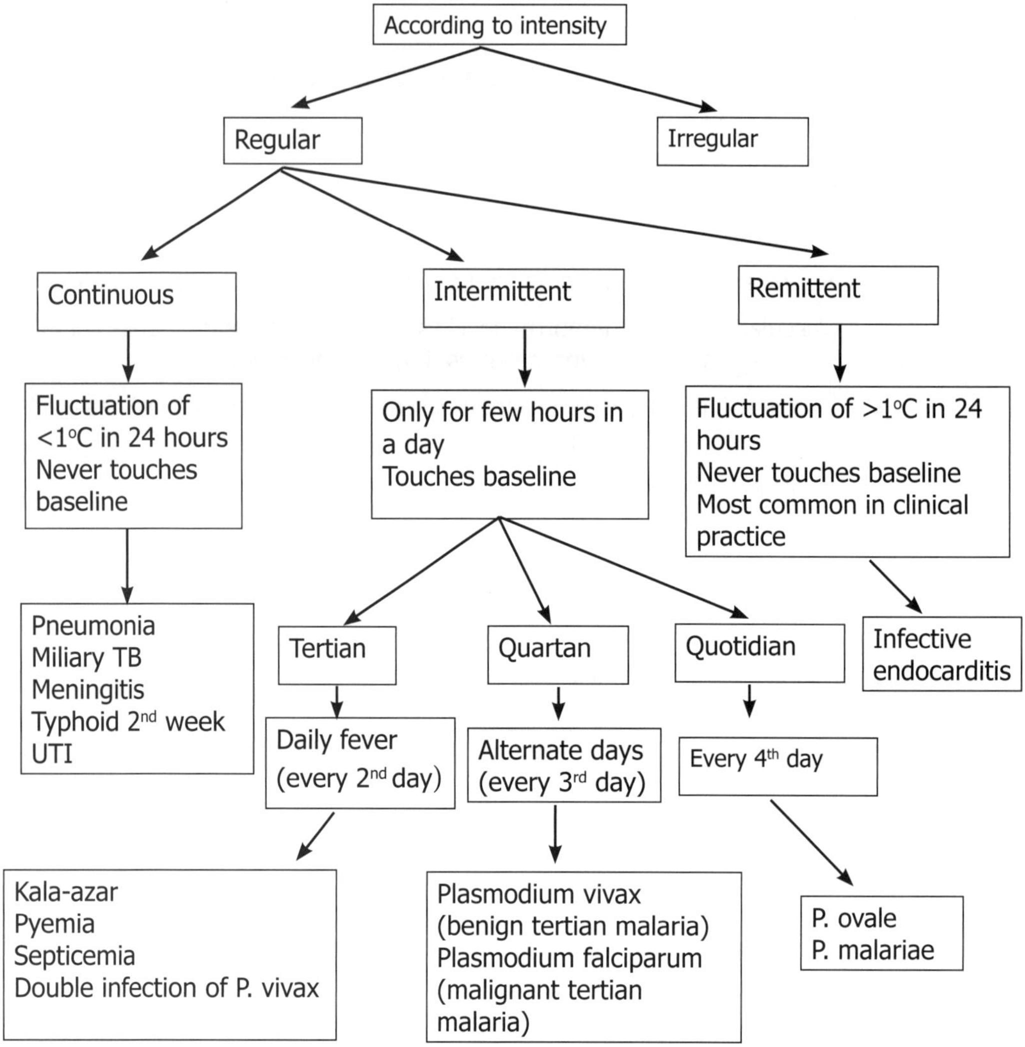

- Special types:

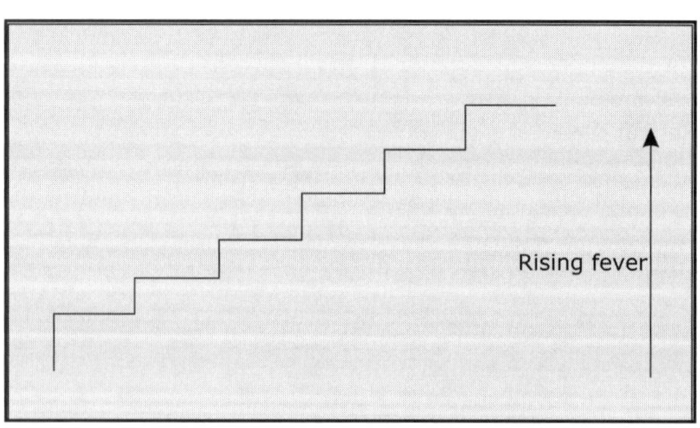

Fig. 2.1: Step ladder pattern of fever

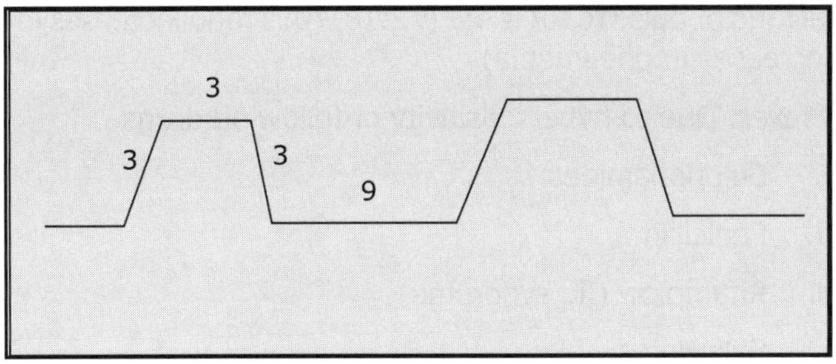

Fig. 2.2: Pel Ebstein fever

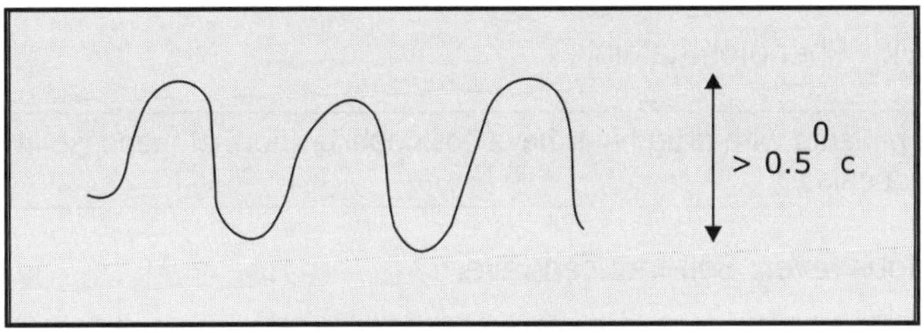

Fig. 2.3: Hectic septic fever

1. Pel-ebstein: Hodgkin's lymphoma, brucellosis, RCC
2. Hectic or septic: Septicemia
3. Step ladder: Typhoid
4. Camel hump fever: Kala-azar

- Stages:
  1. Onset:
     i. Abrupt - viral, malaria, pneumonia
     ii. Slow - typhoid, bacterial
  2. Decline (defervescence):
     i. Abrupt (very quickly within 6-12 hours with profuse sweat)
        - Seen in pneumonia, septicemic shock, dengue
     ii. Slow (over several days)
        - Typhoid, rheumatic fever
- Black fever: kala-azar
- Black water fever: malaria
- Camel hump fever:
  i. Double quotidian fever
  ii. Two fever spikes in a day
  iii. Seen in kala-azar

- Normal ratio of pulse to RR is 4:1 (72:18) (this ratio increases in narcotic poisoning and decreases in pneumonia)
- 'Drug' fever: Due to hypersensitivity of following drugs
    i. Sulphonamides
    ii. Penicillin
    iii. Rifampicin (flu syndrome)
    iv. Salicylates
    v. Barbiturates
    vi. Phenolphthalein

50% patients with drug fever have eosinophilia (normal response in fever is eosinopenia.

- Factitious fever: Self-induced fever
- Fraudulent fever: Patient is normothermic but manipulates the thermometer
- PUO:
    1. New definition:
        i. Fever >38.3°C (101°F) on at least two occasions
        ii. Illness duration of ≥3 weeks
        iii. No known immunocompromised state
        iv. Diagnosis remains uncertain after a thorough history, physical examination and obligatory investigations
    2. Original definition:
        i. Fever ≥38.3°C (101°F) on two occasions
        ii. Illness >3 weeks
        iii. Uncertain diagnosis despite 1 week of IPD evaluation
- Prolonged fever: Fever persisting >2 weeks
- Recurrent fever: Repeated episodes of fever interspersed with fever-free intervals of at least 2 weeks and apparent remission of the underlying diseases

PULSE

- Say "Pulse is ___ beats per minute in right radial artery, regular rhythm, adequate volume, normal force, tension, and character, bilaterally symmetrical with no radio-radial or radio-femoral delay, no apex pulse deficit, all peripheral pulses well felt"
- Definition: Wave of pressure change transmitted along the arterial wall due to left ventricular systole

- Parameters to be assessed:
    1. Rate
    2. Rhythm
    3. Volume
    4. Force
    5. Tension
    6. Character
    7. Condition of vessel wall
    8. Peripheral pulses
    9. Symmetry/delay
    10. Apex pulse deficit

- Significance of three finger method:
    - Proximal finger: Compress the artery fully for assessing force
    - Middle finger: Feel the pulsations
    - Distal finger: Compress to prevent back flow from radio-ulnar anastomosis

- Rate:
    - Normal: 60-100 bpm
    - Tachycardia: >100 bpm
    - Bradycardia: <60 bpm (<50 if on BETA BLOCKERS)
      (for causes, refer standard books)
    - Relative bradycardia (FAGET SIGN): Typhoid, yellow fever, brucellosis, lyme disease
    - Relative tachycardia: Rheumatic carditis, diphtheric myocarditis, TB, PAN

- Rhythm:
    - Regular
    - Irregular
        - Regularly irregular
            1. Sinus arrhythmias
            2. Pulsus bigemini
            3. Pulsus trigemini
            4. Partial AV blocks
        - Irregularly regular
            1. Atrial fibrillation

- Volume:
    - Indicates pulse pressure
    - Normal: 30-50 mmHg
    - Types: Normal, hypokinetic, hyperkinetic

      (for causes, refer standard books)

- Force:
    - Indicates SBP
    - Method: Compress by proximal finger

      OR

      Compress brachial and palpate radial artery

- Tension:
    - Indicates DBP
    - Feel of the artery between two beats

- Condition of vessel wall:
    - First compress by proximal finger → then empty the artery by sliding distal finger distally → then roll the artery side to side by middle finger to feel its condition
    - Normally it is not palpable
    - In atherosclerosis: Smooth or hard (can be both), cord-like feel with continuous segment of at least 7.5-10 cm

- Character:

  (Normal pulse consists of two waves - percussion wave and dicrotic wave but one can palpate only percussion wave.)

    1. Pulsus parvus: Low amplitude : In LVF
    2. Pulsus tardus: Slow rising + slow falling : In AS (severe)
    3. Pulsus parvus et tardus: Combination of both : In AS (severe)
    4. Anacrotic pulse: 2 waves in systole + slow rising : In AS (severe)
    5. Pulsus bisferens: 2 waves in systole + rapid rising : In HOCM, AS + AR, severe AR
    6. Dicrotic pulse: 2 waves, one in systole, other in diastole : In typhoid, CCF, myocarditis
    7. Pulsus alternans: Alternate small and large volume beats with normal rhythm : In acute LVF
    8. Water hammer pulse (Corrigan's pulse):
        - Rapid upstroke + high volume + rapid down stroke

- Detect by two hand method: One on radial artery, other on forearm, suddenly raise the forearm and arm up (radial pulsations disappear while forearm pulsations appear)
- Seen in conditions with WIDE PULSE PRESSURE:

Cardiac	Non-cardiac
1. AR 2. PDA 3. RSOV	1. Anemia 2. Beri-beri 3. Thyrotoxicosis 4. Fever 5. Pregnancy 6. Arteriovenous (AV) fistula 7. Paget's disease

9. Pulsus paradoxus:
   - It is decrease in SBP by ≥10 mmHg during inspiration
   - Method: Raise pressure in sphygmomanometer to 10 mmHg below SBP

     as we lower the pressure, we hear

     ↓

     tuk tuk - silent - tuk tuk - silent

     (Korotkoff sounds are present during expiration, but absent during inspiration.)
   - Seen in: Cardiac tamponade, constrictive pericarditis (one-third patients), pericardial effusion, tension pneumothorax, asthma, emphysema, SVC obstruction
   - It is merely an exaggerated form of normal phenomenon, not a paradox
   - What is the paradox: At times, pulse is not palpable (since low volume) even though heartbeat is audible

- Peripheral pulses (Refer Chapter 11 in Section IV for details)
- Delay:
  - Radio - radial: Subclavian artery compression, peripheral embolism, pre-ductal coarctation of aorta
  - Radio - femoral: Coarctation of aorta, atherosclerosis
- Apex pulse deficit:
  - Method: Simultaneously palpate radial artery and auscultate heart sounds but count only missed beats (do not count individual rate)
  - Ideally two examiners are required
  - Normal: Up to 10 due to occasional VPCs
  - Significant: More than 10, seen in atrial fibrillation

RESPIRATORY RATE

- Say "Respiratory rate is ___ cycles per minute with regular rhythm, abdomino-thoracic with no accessory muscles of respiration used"
- Parameters to be assessed:
  1. Rate
  2. Rhythm
  3. Type
  4. Accessory muscles of respiration (laboured breathing)

❖ Rate (in cycles per min):

1. Normal:
   - Adults: 12-18 cycles per minute (cpm)
   - Neonate: 40-45 cpm
   - Infant: 30-40 cpm
   - Children of age >12 years: 16-20 cpm
2. Tachypnea: >24 cpm

Causes of tachypnea	
Physiological	**Pathological**
1. Exertion	1. Fever
2. Excitement	2. Pain
	3. Anemia
	4. Hypoxia
	5. Diseases of lungs and heart
	6. Anxiety

3. Bradypnea:
   - RR of <12 cpm
   - Causes:
     i. Narcotic poisoning
     ii. Diabetic coma
     iii. Brain tumor, raised ICT
     iv. Conditions of hypometabolism

- Rhythm:
    1. Regular
    2. Irregular: Respiratory rhythm
        i. Biot (chaotic, ataxic):
            - Irregularly irregular
            - Raised ICT, meningitis
        ii. Kussmaul:
            - Deep and rapid
            - Acidosis, uremia
        iii. Cheyne - Stokes:
            - Cyclical apnea and hyperpnea
            - Periodic breathing
            - CHF, raised ICT, uremia, deep sleep, opium, barbiturates
        iv. Apneustic:
            - Full inspiration → pause (2-3 seconds) → full expiration → pause (2-3 seconds)
            - Pontine lesion
        v. Spurious (sighing):
            - Illusion of restricted chest movement
            - Each inspiration seems to fall short of its target, till the desire to take deep breaths is satisfied

- Types:

Abdomino - thoracic (diaphragmatic)	**Thoraco-abdominal (costal)**
Males, children - normal	Females - normal
Abnormal: 1. Pleurisy 2. Lung collapse	Abnormal: 1. Peritonitis 2. Severe ascites 3. Diaphragmatic paralysis 4. Abdominal pain

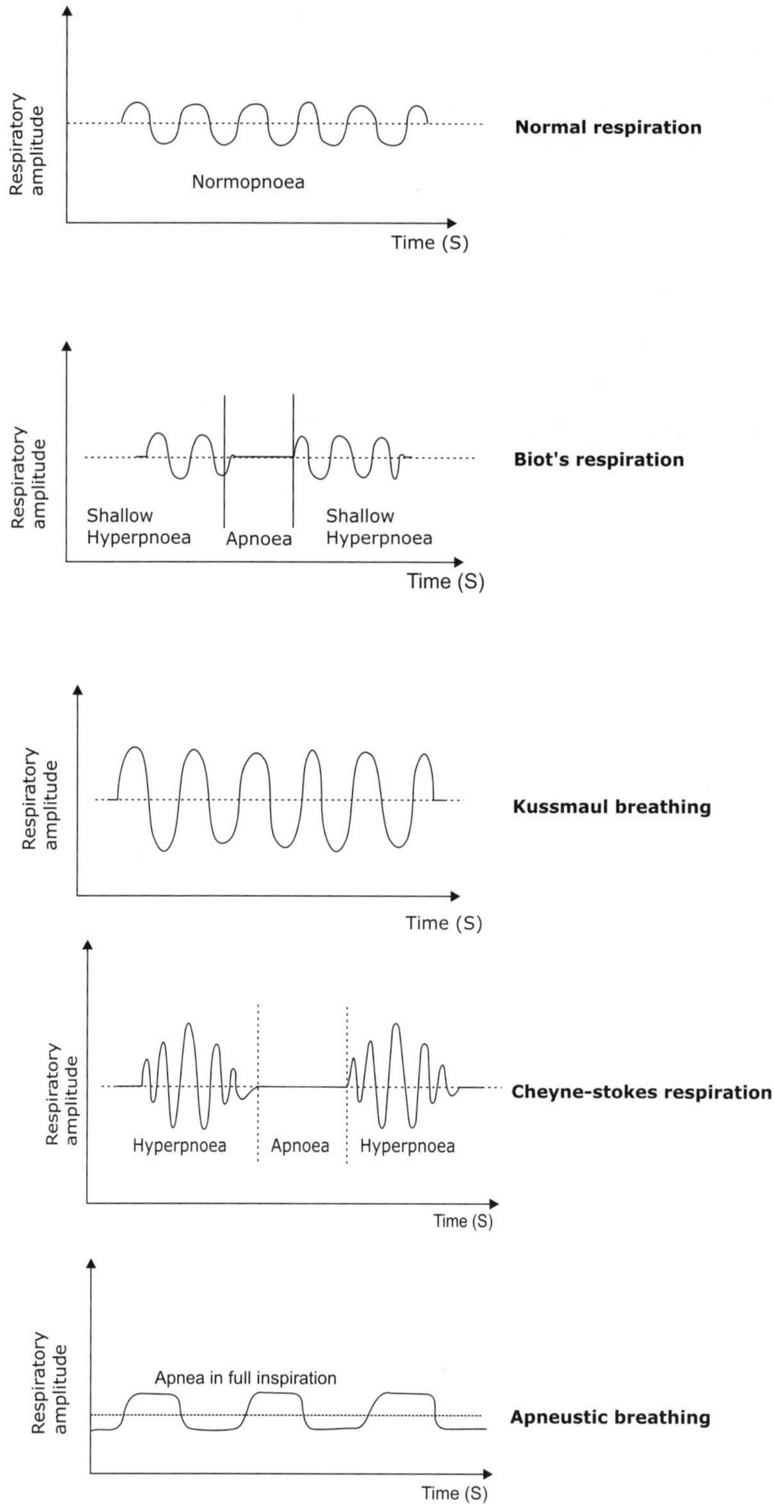

Fig. 2.4: Respiratory rhythms

- Accessory muscles of respiration:
  - Assist but do not play a primary role
  - Sign of respiratory distress: Retractions (in sequence: subcostal → intercostal → supracostal)
  - Muscles (up to down): Alaeque nasi, sternocleidomastoid, trapezius, scalene muscles (anterior, middle, posterior), subclavius, levatorus costarum, transversus thoracis, pectoralis major - minor (in tripod position), serratus anterior, latissimus dorsi, serratus posterior (superior, inferior)

- Prolongation of respiratory phases:
  1. Inspiratory phase: Obstructive lesion of upper airways (glottis, larynx)
  2. Expiratory phase: Obstructive lesion below the level of larynx (asthma, emphysema)
  3. Both phases phase: Acute alcoholism, uremia, narcotic poisoning

- Respiratory sounds:

Vesicular	Bronchovesicular	Bronchial
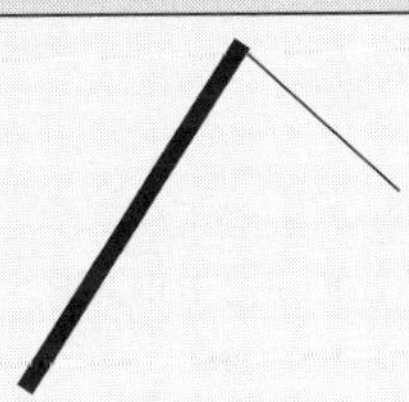	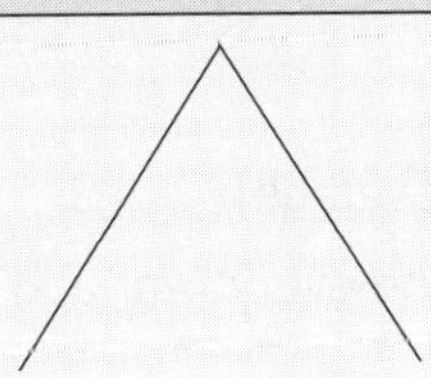	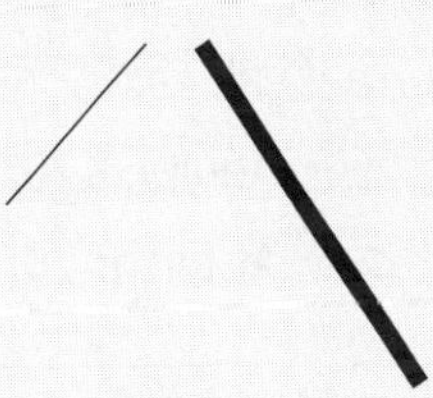
Rustling of leaves		Blowing in a pipe
1. Inspiratory - long and loud 2. No gap 3. Expiratory - soft and short	1. Equal inspiratory and expiratory 2. No gap	1. Inspiratory - soft and short 2. Gap 3. Expiratory - long and loud
- Over most of lungs		- Upper sternum - Trachea - Posterior interscapular space

- Wheeze: Expiratory sound due to obstruction of intrathoracic airway
- Stridor: Inspiratory sound due to obstruction of extrathoracic airway
- Leibermeister rule: Ratio of RISE in temperature : pulse : RR = 1:10:4
- Ratio of RR : pulse = 1:4
  - Increased in: CHF, pneumonia, heart block
  - Decreased in: Opioid poisoning

- Sleep disordered breathing:
  - Apnea: Cessation of airflow for at least 10 seconds
  - Hypopnea: 50% reduction in airflow for at least 10 seconds
  - Apnea (hypopnea) index: $\frac{\text{Number of episodes}}{\text{Hours of sleep}}$

    (>5 is abnormal)

- Platypnea: Dyspnea relieved on lying down (worsens on standing/sitting)
  1. Atrial myxoma
  2. Hepatopulmonary syndrome
  3. Anatomical CVS defect increasing positional R-L shunt

- Trepopnea: Dyspnea on lying on one side (lateral decubitus) but not on the other

BLOOD PRESSURE

- Say "Blood pressure is ___ / ___ millimetres of mercury in right brachial artery in supine position" (avoid saying mm of Hg)

- Definition: Pressure exerted by circulating blood on the walls of vessels (arteries)

- Normal values:
  1. Adults: 120/80 mmHg (average)
  2. At birth: 70/45 mmHg and every year add +3 to SBP and +2 to DBP

Normal range:
SBP is 90-120 mmHg
DBP is 60-80 mmHg

- Variability: Time of day, anxiety, smoking, temperature, meals, activity (lowest during sleep)

- Methods of measurement:
  - Invasive methods: Involve use of arterial catheter which gives a continuous pressure recording
  - Non-invasive methods:
    1. Manual methods:
       i. Mercury sphygmomanometer
       ii. Aneroid sphygmomanometer
    2. Electronic and digital methods
    3. Continuous non-invasive arterial pressure (CNAP)
    4. Non-occlusive techniques - pulse wave velocity principle

> Sphygmomanometer cuff invented by Riva Rocci.
>
> Use of stethoscope to hear sounds for BP described by Korotkoff.

- Continuous invasive BP monitoring:
  - Gold standard
  - Beat-to-beat measurement
  - Principle: Connection of liquid column from arterial blood to pressure transducer (hydraulic coupling)
  - Both numerical and graphical representation

> Sphygmomanometer underestimates SBP while it overestimates DBP.

- CNAP (continuous non-invasive arterial pressure):
  - Current techniques:
    1. Vascular unloading technique
    2. Tonometry
    3. Pulse transit time
- PWV principle (pulse wave velocity):
  - Velocity at which arterial pulse travels is dependent on BP
- Digital (electronic, automated) measurement:
  - Principle: Measure BP by oscillometric detection, using piezoelectric pressure sensor
  - Does not calculate SBP and DBP directly but measures them from mean pressure and empirical statistical oscillometric parameters
- Aneroid sphygmomanometer:
  - Mechanical type with dial
  - Less accurate but safer

- Techniques for BP measurement by sphygmomanometer:
  1. Palpatory: Gives only SBP, not DBP
  2. Auscultatory
  3. Oscillatory (visual)

> SBP by palpation is 10 mmHg lower than auscultatory method.

> Palpatory followed by auscultatory method of BP measurement:
>
> This sequence is followed to avoid false readings due to auscultatory gap.

- Auscultatory gap (silent gap):
  - Period of diminished/absent Korotkoff sounds during BP measurement
  - Leads to underestimation of SBP and overestimation of DBP
  - Between phases II and III of Korotkoff sounds
  - Causes:
    1. Carotid atherosclerosis
    2. Increased arterial stiffness in hypertension
  - Can be abolished by opening and closing the wrist ten times

- Auscultatory method precautions:
  - Patient should be at rest, no recent stimulants/smoke/meals
  - Clothing: Remove or keep it as it is (do not fold to tighten the arm)
  - Cuff to be tight enough only for tip of finger to be passed
  - Sitting or lying position makes no difference
  - Optimal time in the position before measurement:
    - i. Lying or sitting: 3 minutes
    - ii. Standing: 1 minute
  - Arm should be at the level of heart
  - BP to be raised to 20-30 mmHg above the findings of palpatory method
  - Release speed: 3 mmHg/sec

> Cuff (bladder) should have length of 80% of the arm circumference and width of 40% of the arm circumference.
> (Note that the above criteria are for bladder of cuff and not for entire cuff.)

  - Errors:
    1. Too tight: Falsely low
    2. Too loose: Falsely high
    3. Too small: Falsely high
    4. Tea, coffee: Increased
    5. Adrenergics: Increased
    6. Anxiety: increased

- Korotkoff sounds: Five phases

  Phase 1: First appearance of faint, repetitive, clear, tapping sounds (for at least two consecutive beats)

  Phase 2: Softening of sounds (swishing quality)

Phase 3: Return of sharp sounds (loud slapping sounds)

Phase 4: Muffled sounds (soft and blowing in quality)

Phase 5: Disappearance of all sounds

> DBP reading is taken at Korotkoff sound of:
> - Phase 5 (in all cases)
> - Phase 4 if:
>   1. Difference between phases 4 and 5 is >10 mmHg
>   2. Pregnant patients

❖ Methods to enhance Korotkoff sounds:
1. Open and close the wrist 10 times (increases flow in forearm)
2. Inflate cuff quickly
3. Elevation of arm before cuff is applied (empties veins to increase flow gradient)

- Lower limb BP:
  - Prone position
  - Cuff at thigh: Auscultate at popliteal areas
  - Larger cuff: According to cuff guidelines

> Clinically:
> 1. Palpable radial indicates SBP of 80-100 mmHg
> 2. Palpable femoral indicates SBP of 60-80 mmHg
> 3. Palpable carotid indicates SBP of 40-60 mmHg

- Reading variation between limbs:
  - Between two upper limbs (ULs) or two lower limbs (LLs), difference should not exceed 10 mmHg of SBP, if it does, evaluate further (e.g. PVD)
  - Between UL and LL, the difference should not exceed 20 mmHg of SBP, if it does, evaluate further, for example.
    1. Hills sign in AR (LL SBP is greater than UL by >20 mmHg)
    2. Reduced BP in LL: Coarctation of aorta, Leriche's syndrome
    3. Reduced BP in UL: Takayasu's arteritis

- Standing BP:
  - For postural/orthostatic hypotension

> Orthostatic hypotension:
> Fall in SBP of ≥20 mmHg or DBP ≥10 mmHg on standing

Postural orthostatic tachycardia syndrome (POTS): Increase in HR by ≥30 bpm on standing

- The right arm is usually chosen for measurement due to convention and no other reason
- Findings on BP:
    1. Hypertension
    2. Hypotension
    3. Pulsus paradoxus
    4. Pulsus alternans
    5. Postural hypotension
    6. Asymmetry in limbs
- Pulse pressure (PP) = SBP – DBP (normally it is 30-60 mmHg)
    - High/wide PP: (Already discussed in table above)
    - Low/narrow PP: If <25% SBP
        1. Reduced LV stroke volume
        2. Reduced preload
        3. Trauma (hypovolemia)
        4. AS
        5. Cardiac tamponade

Wide pulse pressure: PP > 40 mmHg Narrow pulse pressure: PP < 25% SBP

- Mean arterial pressure (MAP):
    - Definition: Average arterial pressure during single cardiac cycle
    - $MAP = DBP + \frac{PP}{3}$
    - Normal: 65-110 mmHg
- BP values:

BP values	SBP		DBP
Hypotension	<90		<60
Normal	90-119		60-79
Prehypertension	120-139	OR	80-89
Stage I HTN	140-159	OR	90-99
Stage II HTN	160-179	OR	100-109
Isolated systolic HTN	≥140	AND	<90

Hypertensive emergency: Clinical syndrome of markedly high BP (>180/120 mmHg) WITH signs of target organ damage

Hypertensive urgency: Clinical syndrome of markedly high BP WITHOUT signs of target organ damage

Malignant HTN (accelerated HTN): Clinical syndrome of markedly high BP with signs of target organ damage. It is an OBSOLETE term

Resistant HTN: Failure to reach BP control after full dose of appropriate three dose regimen

JVP

- Say "No neck veins seen"

  OR

  "Prominent neck veins seen with raised JVP of __ cm of water and Kussmaul sign __ (positive or negative) and hepatojugular reflux __ (positive or negative)"

- Definition: Jugular venous pulse is defined as the oscillating top of vertical column of blood in the right internal jugular vein (IJV) that reflects the pressure changes in the right atrium during the cardiac cycle

- Seen in right IJV because:
  1. IJV has no valves allowing pulsations to be visible
  2. Right IJV extends in almost a straight line to SVC and right atrium

- Method:
  - Jugular venous pulse:
    1. Direct visualization
    2. Waves tracing method: Place a white paper behind the neck of patient and throw torch light from the front, tangential to IJV such that waves of JVP can be seen as shadows on white paper

- Jugular venous pressure: two-scale method

  At 45° inclinations (semi-recumbent position), measure vertical distance from sternal angle of Louis till top of oscillating column of IJV. Add 5 cm to it (Because center of right atrium lies 5 cm below the sternal angle at 45° inclination.)

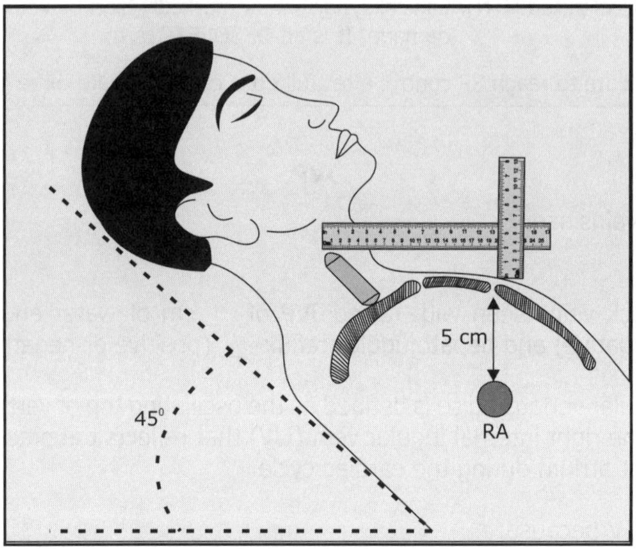

Fig. 2.5: Method of measuring JVP

- Normal value: Up to 8 cm (note that this is from center of right atrium i.e. after adding +5 cm)

Normally, up to 3 cm (i.e. 3 + 5 = 8), pulse is not visible. (Since it lies below the level of clavicle.) So if neck veins are visible, JVP HAS TO BE ELEVATED (ABNORMAL).

- Waves:

  a - Atrial contraction

  c - Closure of tricuspid valves

  v - Venous return

  x, x′ - Emptying of veins, dilation of atria

  y - Passive blood flow from atria to ventricles

- Abnormalities of pressure:

  1. Increased JVP:
     - Exercise, cough (physiological)
     - Right heart failure
     - TS, TR
     - CP, CT, restrictive cardiomyopathy

- Volume overload (e.g. IV fluids)
- SVC obstruction
- Hyperdynamic states

2. Unilateral raised JVP:
   - Innominate vein compression
   - Old age due to aortic arch dilation

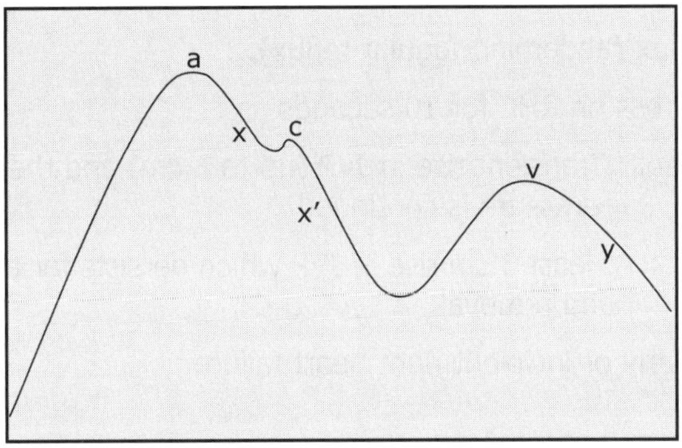

Fig. 2.6: JVP waveforms

- Abnormalities of waveform:
  1. a wave:
     - Absent: Atrial fibrillation
     - Giant a waves (seen in all a waves): TS, PS, pulmonary hypertension, RV diastolic dysfunction
     - Cannon a waves (seen in only few waves): Ventricular ectopic, AV dissociation (complete heart block, VT)
  2. c wave:
     - cv complex: TR (on palpation of radial pulse, JVP does not collapse)
  3. v wave:
     - Tall v wave: TR, ASD, TAPVC
  4. x descent:
     - Rapid: Cardiac tamponade, constrictive pericarditis
     - Slow: RV failure
  5. y descent:
     - Rapid: Constrictive pericarditis
     - Slow: TS, cardiac tamponade

Pay Tax:
Rapid **y** descent: Constrictive **p**ericarditis
Rapid **x** descent: Cardiac **t**amponade

- Kussmaul sign:
    - Increase in JVP during inspiration
    - Causes:
        1. Constrictive pericarditis
        2. Severe RHF
        3. Severe TS
        4. Restrictive cardiomyopathy

- Hepato-jugular reflux (abdomino-jugular reflux):
    - Method: Press on RHC for 10 seconds
    - Normal result: Transient rise in JVP (up to 3 cm) and then falls down even when pressure is continued
    - Positive test: At least 3 cm rise in JVP which persists for at least 15 seconds after hand removal
    - Seen in: Early or incipient right heart failure

- Friedrich sign (square root sign):
    - Rapid x and y descent in constrictive pericarditis

- Differentiation between JVP and carotid pulse:

JVP	Carotid pulse
Definite upper level	No definite upper level
Falls during inspiration	No change with respiration
Wavy column with 2 or 3 positive waves	Jerky with only one positive wave
Two descents seen	One descent seen
Not palpable	Well palpable
Obliterated by mild pressure at root of neck	Not obliterated by pressure at root of neck
Hepatojugular reflux seen	Not seen
Changes with position	Not seen

PALLOR

- Definition: Paleness of skin or mucous membrane due to reduced hemoglobin

- Causes:
    1. Due to reduced hemoglobin:
        - Anemia

2. Due to reduced blood flow:
    - Cold exposure
    - Hypotension
    - Shock (hypovolemia)
    - Vasoconstriction or arterial occlusion
3. Thickening of skin/mucous membranes:
    - Edema
    - Myxedema

- Sites:

Mucous membranes	**Skin**
1. Lower palpebral conjunctiva	1. Palms (skin and palmar creases)
2. Tongue (tip, dorsum)	2. Nail beds
3. Soft palate	3. Soles (skin and plantar creases)
4. Rectal vaginal mucosa	

- For skin creases, compare the color of crease with adjacent skin
- Why to see pallor in lower palpebral conjunctiva:
    1. Lower because it is easier to retract lower lid than upper which requires eversion (and not retraction)
    2. Palpebral because mucosa over this region is very thin and underlying vessels are clearly seen
- Grades:

Clinical grades	**Site of pallor**	**Approximate Hb content**
Mild	Conjunctiva, mucous membranes	<10 g%
Moderate	(above) + skin	7-10 g%
Severe	(above) + palmar crease	<7 g%

- Definition of anemia according to WHO:
    1. Males (>15 years): Hb < 13 g%
    2. Females (>15 years): Hb < 12 g%
    3. Children (12-15 years): Hb < 12 g%
    4. Pregnant females: Hb < 11 g%
       (For Indian pregnant females: Hb < 10 g%)
    5. Children (5-12 years): Hb < 11.5 g%
    6. Children (<12 years): Hb < 11 g%

OEDEMA

- Definition: Collection of fluid in extravascular compartment of tissues in abnormal quantity
- Pathophysiology: According to Starling forces (4)
    1. Increased hydrostatic pressure
    2. Decreased oncotic pressure
    3. Lymphatic obstruction
    4. Increased vascular permeability
- Sites:
    - Subcutaneous:
        1. Localized (dependant areas: legs, sacrum)
        2. Generalized (anasarca)
    - Peritoneal cavity (ascites)
    - Pericardial cavity (pericardial effusion)
    - Pulmonary (pulmonary edema)

> Dependant areas show edema:
> In ambulatory patient: Legs (pedal edema)
> In bed-ridden patient: Sacral (presacral edema)

- Pitting edema:
    - Fluid displaces away and fills back
    - Apply pressure for 30 seconds and observe for filling back:
        1. Fast refill (<40 seconds): Hypoalbuminemia
        2. Slow refill (>40 seconds): Congestive causes
- Non-pitting edema:
    - Fluid does not displace
    - Causes: Myxedema, filariasis, chronic venous edema, Milroy's disease, inflammatory edema

> Grades of edema:
> Grade 1: Up to ankle
> Grade 2: Up to knee
> Grade 3: Above knee
> Grade 4: Generalized

- Timing of edema:
  - Morning > evening: Renal pathology
  - Evening > morning: Cardiac pathology
- Sequence:
  - Cardiac pathology: Dependent portions affected first (pedal edema in ambulatory person and sacrum in bed-ridden patient)

    (This is due to higher hydrostatic pressure at dependant areas)
  - Renal pathology: Face affected first (periorbital edema)

    (This is due to loose connective tissue around eyes)
  - Hepatic pathology: Ascites occurs first

    (This is due to involvement of portal venous system)
- Etiology:
  1. Cardiac
  2. Hepatic
  3. Renal
  4. Nutritional: Anemia, beriberi, hypoproteinemia (malnutrition)
  5. Drugs:
     i. NSAIDs
     ii. Steroids (estrogen, progesterone, cortisol)
     iii. Arteriolar dilators (alpha blockers, K^+ channel openers, CCBs)
  6. Allergy: Angioneurotic edema, etc.
  7. Venous obstruction:
     i. DVT
     ii. Varicose veins
     iii. IVC/SVC obstruction
  8. Lymphatic edema:
     i. Primary (no known cause):
        a. Congenital (<1 year): Milroy's disease
        b. Praecox (1-35 years): Meige's disease
        c. Tarda (>35 years)
     ii. Secondary (known cause e.g. filariasis, mastectomy)
  9. Inflammation: Trauma, infection, arthritis, insect/snake bites, etc.
  10. Hypothyroidism (myxedema)

11. Immobility
12. Post-operative
13. Epidemic dropsy
14. Pregnancy
15. Cyclical premenstrual
16. Idiopathic

- To rule out etiology of edema: Do systemic examination

LYMPHADENOPATHY

- Note that lymphadenopathy in general examination implies 'generalized' lymphadenopathy. If only certain group of lymph nodes are palpable, say "There is no generalized lymphadenopathy, but ___ lymph nodes are palpable which will be commented upon in local examination."
- Generalized lymphadenopathy: ≥3 non-contiguous lymph node involvement
- Significant lymphadenopathy:
  - Palpable cervical LN of ≥1 cm
  - Palpable inguinal LN of ≥2 cm
  - Palpable axillary or supraclavicular LN of ANY size
  - Any palpable LN which is hard, matted, ulcerated, or fixed
- Parameters to be assessed in LNs: Describe it in the same way as a swelling (refer to Chapter 9 in Section IV for more details)
- GIT malignancy:
  - Left supraclavicular LN: Virchow's LN (Troisier's sign)
  - Axillary LN: Irish nodules
  - Umbilicus: Sister Mary Joseph nodules
- Characteristic sites involved in syphilis: Epitrochlear LN and occipital LN
- Levels of cervical LNs:
  - Level 1a: Submental
  - Level 1b: Submandibular
  - Level 2: Upper jugular (jugulodigastric) (first affected by TB)
  - Level 3: Middle jugular
  - Level 4: Lower jugular (juguloomohyoid)
  - Level 5: Posterior triangle (includes supraclavicular LN)

- Level 6: Anterior triangle
- Level 7: Mediastinal

First LN to be affected by TB - jugulodigastric

LN involved in tongue pathologies - juguloomohyoid

LN involved in tonsil pathologies - jugulodigastric

JAUNDICE/ICTERUS

- Definition: Jaundice is a symptom complex involving yellowish discoloration of tissue due to accumulation of bile pigment (bilirubin)
- Bilirubin has affinity for:
  1. Nervous tissue: Kernicterus in neonates (due to weak blood brain barrier)
  2. Elastin: Found in bulbar conjunctiva (not sclera), blood vessels, skin
- Differentials of icterus:
  1. Carotenemia:
     - Spares sclera, involves skin (best on palms, soles)
     - Seen in high intake of vitamin A, myxedema
  2. Muddy sclera: In exposed part of sclera only i.e. interpalpebral part
  3. Mepacrine, acriflavine, picric acid ingestion, tetracycline, quinacrine toxicity: Skin yellow, sclera spared
  4. Diffuse xanthomatosis
  5. Old subconjunctival hemorrhage
  6. Household turmeric (palms)
- Sites:
  - Bulbar conjunctiva
  - Ventral surface of tongue
  - Hard palate, soft palate
  - Uvula
  - Skin (check after blanching skin by digital pressure)

1st site to be jaundiced is bulbar conjunctiva.

'Scleral' icterus is a misnomer.

Bulbar icterus is the correct terminology because bilirubin accumulates in blood vessels of bulbar conjunctiva which has elastin.

- Grading in pediatrics: Kramer's dermal grading (cephalo-caudal)

Grades	Bilirubin in mg%	Site
I	4-6	Head and neck
II	6-8	Torso up to umbilicus
III	8-12	Umbilicus to knees
IV	12-15	Knees to ankle, shoulder to wrist
V	>15	Palms and soles

- Silent/latent jaundice is till bilirubin level of 3 mg/dL (because icterus is not seen) but, in resolving phase of disease, icterus may be seen despite bilirubin <3 mg/dL

- In OJ: Bile salts depress SA node to cause bradycardia

Finding in pulse suggestive of OJ: Bradycardia

Icterus seen despite bilirubin level of <3 mg/dL: Resolving phase of jaundice

- Differentiating features of types of jaundice:

Type	Color	Feces	Urine
Prehepatic	Lemon yellow	Dark	- Normal - Acholuric urine on standing (because colorless urobilinogen is oxidized to yellow urobilin)
Hepatic	Orange yellow	Dark (can be light if intrahepatic cholestasis is also huge)	Normal
Posthepatic (OJ)	Greenish yellow (due to biliverdin)	Pale (clay)	Dark (due to conjugated bilirubin)

- Pathological types of jaundice:

Type	Direct/conjugated	Indirect/unconjugated	Total
Normal	0-0.3 mg/dL	remaining	<1 mg/dL
Conjugated hyperbilirubinemia	>15% of total	remaining	>1 mg/dL
Unconjugated hyperbilirubinemia	<15% of total	remaining	>1 mg/dL

CYANOSIS

- Definition: Bluish discoloration of skin and/or mucosa due to increased deoxy-hemoglobin >4 g/dL
- Sites:
    - For central cyanosis: Mucosa of inner lip (beyond vermillion border), tongue, buccal, nasal, rectal, vaginal (warm sites)
    - For peripheral cyanosis: Tips of fingers, outer lips (before vermillion border), tip of nose, ear lobule (cool sites)

> Note that minimum level of deoxyhemoglobin required for cyanosis is 4 mg/dL (NOT 5 mg/dL).
>
> Reference: Harrison's 19th edition

- Types of clinical presentation of cyanosis:
    1. Central
    2. Peripheral
    3. Mixed
    4. Differential
    5. Local: Due to sluggish/reduced blood flow (e.g. PVD)

❖ Differential cyanosis:
1. Only lower limbs: PDA + shunt reversal
2. Only upper limbs: PDA + shunt reversal + TGA
3. Left arm + lower limbs: Preductal coarctation + PDA + shunt reversal

Central	Peripheral	Mixed
- Pathophysiology: Inadequate oxygenation of blood (despite adequate blood flow) - Sites: (mentioned before) - Temperature of cyanosed part: Warm - Clubbing seen - Polycythemia seen (if chronic condition) - On application of local heat: Cyanosis unchanged - On increasing FiO_2: Cyanosis disappears	- Pathophysiology: Reduced or sluggish flow through vessels causes excess removal of O_2 - Sites: (mentioned before) - Temperature of cyanosed part: Cool - Clubbing not seen - Polycythemia not seen - On application of local heat: Cyanosis disappears - On increasing FiO_2: Cyanosis unchanged	- Pathophysiology: When both these mechanisms coexist - Sites: Both together

(Continued...)

Central	Peripheral	Mixed
Causes: - RS: 1. Any cause of respiratory failure (type 1 or 2) 2. High altitude (>4000 m) - CVS: 1. Cyanotic heart disease - Blood: 1. Abnormal Hb (sulfhemoglobin, methemoglobin) 2. Polycythemia	Causes: 1. Reduced cardiac output: CCF, AS 2. Peripheral vasoconstriction: Cold, Raynaud's, PVD, drugs	Causes: 1. Acute LVF 2. MS (causing pulmonary edema) 3. Cor pulmonale

- Although central cyanosis occurs at both central and peripheral sites, we see it first at central sites, and later if it is severe, we see it at peripheral sites. Hence to distinguish central vs. peripheral, one best place to look is mouth/tongue.

- Abnormal Hb:
  1. Methemoglobin:
     - Cyanosis seen if levels >1.5 g/dL
     - Chocolate brown to black color
     - Congenital cause: Hereditary deficiency of enzyme methemoglobin reductase
     - Acquired cause: Sulphonamides, nitrites (well water), aniline dyes
  2. Sulfhemoglobin:
     - Cyanosis seen if levels >0.5 g/dL
  3. Carboxyhemoglobin (carbon monoxide): Cherry red (not cyanosed)
  4. Cyanmethemoglobin: Bright red (not cyanosed)

- D/Ds of cyanosis: Bluish discoloration of skin by amiodarone, nitrates, dapsone, metoclopramide

Clubbing without cyanosis: IBD, lung carcinoma
Clubbing with cyanosis: Chronic cause of central cyanosis
Cyanosis without clubbing: Peripheral cyanosis, acute central cyanosis

Effect of RBC/Hb on cyanosis:
In polycythemia: Cyanosis seen in spite of no abnormality
In severe anemia: Cyanosis not seen despite the abnormality

Intermittent cyanosis: Seen in Ebstein's anomaly Orthocyanosis: Seen on sitting/standing (upright) cyanosis Seen in pulmonary AV fistula

CLUBBING

- Also called as Hippocratic fingers or serpents head deformity
- Definition: Selective bulbous enlargement of distal finger due to proliferation of connective tissue is called clubbing
- Pathophysiology:
  1. PDGF (most accepted) → vasodilatation, capillary permeability increases → hypertrophy/hyperplasia of soft tissues
  2. Hypoxemia → HIF → hypertrophy/hyperplasia
  3. Ferritin
  4. Neurogenic
- Stages:

Stages	Features
1st	Softening of nail bed as seen by fluctuation
2nd	- Obliteration of diamond shaped window by Schamroth test - Lovibond angle >180°
3rd	Parrot beak or drumstick appearance
4th	- Hypertrophic osteoarthropathy (HOA) - Swelling and pain of joints like wrist (most common), ankle, elbow, etc. - Radiological evidence of subperiosteal bone deposition

- Causes:
  - CVS:
    1. Cyanotic heart disease
    2. ASD/VSD/PDA + shunt reversal
    3. Infective endocarditis
    4. Atrial myxoma
  - RS:
    1. Bronchiectasis (most common cause in young)
    2. Lung abscess
    3. Empyema
    4. Cystic fibrosis

Note that COPD does not cause clubbing

5. TB
6. ILD
7. Asbestosis
8. 1° or 2° lung malignancy (most common cause in old)
9. Mesothelioma
10. Sarcoidosis

- GIT:
  1. Ulcerative colitis (UC > Crohn's disease)
  2. Crohn's disease
  3. Cirrhosis (biliary > nonbiliary)
  4. Celiac disease
  5. Hepatopulmonary syndrome
- Idiopathic
- Hereditary
- Occupational: Jackhammer operators

Finger affected 1st: Index finger

Reversible clubbing: Lung transplant after cystic fibrosis

- Unilateral clubbing: Pancoast tumor, subclavian aneurysm, PVD, etc.
- Unidigital clubbing: Trauma, tophaceous gout, sarcoidosis
- Differential clubbing: Same as cyanosis
- Pseudo clubbing:
  - Hyper parathyroidism (due to resorption)
  - Vinyl chloride workers
  - Leprosy (due to resorption)

- Tests:

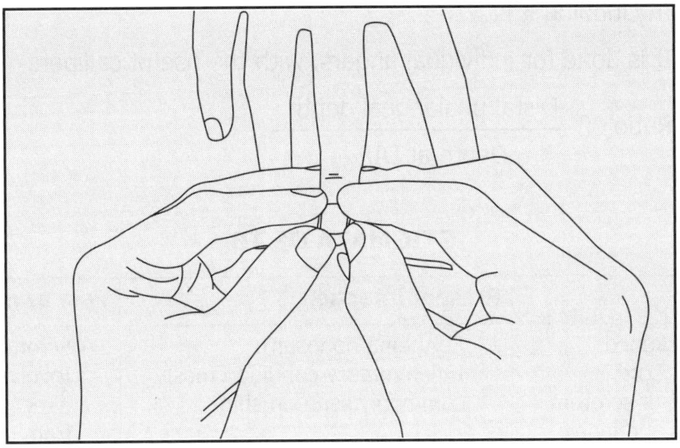

Fig. 2.7: Method to test fluctuation for clubbing of fingers

1. Fluctuation test:
   - Seen in grade 1
   - It has a specific method
2. Schamroth test:
   - Oppose the distal phalanx of same finger of both hands and look for diamond-shaped window
   - Test is positive if window is obliterated (indicates Lovibond's angle is >180°)
3. Lovibond's profile sign:
   - Seen in grade 2
   - See the finger tangentially from side to note the ONYCHODERMAL angle or LOVIBOND's angle or PROFILE angle
   - Normally it is <160°
   - In clubbing it is >180°
4. Curth's modified sign:
   - Tangentially check for angle between distal phalanx and middle phalanx at DIP (same as above)
   - Normally it is 180°
   - In clubbing it is 160°
5. Digital index:
   - In clubbing it is >1
   - Ratio of circumference = $\frac{\text{Circum. at nailbed (sum of all fingers)}}{\text{Circum. at DIP (sum of all fingers)}}$

6. Phalangeal depth ratio:
   - In clubbing it is >1
   - It is done for individual fingers, with the use of callipers
   - Ratio of $\frac{\text{Distal phalangeal depth}}{\text{Depth at DIP}}$

STIGMATA OF TB

Past infection	Present infection	Past or present infection
1. Beaded and thickened spermatic cord: Cord is palpated at root of scrotum between thumb and index finger simultaneously on both sides	1. Erythema nodosum: Inflammatory condition most commonly seen on shin	1. Scrofuloderma: Involvement of skin by direct extension, usually from underlying TB lymphadenopathy
2. Old scar or sinus reflecting TB lymphadenopathy	2. Phlyctenular conjunctivitis: It is a nodular inflammation of cornea/conjunctiva due to hypersensitivity to a foreign antigen and it is best seen in interpalpebral area near limbus Treatment: topical steroids	2. Gibbus, knuckle, kyphus

STIGMATA OF SYPHILIS

- Head:
  1. Alopecia
  2. Frontal bossing
- Eyes:
  1. Interstitial keratitis
- Nose:
  1. Saddle nose due to depression of bridge of nose

     Treatment: Augmentation rhinoplasty
  2. Snuffles: Syphilitic rhinitis
  3. Perforation of nasal septum
- Oral:
  1. Gothic palate: Abnormally high arched palate
  2. Perforation of hard palate

3. Hutchinson teeth: Widely spaced small teeth with notches in incisors
4. Mulberry molars: Multiple rounded rudimentary enamel cusps on the permanent first molars
5. Maxillary hypoplasia
6. Glossitis
7. Mucous patches
8. Condyloma
9. Perioral rhagades: Lines, fissures, cracks, scars in skin at angles of mouth and nose due to bacterial infection of skin lesions

- Genitals:
  1. Gummatous orchitis (epididymis is not involved, or involved late)
  2. Condyloma lata
- Lymphadenopathy:
  1. Often generalized lymphadenopathy seen, with most characteristic sites being epitrochlear and occipital lymph nodes

STIGMATA OF HIV

1. Tattoo marks, puncture marks
2. Generalized wasting
3. Generalized lymphadenopathy
4. Candidiasis
5. Kaposi's sarcoma: Purplish vascular nodules on skin/mucous membranc
6. Polymyositis (muscle pain)
7. Polyarthritis (joint pain)
8. Signs of anemia, neutropenia, thrombocytopenia
9. Seborrheic dermatitis
10. Psoriasis, molluscum contagiosum
11. HIV peripheral neuropathy

SIGNS OF VITAMIN DEFICIENCY

Vitamin A	Conjunctival xerosis Corneal xerosis Bitot's spots Corneal scarring
Vitamin B complex	Stomatitis Angular stomatitis Cheilitis Glossitis Oral ulcers HYPERPIGMENTED KNUCKLES (B12 only)
Vitamin C	Bleeding gums Bone tenderness Petechiae, purpura Scorbutic rosary
Vitamin D	Rickets Osteomalacia
Vitamin K	Petechiae, purpura

STIGMATA OF ATHEROSCLEROSIS

1. Xanthelesma
2. Arcus senilis
3. Locomotor brachialis
4. PVD
5. Chord-like arteries (≥10 cm radial artery)
6. Carotid bruit

MARFAN'S SYNDROME

- Mutation of fibrillin gene
- Triad:
    1. Ectopia lentis
    2. Aortic aneurysm
    3. Skeletal changes

- GHENT criteria for diagnosis:

Skeletal:	CVS:
- Long limbs - Tall stature - Reduced US:LS - Arm span > height - Arachnodactyly - Pectus excavatum - Kyphoscoliosis - Pes planus or cavus - High arched palate - Hypermobility of joints: 1. Thumb sign 2. Wrist sign	- MV prolapse - MR - AR (aortic root dilation) - Dissection of aorta - Aneurysm of aorta
Ocular: - Ectopia lentis - Cataract - Retinal detachment - Elongated eyeball	Others: - Spontaneous pneumothorax - Hernia - Striae on shoulder and back

Section II

MEDICINE

A system based approach is followed here. Since cases in each system share a common approach and comparable findings, a non case-based approach is adopted. Each system starts with specific points on general examination followed by a detailed systemic examination. The beauty of system based approach is that comparable findings of all cases are given at every step of examination. Thus it gives the dual benefit of understanding individual cases while simultaneously comparing them.

3

Cardiovascular System

General Examination

[Only additional points on CVS general examination have been mentioned below. Refer Chapter 2 in Section I beforehand.]

- Body mass index: Ischemic heart disease, atherosclerosis
- Decubitus:
  - Orthopnea (sitting): Left ventricular failure (LVF), pericardial effusion, mitral stenosis (MS)
  - Platypnea (supine): Atrial myxoma, pulmonary AV shunts
  - Leaning forward: Pericarditis
  - Squatting: TOF
- Temperature: Infective endocarditis
- Cheyne-Stokes respiration: Severe heart failure
- Blood Pressure:
  - Increased in hypertension
  - Decreased in arrhythmia, AS, severe MS, LVF
  - Wide pulse pressure in aortic regurgitation (AR)
- Edema
- Cyanosis:
  - Cyanotic heart disease
  - Pulmonary edema
  - Left to Right shunt + reversal (eisenmengerization)
- Clubbing: Refer Chapter 2 in Section I
- Oral cavity: Unhygienic (infective endocarditis), tobacco chewing, smoking
- Tobacco staining (hands): Ischemic heart disease
- Tattoo marking: Right sided infective endocarditis

- Atherosclerotic stigmata:
  - Locomotor brachialis
  - Xanthelasma, xanthomata
  - Chord-like arteries
  - Peripheral vascular disease (embolic, thrombotic)
  - Tobacco staining
  - Arcus senilis

> Peripheral signs of infective endocarditis:
>
> - Immunologic lesions: Roth's spots, Osler's nodes (pulp of fingers, painful)
> - Vascular lesions: Janeway lesions (palm and sole, painless), petechiae, purpura, splinter hemorrhage, splenomegaly, PVD
>
> [Refer Duke's criteria in standard books]
>
> Peripheral signs of AR: Refer standard books

SYSTEMIC EXAMINATION

> Systemic exam in any case should start by saying the following:
>
> "Patient was examined with due consent under adequate illumination, well exposed till umbilicus, in sitting and supine positions, in presence of female attendant (only in female patients)."

- Inspection:
  1. Shape
  2. Symmetry:
     i. Kypho-scoliosis
     ii. Straight back syndrome
     iii. Pectus carinatum
     iv. Pectus excavatum
  3. Precordium: Bulge or depression
  4. Pulsation:
     - Apex impulse (discussed below)
     - Other precordial impulse: Left parasternal (in right ventricular hypertrophy)
     - Other pulsation:
       i. Epigastric pulsations seen in:
          - RVH
          - Abdominal aorta aneurysm
          - Pulsatile liver mass

ii. Supraclavicular pulsations seen in:
   - Supraclavicular aneurysm
   - Hyperkinetic state
   - Coarctation of aorta

iii. Suprasternal pulsations seen in:
   - Physiological
   - Hyperdynamic states
   - Aneurysm of aorta
   - Coarctation of aorta
   - AR
   - Pulsatile thyroid

iv. Carotid pulsations seen in:
   - Corrigan's sign (AR)
   - Carotid body tumor
   - Hyperdynamic states
   - Coarctation of aorta

5. Skin, scars, sinus, dilated veins

❖ Apex impulse:
   - Say "Apex impulse seen just below the left nipple in MCL"
   - Definition: Lowermost and outermost part of precordium where pulsation/systole is best felt
   - Normally seen below the nipple
   - It is seen in one ICS only and has area of 2.5 cm diameter

Abnormality	**Causes**
Diffuse apex (more than one ICS)	Hyper dynamic states AR Volume overload Not seen in left ventricular hypertrophy (LVH) due to pressure overload
Increased/forceful apex	LVH (pressure overload) Thin chest wall
Absent	MI (due to weak pulsations) Thick chest wall Breast tissue Pneumothorax, pleural effusion, emphysema Pericardial effusion

(Continued...)

Abnormality	Causes
Displaced apex	Cardiac causes: - LVH (down and out) - RVH (out) - Dextrocardia Extra cardiac causes: - Causes of mediastinal shift (push and pull effect) - Kypho-scoliosis - Pectus excavatum/carinatum - Straight back syndrome - Ascites, pregnancy
Bifid apex	HOCM
Retraction of apex (Broadbent's apex)	Adhesive pericarditis

Apex impulse: Inspectory finding Apex beat: Palpatory finding

- Palpation:
  - Say "Inspectory findings confirmed"
  - Say "No local rise of temperature or tenderness on superficial palpation"
  - Points to be covered:
    1. Apex beat
    2. Other pulsations like parasternal heave, epigastric pulsation, etc.
    3. Palpable heart sounds
    4. Thrill (palpable murmur) (discussed later)
    5. Tracheal tug
    6. Carotid artery shudder

❖ Apex beat:

- Say "Apex beat is localized at ___ site and of ___ type"
- Definition: Lowermost and outermost part of precordium where pulsation systole is best felt
- First palpated in supine position. If not felt, ask the patient to bend forward or shift to left lateral position. These enhance palpation of apex beat, but also shift it from normal position.
- Correct method for localization: First palpate by palm then by ulnar border of hand and then by tip of index finger
- Normal location is at 5th left ICS, 1 cm medial to left MCL. In tall patients at 6th ICS, and in children at 4th ICS.

- Types:

Type	Features, causes
Normal	Brief gentle thrust, not forceful, palpable with certainty
Hypokinetic	Minimal thrust is seen in: - Thick chest wall - Pleural effusion, thick pleura, chronic obstructive pulmonary disease - Pericardial effusion - MI
Tapping	Ill sustained (<2/3rd of systole) and non-forceful (doesn't lift the finger), seen in: - MS (only one cause)
Heaving	Well sustained (>2/3rd of systole) and localized to one ICS and forceful (lifts the finger), seen in: - Pressure overload (LVH)
Hyper dynamic	Ill sustained (<2/3rd systole), forceful and diffuse (more than one ICS), seen in: - Volume overload
Retractile impulse	Also known as Broadbent sign, seen in: - Adhesive pericarditis
Double impulse	HOCM

❖ Parasternal heave:

- Methods:
  1. Ulnar border of hand
  2. Pen method: Oscillatory movement of pen kept parasternally
  3. Base of hand (according to some authorities)
- Causes: RVH (most common), aortic aneurysm, left atrial enlargement
- Grading:

1	Palpable
2	Palpable and obliterable
3	Palpable but not obliterable

❖ Epigastric pulsation:

- By 3 finger method to differentiate RV pulsations from abdominal aorta aneurysm and pulsatile liver mass
- Index finger: Pulsatile liver mass
- Middle finger: RVH
- Ring finger: Abdominal aorta aneurysm

- Palpable heart sounds:
  - S1: At mitral area: MS
  - S2 (palpable P2) (diastolic shock): At pulmonary area: pulmonary HTN
  - S3:
    - i. at mitral area: LV failure
    - ii. at tricuspid area: RV failure
  - S4: at mitral area: LV failure

- Thrill:
  - It is a palpable murmur of low frequency
  - Say "site" and "timing (diastolic/ systolic)"
  - Same as murmurs (discussed in auscultation)

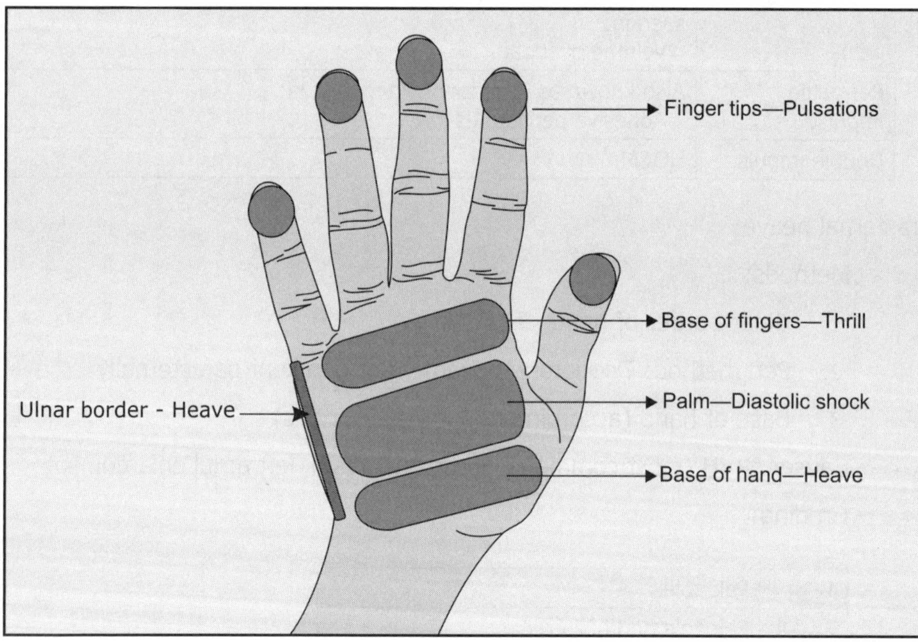

Fig. 3.1: Areas of hand used for CVS palpation

- Tracheal tug (Oliver's sign):
  - Seen in aortic arch aneurysm
  - Method: On upward traction of cricoid, we feel downward tug with systole

- Carotid shudder:
  - Vibration felt at height of carotid pulse
  - Pathognomic sign of AS + AR

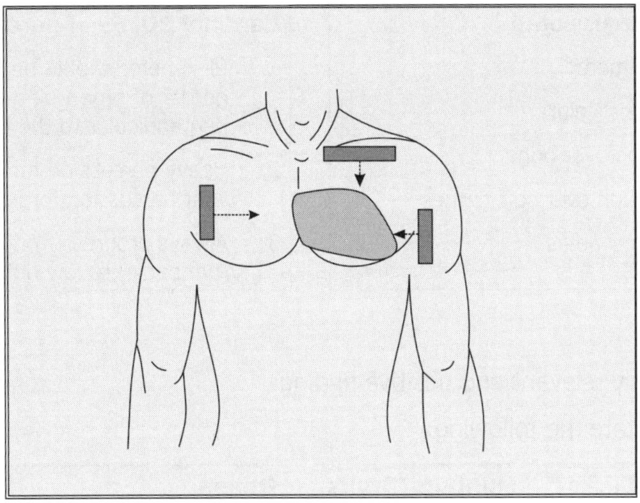

Fig. 3.2: Percussion of heart borders

- Percussion:

  Say "Heart borders are normal with no cardiomegaly"

Base of heart	**Right border**	**Left border**
(Normal - left 3rd ICS) if 2nd left ICS is dull ↓ Pericardial effusion Atrial enlargement	(Normal - retrosternal) Start - percussion on right MCL to find liver dullness, then - one ICS above it, continue percussion leftward ↓ If dullness in right parasternal area, it indicates: - RA enlargement - RVH - Ascending aorta aneurysm - Pericardial effusion	(Normal - 1 cm medial to MCL, i.e. at apex) Start from mid axillary line, then go rightward ↓ If both apex and left border are shifted to left, it indicates LVH or RVH or mediastinal shift If both apex and left border are shifted to right, it indicates mediastinal shift or dextrocardia If only left border is shifted to left, but apex is at normal location, it indicates pericardial effusion

Dorendorf's sign: Supraclavicular fullness due to an aortic arch aneurysm Potain's sign: Dullness at the right upper sternal border due to aortic arch aneurysm

PRINCIPLES of percussion:

1. Plexor and pleximeter
2. Movement at wrist joint
3. Direct percussion over bone
4. Indirect percussion over soft tissues
5. Compare identical areas

Cardinal RULES of percussion:

1. Pleximeter should be parallel to the border of organ, and it should be moved perpendicular to the border of organ
2. Heavy percussion for deep organs and light percussion for light organs
3. Always progress from high note (tympanic) to low note (dull note)

- Auscultation:
  - Say only relevant and positive findings
  - Auscultate the following:

Heart sounds	Snaps/Clicks	Murmurs/Bruits	Others	Adventitious sounds
S1	Ejection click	Systolic	Pericardial rub	Due to technical errors like rubbing of clothes, etc.
S2	Opening snap	Diastolic	Pericardial knock	
S3		Continuous	Prosthetic valve sound	
S4			Tumor plop	

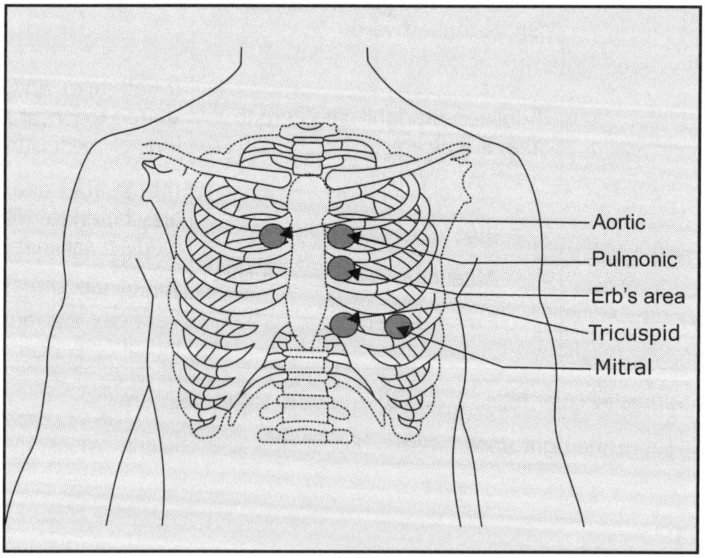

Fig. 3.3: Areas of auscultation on chest

- Areas of auscultation:
  - Mitral (start from here): Left 5th ICS, 1 cm medial to MCL, apex (thus palpation is must before auscultation to note if the apex is shifted)
  - Tricuspid: Left 4th ICS, parasternal
  - Aortic: Right 2nd ICS, parasternal
  - Pulmonary: Left 2nd ICS, parasternal
  - Erbs neoaortic area: Left 3rd ICS, parasternal (in patient of AR) (by leaning forward in expiration)
  - Gibsons: Left 1st ICS, parasternal (in patient of PDA)

Heard best in:

Right sided auscultation (sounds, murmur): In inspiration

Left sided auscultation (sounds, murmur): In expiration

- Heart sounds:

S1	**S2**
Lubb	Dup
Longer	Shorter
Low frequency	High frequency
Softer	Louder

How to identify S1:

1. Correlate sounds with pulse on arteries
2. S1 to S2 gap is shorter than S2 to S1 gap
3. Nature of S1 and S2 are different
4. S1 is better heard at mitral and tricuspid area while S2 is better heard at aortic and pulmonary area

Use of bell: For low pitch sounds like

- Mid diastolic murmur
- S3 sound
- S4 sound
- Fetal heart sounds

Use of diaphragm: For high pitch sounds like

- Rest all sounds

- S1:
  - Normally M1 precedes T1
  - Loud:
    1. MS, TS
    2. Hyper dynamic states
    3. Tachycardia
    4. Short PR interval
  - Soft:
    1. MR
    2. TR
    3. MS + MR
    4. MI (LVF)
    5. Bradycardia
    6. Prolonged PR interval
    7. Calcification
    8. Poor conduction due to thick chest/lung/pericardium
  - Variable:
    1. Atrial fibrillation
    2. Complete heart block
  - Wide split:
    1. RBBB
    2. LV pacing
    3. Ebstein's anomaly
  - Reverse split:
    1. LBBB
    2. RV pacing
    3. Severe MS

- S2:
  - Normally A2 is followed by P2
  - Normal split in expiration is not heard because it is <20 millisecond
  - Normal split in inspiration can be heard because it is >20 millisecond

Abnormality	A2	P2
Loud	HTN Hyper dynamic states Ascending aorta aneurysm	Pulmonary HTN Pulmonary artery dilation
Soft	AS AR Poor conduction due to thick chest, pleura, lung	PS PR Poor conduction due to thick chest, pleura, lung
Wide split	(Early A2) MS MR (important) VSD	(Delayed P2) Pulmonary HTN PS RBBB LV pacing LV ectopic
Narrow or reverse split or single S2	(Late A2) AS HTN HOCM (important) Coarctation of aorta LBBB RV ectopic RV pacing PDA	(Early P2) TS Eisenmengerization

ASD: Wide fixed split

TR: Normal split

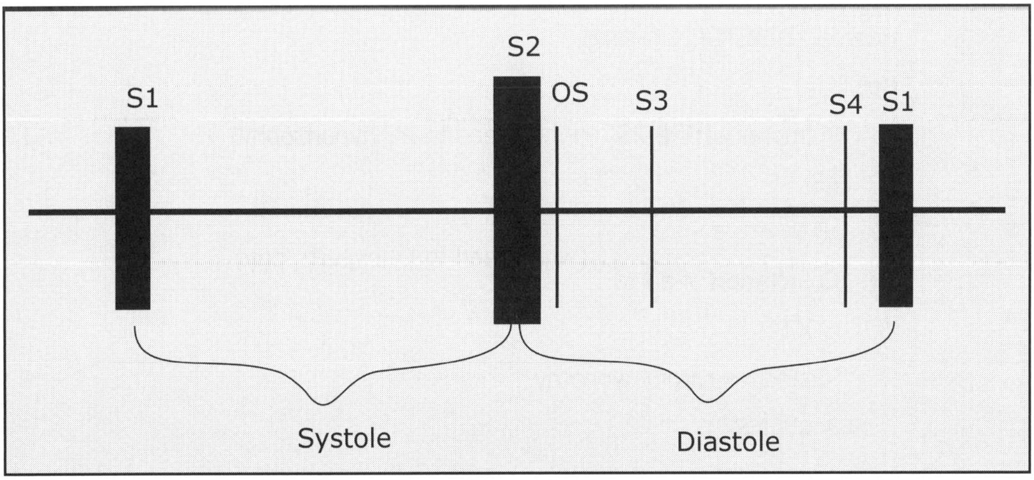

Fig. 3.4: Heart sounds

❖ S3:

- 0.2 sec after S2 (early diastole)
- Low pitch
- Can be heard physiologically in athletes, pregnancy, and up to 30 years
- Heard due to: 1st rapid filling of heart in a prefilled ventricle
- Heard in SYSTOLIC failure
- Heard in:
  1. High cardiac output
  2. MR (chronic)
  3. AR (chronic)
  4. LVF (MI)
  5. Dilatation cardiomyopathy
  6. ASD
  7. TR
  8. PR
- Never heard in MS

❖ S4:

- In late diastole
- Low pitch
- NEVER physiological
- Seen due to 2nd rapid filling of heart in a noncompliant ventricular wall
- Heard in DIASTOLIC failure
- Heard in:
  1. Pulmonary HTN, PS (which lead to RV hypertrophy)
  2. AS
  3. HTN
  4. Coarctation of aorta
  5. HOCM

  (2–5: which lead to LV hypertrophy)

  6. Restrictive cardiomyopathy
  7. Acute MR

- Gallop:
  - Cadecence of 3 or more heart sounds
  - Triple gallop:
    1. S3 gallop: S1+ S2 + S3
    2. S4 gallop: S1 + S2 + S4
    3. Summation gallop: S1 + S2 + (S3-S4) (because S3 and S4 merge in tachycardia)
  - Quadruple gallop: S1 + S2 + S3 + S4

- Opening snap (OS):
  - At apex beat
  - After S2
  - Seen in TS, MS
  - Sudden clicking sound, high pitch
  - Not affected by respiration, posture
  - Affected by:
    1. Condition of valve (thickness)
    2. LA to LV pressure gradient
  - Severity of MS is INVERSELY proportional to time gap of S2 to OS
  - To distinguish S2 to OS gap from S2 split, we use respiration (S2 split varies with respiration, while the other does not)

- Ejection click (EC):
  - High pitched, loud
  - Aortic EC heard in AS, HTN
  - Pulmonary EC heard in PS, pulmonary HTN

    ] (immediately after S1) (due to cusps of valves)
  - Late/mid systolic click heard in MVP, TVP (Post ejection click) (non-ejection click)

    ] (due to tightening of chorda tendinae)

- Pericardial rub:
  - To-and-fro sound (i.e. twice in each cardiac cycle)
  - Intensifies on pressing the diaphragm of stethoscope
  - Grating sound/leathery sound
  - Heard over precordium
  - Best heard at lower left parasternal area (bare area of heart)
  - Cause: Pericarditis

- To differentiate from pleural rub, ask the patient to hold breath; now the pleural rub stops, but pericardial rub is heard
- Causes of pericarditis:
  1. Idiopathic
  2. Infectious (viral, bacterial, TB)
  3. Uremic
  4. Post MI (Dressler's syndrome)
  5. Post trauma, post surgery
  6. Rheumatic pericarditis
  7. Collagen vascular diseases

❖ Pericardial knock:
- All over precordium, best over left lower parasternal
- Early diastole
- Cause: Constrictive pericarditis

❖ Tumor plop:
- Late diastole
- Cause: Atrial myxoma

❖ Prosthetic valve clicks:
- Sharp sound heard with S1 or S2
- Types of prosthetic valves and sounds produced:
  1. Tissue: No sound
  2. Discs: Opening sound heard
  3. Ball: Opening + closing sound heard

❖ Murmur:
- Say "A diastolic (don't say mid diastolic) murmur heard best at mitral area, of grade ___ (never say 1 or 2 as they are difficult to appreciate) with no radiation, better heard with diaphragm and in left lateral position."
- Definition: Abnormal cardiac sounds produced due to turbulent flow in heart valves, walls of heart, walls of great vessels
- Classification:
  1. Systolic
  2. Diastolic
  3. Continuous

- Grading: LEVINE'S GRADING

Systolic grades	Features	Diastolic grades
1	Very faint, audible with effort, in a quiet room only	1
2	Soft, clear, immediately heard	2
3	Loud murmurs	3
4	Palpable thrill present	4
5	Rim of stethoscope touches precordium	-
6	Diaphragm is just off the chest	-

Important dictum:

All diastolic murmurs are pathological

Systolic murmurs: Grade 1, 2: MAY BE physiological

Grade 3 and more: ALWAYS pathological

❖ Systolic murmurs:
  - Pan: MR, TR, VSD
  - Early: Small VSD (muscular VSD), VSD + pulmonary HTN
  - Mid: AS, HOCM, coarctation of aorta, PS, TOF

    (Better called as ejection systolic murmur)
  - Late: MV prolapse, TV prolapse

❖ Diastolic murmurs:
  - Early: AR, PR
  - Mid: MS, TS
  - Late: Atrial myxoma

❖ Continuous murmurs:
  - PDA
  - AV fistula
  - Aorto-pulmonary window
  - RSOV (ruptured sinus of Valsalva)

❖ Eponymous murmurs:
  - Carey Coombs: In rheumatic carditis (due to MS): MDM
  - Austin Flint: In severe AR: MDM
  - Graham Steel: In severe PR: Early diastolic murmur
  - Stills murmur: Physiological (school age): Ejection systolic

- Cole Cecil murmur: In severe AR: Radiation to apex, left axilla
- Gallaverdin effect: In AS: Radiation to mitral area
- Cabot-Locke murmur: Early diastolic murmur, occasionally heard in severe untreated anemia (functional murmur)

❖ Patterns:

- Crescendo decrescendo: AS, PS: mid-systolic/ejection systolic
- Presystolic accentuation: MS (due to 2nd rapid filling)

❖ Radiation sites:

- AS: Carotid, mitral area (Gallavardin effect)
- AR: Mitral and left axilla (Cole Cecil Murmur)
- MS: NO RADIATION
- MR: Anterior leaflet - axilla, back (inferior tip of scapula)
  posterior leaflet - base of heart
- TS: No radiation
- TR: Right sternal border
- PS: Left shoulder
- PR: No radiation

❖ Eponymous signs:

1. De Carvallo's sign:
   - Inspiration increases the pan systolic murmur
   - Seen in TR
2. Suzzman's sign:
   - Pulsations of posterior intercostal artery seen at the back when light is shown tangentially
   - Seen in coarctation of aorta
   - It is an inspectory sign

❖ Bruit:

≈ Extra cardiac murmur

≈ Vascular murmur

Causes:

- Atherosclerosis
- Aneurysm
- Stenosis: Coarctation of aorta, femoral, carotid, renal artery

- AV fistula
- Paget's disease
- Hyperthyroidism (upper pole of thyroid)

❖ Carotid bruit:
  - Suggests high risk for stroke
  - Important to first auscultate carotids before palpating to avoid generating embolus

4
Central Nervous System

GENERAL EXAMINATION

[Only additional points on CNS general examination have been mentioned below. Refer Chapter 2 in Section I beforehand.]

- Decubitus:
  - Opisthotonos: Meningitis
  - Decerebrate: Extended elbow + pronated forearm + extended knees
  - Decorticate: Flexed elbow + supinated forearm + extended knees
  - Hemiplegia: Arms are flexed, adducted, semipronated
    Legs are extended, adducted, plantiflexed
  - Paraplegia in flexion: Worse prognosis
  - Paraplegia in extension: Better prognosis

- Temperature:
  - Meningoencephalitis
  - Pontine hemorrhage (**3P**s: **p**yrexia, **p**aralysis, **p**in point pupils)
  - Hypothalamic stroke
  - Infective endocarditis

- Pulse:
  - Bradycardia: Cushing's reflex due to raised ICT
  - Bradycardia, arrhythmia: Autonomic features of GBS (these are an indication to admit patient to ICU)
  - Irregularly irregular pulse: Atrial fibrillation (embolic stroke)
  - Carotid bruit: Carotid atherosclerosis
  - Weak pulse on left arm: Subclavian steal syndrome

- Respiration:
  - Ataxic rhythm: Cushing's reflex due to raised ICT
  - Ondine's curse: Brainstem stroke (loss of involuntary respiratory drive)

- Blood pressure:
  - Raised BP: Cushing's reflex and stroke (especially of hemorrhagic type)
- Skull:
  - Trauma to calvarium
  - Trauma of base of skull:
    1. Raccoon's eye: Periorbital ecchymosis
    2. Battle's sign: Mastoid ecchymosis
    3. Otorrhea
    4. Rhinorrhea
    5. Cranial nerve entrapment
- Skin:
  - Neurocutaneous syndromes (phacomatosis):
    1. Neurofibromatosis:

       Café au lait spots (significant if there are >5 spots of >5 mm diameter before puberty or >15 mm after puberty)
    2. Von Hippel - Lindau syndrome
    3. Tuberous sclerosis: Shagreen patch, adenoma sebaceum, ash leaf macules
    4. Sturge - weber syndrome
    5. Ataxia telangiectasia
  - Petechia: Meningococcemia
  - Trophic ulcer: Peripheral neuropathy
  - Charcot's joint (neuropathic arthropathy): Peripheral neuropathy
- Spine:
  - Kyphosis:
    1. Knuckle: 1 vertebra involved
    2. Gibbus: 2 - 3 vertebrae involved
    3. Angulated kyphus: 4 vertebrae involved
    4. Rounded kyphus: >4 vertebrae involved
  - Paravertebral cold abscess
  - Trauma
  - Tuft of hair: Occult spina bifida
  - Pressure ulcers at sacrum (in bedridden patients)

- Vitamin deficiency:
  - B_1: Wernicke - Korsakoff psychosis, peripheral neuropathy
  - B_6: Peripheral neuropathy
  - B_{12}: PIGMENTATION OF KNUCKLES, dementia, paresthesia, anemia, SACD

❖ Effects of Alcohol:

- On CNS:

Acute intoxication	Chronic dependence	Withdrawal
1. Slurred speech	1. Dementia	1. Delirium tremens
2. Blurred vision	2. Cerebellar atrophy	2. Rum fits
3. Seizures	3. Peripheral neuropathy	3. Alcoholic hallucinosis
4. Trauma	4. Wernicke - Korsakoff psychosis	4. Central pontine myelinolysis
5. Saturday night palsy (radial nerve)	5. Marchiafava Bignani disease (corpus callosum demyelination)	
6. Coma		

- On CVS:
  1. IHD
  2. Dilatational cardiomyopathy
  3. Holiday heart syndrome (atrial fibrillation)
  4. Wet beri-beri (edema)

SYSTEMIC EXAMINATION

- Proforma:
  - Higher functions:
    1. Consciousness
    2. Orientation (time, place, person)
    3. **B**ehavior
    4. **M**emory
    5. **I**ntelligence
    6. **S**peech
    7. **H**andedness
    8. Visuo-spatial - **A**gnosia, **A**praxia
    9. **P**erception
    10. **E**motional status

BMI SHAPE

- Cranial nerves: All 12
- Motor:
  1. Nutrition
  2. Tone
  3. Power
  4. Coordination (includes cerebellum)
  5. Involuntary movements
- Sensory:
  1. Superficial (3): Pain, touch, temperature
  2. Deep (3): Vibration, pressure, proprioception
  3. Cortical (6):
     i. One-point localization
     ii. Two-point discrimination
     iii. Stereognosis
     iv. Graphesthesia
     v. Sensory extinction (perceptual rivalry)
     vi. Baragnosis
- Reflexes:
  1. Superficial
  2. Deep
  3. Visceral
  4. Primitive
- Peripheral nerves
- Gait
- Miscellaneous:
  1. Raised ICT signs
  2. Meningeal irritation signs

HIGHER FUNCTIONS

- Say: "Higher functions are normal with MMSE score of __/30, well oriented to TPP, normal behavior, memory, intelligence, unaffected speech, and no perceptual or emotional abnormality"

  (Some teachers expect MMSE scores in all CNS cases, while most teachers expect GCS scores in all cases.)

1. MSE: Mental status examination (for psychiatry)
2. MMSE (Folstein's test):
    - Mini-mental state examination
    - For cognitive impairment (dementia): Screening and follow-up
    - 30 points, 5 categories
    - Calculation is as follows: **ORRAL**
        i. **O**rientation to time and place: 10 points (5 + 5)
        ii. **R**egistration: 3 points
        iii. **R**ecall: 3 points
        iv. **A**ttention and calculation: 5 points
        v. **L**anguage: 9 points
    - Score ≥21 is normal
    - Score <21 indicates dementia

- Consciousness:
    - GCS to be done in all patients (mainly in head injury)
- Orientation (Refer Chapter 2 in Section I)
- Behavior:
    - Kluver-Bucy syndrome (bilateral amygdala lesion)
    - Frontal lobe lesion
- Memory:

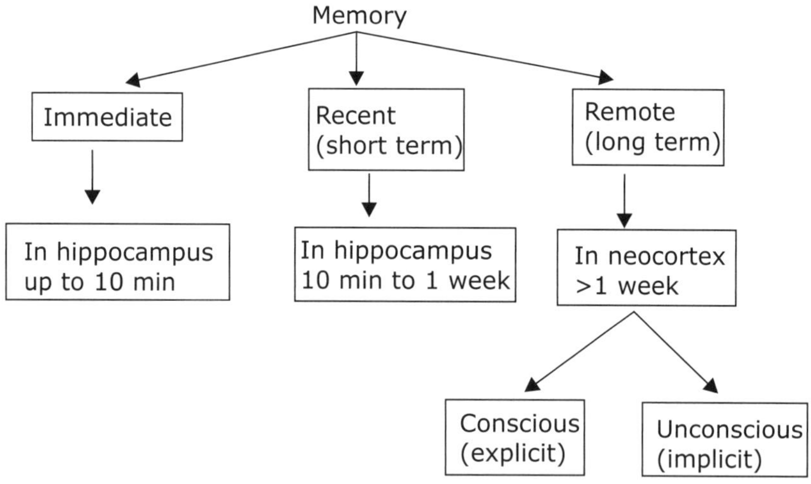

- Dementia:

Reversible	Irreversible
- B_{12} deficiency	- Alzheimer's disease
- Hypothyroidism	- Lewy body dementia
- Nutritional deficiencies	- Fronto-temporal dementia
- Trauma	- Vascular/multi-infarct dementia
- Infection	- Infections: SSPE, prions, AIDS
- Vasculitis	- Multiple sclerosis
- Tumor	
- Metabolic	
- Drugs	

- Intelligence:
  - Reasoning (ask difference and similarities between two things)
  - Judgment (ask what he/she will do in case of fire)
  - Calculation (ask arithmetic questions e.g. 100 minus 7)
  - Abstract thinking (ask him/her the meaning of any proverb)
- Speech:
  - Speech consists of three components:
    1. Fluency: Requires Broca's area + motor association area
    2. Comprehension: Requires Wernicke's area + sensory association area
    3. Repetition: Requires Broca's area + Wernicke's area + arcuate fasciculus
  - Based on these there are 7 types of aphasia:

Type of aphasia	Lesion at	Fluency	Comprehension	Repetition
Pure sensory (Wernicke's)	W	(+)	(−)	(−)
Pure motor (Broca's)	B	(−)	(+)	(−)
Transcortical sensory	SA	(+)	(−)	(+)
Tanscortical motor	MA	(−)	(+)	(+)
Conductive	AF	(+)	(+)	(−)
Global	All areas	(−)	(−)	(−)
Multiple trans cortical	SA + MA	(−)	(−)	(+)

(*W - Wernicke, B - Broca, SA - sensory association, MA - motor association, AF - arcuate fasciculus)

- D/Ds of defective speech:
    1. Aphasia
    2. Dysphonia: Defect in voice production - 10th nerve palsy
    3. Dysarthria:
        - Defect in articulation - lesion of 7th, 10th, 12th nerve or cerebellum
        - Types:
            i. Flaccid
            ii. Spastic
            iii. Cerebellar: Staccato, scanning, explosive
    4. Mutism (psychiatric): Akinetic mutism in ACA infarct

- Handedness:
    - 90% are right handed: Of them, 95% have Broca's area on left side while 5% have on right side
    - 10% are left handed: Of them, 50% have Broca's area on right side while 50% have on left side
    - Handedness of an individual: Is fixed at 3 years

- Agnosia, apraxia (defective visuospatial ability):

Agnosia	**Apraxia**
Impaired interpretation of sensory stimuli	Impaired motor planning
Non-dominant hemisphere	Dominant hemisphere (except constructional apraxia: Non-dominant hemisphere)
Types: 1. Spatial (hemi-neglect) 2. Visual 3. Prosopagnosia (for faces) 4. Auditory 5. Tactile (astereognosis)	Types: 1. Constructional 2. Oculomotor 3. Gait 4. Ideational 5. Ideomotor

- Perception

- Emotional status:
    - Emotional lability (in pseudobulbar palsy)
    - Euphoria

- Depression
- Agitated
- Causes: Dementia, multiple sclerosis, frontal lobe lesions

Brodmann areas:	
3, 1, 2	1° somatosensory
4	1° motor
6	Premotor and supplementary motor
5	2° somatosensory
8	Frontal eye field
17	1° Visual
18, 19	2° Visual
41, 42	1° auditory (Heschl's gyrus) (superior temporal)
22	2° auditory
43	Gustatory (inferior parietal)
44, 45	Broca's
22 (main), 39, 40	Wernicke's area
34	1° olfactory
28	2° olfactory

CRANIAL NERVES

- Olfactory nerve:
  - Method: Close eyes, close mouth and test one nostril at a time with other nostril closed
  - Materials: Tea, coffee, camphor, clove, elaichi (cardamom)

    (Do not use onion, lemon, and ammonia because they irritate nerves)
  - Anomalies:
    1. Anosmia:
       i. Central: CNS lesions, early Alzheimer's, early Parkinson's, Kallmann syndrome
       ii. Peripheral: Nerve lesion (# cribriform plate)
    2. Hyperosmia: Mucoviscidosis, Addison's disease
    3. Parosmia: CNS lesions (head injury)
    4. Cacosmia: Atrophic rhinitis
    5. Hallucination of smell: Psychosis, temporal lobe epilepsy, migraine aura

- Course: Olfactory epithelium (supreme meatus)

(Bipolar neurons are receptor as well as first order)

↓

Cribriform plate

↓

Olfactory bulb (synapse with mitral cells which form second order)

↓

Olfactory tract (mitral cells, tuft cells)

↙ ↘

Medial stria — Lateral stria (to 1° olfactory cortex)

- Optic nerve: Five parameters to test
  1. Visual acuity
  2. Visual field
  3. Color vision
  4. Reflexes: Light (direct, indirect), accommodation
  5. Fundoscopy (not to be done in exam)

❖ Acuity of vision:

1. Far: Snellen's chart (6 m), E chart and Landolt - C (for illiterate)
2. Near: Jaeger's chart (35 cm), Roman chart

Snellen's: 6/3 → 6/6 → - - - - → 6/60 → 1/60 → finger counting (at 50, 40, 30, 20 cm) → hand movement close to face → perception of light → blind

Jaeger's: N6 → N8 → N10 → N12 → - - - -

Binocular vision is achieved by child at 6 - 8 months

❖ Visual field:

- By confrontation test and Humphreys' perimetry
- Normal range:
  1. Superior - 60°
  2. Nasal - 60°
  3. Inferior - 70°
  4. Temporal - 100° (highest)

❖ Color vision:

- Ishihara charts: Only for red and green colour blindness (not blue)
- Nagel's anomaloscope
- Clinically tested by using colored objects (R-G-B)
- Achromatopsia (color blindness)
- Most common pure colour blindness: Green
- Most common colour blindness overall: Red + green

• Oculomotor, trochlear, abducens nerves (S0 - 4, LR - 6):

- Check following four things:

1. Extraocular muscles:

i. Position at primary gaze

Nerve palsy	Position of squint
3	Down and out
4	Up and in with head tilt
6	Adducted

ii. Movements to be examined in all directions

2. Pupillary examination:

i. Pupillary - size and shape

ii. Light reflex - direct and consensual

iii. Accommodation reflex

iv. Ciliospinal reflex

3. Nystagmus

4. Ptosis:

- 2 types: Partial, complete
- Causes: 3rd nerve lesion, Horner syndrome, myasthenia gravis

❖ Horner syndrome:

Components:
1. Ptosis
2. Miosis
3. Anhidrosis
4. Enophthalmos
5. Loss of ciliospinal reflex

Causes:

1. Cervical rib
2. Trauma
3. Pancoast tumor
4. Wallenberg syndrome
5. Multiple sclerosis
6. Syringomyelia
7. Cavernous sinus thrombosis
8. Surgery : sympathectomy
9. Congenital

- Trigeminal nerve: Test for following 3 parameters
  1. Sensory:
     - Face: Vertex-to-lateral canthus (ophthalmic), lateral canthus to angle of mouth (maxillary), below angle of mouth EXCEPT angle of jaw (mandibular)
     - Angle of jaw supplied by great auricular nerve - C2 C3
     - Anterior two-third of tongue (mandibular nerve)
     - Buccal mucosa (mandibular nerve)
     - Gingiva (mandibular nerve)
  2. Motor:
     - Temporalis: Retracts and closes jaw
     - Masseter: Closes jaw
     - Lateral pterygoid: OPENS mouth, pushes jaw to opposite side
     - Medial pterygoid: Closes mouth, pushes jaw to opposite side
  3. Reflexes:
     - Conjunctival: Checked on sclera (away from limbus)
     - Corneal: Checked at limbus (do ONLY if conjunctival reflex is ABSENT)
     - Jaw jerk

Significance of jaw jerk reflex:

It helps us differentiate between bulbar (LMN) from pseudobulbar palsy (UMN).

It is absent in bulbar palsy, but exaggerated in pseudobulbar palsy.

Deviation	Presentation
Toward side of lesion	Jaw deviation in 5th nerve palsy
	Tongue deviation in 12th nerve palsy
	Angle of mouth deviation in 7th nerve palsy UMN type
Away from side of lesion	Uvula in 10th nerve palsy
	Angle of mouth in 7th nerve palsy LMN type

- Facial nerve: Test for following three parameters:
  1. Sensory:
     i. Taste of anterior two-thirds of tongue
     ii. Hyperacusis
  2. Motor:
     i. Wrinkles (frontalis, procerus)
     ii. Closure of eyelids (orbicularis oculi)

     } Upper part of face i.e. above lateral canthus of eye is spared in UMN lesion due to bilateral cortical representation

     iii. Blowing of cheeks (buccinator)
     iv. Pursing of lips/whistle (orbicularis oris)
     v. Smile (levator anguli oris)
     vi. Nasolabial fold
     vii. Drooling of saliva
     viii. Platysma
     ix. Dysarthria
  3. Reflexes: Conjunctival, corneal
  4. ANS:
     i. Xerostomla
     ii. Loss of tears
     iii. Epiphora (due to lacrimal pump failure)

> Bell's phenomenon: Up rolling of eyes seen in LMN palsy (seen due to ptosis)

> Localization:
> UMN lesion: Contralateral lower half of face affected
> LMN lesion: Ipsilateral upper + lower half of face affected

LMN lesion localization:

1. Beyond stylomastoid foramen: Facial palsy only
2. Mastoid part: Facial palsy + loss of taste (chorda tympani nerve affected)
3. Tympanic part: Facial palsy + loss of taste + hyperacusis (stapedial nerve affected)
4. Labyrinthine/meatal part: Facial palsy + loss of taste + hyperacusis + dryness of mouth/nose (GSP Nerve affected)
5. In brainstem: Diplopia

- Auditory nerve: Test for the following two functions:
    1. Cochlear functions:
        i. Simple: Watch, whisper, finger snap
        ii. Tuning fork tests: Rinne's, Weber's, Schwabach, ABC tests
    2. Vestibular functions:
        i. Nystagmus
        ii. Caloric test (COWS - cold opposite, warm same)

- Glossopharyngeal nerve:
    1. Taste + tactile sensations on posterior one-third tongue and circumvallate papilla
    2. Tactile sensations on tonsils
    3. Gag reflex
    4. Xerostomia

- Vagus nerve:
    1. Gag reflex
    2. Uvula deviation
    3. Depressed soft palate
    4. Hyper-nasality/nasal twang in voice
    5. Dysphonia

- Spinal accessory nerve:
    1. Shrugging of shoulders against resistance (stand behind the patient) for testing trapezius
    2. Move neck to opposite side against resistance for testing SCM

- Hypoglossal nerve:
    1. Check for deviation (toward side of lesion)
    2. Check for movement: Protrusion, sideways movement
    3. Fasciculation: LMN palsy (Keep tongue INSIDE the mouth to elicit fasciculation)
    4. Atrophy: Bulbar palsy (LMN palsy)
    5. Spastic: Pseudobulbar palsy (UMN) - tongue stays within mouth and it is small, conical shaped
    6. Chorea: Jack in the box phenomenon

PATHWAYS

- Visual pathway:

Retina {
Cones, rods (receptors)
↓
Bipolar cells (first order)
↓
Ganglion cells (second order)
}
↓
Optic nerve
↓
Optic chiasma (only nasal fibers decussate)
↓
Optic tract
↓
Lateral geniculate body (third order)
↓
Optic radiation
(Retrolentiform part of internal capsule)
↓
Primary visual cortex (area 17)

❖ Abnormalities:
1. Heteronymous hemianopia:
    - Bitemporal hemianopia (pituitary adenoma)
    - Binasal hemianopia (bilateral carotid artery aneurysm)

2. Homonymous hemianopia:
   - Congruent (lesion from LGB to cortex)
   - Incongruent (lesion up till LGB)
   - With sparing of macula (lesion of visual cortex)
3. Homonymous quadrantanopia (lesion at optic radiation)
4. Unilateral anopia (lesion of eye or optic nerve)

- Light reflex: Direct and consensual (indirect)

Same pathway till optic tract

↓

Pretectal nucleus (of both sides)

(Note that LGB is bypassed)

↓

Edinger Westphal nuclei (of both sides)

↓

Third nerve

↓

Travel via verve to inferior oblique

↓

Branch to ciliary ganglion (synapse)

↓

Short ciliary nerves

↓

Miosis (no ciliary contraction)

- Accommodation reflex ≈ triple response ≈ near response:
  - It has three components:
    1. Convergence
    2. Miosis
    3. Ciliary muscle contraction (increase in curvature of lens)
  - Accomodation reflex can be initiated in two ways. First way is if eyes are in pursuit of an object which approaches close to face (smooth pursuit movement, which is involuntary). Thus bilateral medial rectus contraction occurs and reflex is initiated. Second way is if eyes are brought into convergence voluntarily (by saccadic eye movements). Thus bilateral medial rectus contraction occurs and reflex is initiated.

Voluntary convergence OR Involuntary convergence

↓

Medical rectus contraction

↓

Proprioception through 3rd nerve

↓

Mesencephalic nucleus (of 5th nerve)

↓

Edinger - Westphal nucleus

↓

3rd nerve

↓

Ciliary ganglion (via nerve to inferior oblique)

↓

Short ciliary nerves

↓

Miosis and ciliary contraction

- **A**rgyll **R**obertson **p**upil:
  - ARP: **A**ccommodation **R**eflex **P**resent

    ARP - PRA
  - PRA: **P**upillary **R**eflex **A**bsent (light reflex absent)
  - Reason: ONLY pretectal nucleus affected (not EW nucleus)
  - Causes: Neurosyphilis, MS, etc.
  - It is a bilateral condition
- Homes Adie tonic pupil:
  - Light reflex is absent
  - Accommodation reflex is slow and persistent (tonic)
  - Reason: Ciliary nerves damaged
  - Cause: Orbital infection, post-surgery
  - Often unilateral
  - Can be associated with Adie's syndrome (Adie's pupil, absent DTRs, absent sweating)

❖ Marcus Gunn pupil:
  - Seen in RAPD (relative afferent pupillary defect)
  - RAPD is partial blindness in one eye due to retinal damage or optic nerve damage
  - Procedure: Swinging torch light test
  - One of the EARLIEST symptoms of optic nerve disease, even when visual acuity is normal

❖ Wernicke's hemianopia:
  - Optic tract lesion
  - Homonymous hemianopic field

❖ Ciliospinal reflex:
  - Lost in Horner's syndrome
  - Enhanced with cluster headache
  - Method: Pinch at nape of neck to see a brief dilatation of pupil

> When homonymous hemianopia occurs in a patient of stroke (due to lesion above LGB), light reflex is PRESERVED, because pretectal nucleus is spared.

MOTOR EXAMINATION

- Nutrition:
  - Circumference of limb at site of maximum diameter which is approximately:

    4 inches above elbow
    4 inches below elbow
    6 inches above knee
    4 inches below knee
    } compare with normal side for unilateral disease

  - Places to look for wasting in a patient of bilateral disease:
    1. Intermetacarpal and intermetatarsal areas
    2. Lateral edge of shin becomes prominent due to wasting of muscles in anterior compartment of leg
    3. Hypothenar and thenar eminences
    4. Temporal fossae
    5. Buccal pad of fat
  - Increased in:
    1. Physiological
    2. Gigantism, acromegaly
    3. Myositis

4. Myotonia
5. Klippel - Trenauny syndrome

- Pseudo-hypertrophy of muscles seen in:
  1. Dystrophinopathies (Duchenne, Becker)
  2. Hypothyroidism
- Decreased in:
  1. Denervation: LMN lesion (lesion of anterior horn cell, nerve roots, nerves, NMJ, muscle)
  2. Devascularization (PVD)
  3. Disuse atrophy (immobilization, UMN lesion - late feature)
- Systemic wasting:
  1. Infections: TB, HIV
  2. Malnutrition
  3. Malignancy

- Tone:
  - Theoretical definition: Resting state of contraction of muscle
  - Clinical definition: Resistance offered by muscle to passive movement
  - Methods:
    1. Feel the tone by palpating the consistency
    2. Passive movements: Feel the resistance to opposite movement
    3. Attitude: e.g. rag doll attitude (in children), lower limb lying in external rotation (inspection)
    4. Gait (explained below)

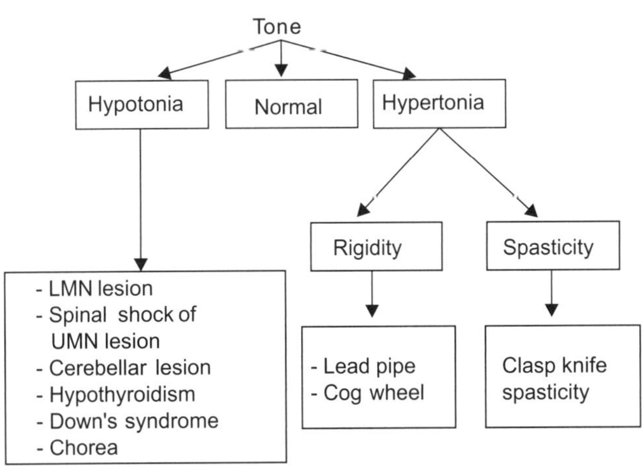

5. Leg dropping: Lift the leg and drop it on bed. A hypotonic leg falls with a 'thud.'
6. Log rolling maneuver (passive internal - external rotation of lower limb)
7. Knee lifting maneuver (on raising the knee, see if the foot follows it or lags behind it)
8. Muscle contour (inspection)

> - Lead pipe rigidity: In all extra pyramidal lesions (also in Parkinson's dis ease)
> - Cog-wheel rigidity: Characteristic of Parkinson's disease. It is lead pipe rigidity mixed with tremors.
> - Clasp-knife spasticity: In UMN lesions
>   Initial resistance (due to muscle spindle activity)
>   Followed by sudden give way of resistance (due to golgi tendon organ)

- Other causes of hypertonia:
  1. Hypercalcemic tetany
  2. Tetanus
  3. Strychnine poisoning
  4. Hysterical
  5. Reflex: Peritonitis, pain, meningism
  6. Gegenhalten: Frontal lobe lesions, encephalitis
  7. Myotonia

> Myotonia:
> - Impaired relaxation
> - Method: Ask the patient to loosen the grip after a handshake or gripping the finger
> - Percussion myokinia: Elicited by percussion of thenar area, deltoid and tongue

- Power:
  - Definition: Maximal forceful contraction of a muscle group
  - MMRC grades: (Modified Medical Research Council)

    0 - No movement at all

    1 - Flicker

    2 - Eliminating gravity

    3 - Against gravity

    4 - Against resistance

    5 - Full power

Grade 4 is further divided as:	
4–	Mild
4	Moderate
4+	Severe

(Note that COMPLETE range of movement should be possible for that grade of power e.g. while testing biceps, if flexion at elbow occurs against gravity with INCOMPLETE range of movement, it should be regarded as grade 2.)

- Decreased in both LMN and UMN lesions

- Coordination:
  - Checked only if power ≥3
  - Points to check:
    1. Ataxia:
       i. Ataxic gait (wide steppage)
       ii. Romberg's test:
          a. Sways to the side of lesion when eyes are open or closed - cerebellar ataxia (lesion in lateral cerebellum)
          b. Sways to the side of lesion only when eyes are closed - sensory ataxia (dorsal column lesion)
       iii. Tandem walking: Sways to the side of lesion (done with eyes open)
    2. Upper limbs:
       i. Finger - nose test (past pointing phenomena seen)
       ii. Finger - finger test (affected finger UNDERSHOOTS)
       iii. Dysdiadochokinesia (rapid supination - pronation)
       iv. Rebound phenomenon (other hand of examiner protects the patients face)
       v. Finger - thumb test
    3. Lower limbs:
       i. Heel - knee test
       ii. Foot pat test
    4. Additional tests for cerebellum:
       i. Truncal ataxia: Getting up from bed
       ii. Vestibular dysfunction: Nystagmus (fast phase towards side of lesion) and caloric test

iii. Speech defects:

a. Explosive speech: Sudden burst of speech

b. Scanning: Due to incoordination of tongue, words are separated by pauses

c. Staccato speech: Due to incoordination of larynx, each syllable is separated by pauses

iv. Tremors: Intention tremors (seen in finger - nose, finger - finger tests) and titubation (head nodding movements)

v. Pendular knee jerk

vi. Dyssynergy: Inability to smoothly do complex tasks like writing thus causing MACROGRAPHIA

(Micrographia is seen in Parkinson's disease.)

Knee jerk is called 'pendular' when it swings for ≥ 2.5 times.

❖ Abnormal movements:

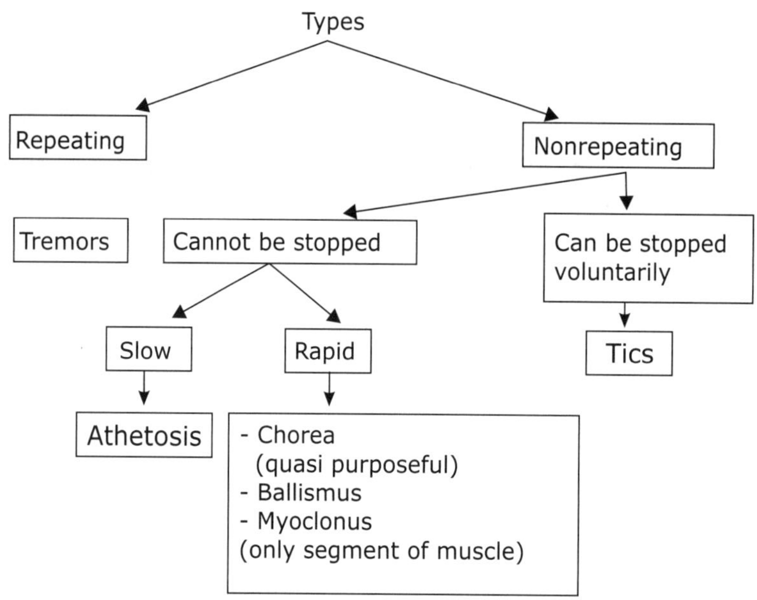

- Types of tremors:

1. Resting tremors: Attenuates on voluntary movement - seen in Parkinson's disease and senility

2. Postural tremors: When limb maintained in a particular position seen in familial, anxiety, hyperthyroidism, and delirium tremens

3. Intention (action) tremors: While doing precise movements near target - seen in cerebellar lesion

- Other abnormal movements: Fasciculation, fibrillation, flexor spasms

Fine tremors:

- Seen in thyrotoxicosis
- Checked by placing paper on the dorsum of outstretched hands

Coarse tremors:

- Seen in extrapyramidal, cerebellar lesions, etc.
- e.g. asterixis

Type of abnormal movement	Site of movements	Lesion at
Athetosis	Distal limb	Putamen
Chorea	Distal limb	Caudate
Ballismus	Proximal limb	Subthalamus

REFLEXES

- Definition: Involuntary contraction of muscle due to stretch of muscle spindles
- Superficial reflexes:
  1. Conjunctival, corneal:
     - Method: Wisp of cotton on bulbar conjunctiva
     - See: Blinking of eyes
     - 5th nerve (afferent route), 7th nerve (efferent route)
     - Do corneal reflex ONLY if conjunctival reflex is absent
     - Corneal reflex to be done AT LIMBUS, not on center of cornea

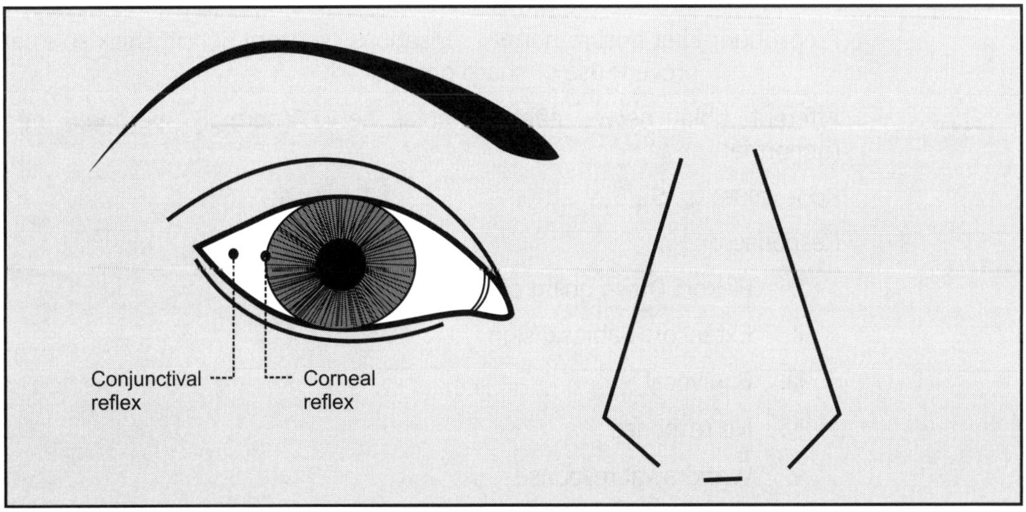

Fig. 4.1: Sites to elicit conjunctival and corneal reflexes

2. Abdominal:
   - Method: Stroke radially TOWARD umbilicus
   - See: Contraction of muscles/movement of umbilicus
   - Root value: T_8, T_9, T_{10} (level of umbilicus), T_{11}, T_{12}
3. Cremasteric:
   - Method: Stroke above downward on upper medial thigh
   - See: Upward movement of testis
   - Root value: L_1, L_2
4. Bulbocavernosus:
   - Method: Squeeze glans or clitoris, tug the foley's catheter
   - See: Anal sphincter contraction
   - FIRST TO RECOVER IN SPINAL SHOCK (hence used for assessing spinal shock)
   - Root value: S_2, S_3, S_4
5. Anal wink:
   - Method: Stimulation of perianal skin
   - See: Anal sphincter contraction
   - Used for assessing spinal shock, as it recovers early
   - Root value: S_4, S_5
6. Plantar reflex (do not confuse with ankle jerk):
   - Method: Stroke lateral side of foot from heel till the ball of great toe
   - See: Great toe, other toes, contraction of tensor fascia lata
   - Precaution: First ensure normal sensations (sensory deficit, thick sole) and prevent use of sharp objects
   - Afferent tibial nerve, efferent tibial nerve (normal), peroneal nerve (abnormal)
   - Root value: L_5, S_1, S_2
   - Responses:
     i. Flexor: Down going plantar (normal)
     ii. Extensor: Babinski sign
     iii. Equivocal
     iv. No response
     v. Withdrawal response

- Other methods of eliciting plantar reflex:
    i. Oppenheim: Stroking downward on medial side of tibia
    ii. Schaeffer: Squeezing Achilles tendon
    iii. Gordon: Squeezing calf muscle
    iv. Chaddok: Pinching skin of lateral malleolus
    v. Cornell: Scratching along inner side of extensor hallucis longus tendon
    vi. Bing: Pricking dorsum of foot
    vii. Silva: Pinching rectus femoris muscle (helpful in amputated limb)

Babinski sign:

- Components: Big toe dorsiflexion, fanning of other toes, taking up of lower limb (due to tensing of fascia lata)
- Seen in:
    1. Physiological till 1 year
    2. Deep sleep
    3. UMN lesion
    4. Coma
    5. Hypoglycemia
    6. Metabolic encephalopathy
    7. Post seizure
- Absent in:
    1. Thick sole
    2. S_1 lesion
    3. Sensory loss
    4. Cauda equina lesions
- Extensor response with absent ankle jerk:
    1. SACD
    2. Tabes dorsalis
    3. Friedrich ataxia
- Pseudo Babinski: Chorea and plantar hyperesthesia
- Similar reflex in upper limb:
    1. Hoffman reflex
    2. Wartenburg reflex

- Visceral reflexes:
    1. Swallowing
    2. Coughing
    3. Bowel
    4. Bladder

- Deep tendon reflexes (DTR) ≈ muscle stretch reflexes (MSR):
    - Increased in: Conditions causing hypertonia
    - Decreased in: Conditions causing hypotonia (except cerebellar lesion)
    - Jendrassik maneuvers: Clench fist, clench jaw, pull fingers apart, squeeze knees together (causes firing of gamma motor neurons and thus increases tone) (also helps in distracting the patient)
    - Grades:

        0 - Absent

        1 - Present but diminished

        2 - Normal

        3 - Exaggerated (brisk)

        4 - Clonus
    - List of reflexes:

Reflex	Root value	Nerve involved
Jaw	Mid-pons	Trigeminal nerve
Biceps	C_5 C_6	Musculocutaneous nerve
Supinator (brachioradialis)	C_5 C_6	Musculocutaneous nerve
Triceps	C_7 C_8	Radial nerve
Knee	L_2 L_3 L_4	Femoral nerve
Ankle	S_1 S_2	Tibial nerve

Theoretically, additional DTR: Pectoralis, finger flexion, tibialis anterior, tibialis posterior

- Clonus:
    1. Definition: Rhythmic, repetitive contraction of muscle associated with increased gamma efferent discharge

2. Mechanism: In UMN lesion, due to hyperactive muscle stretch reflex, the muscle is kept under tension. This leads to cyclical contraction (stretch reflex) and relaxation (due to Golgi tendon reflex) causing repetitive movements.
3. Types:
    a. Ankle clonus: True (well sustained) or false (ill sustained)
    b. Patellar clonus
4. Method to elicit:
    a. Suddenly dorsiflex the ankle with a jerk
    b. Suddenly pull down the patella with a jerk

- Primitive reflexes:
    - Seen in frontal lobe lesions
    - Reflexes:
        1. Sucking reflex
        2. Rooting reflex
        3. Grasp reflex
        4. Palmomental reflex
        5. Glabellar tap

SENSORY SYSTEM

- Always remember:
    - Compare on other side
    - Eyes should be closed
    - Go along the dermatomes
- Dermatomes:

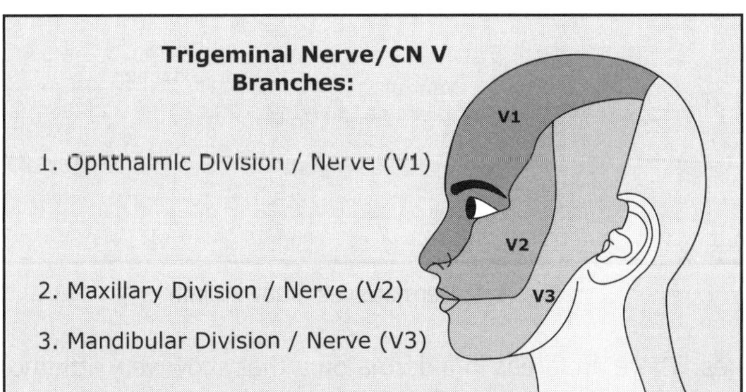

Fig. 4.2: Dermatomes of head and face

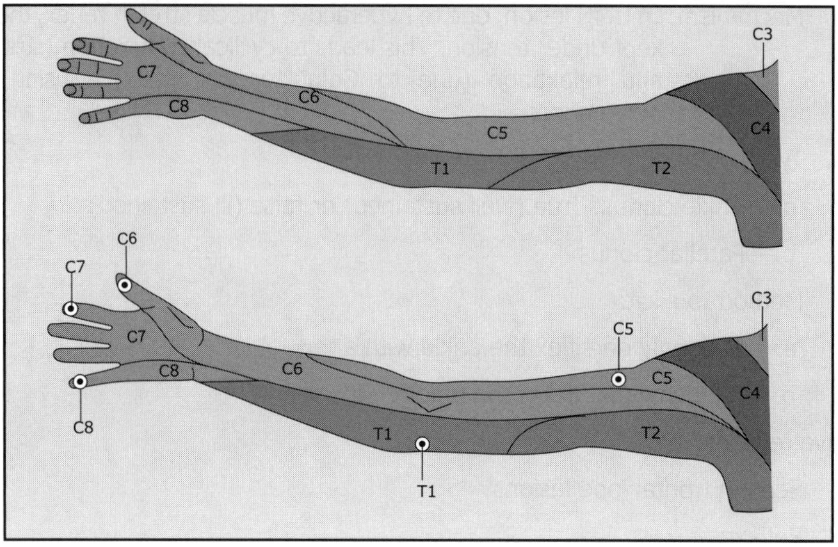

Fig. 4.3: Dermatomes of upper limb showing autonomous zones

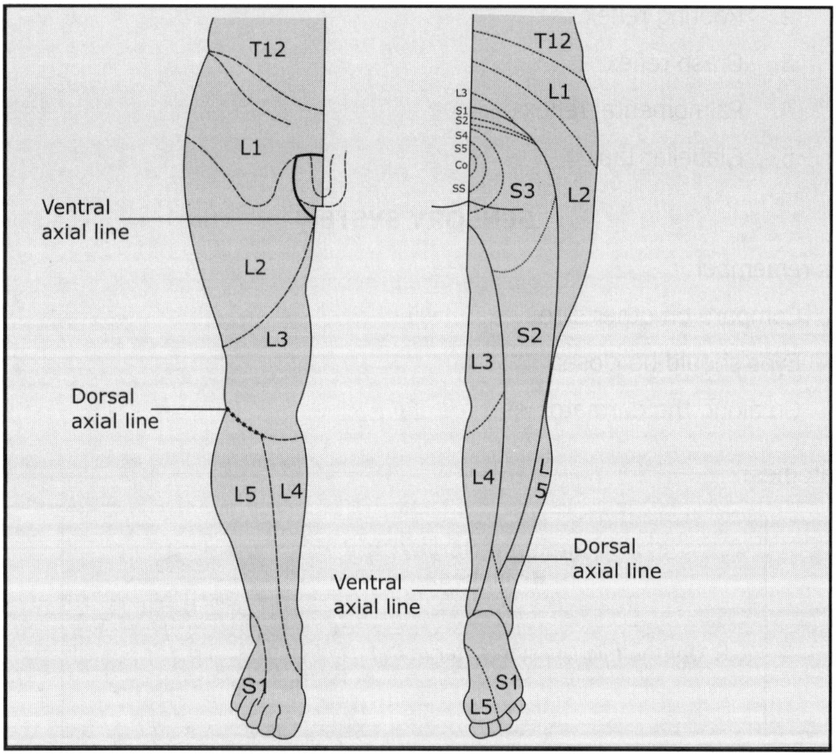

Fig. 4.4: Dermatomes of lower limb

Autonomous zones: There are areas in a dermatome that show very little/no overlap with other dermatomes. Thus they reliably represent if a particular dermat ome is affected or not.

C1	- No dermatome
C2, C3	- Neck (C2 - occiput, C3 - lateral neck)
C4	- Tip of shoulder
C5, C6, C7	- Hand (C5 - thumb, C6 - middle three fingers, C7 - little finger)
T4	- Nipple
T6, T7	- Xiphoid
T10	- Umbilicus
T12	- Inguinal ligament
L1	- Pubis
L3	- Knee
S1	- Lateral foot, sole of foot
S3, S4, S5	- Perianal

- Superficial sensations:
  1. Touch:
     - Fine touch: Wisp of cotton, back of pin
     - Crude touch: Can not be checked clinically
     - Ask yes/no and localize
  2. Pain:
     - Superficial pain: Pin prick
     - Deep pain: Squeeze muscles, tendons, testis
  3. Temperature:
     - Two test tubes: Hot and cold water
     - If not available: Ask if he can feel hot/cold water while bathing

> Dissociative anesthesia:
>
> - Touch sensation intact but pain/temperature lost
> - Dorsal column is intact
> - Causes: Syringomyelia, intramedullary tumor, anterior spinal artery thrombosis
> - Lesion of lateral spinothalamic tract (or its decussating fibers in anterior commissure)

Relation of spinal segments with vertebrae:
- Upper cervical: At same level
- Lower cervical: +1 (i.e. add 1 to vertebral level to get corresponding spinal segment)
- Upper thoracic: +2
- Lower thoracic: +3
- T_{10} vertebra → T_{12} spinal segment
- T_{12} vertebra → L_5 spinal segment
- L_1 vertebra → Spinal cord ends (in adults) (Spinal cord ends at L_3 in children)

- Deep sensations:
  1. Vibration:
     - Pallesthesia is perception of vibration
     - Test with tuning fork of 128 Hz
     - Place it on bony prominences
     - Sites: Big toe, malleoli, shin of tibia, patella, ASIS, sternum, radial/ulnar styloid, olecranon, mastoid, forehead

     1st sensation to be lost in diabetic neuropathy is vibration sense.

  2. Pressure: Test with back of pin
  3. Proprioception:
     - Joint position sense
     - Methods:
       i. Patient tells the position of joint
       ii. Patient reciprocates same position in opposite limb
     - Technique:

Eyes closed

↓

First immobilize proximal joint

↓

Specific way to hold great toe (grip the toe on sides, do not touch dorsal or plantar aspect)

↓

Follow method i. or ii.

↓

Repeat it 10 times (always start from the neutral position)

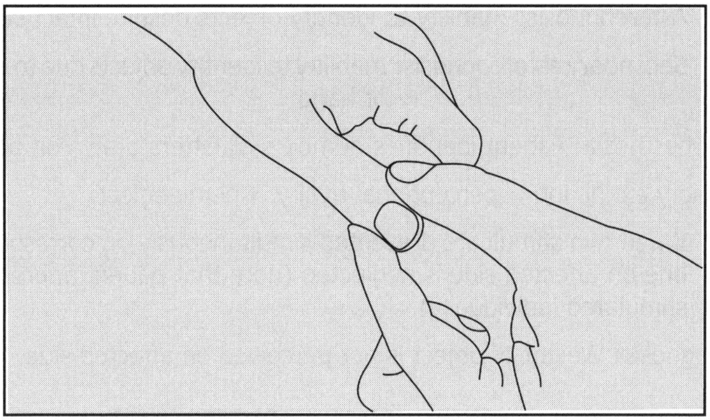

Fig. 4.5: Method to check proprioception

- Interpretation:
    i. Consecutive 5 +ve indicates normal
    ii. Consecutive 3 -ve indicates abnormal

> Conscious proprioception is a function of dorsal column (which relays information to cortex).
> Unconscious proprioception is a function of spinocerebellar and cuneocerebellar tracts which relays information to cerebellum.

- Cortical sensations: Parietal lobe lesions
    1. One-point localization: Topognosis
    2. Two-point discrimination:
        - By compass or 2 pins
        - Technique: Place pins wide apart → bring them closer gradually → when patient perceives them as one point → measure the distance between the pins
        - Ideal distances:
            i. Pulp of fingers and lips: 3 - 5 mm
            ii. Palm: 2 cm
            iii. Dorsum of foot: 3 cm
            iv. Sole: 4 cm
            v. Back: 5 cm
    3. Stereognosis:
        - Place objects in hand and with closed eyes
        - Use familiar objects like coin, key, pen, mobile
        - Do not give bunch of keys as the sound will hint the patient

  - Astereognosis: Inability to identify objects despite intact sensation
  - Secondary astereognosis: Inability to identify objects due to loss of sensations of hand

4. Graphesthesia: Patient identifies numbers or letters drawn on back
5. Sensory extinction ≈ perceptional rivalry ≈ hemineglect:
    - When two stimuli are presented simultaneously on corresponding parts, the one on affected side is neglected (note that patient appreciates both when stimulated individually)
6. Baragnosis: Weight of object is not perceived on affected side

PERIPHERAL NERVES

- Sites to examine:
    1. Greater auricular nerve
    2. Ulnar nerve
    3. Radial nerve
    4. Common peroneal nerve
    5. Sural nerve
    6. Tibial nerve
- Parameters to note:
    - Thickening:
        1. Acquired causes: Leprosy, DM, acromegaly, sarcoidosis
        2. Hereditary causes: NF, CMTD, amyloid, Refsum's disease
    - Nodularity
    - Tenderness: Post herpetic neuralgia
    - Tinel's sign:
        1. Percussion on nerve gives tingling in distal part
        2. Causes:
            i. CTS (carpal tunnel syndrome)
            ii. Tarsal tunnel syndrome
            iii. Guyon's canal - ulnar nerve
            iv. Recovering nerve (sign of recovery)
    - Nerve stretch tests:
        1. SLRT
        2. Crossed SLRT
        3. Lasegue's test

4. Braggard's test
5. Bow string sign
6. Tripod test
7. Femoral nerve stretch test

GAIT

- Definition: Attitude of patient while walking
- Gait and stance are checked only if lower limb power is ≥3
- Types:
  - Spastic gait (due to UMN lesion):
    1. Hemiplegic gait (circumduction gait):
       i. Due to unilateral spasticity
       ii. Arm is flexed at elbow and immobile
       iii. Legs circumduct while walking
    2. Paraplegic gait (sticky gait):
       i. Due to bilateral lower limb spasticity
       ii. Walks stiffly
    3. Scissor's gait (cross legged gait):
       i. Due to bilateral lower limb spasticity and resultant excess adductor spasm
       ii. Crossing of legs on each step
       iii. Seen in spastic type of cerebral palsy
  - Parkinsonian gait:
    1. Also called as extra pyramidal gait, shuffling gait, festinant gait
    2. Universal flexion attitude i.e. stooped posture, stiff posture
    3. Absent/reduced arm movements
    4. Narrow base
    5. Short steps (reduced stride length)
    6. Speed of walking is generally slow but sometimes fast, as if chasing center of gravity (shuffling gait, festinant gait)
    7. Freezing episodes i.e. hesitancy/inability to initiate walking
    8. Turning en bloc i.e. whole body turns as one mass

- Ataxic gait:
  1. Cerebellar ataxic gait:
     i. Also called a drunken gait, reeling gait, staggering gait
     ii. Wide based
     iii. Swaying toward the side of lesion
     iv. Compass gait: Patient walks in circles
     v. Causes: Cerebellar lesions, labyrinthine lesion, alcoholism
  2. Sensory ataxic gait:
     i. Also called as tabetic gait
     ii. Wide based
     iii. Swaying
     iv. Stamping gait (patient stomps ground to hear the foot)
     v. Cause: Bilateral dorsal column lesion
- Foot drop gait: Peroneal nerve injury (inability to dorsiflex)
- Heel drop gait: Tibial nerve injury (inability to plantiflex)
- Flail foot gait: Sciatic nerve injury (inability to dorsiflex and plantarflex)
- Stamping gait: Sensory deficit on sole of foot, etc.
- Waddling gait (oscillating gait, pride of pregnancy gait):

  If unilateral: Lurching gait

  If bilateral: Waddling gait (Patient lurches/waddles on both sides like a duck)

  Causes:
  1. Proximal muscle weakness of both limbs (muscle dystrophy, etc.)
  2. Trendelenburg gait
  3. Ascites
  4. Late pregnancy

• Phases of gait cycle:
  1. Stance phase (60%):
     i. Heel strike
     ii. Foot flat
     iii. Mid stance
     iv. Heel off
     v. Toe off

2. Swing phase (40%):
   i. Acceleration
   ii. Mid swing
   iii. Deceleration

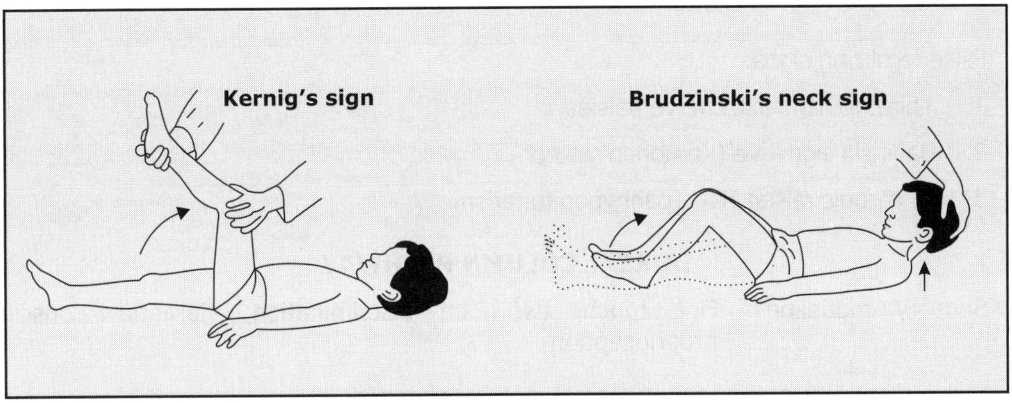

Fig. 4.6: Signs of meningitis

MENINGEAL IRRITATION SIGNS

- Neck rigidity:
  - Resistance to neck's passive flexion
  - Due to extensor neck rigidity
  - Note that in local neck pathology, ALL movements are restricted

- Kernig's sign:
  - Method: Patient lies supine with flexed hip → extend knee passively
  - In meningism, there is resistance to passive extension at knee
  - Interpretation:

    Normal: ≥135° between thigh and leg

    Abnormal: <135° between thigh and leg
  - Cause: Meningeal irritation causes rigidity of hamstrings

- Brudzinski sign:
  - Brudzinski neck sign: On passive flexion of neck → both hips flex
  - Brudzinski leg sign: On passive flexion of hip → other hip flexes

- SLRT and other nerve stretch tests (Refer standard orthopaedic books)

SIGNS OF RAISED ICT

- Cushing's reflex: Triad of hypertension, bradycardia, irregular breathing
- Papilledema: Visual field testing for blind spot enlargement or fundoscopy (ask for visual problems)
- Pupils: Nonreactive to light, unequal
- False localizing signs:
  1. Third, fourth, sixth nerve palsies
  2. Babinski sign +ve (Kernohan's notch)
  3. In chronic raised ICT - panhypopituitarism

DORSAL COLUMN PATHWAY

- Sensory modalities: Fine touch, two-point discrimination, vibration, conscious proprioception
- Cell body of first order neuron: Dorsal root ganglion (DRG)
  Cell body of second order neuron: Nucleus gracilis and cuneatus
  Cell body of third order neuron: VPL nucleus of thalamus
- Pathway:

Receptor

↓

Nerve

↓

DRG

↓

Posterior white column (fasciculus gracilis ≈ tract of Gall: Below T6)

(fasciculus cuneatus ≈ tract of Burdah: Above T6)

↓

Nucleus gracilis and nucleus cuneatus (some uncrossed fibers go to cerebellum via inferior peduncle which is cuneo-cerebellar tract ≈ posterior external arcuate fibers)

↓

Great sensory decussation (≈ internal arcuate fibers) in medulla

↓

Medial lemniscus

↓

VPL of thalamus

↓

Posterior limb of internal capsule

↓

Corona radiata

↓

Brodmann areas 3, 1, 2 (primary somatosensory area)

ANTERIOR SPINOCEREBELLAR PATHWAY

- Sensory modalities: Proprioception (unconscious type) (upper limb + lower limb + trunk)
- Cell body of first order neuron: Dorsal root ganglion (DRG)
  Cell body of second order neuron: Nucleus dorsalis (Clarke's nucleus)
- Pathway:

Receptor

↓

Nerve

↓

DRG

↓

Nucleus dorsalis (nucleus of Clarke)

↓

First decussation through anterior commissure of spinal cord at same level

↓

Anterior spinocerebellar tract

↓

Midbrain

↓

Superior cerebellar peduncle

↓

Second decussation within cerebellum

POSTERIOR SPINOCEREBELLAR PATHWAY

- Sensory modalities: Proprioception (unconscious type) (lower limb + trunk)
- Cell body of neurons: Same as anterior spinocerebellar tract
- Pathway:

Receptor

↓

Nerve

↓

Dorsal root ganglion

↓

Nucleus dorsalis (Clarke's nucleus)

↓

No decussation

↓

Posterior spinocerebellar tract

↓

Medulla

↓

Inferior cerebellar peduncle

↓

Cerebellum (no decussation)

CORTICOSPINAL PATHWAY

- Cell body of first order neuron: Pyramidal cells of Betz in Brodmann area 4
  Cell body of second order neuron: Anterior horn cell
- Pathway:

Brodmann area 4 (primary motor area) (some fibers arise from areas 3, 1, 2 and 6)

↓

Posterior limb of internal capsule (fibers for upper limb are near genu and fibers for lower limb are away from genu)

↓

Crus cerebri in midbrain

(Middle section of crus cerebri)

(Upper limb fibers are arranged medially)

(Lower limb fibers are arranged laterally)

↓

Lower medulla (at pyramids)

↓

85% fibers decussate (pyramidal decussation)

↓

Lateral corticospinal tract

↓

Anterior horn cell

↓

Nerve

↓

Muscle

(15% fibers do not decussate in medulla. They continue downward to form anterior corticospinal tract and decussate in spinal cord at the level of anterior horn cell.)

LATERAL SPINOTHALAMIC TRACT

- Sensory modalities: Pain and temperature
- Cell body of first order neuron: Dorsal root ganglion (DRG)
  Cell body of second order neuron: Substantia gelatinosa of Rolando
  Cell body of third order neuron: VPL nucleus of thalamus
- Pathway:

Receptor

↓

Nerves - A delta fibres (fast pain), C fibres (slow pain)

↓

DRG

↓

Substantia gelatinosa of Rolando

↓

Decussation through anterior commissure within one segment (above and below) to form lateral spinothalamic tract

↓

Spinal lemniscus in medulla

↓

VPL nucleus of thalamus

↓

Posterior limb of internal capsule

↓

Areas 3, 1, 2 (primary somatosensory area)

ANTERIOR SPINOTHALAMIC TRACT

- Sensory modalities: Light touch (crude touch), pressure, itching
- Cell body: Same as lateral spinothalamic tract
- Pathways:

Receptors

↓

Nerves

↓

Dorsal root ganglion

↓

Substantia gelatinosa of Rolando

↓

Decussate through anterior commissure within several segments (above and below) to form anterior spinothalamic tract

↓

Spinal lemniscus in medulla

↓

VPL nucleus of thalamus

↓

Posterior limb of internal capsule

↓

Areas 3, 1, 2 (primary somatosensory area)

5

Respiratory System

GENERAL EXAMINATION

[Only additional points on RS examination have been mentioned below. Refer Chapter 2 in Section I beforehand.]

- Decubitus:
  - Lateral: On the side of pleural effusion, abscess, cavity, pleurisy
  - Tripod posture: Dyspnea
- BMI: Obstructive sleep apnea
- Raised JVP:
  - Cor pulmonale
  - Tension pneumothorax
- Pulsus paradoxus: Severe asthma/severe COPD
- Respiration:
  - Rhythm: Four types (discussed in Chapter 2 in Section I)
  - Two types: Abdomino-thoracic, thoraco-abdominal
  - Labored breathing ≈ air hunger ≈ respiratory distress
- Edema: Seen in cor pulmonale
- Clubbing: Empyema, bronchiectasis, abscess, lung cancer, ILD, etc.

  [Refer clubbing in Chapter 2 in Section I for more details]
- Skin:
  - Tobacco staining
  - Subcutaneous nodules in RA (Caplan syndrome = RA + pneumoconiosis)
- Asterixes: Hypercapnic encephalopathy (CO_2 narcosis)
- Spine: Kyphoscoliosis
- TB stigmata: Important in all respiratory cases
- Facies: Pursed lips in COPD

- Treatment:
  - ICD (in triangle of safety, fifth ICS, midaxillary line)
  - Site for diagnostic or therapeutic tap (at the site of maximal fluid collection as identified by USG or clinical methods)
  - O_2 delivery devices or ventilator

SYSTEMIC EXAMINATION

> Systemic exam in any case should start by saying the following:
>
> "Patient was examined with due consent under adequate illumination, well exposed till umbilicus, in sitting position, in presence of female attendant (only in female patients)."

UPPER RESPIRATORY TRACT EXAMINATION

[ALWAYS examine upper respiratory tract before lower respiratory tract]

1. Nose
2. Oral cavity:
   - Say "Oral cavity is hygienic or dirty"
   - Check for gingiva, teeth, buccal, floor, tongue, palate
   - Smoking causes:
     i. Tobacco-stained teeth
     ii. Smoker's keratosis
     iii. Leukoplakia
     iv. Erythroplakia
     v. Submucosal fibrosis
     vi. Oral cancer
3. Oropharynx:
   i. Pharyngitis
   ii. Reflux pharyngitis
   iii. Postnasal drip
4. Sinus:
   i. Ethmoid (palpate on the sides of root of nose)
   ii. Sphenoid (cannot be palpated)
   iii. Maxillary (palpate on malar prominences)
   iv. Frontal (palpate on the medial end of superior orbital margin, by applying pressure in upward direction)

LOWER RESPIRATORY TRACT EXAMINATION

- Inspection:
  1. Shape:
     - See tangentially from the feet of patient while he lies supine. Normally AP < transverse diameter, but in COPD (barrel-shaped chest), AP > transverse diameter
     - Pectus excavatum (cobbler's chest)
     - Pectus carinatum (in childhood obstructive diseases, forceful respiration leads to abnormal molding of chest wall)
     - Bulging precordium (in congenital heart disease)
     - Kyphoscoliosis causes restrictive lung disease and type 2 respiratory failure (ALWAYS EXAMINE BACK IN RS EXAMINATION TO CHECK FOR KYPHOSCOLIOSIS)
  2. Symmetry: Compare these on opposite sides
     - Nipple level
     - Shoulder level
     - Inferior angle of scapula level
     - Spino scapular distance
     - Chest depression/fullness
  3. Movements: Just note if movements are restricted on one side
  4. Respiration:
     - Labored breathing:
       1. Accessory muscles of respiration like SCM, scalene, intercostal muscles, pectoralis major (by stabilizing the upper limbs in a tripod position), etc.

          [Refer respiration in Chapter 2 in Section I for details]
       2. Dilation of nares (nasal orifices)
       3. Noisy breathing
       4. Retraction of: Subcostal → intercostal → apical spaces (in sequence)
       5. Breathing with open mouth
       6. Breathing with pursed lips seen in COPD (pursing of lips helps to increase positive intrathoracic pressure to expire the trapped air)
     - Rhythm: Kussmaul, Biot's, Cheyne-Stokes, ataxic, etc.

       [Refer respiration in Chapter 2 in Section I for details.]
     - Observe for duration of phases (inspiration vs. expiration). Normally expiration is longer than inspiration.

       In obstructive lung diseases, expiration is prolonged.

- Audible sounds:
  1. Wheeze: Expiratory sound due to obstruction of intrathoracic airway
  2. Stridor: Inspiratory sound due to obstruction of extrathoracic airway
  3. Bubbling/rattling: Due to severe pulmonary edema (cardiogenic or noncardiogenic)

5. Tracheal deviation (Trail's sign): Observe prominence of sternal head of SCM, which denotes deviation of trachea to that side
6. Apex impulse: For deviation
7. Skin, sinus, scars, dilated veins: Empyema necessitans (painful red intercostal swelling) precedes formation of fistula

> (It is called empyema "necessitans" as urgent drainage is necessary)

> During examination of chest expansion and auscultation, ask the patient to take deep breaths (if required with open mouth)

> Deviation of trachea and apex beat is governed by PUSH - PULL EFFECT:
> - Trachea indicates push or pull in upper part of thorax
> - Apex beat denotes push or pull in lower part of thorax
> - Push: pleural effusion, pneumothorax, lung carcinoma
> - Pull: lung collapse

- Palpation:
  1. Inspectory findings confirmed
  2. Superficial palpation: Local rise of temperature or local tenderness
     - Sternal tenderness: For causes refer standard books
     - Costochondral tenderness: Tietze syndrome
     - Intercostal tenderness: Pleuritis
     - Intercostal swelling, redness, and tenderness in empyema necessitans
     - Bone tenderness
  3. Measurements: Measurements to be taken:
     i. AP diameter
     ii. Transverse diameter
     iii. AP: Transverse diameter ratio (normally 5:7)
     iv. Hemithorax diameter
     v. Chest expansion

vi. Hemithorax expansion

- AP: Transverse diameter is >5:7 in hyperinflated lungs (COPD)
- Chest expansion assessed by measuring circumference of chest at nipple level at maximal inspiration and expiration. Normally, it is >5 cm. If <5 it indicates poor chest expansion.
- Similarly, circumference of hemithorax can be measured (from sternum to vertebral spine at nipple level) and compared with opposite side to assess unilateral disease
- For i, ii, iii, iv: Ask patient to hold breath in mid-respiration and use a cardboard
- For v, vi: Use a measuring tape with crossed tape method

4. Movements:
   - Check for expansion at upper anterior chest, lower anterior chest, apex, suprascapular, interscapular, and infrascapular regions. Note that upper chest has predominant bucket handle movement, while lower chest has predominantly pump handle movement.

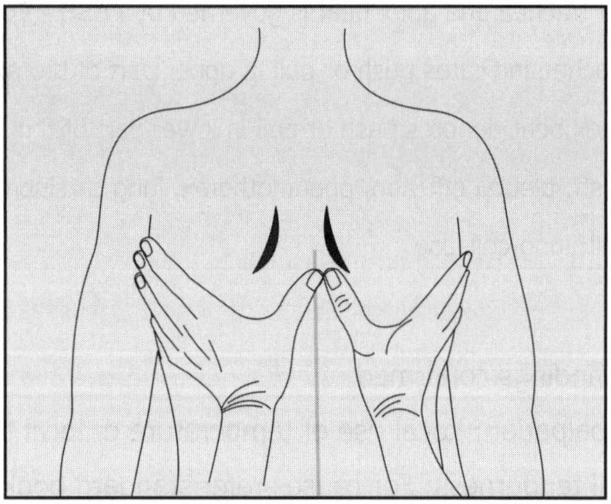

Fig. 5.1: Chest movements- posterior

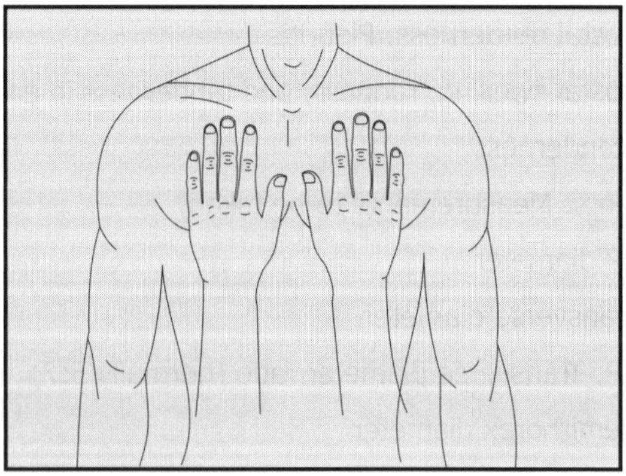

Fig. 5.2: Chest movements- upper anterior

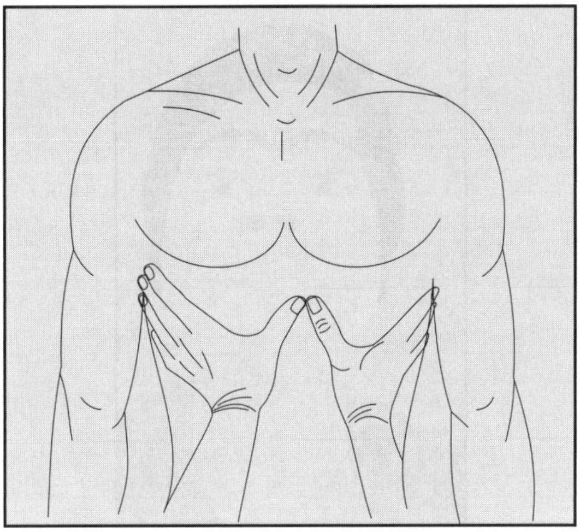

Fig. 5.3: Chest movements- lower anterior

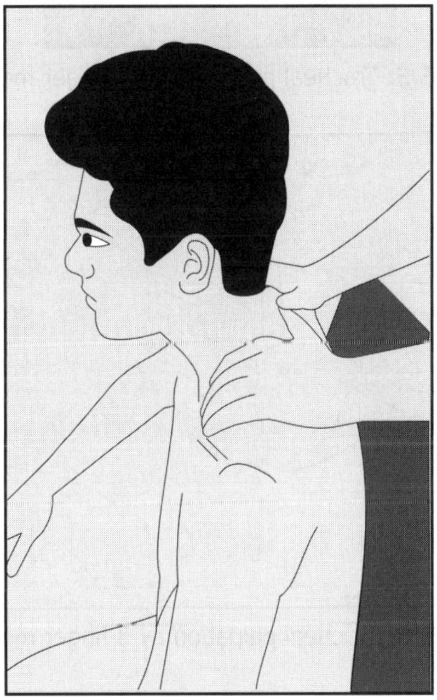

Fig. 5.4: Chest movements- apical

5. Tracheal position by: (TRAIL'S SIGN IS INSPECTORY finding and not palpatory)
   - Two-finger method: Index and middle fingers are insinuated in the groove between trachea and SCM and compared with the opposite side to judge deviation
   - Three-finger method: Index and ring fingers are placed on medial end of each clavicle and middle finger is rolled downward from thyroid cartilage to suprasternal notch to note deviation

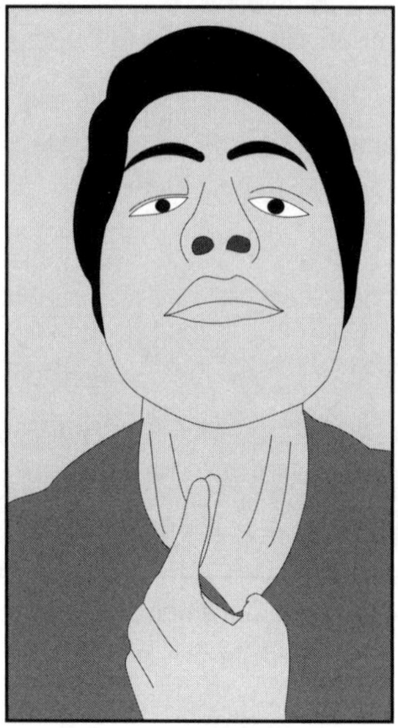

Fig. 5.5: Tracheal palpation by 2 finger method

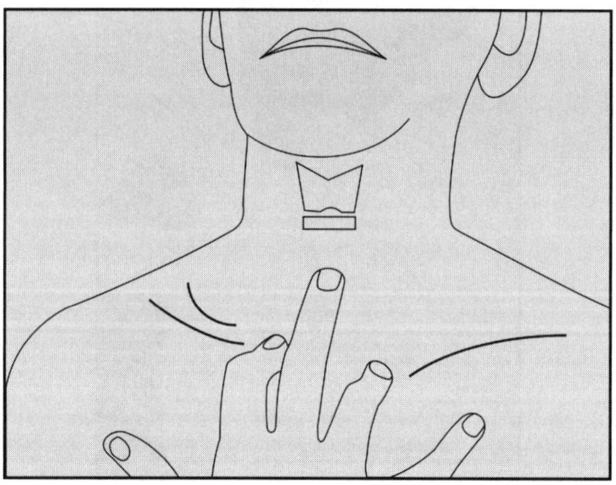

Fig. 5.6: Tracheal palpation by 3 finger method

6. Apex beat:
   - Displaced to left or right (push - pull effect)
   - Displaced outward in RVH due to cor pulmonale
   - Absent or poorly felt in massive pneumothorax or tension pneumothorax
   - Parasternal heave seen in cor pulmonale due to RVH
7. Tactile vocal fremitus (TVF):
   - Patient says "9-9-9 . . . or 1-1-1 . . ."
   - Ulnar border of hand is used by examiner

- ALWAYS COMPARE RIGHT AND LEFT SIDES. Do not percuss one side completely and then the other. Each ICS examined on one side should be immediately followed by examination of the corresponding ICS on opposite side.
- TVF increases with increase in density of lung parenchyma i.e.
  - i. Increase in solid component of parenchyma: Consolidation, pulmonary edema, interstitial lung disease (it is NOT seen pleural effusion as pleural fluid is OUTSIDE lung parenchyma, and creates an interface/barrier for transmission of sound to the examiner)
  - ii. Decrease in air within the alveoli: Compression of lung (seen in normal lung JUST ABOVE the level of pleural effusion, collapse)
- Decreased TVF with:
  - i. Decrease in density of lung parenchyma i.e. air trapping seen in COPD, severe asthma
  - ii. Interface/barrier between lung parenchyma and chest wall leads to loss of sound energy and reduced TVF: Pleural effusion, pneumothorax
  - iii. Thick chest wall: Thickened pleura, obesity, breast tissue
- TVF ALWAYS GOES HAND IN HAND WITH VOCAL RESONANCE

8. Tracheal descent (laryngeal height): From suprasternal notch to thyroid cartilage
9. Other: Subcutaneous emphysema around ICD or central venous catheter

- Percussion:
  - Method:

Start with direct percussion of clavicle

↓

Anterior chest wall (all intercostal spaces from up to down in MCL)

↓

Axilla (up to down in MAL) (patient places hands over his head)

↓

Back (suprascapular, interscapular, infrascapular) (done by asking the patient to protract his scapulae by placing his hands on his opposite shoulders)

↓

Apex (done by standing at the back)

(ALWAYS COMPARE RIGHT AND LEFT SIDES. Do not percuss one side completely and then the other. Each ICS percussed on one side should be immediately followed by percussion of the corresponding ICS on opposite side.)

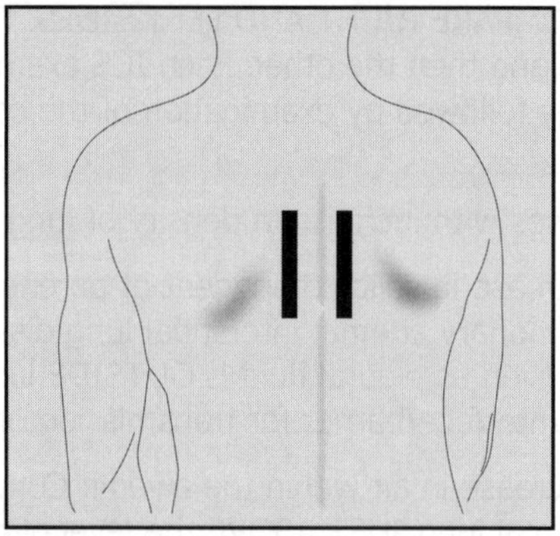

Fig. 5.7: Site of percussion of interscapular area

- Normal notes on chest percussion:
  1. Tympanic: Traube's area
  2. Dull:
     i. Cardiac dullness
     ii. Liver dullness
     iii. Apical dullness (except Kronig's isthmus)
  3. Resonant: Everywhere else
- Abnormal notes on chest percussion:
  1. Tympanic note: Seen in diaphragmatic hernia and eventration of diaphragm
  2. Hyper-resonant note: Seen in
     i. Emphysema (COPD)
     ii. Pneumothorax
     iii. Severe asthma attack causing air trapping
  3. Dull note: Seen in
     i. Pleural thickening, ILD (impaired resonance)
     ii. Consolidation (woody dull)
     iii. Pleural effusion (stony dull)
- Special types of percussion:
  1. Tidal percussion: Done in right MCL
     - To note the upper border of liver
     - It helps to distinguish between subdiaphragmatic pathology and supradiaphragmatic pathology
     - On inspiration, a subdiaphragmatic pathology or liver dullness shifts down to lower space

  - In case of supra diaphragmatic pathology (pleural effusion) or hemidiaphragmatic palsy, dullness stays at the same level

2. Shifting percussion/shifting dullness: For hydropneumothorax
3. Coin percussion: For pneumothorax. Patient holds the chest piece of stethoscope on anterior chest wall. Doctor percusses by hitting a coin over another coin placed flat on the posterior wall of thorax. A tinkling sound is heard in the stethoscope, indicating presence of air.

Grades of percussion notes (high to low):

Tympanic - due to hollow viscus

↓

Hyper resonant - due to pneumothorax or COPD

↓

Resonant - due to air-filled alveoli

↓

Dull (impaired resonance) - due to pleural thickening, ILD

↓

Dull (woody dull) - due to consolidation

↓

Stony dull - due to pleural effusion

(Sound which is produced on percussion on thigh)

- Auscultation:

  Ask patient to take DEEP breaths (to amplify sounds) with an OPEN mouth (to prevent adventitious sounds)

  - Following sounds are to be auscultated:
    1. Normal breath sounds
    2. Abnormal breath sounds
    3. Adventitious breath sounds (rhonchi, crepitation, pleural rub)
    4. Vocal resonance
    5. Others: Succussion splash (heard in hydro-pneumothorax)

❖ Normal breath sounds:

  Describe the following points:

  1. Type of normal breath sound (bronchial, bronchovesicular, vesicular)

2. Site: Trachea, sternum, right or left supramammary, mammary, inframammary, upper axilla, lower axilla, apex, suprascapular, interscapular, infrascapular
3. Intensity: Reduced, normal, increased

Difference between bronchial and vesicular sounds:

Vesicular	**Bronchovesicular**	**Bronchial**
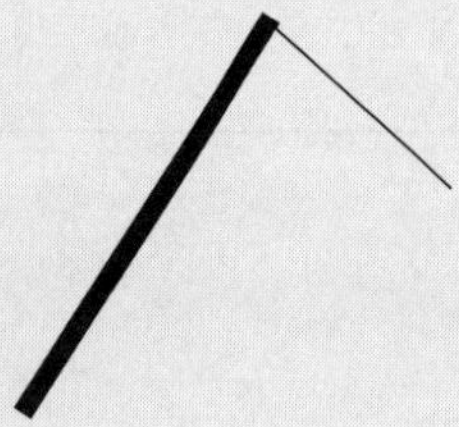	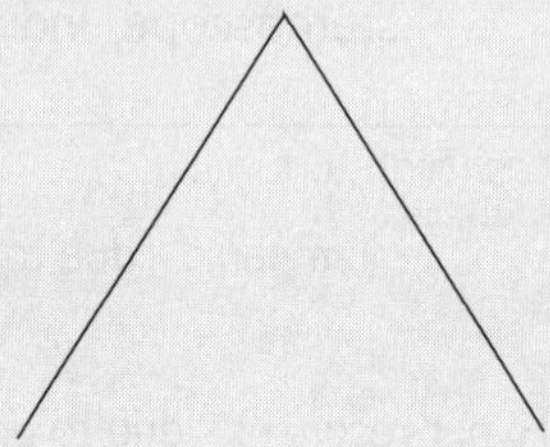	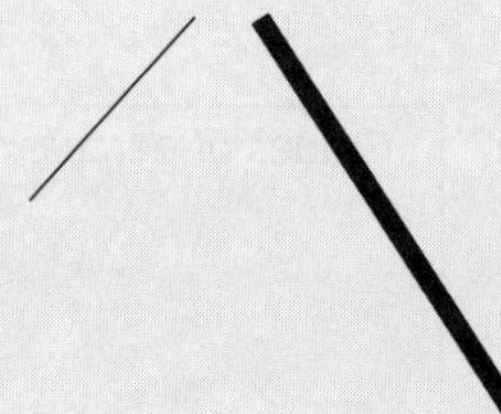
Rustling of leaves		Blowing in a pipe
1. Inspiratory - long and loud 2. No gap 3. Expiratory - soft and short	1. Equal inspiratory and expiratory 2. No gap	1. Inspiratory - soft and short 2. Gap 3. Expiratory - long and loud
- Over most of lungs	Normally not heard	- Upper sternum - Trachea - Posterior interscapular space

❖ Abnormal breath sounds:

1. Bronchial breath sounds (tubular type) heard over periphery:
   - Consolidation of lung
   - Compression of lung (just ABOVE the level of pleural fluid)
2. Reduced/absent breath sounds:
   - Reduced ventilation due to lung collapse/atelectasis/severe asthma (silent chest), or poor expansion (restrictive lung disease - ILD, kyphoscoliosis)
   - Interface (pleural effusion, pneumothorax, thick pleura)
   - Thick chest wall (breast tissue, obesity)
3. Cavernous sounds: It is a type of bronchial breath sound heard when a small cavity (e.g. TB) communicates with respiratory tree

4. Amphoric sounds: It is a type of bronchial breath sound heard when a large cavity communicates with respiratory tree (e.g. bronchopleural fistula causing a pneumothorax)

❖ Adventitious sounds:

i. Rhonchi

ii. Crepitation

iii. Pleural rub

1. Rhonchi:
   - Musical sounds, heard best in expiration (but can also be heard in inspiration)
   - Due to narrowing/obstruction of airways
   - Although in severe narrowing, no sound is heard (e.g. severe attack of asthma - SILENT CHEST)
   - Can be MONOPHONIC (due to obstruction of a single bronchi)
   - Can be POLYPHONIC (due to multiple airway obstruction, leading to multiple frequencies, thus a musical sound)
   - Most commonly we hear bilateral polyphonic rhonchi
   - Causes of monophonic rhonchi: Foreign body, endobronchial growth, external compression of bronchi by lymph node
   - Causes of polyphonic rhonchi: Bronchitis, asthma, bronchiectasis
2. Crepitation:
   - Bubbling or crackling sound best heard in inspiration (sometimes in expiration too)
   - Two subtypes: Rales and crackles

Rales	**Crackles**
Bubbling sounds	Crackling sound
Due to bubbling of air in fluid filled in respiratory tree	Due to sudden opening of fibrotic collapsed respiratory tree
Mid-inspiratory	End inspiratory
Character changes on coughing	Character remains the same on coughing

Seen in: 1. Pneumonia (only in resolution phase) 2. Pulmonary edema 3. Bronchitis (due to secretions) 4. Bronchiectasis (due to secretions)	Seen in: 1. ILD 2. Early stage of pulmonary edema (only interstitial edema)
• Fine basal crepitation: Due to LVF causing cardiogenic pul monary edema • Velcro crepitations are fine crepitations heard in ILD • Coarse crepitations are heard in bronchiectasis	

3. Pleural rub:
   - Coarse leathery sound heard in both inspiration and expiration
   - Heard at only those sites with pleuritis (hence often confined to an area)
   - Accentuates on pressing the stethoscope on ICS
   - Does not change after coughing
   - Important to differentiate it from pericardial rub (ask the patient to hold breath. Pericardial rub continues, but the pleural rub stops.)

> Wheeze and stridor are adventitious sounds heard WITHOUT a stethoscope.
>
> Rhonchi, crepitation and pleural rub are adventitious sounds heard WITH stethoscope on auscultation.

❖ Vocal resonance:
- Similar concept as TVF
- Similar method as TVF
- Similar findings and causes as TVF
- ONLY in cases of increased vocal resonance, ask the patient to whisper (to check for WHISPERING PECTORILOQUY)
- If we hear CLEAR and LOUD words: BRONCHOPHONY, seen in: Consolidation
- If we hear UNCLEAR and LOUD words: EGOPHONY, seen in: Communicating cavity and bronchopleural fistula

Important concept in pleural effusion:

There is compression of lung parenchyma just above the level of fluid.

Below the level there is reduced TVF and vocal resonance, stony dull note and absent/ reduced breath sounds.

This compression causes increased density of lung parenchyma, thus the clinical findings JUST ABOVE level of fluid are:

1. Increased TVF and vocal resonance
2. Dull note (impaired resonance)
3. High intensity of bronchial breath (tubular type) sounds

(Although sometimes these changes can be partially seen or not seen, there can be compensatory hyperinflation of the lung above the pleural fluid level, giving a hyper resonant note called SKODIAC RESONANCE.)

Following table compares the clinical findings of common chest pathologies:

	Consolidation	**ILD**	**Pleural effusion**	**Pneumothorax**
Inspection	Normal shape	Normal shape	Normal shape	Normal shape
	Normal symmetry	Asymmetrical with drooping of shoulders on affected side	Normal symmetry (can have bulging intercostals spaces)	Normal symmetry
	Not affected	Movements reduced on affected side	Movements reduced on affected side	Movements reduced on affected side
	No deviation of trachea or apex beat	Deviation seen in unilateral disease, but since most ILD are bilateral, no deviation seen	Trachea and apex beat deviated to contralateral side (push effect)	Trachea and apex beat deviated to contralateral side (push effect)
Palpation	TVF increased	TVF increased	TVF decreased	TVF decreased
	Normal chest expansion	Reduced chest expansion	Reduced chest expansion	Reduced chest expansion
	AP: Transverse ratio is normal	AP: Transverse ratio is normal	AP: Transverse ratio is normal	If underlying COPD present, then AP: Transverse ratio is ≥5:7 (barrel shaped chest)

(Continued...)

	Consolidation	ILD	Pleural effusion	Pneumothorax
Percussion	Dull (woody dull)	Dull (impaired resonance)	Dull (stony dull)	Hyperresonant
Ausculta-tion	Bronchial breath sounds	Reduced breath sounds	Reduced or absent sounds	Reduced or absent sounds (± Amphoric sounds heard in case of broncho-pleural fistula)
	Crepitation (+) mid-inspiratory rales	Crepitation (+) end inspiratory crackles	(−)	(−)
	Vocal resonance increased	Vocal resonance increased	Vocal resonance decreased	Vocal resonance decreased
	Whispering pectoriloquy (+) Bronchophony (+)	Whispering pectoriloquy (−)	Not applicable	Not applicable Egophony (+) if a cavity or bronchopleural fistula)

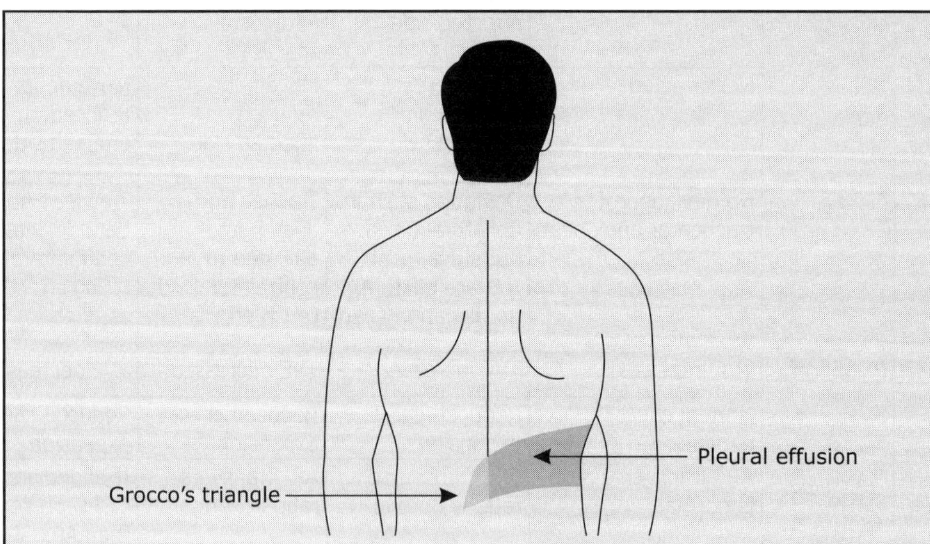

Fig. 5.8: Grocco's triangle

Eponymous sites on thorax:

1. Traube's area: Refer to Chapter 6 in Section II
2. Kronig's isthmus: Medial part of supraclavicular space. It lies above the apex of lung, and gives resonant note on percussion. Dull note in this area signifies apical pathology (secondary TB, pancoast tumor)
3. Grocco's triangle: Seen in pleural effusion. It is a small triangular area on the back (paraspinally) on the contralateral side. It occurs be cause the pleural fluid pushes the mediastinal contents to opposite side.

Anatomically/pathologically:
Lungs are divided into lobes and segments. But clinically these cannot be ascertained, hence do not use these terms to describe findings on examination.

Radiologically:
Lungs are divided into zones. Hence use this term only for X-ray and CT scan findings and not for describing findings on examination.

Clinically areas on chest are:
Supramammary, mammary, inframammary, upper axilla, lower axilla, apical, suprascapular, interscapular, infrascapular.
Use these terms while describing clinical findings.
In case of TVF and percussion describe the findings in terms of ICS.

Difference between pleural effusion and hydropneumothorax:

(Triple **S**)

1. **S**uccussion splash
2. **S**hifting dullness
3. **S**traight line (air fluid level) on X-ray

Paradoxical movement of chest wall:
Seen in flail chest because the independent piece of chest wall gets sucked in during inspiration and pushed out during expiration.

Paradoxical movement of abdomen with respiration:
Seen in diaphragmatic palsy, due to upward movement of diaphragm on inspiration and downward movement during expiration.

6

Gastrointestinal System

GENERAL EXAMINATION

[Only additional points on GI general examination have been mentioned below. Refer Chapter 2 in Section I beforehand.]

- CCC and orientation:
    - ❖ Hepatic encephalopathy:
        - Definition: It is a neuropsychiatric syndrome with abnormality of sleep, behavior, consciousness and other neurological signs, with distinct EEG pattern
        - Know the cause, mechanism, precipitating factors, and treatment [Refer standard books]
        - WEST HAVEN grading:

Grade	Features	Asterixis	EEG
1st	Disordered sleep cycles, micrographia, constructional apraxia, euphoria, depression, mild confusion	May or may not be seen (seen in later part of 1st grade)	Triphasic
2nd	Moderate confusion, drowsiness	Seen	Triphasic (theta > delta)
3rd	Severe confusion, stupor	Seen	Triphasic (delta > theta)
4th	Coma	Not seen	Delta waves

- Nourishment: Cachexia seen in chronic liver disease
- Decubitus:
    - Orthopneic posture (propped up) due to severe ascites causing respiratory distress
    - Still abdomen in peritonitis (rigid dorsal decubitus)
    - Left lateral in amoebic liver abscess
- Temperature:
    - Hodgkin's lymphoma (hepatosplenomegaly) shows Pel-Ebstein fever pattern
    - Spontaneous bacterial peritonitis (SBP)

- Hepatitis
- Chills/rigors seen in liver abscess (pyogenic and amoebic), malaria, etc.
- In alcohol intoxication we find warm periphery with hypothermia

- Pulse:
  - Low volume in ascites (due to hypovolemia)
  - Bradycardia (obstructive jaundice)
  - Tachycardia: Fever, SBP, hepatitis

- Respiratory rate:
  - Labored breathing, tachypnea, thoracoabdominal breathing (in ascites)
  - Ataxic in terminal hepatic encephalopathy
  - Ascites can cause hydrothorax leading to respiratory distress

- BP:
  - Hypotension due to severe hematemesis and 3rd space loss (in case of ascites)

- JVP:
  - Raised JVP in case of cardiac cirrhosis

- Pallor: Seen in liver disease

- Edema: Seen in liver disease

- Lymphadenopathy:
  - Irish nodules (axilla)
  - Sister Mary Joseph nodules (umbilicus)
  - Troisier's sign/Virchow's lymph node (left supra clavicular lymph node)
  - Causes of hepato-splenomegaly, which also involve lymph nodes, e.g., lymphoma

- Icterus: Refer Chapter 2 in Section I

- Cyanosis: Seen in hepatopulmonary syndrome

> Hepatopulmonary syndrome:
> - It is a triad of:
>   1. Liver disease
>   2. Hypoxia
>   3. Pulmonary AV fistula (due to pulmonary vasodilation)
> - Clinical feature: Platypnea (orthodeoxia)

Hepatorenal syndrome:

- Deranged RFTs in absence of renal pathology or shock
- Caused by defective clearance of vasoconstrictors by the liver leading to intrarenal vasoconstriction

- Clubbing: Primary biliary cirrhosis, inflammatory bowel disease, celiac sprue
- Skin and nails:
  - Terry's sign/Terry's nail (hypoproteinemia)
  - Blue nail in Wilson's disease
  - Pigmentation (primary biliary cirrhosis, primary sclerosing cholangitis)
  - Dark skin in hemochromatosis
- Eyes: KF rings (Wilson's disease)
- Gait: Short steppage gait (due to peritonitis)
- Vitamin deficiency: Thiamine deficiency, vitamin K deficiency
  [Refer Chapter 2 in Section I]
- Tattoo, multiple puncture marks: HBV, blood-borne diseases

Signs of liver cell failure:

(Listed in order from hand to shoulder to HFN to chest to abdomen to lower limbs)

- Ridged, brittle nails, Terry's nail
- Flapping tremor
- Loss of hair
- Palmar erythema
- Loss of axillary hair
- Alopecia
- Fetor hepaticus
- Hepatic facies:
  1. Icterus
  2. Hollowing of temporal fossa
  3. Sunken eyes
  4. Loss of buccal fat pad
- Spider nevi
- Paper money skin

(Continued...)

- Petechiae
- Gynecomastia
- Abdominal distension
- Dilated veins
- Testicular atrophy
- Menstrual irregularity
- Pedal edema
- Dupuytren's contracture (sign of alcoholic cirrhosis)
- Parotid enlargement (sign of alcoholic cirrhosis)

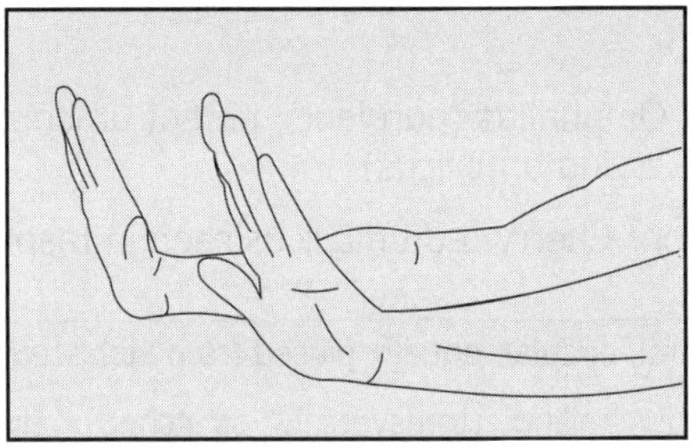

Fig. 6.1: Method to check for flapping tremors

SYSTEMIC EXAMINATION

Systemic exam in any case should start by saying the following:

"Patient was examined with due consent under adequate illumination, well exposed from nipple to knees, in supine and standing positions, in presence of female attendant (only in female patients)."

[Always mention upper GI examination before lower GI examination]

UPPER GI EXAMINATION

- It includes teeth, tongue, tonsils, oropharynx
- Check for effects of tobacco [Refer Chapter 5 in Section II for details], vitamin deficiencies, icterus, pallor, etc.

D/Ds of abdominal distension: 7 Fs + others

F fat	Down syndrome
F fluid	Hypothyroidism
F fetus	Rickets
F feces	Hypokalemia
F flatus	
F full bladder	
F fatal growth (malignant growth)	

LOWER GI EXAMINATION

- Inspection:
  1. Shape/contour:
     - Flat
     - Globular
     - Scaphoid
  2. Symmetry:
     - Can be asymmetrical due to lump in abdomen
     - Visceroptosis (hollowing of right and left hypochondrium)
  3. Umbilicus:
     - Discharge: Omphalitis (purulent), patent urachus (clear fluid) (called as crying umbilicus)
     - Discoloration: Cherry red umbilicus seen in raspberry tumor

> Normal shape: Inverted, central, circular, equally placed from xiphisternum and pubic symphysis
>
> In ascites: Flat or everted, smiling (transversely stretched), distance from umbilicus to xiphoid is more than distance from umbilicus to pubic symphysis
>
> In ovarian cyst: Flat, everted, vertically stretched, distance from umbilicus to xiphisternum is less than distance from umbilicus to pubic symphysis
>
> In obesity: Buried

  4. Movements:
     - Normally: Inspiration causes bulge, expiration causes hollow
     - Paradoxical movement: Diaphragmatic palsy
     - Absent movement (still abdomen): Peritonitis
  5. Pulsations:
     - Epigastrium
     - RHC in pulsatile liver
  6. Peristalsis: to elicit visible peristalsis by use of topical ether or gentle flicking

> Directions of various peristalses:
> 1. Stomach: Left top to right bottom
> 2. Small intestine: Ladder pattern
> 3. Ascending colon: Down to up
> 4. Transverse colon: Right to left
> 5. Descending colon: Up to down

7. Skin:
   - Tense shiny skin due to distension
   - Wrinkled and stria albicantes due to old distension
   - Ecchymosis at various sites
   - Purple stria due to Cushing's syndrome

> Ecchymosis at various sites:
>
> Cullen's sign: Periumbilical
>
> Grey turner's sign: Flanks
>
> Fox sign: Inguinal region

8. Scars
9. Sinus:
   - Fistula in Crohn's disease
   - Patent urachus
   - Raspberry tumor
   - Entero-cutaneous fistula
10. Dilated veins: 2 types

Radially arranged (caput medusae)	**Longitudinally arranged**
Around umbilicus	At flanks
Due to portal hypertension	Due to IVC or SVC obstruction
Direction: Radially outward (to be checked in palpation by Harvey's sign)	Direction: Down to up (IVC block), up to down (SVC block)

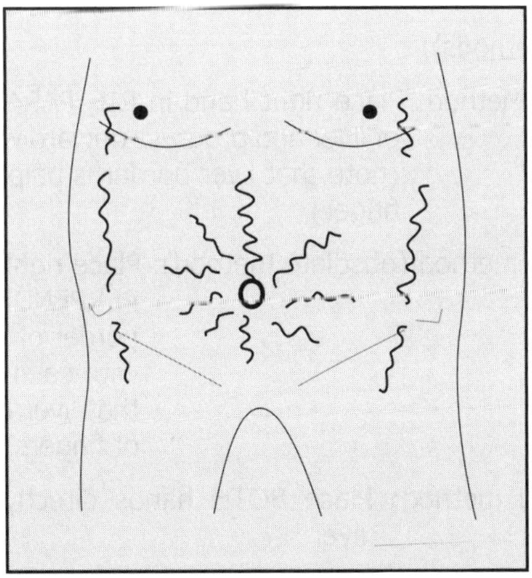

Fig. 6.2: Dilated veins over abdominal wall

11. Hernial orifices + divarication of recti
    External genitalia
    Renal angle fullness
    Supraclavicular fossa
    [These 4 points are to be examined in ALL abdominal cases]

- Palpation:

  (Abdominal palpation should always be done in DORSAL POSITION i.e. knees and hips FLEXED and with warm sanitized hands)

  - Always start by saying "On palpation inspectory findings were confirmed"
  - Measurements: As mentioned on page 141
  - Superficial palpation: Say "On superficial palpation, there is no local rise of temperature or tenderness. There is no obvious lump or guarding/rigidity of the abdomen."
    1. Local rise of temperature
    2. Local tenderness (shifting tenderness seen in mesenteric lymphadenitis)
    3. Obvious lump
    4. Guarding and rigidity
    5. Edema of abdominal wall
  - Deep palpation:
    [Refer Chapter 9 in Section IV for details on swelling]
    1. Liver palpation
    2. Spleen palpation
    3. Kidney palpation
    4. Any other lump

❖ Liver palpation: (Do not forget to palpate the left lobe of liver which lies in epigastrium)

  - Methods (5 methods):
    1. Classical Method: Place right hand in RIF, PARALLEL to the inferior border of liver and progress upward with each cycle of respiration (note that liver border is palpated by radial side of index finger)
    2. Alternate method (obsolete method): Place right hand in RIF, PERPENDICULAR to the inferior border of liver and progress upward with each cycle of respiration (note that liver border is palpated by tips of fingers)
    3. Two-hand method: Place BOTH hands directly in RHC and palpate the liver
    4. Dipping method: For ascites

5. Bimanual palpation: For pulsatile liver in tricuspid regurgitation

- Degrees of enlargement:
  1. Mild: Up to 2 fingers
  2. Moderate: 2 - 5 fingers
  3. Severe: >5 fingers
- Liver fremitus can be felt when a palpable liver with perihepatitis moves on respiration
- Important to differentiate from other d/ds of RHC lump:
  1. Gall bladder lump
  2. Mass at hepatic flexure of colon
  3. Parietal swellings (lipoma, fibroma, etc.)
- Important to differentiate hepatomegaly from downward displacement of liver: by percussion of upper border of liver (to note the liver span)
- Liver is enlarged in early cirrhosis but shrinked in advanced cirrhosis

❖ Spleen palpation:
- Methods:
  1. Classic method: Palpate from RIF to LHC by right hand such that fingers point toward LHC
  2. Bimanual method: In right lateral decubitus
  3. Hooking method (Middleton method): In right lateral decubitus position, standing on left side of patient, examiner can choose to use any hand for hooking
  4. Dipping method: For ascites
- Splenic fremitus when a palpable spleen with peri-splenitis moves on respiration
- Harris dictum: 1, 3, 5, 7, 9, 11

  Size: 1 × 3 × 5 inches

  Weight: 7 oz (200 g)

  Extent: 9th to 11th rib

  Axis: 10th rib

- Grades of splenomegaly:

Classification	Grades	Splenomegaly
Hackett classification	1	Just palpable
	2	Between costal margin and umbilicus
	3	At umbilicus
	4	Beyond umbilicus
Other classification	Mild	Up to 2 fingers
	Moderate	2 - 5 fingers
	Severe	>5 fingers
Other classification	Mild	Up to 2 cm
	Moderate	3 - 7 cm
	Severe	>7 cm

- Difference between splenic and left renal lump:

Spleen	Left kidney
Anterior notch palpable	No notch
Moves with respiration	Restricted movement with respiration
Enlarges obliquely toward RIF	Enlarges downward toward LIF
Can cross midline	Cannot cross midline
No renal angle swelling	Renal angle swelling may be seen
No colonic band of resonance, hence percussion note is always dull	Colonic band of resonance can be elicited
Cannot insinuate fingers deep to costal margin	Fingers can be insinuated
Not ballotable	Ballotable

Spleen enlarges OBLIQUELY due to PHRENICO-COLIC ligament

❖ Kidney palpation:

- Methods:

1. Bimanual palpation: Place both hands on lumbar region (one on anterior abdominal wall and other on posterior abdominal wall), palpate with the hand on anterior abdominal wall while other hand only supports (slight movement of kidney during respiration can be noticed as slipping of the mass between two hands)

2. Ballottement method: Place both hands on lumbar region (one on anterior abdominal wall and other on posterior abdominal wall), PUSH the mass anteriorly with the hand placed on posterior wall and palpate with the hand on anterior wall (kidney lump is ballotable because it has a pedicle)

3. Dipping method: For ascites

- Pasternacki sign: Tenderness in renal angle, seen in pyelonephritis

Dipping method (in case of ascites): Place both hands on anterior abdominal wall one above the other (left hand above right hand), suddenly flex the fingers at MCP joints (dipping) to feel the lump (left hand applies pressure to displace fluid while right hand feels for the mass).

[Note that dipping maneuver may be required more than once or twice at the same place for displacing the fluid.]

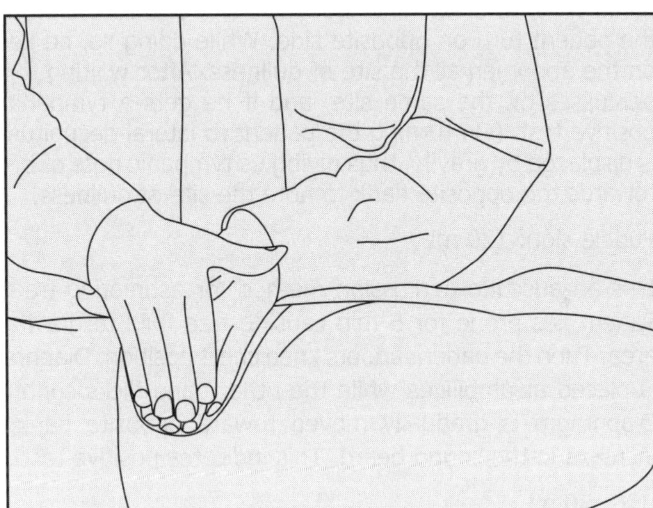

Fig. 6.3: Dipping method of abdominal palpation

❖ Measurements:

1. Abdominal girth: At the level of umbilicus
2. Spino-umbilical distance (ASIS to umbilicus)
3. Xiphisternum to umbilicus
4. Pubic symphysis to umbilicus

Liver is clinically palpable after enlarging 2 - 2.5 times its normal size.

Spleen is clinically palpable after enlarging 3 times its normal size.

- Percussion:
  - Of free fluid:
    1. Fluid thrill: 1500 mL

       Patient's ulnar border of hand is placed in the midline (to dampen vibrations from anterior abdominal wall). One side of abdomen is tapped by the examiner. The other hand of examiner placed on opposite side feels for transmitted thrill which indicates a positive test.

    2. Horse shoe dullness: 1000 mL

       Percussion is carried out from xiphisternum downward to the point of dullness which is noted. Similarly, we percuss FROM XIPHISTERNUM to each point on both sides of abdomen. Thus, we obtain a horse shoe shaped area demarking the level of ascitic fluid.

    3. Shifting dullness: 500 mL

       Start percussion from xiphisternum to pubic symphysis to ensure there is no dullness due to fluid. Then percuss from umbilicus and go laterally to flank. When the examiner notices a site of dullness on the flank, he makes the patient turn on opposite side. While doing so, he keeps the pleximeter on the abdomen at the site of dullness. After waiting for at least 1 min, he percusses on the same site, and if he gets a tympanic note, it indicates positive test. (On turning the patient to lateral decubitus, fluid in the flanks is displaced by gravity, thus giving us tympanic note of bowels) Now percuss towards the opposite flank to note the site of dullness.

    4. Puddle sign: 120 mL

       It is an ausculto-percussion method for estimating free fluid in abdomen. Patient lies prone for 5 min causing free fluid to gravitate to periumbilical area. Then the patient adopts knee chest position. Diaphragm of stethoscope is placed at umbilicus while the other hand flicks continually at one flank. Diaphragm is gradually moved toward opposite flank, and we note an increase in the sound heard. This indicates positive test.

    5. USG: 50 mL

Balance's sign: Unilateral shifting dullness, seen in splenic rupture

Tympanites or meteorism: Exaggerated tympanic note on abdominal percussion

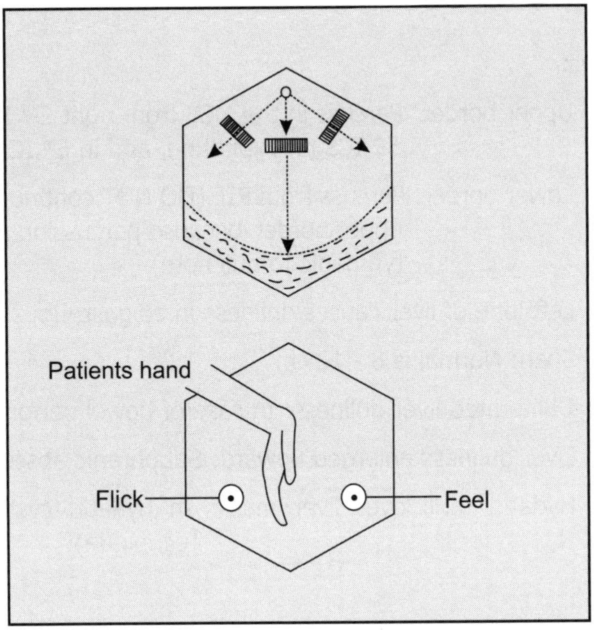

Fig. 6.4: Method to elicit horse shoe dullness and fluid thrill

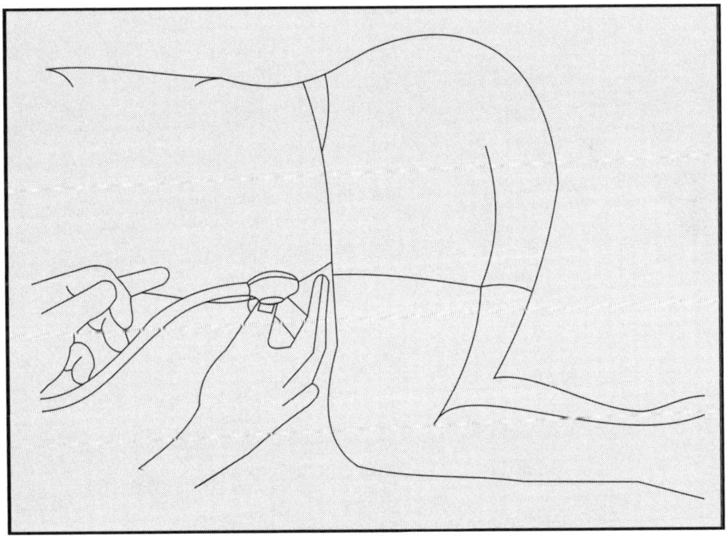

Fig. 6.5: Puddle sign

- Of organs:

1. Liver:

    - Upper border: Percuss in the MCL from right 2nd ICS, normally it lies in 5th ICS on expiration, and in 6th ICS on inspiration
    - Lower border: Percuss from RIF (DO NOT continue percussing from the upper border, because percussion always proceeds from tympanic to dull note)
    - Left lobe of liver causes dullness in epigastrium and Traube's space
    - Span: Normal is 8 - 12 cm
    - Obliterated liver dullness: In case of bowel perforation
    - Liver dullness enlarged upward: Subphrenic abscess
    - Hydatid thrill over liver mass: In hydatid cyst (elicited by special technique)

2. Spleen:

   - Methods:

1. Castell's method	- Most sensitive method - In supine position - Percuss in 8th or 9th left ICS in anterior axillary line - Positive if: Resonant note on expiration (due to stomach) and a dull note in inspiration (due to spleen)
2. Nixon's method	- In right lateral position - Start from midpoint of anterior costal margin - Percuss perpendicular to costal margin upwards - If dullness extends for >8 cm, it is positive
3. Traube's space	- It is a semilunar-shaped area - Internal boundaries are: 1. Spleen (on left) 2. Left lobe of liver (on right) 3. Left costal margin (below) 4. Left lung border (above) - External boundaries are: 1. Left costal margin (below) 2. Left 6th rib (above) 3. Left mid-clavicular line (on right) 4. Left mid-axillary line (on left) - Positive test: Dullness in this space - False positive: 1. After meals (due to a filled gastric fundus) 2. Left lobe liver enlargement 3. Gastric mass 4. Left pleural effusion
4. Classical method	- Start from uppermost ICS in left mid-axillary line and proceed downward till 8th ICS - Normally 8th ICS is resonant - Dull note in 8th ICS indicates splenomegaly, specifically posterior enlargement of spleen

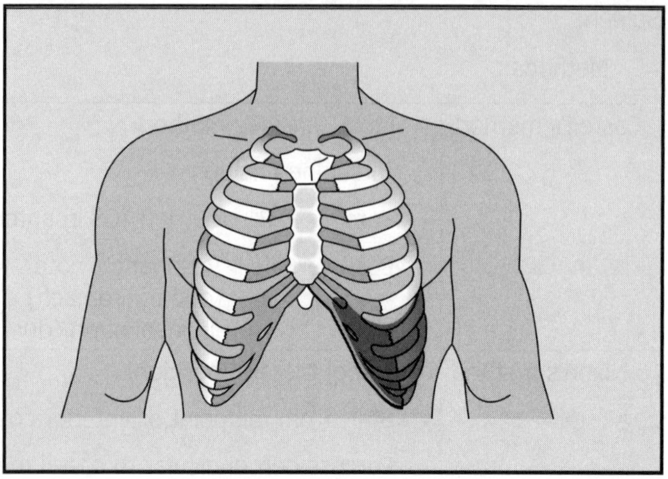

Fig. 6.6: Traube's space

- Auscultation:
  1. Peristalsis:
     - Normal rate: 3 - 5/min
     - Hyperactive: Seen in intestinal obstruction, gastroenteritis, diarrhea, GI bleed
     - Borborygmi: Gurgling noise made by the movement of fluid and gas in the intestines which can be heard by bare ears
     - Tinkling abdomen: Seen in paralytic ileus
     - Reduced sounds:
       i. Auscultate for at least 1 min
       ii. Seen in constipation, paralytic ileus, hypokalemia, hypercalcemia
  2. Arterial bruit:
     - Renal artery stenosis
     - Vascular tumors of liver
  3. Venous hum:
     - Portosystemic shunts over liver, umbilicus
  4. Succusion splash:
     - Gastric outlet obstruction
  5. Liver rub
  6. Splenic rub

Section III

PEDIATRICS

Since uniqueness of pediatric case taking centres mainly around history and general examination, high yield topics are covered with special emphasis on Birth History, Developmental History, Dietary History and Anthropometry

7
Pediatric History Taking

[Only additional points on pediatric history have been mentioned below. Refer Chapter 1 in Section I beforehand.]

- Proforma:
  1. Personal profile (PP)
  2. Chief complaints (CC)
  3. HOPI
  4. Past history
  5. Personal history
  6. Family history
  7. **B**irth history (perinatal)
  8. **I**mmunization history
  9. **D**evelopmental history
  10. **D**ietary history
  11. **S**ocioeconomic history

There is nothing like LHS and RHS history

BIDDS

- Personal profile:
  1. Born of consanguineous or non-consanguineous marriage
  2. Informant:
     - Who is it?
     - If reliable/not reliable
  3. Birth order

❖ Consanguinity:
  - High risk of autosomal recessive (AR) diseases
  - Degrees of consanguinity:

1st	Parents and children, siblings
2nd	Uncle - aunt, nephew - niece
3rd	First cousin

- Most common form is 3rd degree
- Non-consanguineous parents have risk of birth defects: 2%
- 3rd degree consanguinity has risk of birth defects: 6%

Risk of transmission of birth defects is high till 3rd degree of consanguinity

❖ Criteria for reliable informant:
1. Blood relative
2. Staying with the child
3. Literate
4. Adult

❖ Birth order: Significance of high birth order–
1. Indicates high maternal age
2. One can enquire for disease in siblings
3. Risk of neglected child

- Chief complaints
- HOPI
- Past history: Do not mention diabetes and hypertension (in contrast to medical history of adults)
- Personal history:
  - Do not mention addiction (in contrast to medical history of adults)
- Family history**:**
  - Draw a pedigree chart
  - Ask for similar illness in family members
  - For X-linked recessive diseases, ask for disease in MATERNAL UNCLE
- Birth history:
  - Antenatal:
    1. Registered or not, month of registration
    2. Calcium, iron, folic acid, tetanus toxoid (TT) vaccine
    3. History of fever, rash, leaking P/V (indicates perinatal infection)
    4. Hypertension, diabetes mellitus (DM), thyroid problems, radiation exposure
    5. Drug intake

- Natal:
  1. Term/ preterm/ post-term
  2. Institutional/home, if home conducted by dai? Aseptic precautions taken?
  3. Vaginal/operative vaginal/cesarean section (operative vaginal means use of forceps/vacuum)
  4. Cried immediately? Resuscitation required?
  5. Birth weight

- Postnatal:
  1. Neonatal intensive care unit (NICU) admission, if yes: reason and duration?
  2. Feeding initiation (breastfeeding to be started within 30 minutes of vaginal delivery and within 4 hours of LSCS)
  3. Any complications: Jaundice, cyanosis, fever, convulsions

- Others:
  1. Maternal age
  2. History of abortion/complication of previous pregnancy

  [Mention birth history in detail only in relevant cases; else say "Birth history not contributory" especially in older children]

- Immunization history:
  1. Ask for immunization card
  2. Birth vaccines taken or not as per National Immunization Schedule (NIS)
  3. Any special vaccines taken?
  4. Most recent vaccine taken

- Developmental history: (discussed later)

- Dietary history: (discussed later)

- Socioeconomic history:
  1. Kuppuswamy (urban), Kulshrestha and Pareek (urban + rural), Prasad (rural), Hollingshed (western countries)
  2. Housing: Kachha/pakka, number of rooms, drinking water, sanitation, nearby areas (dump yard, open drains)
  3. Family: Number of members
  4. Education of mother

  (Say "Patient belongs to Kuppuswamy class _____")

Kuppuswamy system
1. Education (7 points)
2. Occupation (10 points)
3. Income of family (12 points)
(For grades, refer standard books)

DEVELOPMENTAL HISTORY

- Milestones:

Gross motor skills	Fine motor skills	Social skills	Linguistic skills
3 - Neck holding **5** - Sit with support **6** - Prone to supine and vice versa (roll over) **8** - Sit without support **9** - Crawl **10** - Creep **11** - Walk with support **12** - Walk without support **2** - Runs well - Upstairs and downstairs with 2 steps **3** - Rides a tricycle - Upstairs with single step **4** - Hopping (jump on one leg) - Downstairs with single step **5** - Skipping (jump on both legs)	**Birth** - Grasp reflex present **3** - Grasp reflex disappears **5** - Bidextrous approach - Mouthing appears **6** - Drop one object when another is offered **7** - Transfers objects - Unidextrous approach **9 - 10** - Pincer grasp appears **12 - 13** - Casting appears - Mouthing disappears - Mature pincer grasp **15** - Feeds with spoon **18** - Feeds from cup - Tower of three **2** - Tower of six - Vertical strokes - Turns one page **3** - Draws O - Tower of nine **4** - Draws + **5** - Draws X, Δ	**2** - Social smile **3** - Identifies mother **7** - Stranger anxiety - Enjoys mirror **9** - Bye bye, clap **12** - Waves head in response to no (nods head) **15** - Hugs parent **18** - Kisses parent **2** - Dry by day **3** - Dry by night **4** - Goes to toilet alone **5** - Dresses and undresses without assistance	**3** - Cooing **6** - Monosyllable **9** - Bisyllable **12** - two words **18** - ten words **2** - Single sentences **3** - Name, age, gender **4** - Tells one story/poem **5** - Identify four colors

- Developmental quotient (DQ):
    - $DQ = \frac{\text{Average age at attainment}}{\text{Observed age at attainment}} \times 100$
    - Delayed milestones: DQ < 70%
    - To be reported for each domain separately and also as average of all domains
- In babies born preterm, "CORRECTED AGE" rather than postnatal age is used for evaluating developmental status TILL 2 years of age.
- Maneuvers to check gross motor development in infants (note that this comes in examination and not history):
    - Ventral suspension: Head in line of trunk: 2 months
      Head above the line of trunk: 3 months
    - Pull to sit: Head in line of trunk: 4 months
      Head above the line of trunk: 5 months
- Grasps:
    - Ulnar grasp: 4 months
    - Palmar grasp: 5 months
    - Radial grasp: 6 months
    - MATURE pincer grasp: 12 months

DIETARY HISTORY

- Breastfeeding history:
    1. Breastfeeds: Frequency; duration of each episode; one breast at a time or alternate; on demand or not; night feeds or not
    2. Exclusively breastfed or not? If yes, for how long?
    3. Top feed:
        - Reason for initiation
        - Cow's milk or formula milk
        - What dilution used
        - Bottle feed or vati-chammach (spoon and cup)
        - Was the bottle/vati-chammach boiled between every feed?
    4. Weaning: Age and type of food
    5. Any breastfeeding complications:
        - Maternal (sore nipple, mastitis, breast abscess)
        - Infant (poor feeds)

- For older child: Regular diet history as in adults (DO NOT elaborate on breastfeeding history)

❖ Important points for dietary history:

- Adequacy of breastfeeding is indicated by:
    1. Urine frequency of 5 - 6 times/day
    2. Sleeps well after breastfeed (not stools)
    3. Good weight gain
- Ideally feed from each breast for 20 min or complete before shifting over to other breast. This ensures complete emptying of both foremilk and hindmilk.
- Differences between foremilk and hindmilk:

Foremilk	Hindmilk
- First to be ejected	- Ejected towards the end of feed
- Watery	- Thick
- Quenches thirst	- Provides satiety
- Rich in proteins, sugars, vitamins, minerals	- Rich in fat (calorie rich)

- Breastfeeding should be initiated within 30 minutes of vaginal delivery and within 4 hours of LSCS.
- Exclusive breastfeeding up to 6 months (i.e. weaning at 6 months)

  (Exclusive means nothing apart from breast milk, NOT even water.)
- Ideally breastfeeding must be continued up to 2 years
- Milk requirement:

  600 mL/day (4 - 5 months)

  750 mL/day (6 months)
- To calculate calorie intake of a breastfed child:

  According to milk output (mentioned above), the calorie content is calculated roughly by multiplying it with calorie content of human milk.
- Energy content of milk:

Type	Energy per 100 mL	Protein per 100 mL
Human milk	67 kcal	1.1 g
Cow milk	65 kcal	3.3 g
Buffalo milk	104 kcal	4.4 g
[TAKE INTO ACCOUNT THE DILUTION]		

- Commonly used weaning foods:
  1. Smashed potatoes
  2. Khichdi
  3. Smashed banana in milk
  4. Mashed roti, biscuit in thick dal + ghee
- Liquid diet used in hospital:
  1. RMP (Rice, Moong dal Powder) (3:2) : Calorie content of it is 50 - 90 kcal
  2. Egg flip
  3. Banana flip
  4. Rice Kanji
- Requirements for infants and children:

	Calorie required with respect to age	**Protein required with respect to age**
Infants	100 kcal/kg/day	2 g/kg/day (up to 6 months)
		1.5 g/kg/day (6 months - 3 years)
Children	Given below	1.4 g/kg/day (3 - 6 years)
		1.3 g/kg/day (6 - 9 years)

- Holliday-Segar formula:
  1. Applicable up to 12 years
  2. To calculate calorie intake and fluid intake
  3. Based on the weight of child

	Calorie requirement	**Water requirement**
For first 10 kg	100 kcal/kg/day	100 mL/kg/day
For next 10 kg (11 - 20 kg)	50 kcal/kg/day	50 mL/kg/day
After that	20 kcal/kg/day	20 mL/kg/day
Example: Child of weight 16 kg	1300 kcal/day (100 × 10 + 50 × 6)	1300 kcal/day

8

Pediatric General Examination

[Only additional points on pediatric general examination have been mentioned below. Refer Chapter 2 in Section I beforehand.]

- In a small child, don't say "Conscious, cooperative, coherent (CCC) and oriented to time, place, person (TPP)"

  Instead say "Child is alert and playful"

  (Child will be apathetic in kwashiorkor and alert in marasmus.)

- Do not say "Averagely built and nourished," since a detailed discussion is presented in anthropometry

- Decubitus:
  - Hemiplegia: Same as adults
  - Pithed-frog position: Hypotonia
  - Turns away from light: Pyogenic meningitis (photophobia)

- Temperature:
  - Young children: Oral temperature is not measured

    Axilla, rectal, groin temperature preferred
  - In PEM: Rectal temperature is to be taken
  - Hypothermia: Rectal temperature < 35.5 °C

    Axillary temperature < 35°C
  - Severe hypothermia: Rectal temperature < 32°C

> Method for rectal temperature measurement:
> - In prone position with child on mother's lap
> - Insert thermometer 2 cm deep

> Ideal time up to which thermometer should be kept at any place for recording temperature is 3 minutes

- Pulse: Varies with age

Age (years)	Pulse rate (bpm)
12	80
10 - 12	85
8 - 10	90
6 - 8	95
4 - 6	100
2 - 4	105
1 - 2	110
1 month to 1 year	120
Neonate	140 (110 - 160)

- Respiration:
  - Varies with age
  - Infants predominantly have abdominal breathing

Normal rate (breaths per min):
- Neonate: 40-50
- 1 month to 1 year: 30 to 40
- 4-6 years: 25
- >12 years: 16 to 20

Tachypnea:
- <2 months: >60
- 2 months to 1 year: >50
- 1-5 years: >40

- Blood pressure (BP):
  - Neonate: 70/45 mmHg
  - Then add +3/2 mmHg every year till 12 years
  - At 12 years, BP is 120/80 mmHg
  - Cuff size is of 4-6 cm in infants, 7 - 9 cm in children

ANTHROPOMETRY

- Mention in the following order:

  Parameter → observed → expected → percentile range in which it falls

  For example, "The patient's weight is ___kg, expected being ___kg, falls between __ to ___ percentile"

- Ordinarily following parameters have to be assessed:
  1. Weight (for age): In all cases
  2. Height (for age): In all cases
  3. Head circumference (HC): Only till 5 years
  4. Chest circumference (CC): Only till 3 years
  5. Mid-arm circumference (MAC): Only till 5 years

- Weight:

2.5 - 4 kg is normal birth weight
<2.5 kg is low birth weight
<1.5 kg is very low birth weight
<1 kg is extremely low birth weight
>4 kg is macrosomia

  - In early neonatal period (0 to 7th day), weight loss occurs (up to 10% in full term and upto 15% in preterm children)
  - Birth weight is regained by 10th day
  - Further weight gain:

    30 g/day till 3 months

    400 g/month till 1 year
  - Progression of weight:

x	at birth
2x	at 6 months
3x	at 1 year
4x	at 2 years
5x	at 3 years
6x	at 5 years
7x	at 7 years
10x	at 10 years

- Formulae:

  For 3 months to 1 year = $\frac{9 + \text{age (months)}}{2}$

  For 1 - 6 years = 2 (age in years) + 8

  For 6 - 12 years = $\frac{7 \text{ (age in years) } - 5}{2}$

- Measuring devices:
  1. Electronic machine: Most preferred (pan/tray used for infants)
  2. Beam balance: Acceptable
  3. Spring balance: Used only by community workers due to portability
- It is a very sensitive parameter for ACUTE nutritional status
- PEM classification that use weight for age: IAP, Gomez, Bengoa, Jellife's, Welcome Trust

• Height:
- Height at birth is 50 cm
- Further height gain:

50 cm - birth
60 cm - 3 months
65 cm - 6 months
70 cm - 9 months
75 cm - 1 year (i.e. birth + 25 cm)
87.5 cm - 2 years (i.e. 1 year + 12.5 cm)
94 cm - 3 years (i.e. 2 years + 7 cm)
100 cm - 4 years (i.e. 3 year + 6 cm)
+6 cm/year - 4th to 12th year
+8 cm/year or +10 cm/ year-growth spurt (girls or boys, respectively)

- Formula: (applicable only for 2 - 12 years)

  Height = 77 + (6 x age in years)

- Formula to predict adult height:
  1. Mid-parental height formula = $\frac{\text{Dad+Mom } \pm 6.5}{2}$ (+6.5 cm) for male (-6.5 cm) for female
  2. Tanner's formula = height at 2 years x 2
- It is a sensitive parameter for CHRONIC nutritional status (Chronic means $\geq$ 6 months)

- Measurement:

  <2 years: Infantometer (length is measured, not height)

  >2 years: Stadiometer (height is measured)

  (By the age of 2 years, most children are able to stand without support)
- Waterlow's classification uses height for age (H/A) and weight for height (W/H)

• Head circumference:
  - To be done only upto 5 years
  - From external occipital protuberance to superior orbital ridges
  - Method: CROSSED TAPE METHOD
  - HC at birth is 35 cm
  - Further growth:

    2 cm/month till 3 months

    1 cm/month till 6 months

    0.5 cm/month till 1 year

    2 cm from 1 - 2 years

    1 cm from 2 - 3 years

    0.5 cm from 3 - 4 years

    0.25 cm from 4 - 6 years

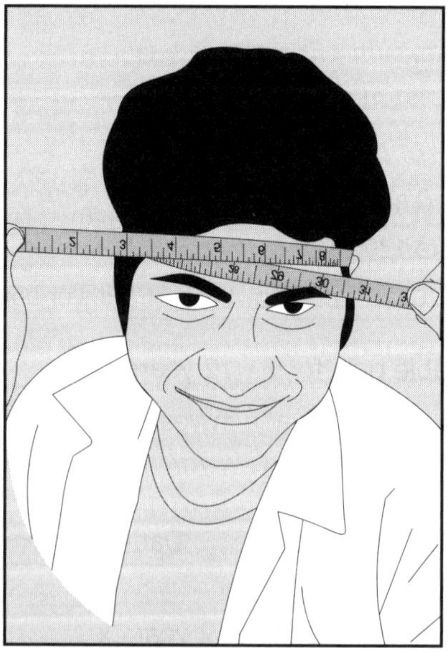

Fig. 8.1: Crossed tape method

- Dine's formula (for infant only):

$$HC\ (\text{in cm}) = \frac{\text{Length}}{2} + 9.5$$

- Affected by:
  1. Soft tissues
  2. Bony disease
  3. Cerebrospinal fluid (CSF)
  4. Brain growth (70% growth occurs in fetal life, 15% in infanthood, 10% in preschool)
- Brain sparing occurs in PEM (except severe chronic PEM). Hence, HC is rarely affected in PEM.

• Chest circumference:
  - To be done only up to 3 years
  - At level of nipples, midway between inspiration and expiration
  - Method: CROSSED TAPE METHOD
  - At <1 year: CC < HC (by 3 cm)

    At 1 year (9 - 12 months): CC = HC

    At >1 year: CC > HC
  - CC is READILY affected by PEM

    Therefore in PEM, CC crosses HC later than normal

• Mid-arm circumference (MAC):
  - Age-dependent parameter
  - To be done only in age group of 1 to 5 years (fat is replaced by muscle. Hence, MAC remains constant.)
  - Normal: >16 cm

    Mild PEM: >13.5 cm

    Moderate PEM: >12.5 cm

    Severe PEM: <11.5 cm
  - Measured at mid arm (midpoint of acromion and olecranon)

- Measured by:
  1. Shakir's tape:

Color codes of Shakir's tape:
Normal: White
Mild: Green
Moderate: Yellow
Severe: Red

  2. Quaker arm circumference measuring (QUAC STICK): Compares height vs. MAC

     $\frac{\text{MAC}}{\text{HT}}$ = QUAC test (age independent)

  3. Bangle test: Quick test to rule out severe PEM

     (Bangle circumference is 12.5 cm)

- False negative result in kwashiorkor (due to edema) and other causes of edema

• Upper segment (US) by Lower segment (LS) ratio:
  - To be done only in relevant cases (short/long stature)
  - Take the ratio of–

    Vertex to pubic symphysis: Pubic symphysis to heel (i.e. trunk: lower limb)
  - At birth it is 1.7:1

    At 3 years it is 1.3: 1

    At 7 years it is 1:1

    In children >7 years and adults it is 0.9:1
  - In newborn, midpoint of body is umbilicus which gradually shifts to pubic symphysis by age of 12 years (limb growth > truncal growth)
  - US: LS ratio higher than normal indicates shorter limbs and longer trunk
    1. Achondroplasia
    2. Bowed leg (rickets) and other limb deformities
    3. Cretinism
    4. Sexually precocious
  - US: LS ratio lesser than normal indicates longer limbs and shorter trunks
    1. Chondrodystrophy
    2. Marfan's syndrome
    3. Hypogonadism, Turner's syndrome, Klinefelter syndrome
    4. Spinal deformity (scoliosis, etc.)

- Arm span:
  - To be done only in relevant cases (short/long stature)
  - Measurement: In horizontally outstretched arms, tape from tip of each middle finger, tape passes from back of child
  - Progression:

    <12 years: Arm span < height (by 2 cm)

    At 12 years: Arm span = height

    >12 years: Arm span > height (by 2 cm)
  - Abnormalities:

    Reduced arm span: Due to causes of short-limb dwarfism

    Increased arm span: Marfan's, Klinefelter's, coarctation of aorta (since upper limb gets good blood supply)

Good to know:

1. Skinfold thickness:
   - Age-independent parameter
   - Poor test, many false results
   - Applicable for age group of 1 - 6 years
   - Sites: Subscapular and triceps
   - Method: Pinch with index finger and thumb and use Harpenden caliper
   - Normal: >1 cm

     Mild to moderate PEM: >0.6 cm

     Severe PEM: <0.6 cm
2. Weight for height:
   - Age-independent parameter
   - Formula:

     $$\frac{\text{Weight of child}}{\text{Weight of child of same height}} \times 100$$
   - It represents ACUTE malnutrition, because in chronic malnutrition, weight for height is normal
   - Used in Waterloo classification of PEM

3. BMI:
   - Waist-to-hip ratio
   - Lorentz index
   - Broca's index
   - Corpulence index
   - Ponderal index
   - Rao and Singh
   - Kanawati

   (All of the above:) Better indicators for obesity rather than malnutrition

4. Indicators of PEM:

Age independent	Age dependant
- Weight for height - MAC - Rao and Singh - Dugdale - Kanawati and McLaren - Jellife	- Weight for age - Height for age - CC - HC - MAC - US:LS

- POLICE
- Head-to-toe examination:

  Say "Head to toe examination normal and BCG mark seen/not seen"

  - Skull:
    1. Shape:
       - Brachycephaly: Reduced AP diameter due to premature closure of coronal suture
       - Dolichocephaly: Increased AP diameter due to premature closure of sagittal suture
       - Plagiocephaly: Unilateral coronal suture premature closure
       - Prominent occiput: Dandy-Walker syndrome
    2. Dysmorphic features: Down syndrome

3. Fontanelles:
    - Total number is 6 (1 anterior, 1 posterior, 2 anterolateral, 2 posterolateral)
    - Anterior is diamond shaped, posterior is triangular shaped
    - Anterior closes by 18 months, posterior closes by 2 - 3 months
    - Open fontanelles (delayed closure) seen in :
        1. Hydrocephalus
        2. Rickets
        3. Down syndrome
        4. Hypothyroidism
    - Bulging fontanelle seen in raised intercranial tumor (ICT)
    - Depressed fontanelle seen in dehydration
    - Method to measure dimensions of anterior fontanelle:

      Say "Anterior fontanelle measures a x b cm" (dotted line)

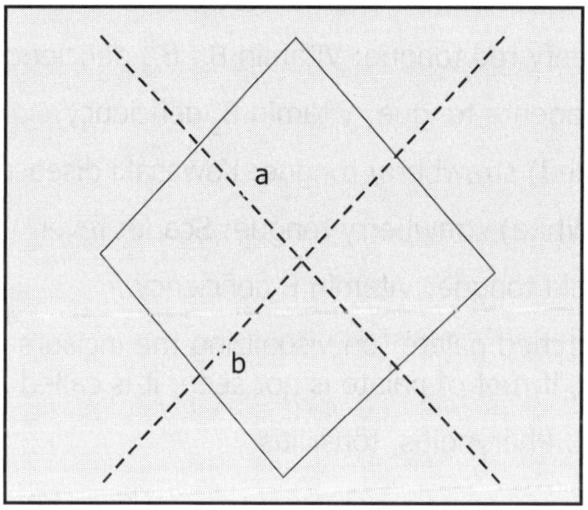

4. Unique signs on skull:
    ≈ Macewen sign (≈ crackpot sign): Seen in chronic raised ICT (Not to be done if open anterior fontanel, in ventriculostomy patient)
    - Craniotabes (≈ ping pong ball): First sign of infantile rickets
    - Trans illumination: Hydrocephalus (>1 inch in frontal area, >½ inch in occipital area)
    - Bruit: Heard in raised ICT

- Eye:
    1. Kayser-Fleischer (KF) ring (Wilson's disease)
    2. Bitot's spots (vitamin A deficiency)
    3. Congenital anomaly: Coloboma iridis, cataract, retinoblastoma

- Ears:
    1. Low set ears (when we draw a horizontal line from palpebral fissure if the whole auricle lies below it, indicates low set ears)
    2. Deformity (microtia, skin tags, preauricular sinus)
- Nose: Syphilis (snuffles, etc.)
- Mouth:
    1. Vitamin deficiency ulcers
    2. Cleft lip, palate
    3. Koplik spots: Seen in measles
    4. Dentition:
        - First deciduous tooth to erupt: Lower central incisor at 6 months
        - First permanent tooth to erupt: Lower first molar tooth at 6 years
    5. Tongue:
        - Coated tongue: Enteric fever, chronic illness
        - Beefy red tongue: Vitamin B_3, B_{12} deficiency
        - Magenta tongue: Vitamin B_2 deficiency
        - (Red) strawberry tongue: Kawasaki disease
        - (White) strawberry tongue: Scarlet fever
        - Bald tongue: Vitamin B deficiency
    6. High-arched palate (on visualizing the incisors and uvula in line in an open mouth, if roof of palate is not seen, it is called high arched-palate)
    7. Throat: Pharyngitis, tonsillitis
- Neck**:**
    1. Swelling: Diphtheria, mumps
    2. Webbed neck: Turner syndrome
    3. Visible veins: Heart failure
    4. Lymph nodes
    5. Thyroid
- Skin:
    1. BCG mark: Has to be mentioned in EVERY case

Mark is not seen in 10% of immunized patients. So absence of mark does not necessarily indicate missed immunization and it is NOT a criterion for reimmunization.

2. Turgor: Dehydration (it is best checked on anterior abdominal wall)
3. Color: Hyper pigmentation: Nevus of Ota, nevus of Ito, Mongolian spots

   Petechiae: <3 mm

   Purpura: 3 mm to 1 cm

   Ecchymosis: >1 cm
4. Rash: Infection (read on exanthematous diseases)
5. Toad skin: Essential fatty acid deficiency
6. Fish skin (ichthyosis): Congenital disease
7. Xanthoma, xanthelesma
8. Subcutaneous nodules: Seen in rheumatic fever

- Nails:
  1. Platonychia, koilonychia: Iron deficiency anemia
  2. Brittle nails: Malnutrition, hypoproteinemia
- Hair: PEM and seborrheic dermatitis
- Bones
- Joints
- Spine

  } kyphoscoliosis, rickets, scurvy, neural tube defects, rheumatic fever, juvenile RA, septic arthritis, osteomyelitis
- Genitalia: Sexual maturity rating scale (SMR scale)
  1. Ambiguous genitalia (e.g. congenital adrenal hyperplasia)
  2. Congenital anomalies like hypospadias, epispadias

• Developmental examination:
  - Done only if patient is suspected to have delayed milestones
  - Consists of:
    1. Primitive reflexes
    2. Muscle tone
    3. Milestone examination

❖ Primitive reflexes:

Reflex	Appearance	Disappearance
1. Moro's reflex	28 weeks IUL	4 months
2. Landau's reflex	6 months	15 - 18 months
3. Parachute reflex	8 months	Never
4. Glabellar tap	28 weeks	6 weeks
5. Rooting and sucking reflex	Birth	4 months
6. Palmar grasp and plantar grasp		
7. Asymmetric tonic neck reflex (ATNR)		
8. Symmetrical tonic neck reflex (STNR)		

❖ Special maneuvers to assess the tone of child:

Maneuver	Interpretation
Lift the child (vertical suspension)	- Child slips: Hypotonia - Stays in hand: Normal - Stiff limbs: Hypertonia
Shake the child	- Excess movement: Hypotonia - Doesn't move much: Hypertonia
Prone suspension	- Ragged doll appearance: Hypotonia - Retracted head: Hypertonia
Ventral suspension	- Head droops: Hypotonia
Pull to sit	- Head lag: Hypotonia
Sling method (hold knee and lift up)	- Ankle comes up with drag: Hypotonia - Ankles come up with knees: Hypertonia
Five special tests in infants only: 1. Scarf sign 2. Heel-ear test 3. Popliteal angle test 4. Adductor angle test 5. Ankle dorsiflexion test	

Section IV

SURGERY

A case based approach has been adopted for Surgery. Each case is discussed under six headings: History, general examination, local examination, diagnosis, discussion, and management

- Only additional points on history taking and general examination pertaining to that case have been mentioned.
- Local examination is discussed in depth with proforma wherever applicable
- Model diagnosis for each case is given
- Discussion part contains basic concepts and details pertaining to that topic
- Management part includes 'management protocol' for algorithmic understanding followed by in-depth discussion on the same

9

General Points

- Swelling:

  Examine and describe any swelling according to the following points relevant to that case:

  - Inspection: **7S M_2INCED**
    1. Site
    2. Size
    3. Shape
    4. Surface
    5. Skin over the swelling
    6. Scar
    7. Sinus
    8. Margin
    9. Movement

    a. With respiration

    b. Peristalsis

    c. Pulsatile swelling: Expansile, transmitted

    d. Impulse on coughing

    10. Illumination (transillumination)
    11. Number
    12. Color
    13. Extent
    14. Dilated veins

    (Note that transillumination should only be done for cystic swellings)

  - Palpation: (9 points: Remember in groups of 2)
    1. Inspectory findings confirmed
    2. Temperature, tenderness
    3. Texture, consistency
    4. Reducibility, compressibility
    5. Fluctuation, fixity

To test fluctuation of:

1. Small swellings → one finger method (Paget's test)
2. Moderate size swellings → two fingers of one hand + one finger of other hand
3. Large size swellings → first fix (peculiar for hydrocele discussed later)

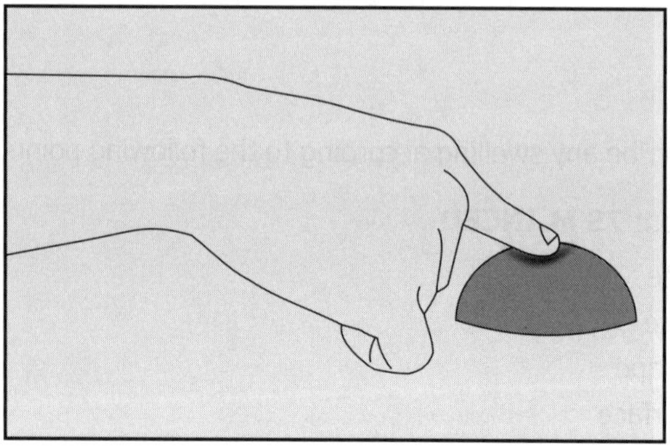

Fig. 9.1: One finger method to test fluctuation in a small sized swelling (Paget's test)

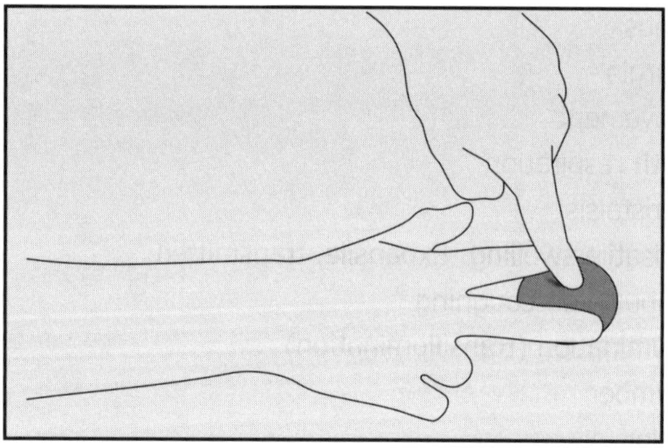

Fig. 9.2: Two hand method to test fluctuation in a moderate sized swelling

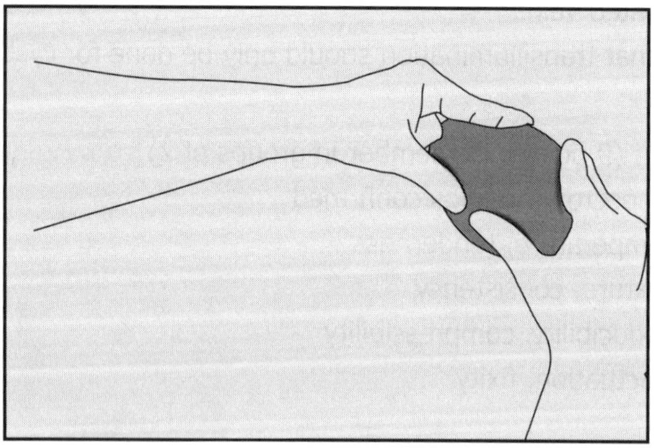

Fig. 9.3: Method to test fluctuation in a large sized swelling

> Difference between lump and swelling:
> - All three dimensions of a lump cannot be known on clinical examination e.g. lump in abdomen (depth cannot be known), lump in breast.
> - All three dimensions of a swelling can be known on clinical examination e.g. thyroid swelling.

- Pain:
  - Mnemonic for history of pain: **SITAR ODP MAN**
    1. Site
    2. Intensity
    3. Timing
    4. Aggravating factors
    5. Relieving factors
    6. Onset
    7. Duration
    8. Progress
    9. Movement: Radiating, referred, migratory
    10. Associated symptoms
    11. Nature of pain
  - Movement of pain:
    1. Radiating pain: Pain that radiates along the length of an organ or nerve e.g. ureteric colic, sciatica
    2. Migratory pain: Pain felt at a site distant from the organ at its embryological dermatome, but later felt at the site of organ (due to local irritation)

       e.g. appendicular pain is felt first around umbilicus, later in RIF
    3. Referred pain: Pain due to irritation of nerve root of a structure adjoining the organ

       e.g. cholecystitis has referred pain to shoulder due to irritation of diaphragm

       In MI, pain is felt along the inner aspect of arm due to irritation of pericardium
  - Nature of pain:
    1. Colicky pain:
       - Severe, intermittent, constricting pain, which appears and disappears suddenly
       - Seen in tubular organs: GB, intestine, appendix, ureter

2. Burning pain: Due to mucosal irritation/inflammation and peripheral neuropathy
3. Dull aching pain: Due to stretching or ischemia of visceral organ
4. Sharp shooting pain: Rupture/perforation, sciatica
5. Throbbing pain: Abscess anywhere (due to pulsation of nearby artery)

- Fever: Mnemonic for history of fever: **ODP AC TRIP**
    1. Onset
    2. Duration
    3. Progress
    4. Associated symptoms: Rash/malaise/myalgia, any localizing symptoms
    5. Chills/rigor
    6. Timing
    7. Response (to medications)
    8. Intensity
    9. Pattern: Continuous, remittent, intermittent, irregular

    [Refer Chapter 2 in Section I for more details.]
- Before starting local examination in every case, always say:
    1. Patient examined with due consent
    2. Under adequate illumination
    3. Well exposed from ____ to ____
    4. In _______ position
    5. In presence of female attendant (for female patients)

    (For any abdominal case: Exposure should be from nipple to knees)
- Abdominal examination: Refer Chapter 6 in Section II for details.
- For any abdominal case (e.g. hernia, lump, portal hypertension, OJ, hydrocele, etc.): Always mention the following four things at the end of inspection:
    1. External genitalia
    2. Hernial orifices
    3. Renal angle fullness
    4. Left supraclavicular fullness

Renal angle should be inspected in sitting position (not in prone).

Hernial orifices refer to:

1. Inguinal region (superficial and deep inguinal rings)
2. Saphenous opening
3. Linea alba
4. Spigelian line
5. Hesselbach's triangle
6. Superior and inferior lumbar triangles
7. Umbilicus

- Difference between guarding and rigidity:

Guarding	Rigidity
Due to voluntary contraction of muscles	Due to involuntary contraction of muscles
Present diffusely all over the abdomen (since only a single muscle cannot be contracted voluntarily)	Can be present over a small region of abdomen or diffusely
Occurs in response to pain, cold hands, tickle, etc.	Occurs in response to local irritation of parietal peritoneum

- Quadrants of abdomen:

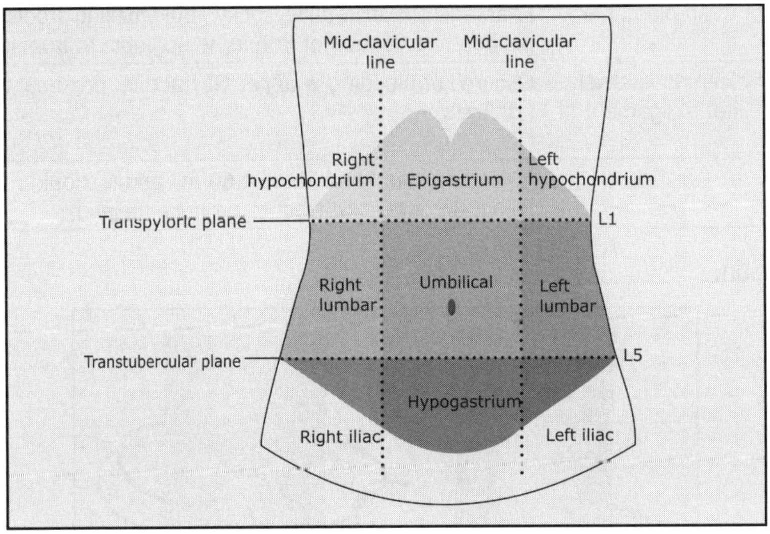

Fig. 9.4: Quadrants of abdomen

- Divided into nine quadrants by four lines: Two mid-clavicular lines, transpyloric plane, transtubercular plane
- Quadrants: LHC, epigastrium, RHC, left and right lumbar, umbilical, right and left iliac fossae, hypogastrium

Mid-clavicular lines: Cross the midpoint of clavicle, tips of 9th costal cartilage and mid-inguinal points

Transpyloric plane (of Addison): Through lower border of L_1 vertebra and tips of ninth costal cartilage

Transtubercular plane: Through L_5 vertebra and tubercles of iliac crest

10th quadrant of abdomen: Perineum (external genitalia)

11th quadrant of abdomen: Left supraclavicular fossa

- Investigations for anesthesia fitness ('A' fitness):
  1. Hemoglobin (Hb), complete blood count (CBC)
  2. Chest X-ray (CXR)
  3. ECG: If age > 35 years
  4. LFTs
  5. RFTs
  6. Blood sugar levels

- Hematochezia vs. melena:

Hematochezia	Melena
Passage of fresh blood per rectum	Passage of black, tarry, sticky, foul smelling stools (black color is due to oxidation of iron in hemoglobin to iron sulfide)
Source of bleeding is lower GI tract i.e. distal to ligament of Treitz	Source of bleeding is upper GI tract i.e. proximal to ligament of Treitz
	Bleeding should be at least 60 mL and it should remain for at least 8 hours in GI tract to produce melena

- Transfixation:

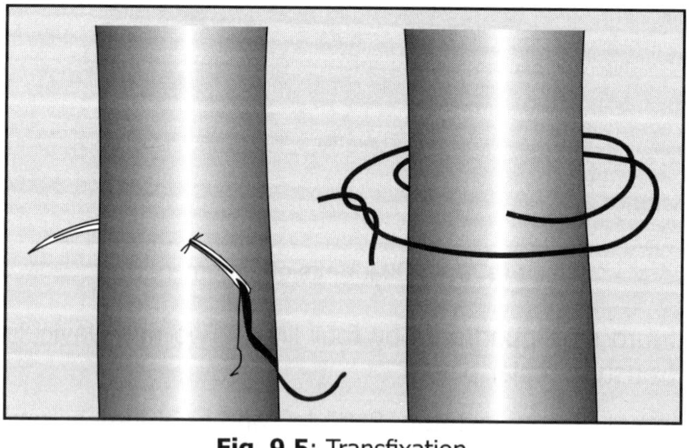

Fig. 9.5: Transfixation

- Special technique of ligature where suture is passed through the stump (e.g. vessel, pedicle, etc.), tied around half the stump and then along the entire circumference
- Advantage: Prevents slippage of ligature (secures it in place)

- Operability vs. resectability

Operability	Resectability
Intent of excision of tumor is cure	Intent of excision is to achieve negative resection margins
Based on patient factors (fitness)	Based on tumor factors (invasion, metastasis, etc.)

- Types of hemorrhage:
  1. Primary:
     - Occurs due to acute severance of blood vessel
     - e.g. on table hemorrhage
  2. Reactionary:
     - Occurs when mechanisms for arrest of primary hemorrhage fail (e.g. clotting, vasospasm, surgical methods)
     - Generally around 48 hours
  3. Secondary:
     - Occurs due to erosion of blood vessel (due to infection, tumor, etc.)
     - Since blood vessel wall is eroded, control by ligature at that site is difficult

> Methods to control hemorrhage:
> Catch, clamp, crush, cauterize, ligate, pack, pressure, pray
> (1st and most important method is pressure)

- Eight mechanisms of action of H_2O_2:
  1. Creates effervescence and reduction in surface tension (so raises slough)
  2. Causes exothermic reaction (local heat production)
  3. Acts as an irritant (promotes granulation tissue)
  4. Produces nascent oxygen (free radical generation)
  5. Causes coagulation of proteins
  6. Destroys cell membranes of gram positive bacteria
  7. O_2 kills anaerobic bacteria
  8. Causes chemical oxidation of cellular components

10
Ulcer

HISTORY

[Only additional points on ulcer history have been mentioned below. Refer Chapter 1 in Section I beforehand.]

- Patient profile:
  1. Age: Can point towards etiology
  2. Sex: Not contributory
  3. Occupation:
     - Macerated skin in fisherman, washerwoman (constant exposure to water)
     - Farmers (mycetoma)
     - Laborers (trauma)
     - Sportsman: Repeated trauma/friction
     - Occupations predisposing to varicose veins → varicose ulcer (Refer Chapter 10, Section IV)
  4. Residence: Not contributory
  5. Religion: Not contributory
- Chief complaints:
  1. Wound (do not say 'ulcer')

> Do not say 'non-healing' ulcer on history; say "Patient complains of a wound which has been persisting since __ months."

- HOPI:
  - ❖ Symptoms:
    1. Wound:
       - i. Number
       - ii. Site
       - iii. Size: Progressing (spreading) or regressing (healing) or same (non-healing)

iv. Shape

v. Color: Pinkish (healing), pale yellow/white (chronic, non-healing)

vi. Onset:

a. Spontaneous: Confirm whether truly spontaneous or preceded by any swelling, itching, discoloration, burns, scars, insect bite, and so on

b. Traumatic: External friction (clothes), scratching

Trauma only once or repetative

Iatrogenic: Amputation, incision site (MELENY'S ULCER)

vii. Duration: In case of genital ulcers, ask for time since exposure

> Incubation period of:
> - Soft chancre is 3 days
> - Hard chancre is 3 weeks

viii. Associated symptoms:

a. Pain

b. Fever/warmth: In acute infection/acute inflammation

c. Discharge:

Type of discharge	To be asked on history (say these words while presenting the case)	Interpretation	Seen in
According to character	Mucoid	Mucoid	
	Thick, odorous, yellow-white, sticky	Purulent	Infected ulcer
	Thin, clear	Serous	Healing ulcer
	Red	Sanguineous	Malignant ulcer, granulation tissue
	Thin with yellowish granules	Sulfur granules	Actinomycosis
	Greenish	Greenish	Pseudomonas
	Yellowish (yellow cheesy)	Caseous	Tuberculosis
According to amount	No need for repeated change of dressing	Scanty	
	Need for repeated change of dressing	Copious	

(Chronology of symptoms is very important, for example, in secondarily infected ulcer, pain/discharge/fever will come later to appearance of wound.)

- Etiology:
    1. Traumatic: Iatrogenic, external trauma, friction
    2. Arterial: Peripheral vascular disease (PVD)
    3. Venous: Varicose veins, deep venous thrombosis (DVT)
    4. Neuropathic (TROPHIC): Peripheral neuropathy, spinal cord, constant pressure (bed sore)
    5. Lymphatic: Inguinal lymphadenopathy
    6. Infection: Pyogenic, TB, syphilis, leprosy
    7. Malignancy
- Complications:
    1. Infection: Fever/warmth, pain
    2. Hemorrhage: Bleeding from ulcer site
    3. Osteomyelitis: Discharge of bony pieces from ulcer
    4. Disability: Difficulty in movement
    5. Malignancy: Rapid growth of ulcer/fungating mass
- Treatment taken: (history of ulcer care)
    1. Cleaning
    2. Dressing: Type, frequency
    3. Rest/immobilization

- Past history: DM can lead to recurrent non-healing ulcers
- Personal history: Smoking and tobacco consumption predispose to PVD and hence arterial ulcers
- Family history: Not contributory

GENERAL EXAMINATION

[Only additional points on ulcer general examination have been mentioned below. Refer Chapter 2 in Section I beforehand.]

- Obesity (BMI): Predisposes to PVD and DM (thus arterial ulcers)
- Temperature: Fever in infection
- Pallor: Indicates poor nutritional status, thus causing a non healing/ slow healing ulcer
- Pulse: For PVD

- Lymphadenopathy:
    1. Infected ulcers can lead to lymphadenopathy
    2. Suppuration of lymph nodes can cause sinus and ulcer
    3. Marjolin's ulcer NEVER causes enlargement of lymph nodes
- Signs of malnutrition: For non-healing ulcer
- Stigmata of TB, syphilis (Refer Chapter 2 in Section I for details)

LOCAL EXAMINATION

	Floor	Base	Edge	Margins	Surrounding skin
Inspection	✓	×	✓	✓	✓
Palpation	✓	✓	✓	✓	✓

- Always say this first:
    1. Examined with due consent
    2. Under adequate illumination
    3. Well exposed from _____ to ____ (only affected part)
    4. Patient in sitting or supine position
    5. In presence of female attendant (for female patients)
- Inspection:

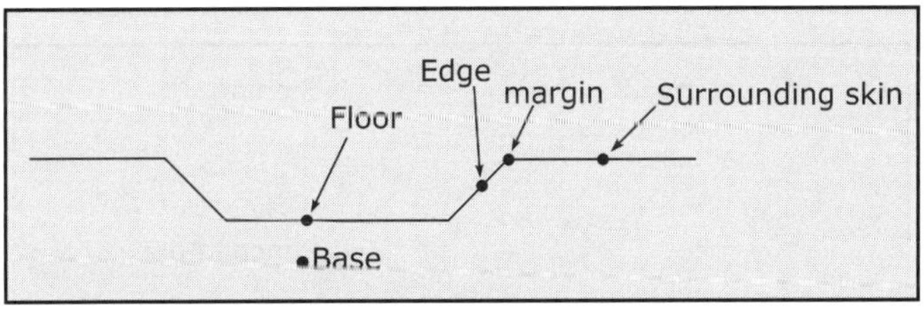

Fig. 10.1: Parts of ulcer

1. Ulcer: Number, site, size, shape, extent

   (Shape: Irregular in malignancy, serpiginous in venous)
2. Floor:
    i. Slough:
        - Color
        - Site: All over the ulcer or only certain edge
        - Indicates non-healing ulcer

- Character:
  a. Soft → slough
  b. Hard → sequestrum (bone)
  c. Wash leather → gumma

ii. Discharge (BEST SEEN ON DRESSING)

iii. Granulation tissue:
- Character: Healthy (pink, pinpoint)/unhealthy
- Amount: Less (pale, smooth)/adequate/excess (proud flesh)

iv. Level (i.e. how deep) (just say up to what tissue, no need to specify in mm)

Structure seen: Subcutaneous tissue (superficial ulcer) or
muscle, bone, tendon (deep ulcer)

(Note that squamous cell carcinoma [SCC] can be raised above surface)

v. Color:
- Black: Melanoma, gangrenous ulcer
- Pink: Healthy
- Pale color: Slow healing, unhealthy

3. Edge:
   i. Filled with discharge (unhealthy)
   ii. Types:

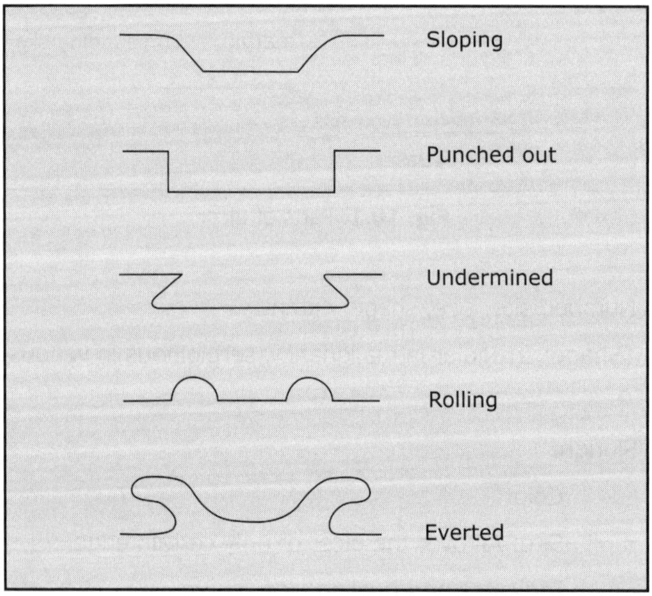

Fig. 10.2: Types of edge of ulcer

a. Sloping: Venous, healing
b. Punched out: Arterial, trophic, traumatic
c. Raised and beaded (pearly white): Rodent ulcer
d. Everted/rolled out: SCC
e. Undermined: TB, amebic ulcer (in GIT)

Punched out edge occurs due to obliterative end-arteritis.

4. Margins:
   i. Color:
      - Red → blue → white (in to out)
        (Red: Granulation tissue with single layer of epithelium
        Blue: Thin squamous epithelium (not cornified) due to Raman effect
        White: Fibrosis, immature collagen yet to be pigmented)
      - Bluish: Tuberculous (because of undermined edge → Raman effect)
   ii. Type:
      - Regular: Most ulcers
      - Irregular: Malignancy

Do not confuse between edge and margin - remember as **EMS** (edge, margin, skin) from inside outwards.

5. Surrounding skin:
   i. Color: Hyperpigmented in chronic ulcer and varicose ulcer
   ii. Edema
   iii. Veins: Seen in varicose veins and malignancy
   iv. Scars, sinuses
   v. Skip lesions

- Palpation:
  Always say this first on palpation: Inspectory findings confirmed
  1. Floor:
     i. Granulation tissue: Healthy/unhealthy
     ii. On pressing: Discharge oozes out

2. Base (pinch the floor between thumb and index finger):
    i. Structure:
        - Soft tissue (muscle)
        - Hard tissue (bone)
    ii. Fixity:
        - Pinch the ulcer and move it → if doesn't move → bone deep
        - Ask patient to contract muscle and move it → if fixed (muscle deep), if moves (superficial)
3. Edge:
    i. Tenderness:
        - Painful: Acute (infection, inflammation)
        - Painless: Chronic, malignancy, neuropathic, trophic, etc.
    ii. Consistency:
        - Hard/firm: Chronic, non-healing, callous ulcer
        - Soft: Acute, healing
    iii. Undermined edge (check with probe)
4. Margin:
    i. Tenderness: Same causes as given in base
5. Surrounding skin: Tenderness, warmth, edema

- Dressing:
    1. Discharge:
        - Character: Purulent, serous, sanguineous, mucoid, caseous
        - Amount: Copious (soaked), scanty (dry)
    2. Type:
        - Dry (absorbent): For exudative lesions
        - Moist dressings: For dry lesions

Do not forget to examine the dressing.

FOCAL EXAMINATION

(Same as in PVD, amputation, varicose veins)

Artery

↓

Veins

↓

Nerves

↓

Lymphatics

↓

Joints

(Trophic and neuropathic ulcers will show decreased sensations on nerve exam.)

DIAGNOSIS

65-year-old male is a case of single, ________ (healing/non-healing) ulcer on the _________ (site, e.g. dorsum of right foot) probably ________ (pathology, e.g. vascular, neuropathic) in origin due to _______ (etiology, e.g. DM) with/without any complications.

DISCUSSION

- Definitions:
  - Ulcer: Breach in the continuity of skin or mucous membrane with molecular death of cells due to underlying inflammation
  - Gangrene: Macroscopic death of tissue with superadded putrefaction
  - Wound: Forcible/traumatic breech in continuity of skin or mucous membrane
  - Floor: Visible part of ulcer
  - Base: Tissue on which the ulcer rests
  - Edge: Area between floor and margin (3D space)
  - Margin: Peripheral limit of ulcer (2D)
  - Slough: Soft necrotic tissue ADHERED to the floor

    (Hard necrotic tissue → sequestrum)

    (Non-adherent → discharge)
  - Granulation tissue: Highly cellular and vascular regenerative tissue with capillaries and fibroblasts intermingled with RBCs and WBCs with a thin fibrin cover over it

Chronic non-healing ulcer: Ulcer persisting for >3 months

- Patient says that ulcer was soft before, but now it is hard → indicates chronic ulcer
- Patient says ulcer developed on:
    1. Scar → Marjolin's ulcer
    2. Swelling → lymphadenopathy, sebaceous cyst, pustule, insect bite
    3. Erythema → skin infection
    4. Blackening → PVD/ischemia

- Pain in various ulcers:
    - Venous: Slightly painful to begin with → painless later (essentially painless)
    - Arterial: Severely painful (pain is out of proportion due to ischemia of nerves)
    - Trophic: Painless
    - Malignant: Painless to begin with → painful later
    - TB: Slightly painful
    - Pyogenic: Severely painful
    - Syphilitic: Painless
- Peculiar sites:
    1. Trophic: (pressure points)
        - Heel, base of metatarsal, malleoli
        - Sacral region
        - Scapula, back of shoulders
        - Elbow (olecranon)
        - Back of head (occiput)
    2. Arterial: Distal limb (toes, inter-digital area)
    3. Venous: Gaiter's area
    4. TB:
        - Sites of lymph nodes, for example, axilla, supraclavicular region, inguinal region
        - Hands, fingers, face (lupus vulgaris)
    5. Syphilis:
        - Subcutaneous bone (gumma)
        - External genitalia (hard chancre)
    6. Hunterian chancre (soft chancre): External genitalia
    7. Rodent ulcer (JACOB ULCER) (basal cell carcinoma): Above angle of mouth (never metastasizes)

8. SCC: Anywhere
9. Melanoma: Exposed part of skin

Almost all cancers metastasize EXCEPT:
1. Rodent's ulcer 2. Marjolin's ulcer 3. Glioma

- Difference between arterial and venous ulcers:

Arterial ulcer	Venous ulcer
1. Painful	1. Painless
2. Below medial malleolus	2. Above medial malleolus
3. Punched out edge	3. Sloping edge
4. Deep (destruction of deep fascia)	4. Superficial
5. Caused as a result of ischemia (PVD)	5. Caused as a result of varicose veins
6. Associated with symptoms like intermittent claudication	6. Associated with symptoms like eczema, pigmentation

- Vasculitis presents as → multiple shallow ulcers
- No lymphadenopathy in Marjolin's ulcer → ∵ It grows in scar tissue
- Hyperpigmentation of surrounding skin:
    1. Chronic ulcer
    2. Varicose ulcer
- Classical TRIAD of diabetic foot:
    1. Neuropathy (polyneuropathy)
    2. Ischemia (microangiopathy)
    3. Infection (sepsis)
- When patient complains of chronic ulcer, always ask for history to rule out causes:
    1. Local causes:
        - Infection
        - Repeated trauma
        - Lack of rest/movement of joint (ulcer on joint)
        - Foreign body
        - Sequestrum

        - Malignancy
    2. Focal causes: Nontreatment of etiology
    3. General causes:
        - Malnutrition (protein, vitamin C)
        - Poor immunity
        - Chronic liver, renal, heart disease
        - DM
        - Hypertension
        - Steroids
        - Radiation

- Granulation tissue:
    - Definition: Highly cellular and vascular regenerative tissue with capillaries and fibroblasts intermingled with RBCs and WBCs with a thin fibrin cover over it
    - Generally forms by 5 to 7 days
    - Delayed formation if hemoglobin is <10 g/dL and serum albumin is <3 g/dL
    - Healthy granulation tissue: **5 Ps**
        1. **Pi**nk
        2. **P**inpoint hemorrhages
        3. **P**ainless
        4. **P**ulseful
        5. No **P**us
        6. Bleeds on touch
        7. Soft
    - Unhealthy granulation tissue: Pale, bumpy
    - Treatment of exuberant granulation tissue (PROUD FLESH):
        1. Scooping (mechanical)
        2. Chemical cauterization with silver nitrate

- Spreading and non-healing ulcers will show edge according to the etiology

- Stages of wound healing:
    1. Stage of hemostasis and inflammation
    2. Stage of proliferation
    3. Stage of maturation

- Rate of ulcer healing is 1 mm/day
- Types of wound healing:
    1. Healing by primary intention:
        - Closing a clean wound by sutures at the first instance
        - Forms good scar
    2. Healing by secondary intention:
        - Leaving the wound open to heal by granulation tissue formation and scarring
        - Done in cases of infected wounds or large tissue loss
        - Forms an ugly scar
    3. Healing by tertiary intention (delayed primary closure):
        - Combination of both
        - Leaving the wound open for a few days followed by subsequent suturing
- Difference between hypertrophic scar and keloid:

Hypertrophic scar	**Keloid**
Growth remains within the margins of wound	Outgrows the wound area
No predominant site	Commonly occur on chest, shoulders, upper back, etc.
Appear 4 to 6 weeks post-injury	Symptom free interval, can take years to appear
Less or no symptoms	Associated with pain, itching or hyperesthesia
Can regress gradually	Do not regress on their own
Contractures are common	Contractures are rare

Eponymous ulcers:

1. Meleny's ulcer: Post-operative progressive bacterial gangrene that forms at incision site
2. Malum perforans: Trophic ulcers: neuropathic ulcers
3. Hunterian chancre: Hard chancre (syphilis)
4. Marjolin's ulcer: Squamous cell carcinoma developing in scar tissue
5. Jacob ulcer: Rodent ulcer - basal cell carcinoma
6. Curling's ulcer: Acute gastric ulcers due to burns (stress ulcers)
7. Cushing's ulcer: Acute gastric ulcers due to raised ICT
8. Martorell ulcer: As a result of hypertension
9. Buruli ulcer: Due to mycobacterium ulcerans

MANAGEMENT

- Investigations:
    1. Local investigations:
        i. SCABS:
            - Swab culture and antibiotic sensitivity
            - Always taken from FLOOR of ulcer (to avoid contamination from skin commensals)

        ii. X-ray: For osteomyelitis and foreign body

        iii. Edge biopsy:
            - Biopsy from ulcer site NOT including surrounding skin
            - Sent for culture (not histopathology)
            - Indication: Strong suspicion of infection when SCABS is negative

        iv. Wedge biopsy:
            - Biopsy from ulcer site INCLUDING surrounding skin
            - Sent for histopathology
            - Indication: Suspected malignancy

        v. Doppler ultrasound:
            - Indication: Ischemic ulcer (clinically poor vascularity)

    2. General investigations:
        i. Hemoglobin: For anemia

        ii. Complete blood count: For leucocytes (infection)

        iii. Total protein/albumin: For hypoproteinemia

    3. Investigations for etiology:
        i. Doppler ultrasound: For PVD, varicose veins

        ii. CXR, sputum examination, swab microscopy and culture: For TB

        iii. Blood sugar levels: For DM

- Treatment:
    ❖ Goals:
        i. Treat the cause

        ii. Convert non-healing to healing ulcer

        iii. Once healing starts → promote healing

        iv. Ulcer care: Cleaning and debridement, regular dressings, pain management, infection control

        v. Management of complications

Desloughing: Removal of dead tissue
Debridement: Removal of infected tissue

- Chemical desloughing:
  1. Hydrogen peroxide (H_2O_2):
     - Eight mechanisms of action: Refer Chapter 9 in Section IV for details
  2. Edinburgh University Solution Of Lime (EUSOL):
     - Active agent: Nascent chloride
     - Requires to be freshly prepared
- When slough disappears

  ↓

  Promote granulation tissue (acriflavine)

  ↓

  Till granulation tissue is complete (prolonged use leads to proud flesh)

- Skin grafting:
  - Graft: Transfer of tissue from one area to another without its blood supply or nerve supply
  - Types:
    1. Partial-thickness graft
    2. Full-thickness graft
  - Partial-thickness graft:
    1. Also called as split-thickness skin graft (STSG) or THIERSCH graft
    2. Includes full epidermis + part of dermis
    3. Indications:
       i. Well granulated ulcer
       ii. Large ulcers which need tissue to heal
       iii. Non-healing ulcers
    4. Taken preferably from thigh of OPPOSITE limb
    5. Skin graft is not useful if ulcer is directly on bone, tendon or over a large area (due to poor vascularity), in such cases pedicled flaps are required
  - Full-thickness graft:
    1. Also called as WOLFE graft
    2. Includes full epidermis + full dermis

- Flaps: Transfer of tissue from one area to another with its intact blood supply
- Dressings:
  - Dressings can be classified as:
    1. Primary dressing: Placed directly on the wound and provide absorption of fluids and prevent desiccation, infection, and adhesion of a secondary dressing
    2. Secondary dressing: Placed on the primary dressing for further protection, absorption, compression, and occlusion
  - Special types of dressings:
    1. Absorbent dressings: To prevent accumulation of wound fluid that can lead to maceration and bacterial overgrowth. It includes cotton, wool, and sponge.
    2. Non-adherent dressings: Impregnated with paraffin, petroleum jelly, or water-soluble jelly for use as non-adherent coverage
    3. Occlusive and

       semi-occlusive dressings: Provide a good environment for clean, minimally exudative wounds. These film dressings are waterproof and impervious to microbes but permeable to water vapor and oxygen.
    4. Hydrophilic dressings: Aids in absorption
    5. Hydrophobic dressings: Waterproof and prevents absorption
    6. VAC: Vaccuum assisted closure involves creating a suction of upto -125 mmHg at the site of ulcer. It reduces edema and promotes healing.

11

Peripheral Vascular Disease (PVD)

HISTORY

[Only additional points on PVD history have been mentioned below. Refer Chapter 1 in Section I beforehand.]

- Personal profile:
  1. Age:
     - Young: Primary Raynaud's (Raynaud's disease) (20-40 years), Buerger's disease (<40 years)
     - Old: Atherosclerosis (>50 years), DM (>40 years)
     - Any age: Secondary Raynaud's (Raynaud's phenomenon)
  2. Sex:
     - Male: Atherosclerosis, Buerger's disease
     - Females: Raynaud's syndrome
  3. Occupation: Involving drilling and vibrations, exposure to cold
  4. Residence: High altitude → polycythemia → prothrombotic state
  5. Religion: Not contributory
- Chief complaints:
  1. Intermittent claudication
  2. Night pain
  3. Rest pain
  4. Ulcer
  5. Gangrene
- HOPI:
  - ❖ Symptoms:
    - Side affected:

      Bilateral - Buerger's disease, Raynaud's syndrome, Leriche's syndrome

      Unilateral - embolism

Atherosclerosis is unilateral to start with but ends as bilateral disease

- Limbs affected:

  Upper limb - Raynaud's syndrome

  Lower limb - Buerger's disease, atherosclerosis

- Important thing in history for gangrene is whether it was:

  Amputated on an emergency basis → wet gangrene

  Amputated electively or allowed to fall off → dry gangrene

- If claudication distance and/or time is not specific on history, ask the patient if he can walk from one end to other in the ward

❖ Etiology:

- Common to both UL and LL:
  1. Buerger's disease: H/o smoking and pain, swelling, discoloration along course of superficial veins (superficial thrombophlebitis)
  2. Raynaud's disease: H/o cyclical color changes with tingling numbness and pain particularly on exposure to cold
  3. Atherosclerosis: H/o giddiness, syncopal attacks, stroke, pain in abdomen after meals, heart attack
  4. Trauma
  5. DM: Polyuria, polydipsia, polyphagia, recurrent episodes of non-healing ulcer
  6. Hypertension
  7. Vasculitis: Skin rash, fever, systemic complaints
  8. Drugs, syphilis, thromboembolism (MR, MS)

     (Drugs: Ergot, thiopentone, non-specific beta blockers)
- Exclusive UL:

  Thoracic outlet syndrome:
  1. Bone: Cervical rib, wide first thoracic rib, fracture first rib or clavicle, costoclavicular syndrome
  2. Muscle: Scalenus anticus syndrome, pectoralis minor syndrome
- Exclusive LL:
  1. Leriche's syndrome: H/o impotency associated with pain in both buttocks and thigh
  2. Hemi-Leriche's syndrome: Pain in one buttock only
  3. Middle aortic syndrome: H/o calf pain, hypertension, oliguria (renal failure)

❖ Complications:
 1. Ulcer
 2. Gangrene

❖ Treatment history:
 1. Amputation
 2. Medications: Mention DETAILS of drugs in case of DM, HTN, MI, or others (which drug, dose, frequency, since when)
 3. Intervention (if any)
 4. Ulcer care

- Past history: DM, hypertension, MI, stroke
- Personal history:
  - Smoking, alcohol → aggravates atherosclerosis

Significant smoking index for PVD is >300 Significant pack years index for PVD is >40 [Refer Chapter 1 in Section I for more details.]

- Family history: Connective tissue disorders (e.g. vasculitis, SLE, etc.)

GENERAL EXAMINATION

[Only additional points on PVD general examination have been mentioned below. Refer Chapter 2 in Section I beforehand.]

- Do not forget to mention posture and attitude
- BMI is important → obesity is a risk factor for hypertension and atherosclerosis
- Mention radial pulse IN DETAIL here, rest all in local examination
  [Say "All other peripheral pulses will be commented upon in local examination"]
- BP: Take 4-limb BP only if you have correct size cuff for lower limb

  [Else do not take lower limb BP and defend by saying cuff criteria:
  - Length of cuff (bladder) should be 80% of arm circumference
  - Breadth of cuff (bladder) should be 40% of arm circumference
  - Length: In children of 6 years age → 12 cm
    : In adults (>18 years) → 36 cm (±5 cm depending on obesity)]
- Do not forget to examine cyanosis

- Skin changes: Mention in local examination
- Gait: Mention in local examination

LOCAL EXAMINATION

- Follow the sequence:
  1. Examined with due consent
  2. Adequate illumination
  3. Well exposed from ___ to ___ (whole limb should be exposed)
  4. Position of patient - sitting and supine
  5. In presence of female attendant (for female patients)

↓

Then "opposite limb appears to be normal"

↓

Then affected limb - pathology (ulcer, gangrene, amputation)

↓

Signs of ischemia

↓

Special tests for circulatory insufficiency

↓

Arteries

↓

Veins

↓

Nerves

↓

Lymphatics

↓

Joints

(Arteries → Joints: Focal examination)

In inspection → don't forget to mention attitude of limb

- Special tests:

Special tests

- **LL**
  - **Inspection**
    1. Buerger's postural test
    2. Capillary filling time
    3. Venous refilling
    4. Crossed leg test (Fuschig test)
  - **Palpation**
    1. Capillary refilling
    2. Venous refilling (Harvey's sign)
- **UL**
  - **Inspection**
    1. Capillary filling time
    2. Roos elevated arms test
    3. Wright's hyperabduction test
    4. Halsted military position
    5. Adson's (face turning) test
  - **Palpation**
    1. Capillary refilling time
    2. Allen's test

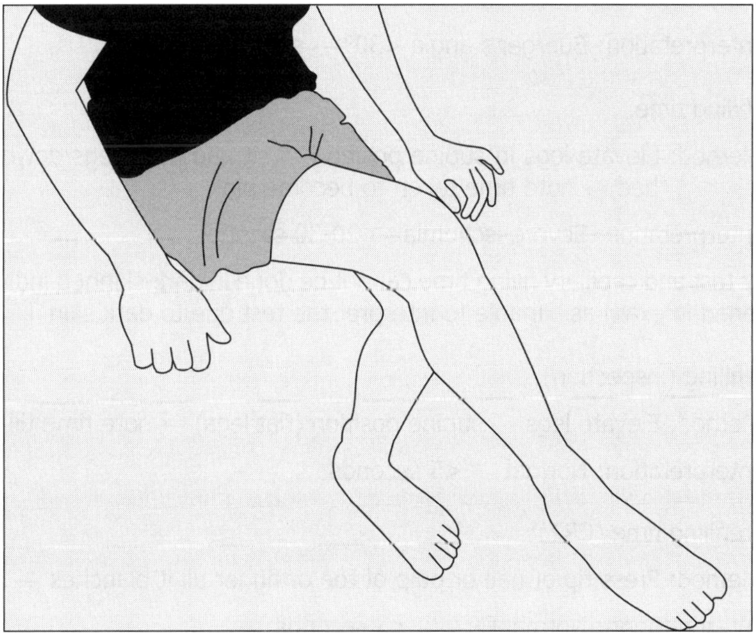

Fig. 11.1: Fuschig's test

❖ Buerger's postural test:

- Method:

Patient supine → lift legs actively

- → Normal
  - ↓ Support patient's legs and ask him to alternately plantar-dorsiflex continuously till fatigue
    - → 1. Pallor 2. Guttering of veins
      - ↓ Feet lowered below bed in sitting position
      - ↓ Cyanotic hue
    - → Normal
- → 1. Pallor 2. Guttering of veins seen at Buerger's angle (Vascular angle)

- Interpretation: Buerger's angle <30° → severe ischemia

❖ Capillary filling time:

- Method: Elevate legs in supine position → sit and hang legs down from edge of bed → note time taken to become pink
- Interpretation: Severe ischemia → 20-30 seconds

[Buerger's test and capillary filling time cannot be done in dark-skinned individuals, so can be mentioned in exam as "unable to interpret the test due to dark skin"]

❖ Venous refilling (inspection):

- Method: Elevate legs → supine position (flat legs) → note time till filling of veins
- Interpretation: Normal → <5 seconds

❖ Capillary refilling time (CRT):

- Method: Press tip of nail or pulp of toe or finger till it blanches → release
- Interpretation: Normal CRT → <3 seconds

❖ Venous refilling (palpation) (Harvey's test):

- Method: Two index fingers placed side by side on a segment of vein → proximal finger moved proximally to empty the vein → distal finger released → observe venous refilling

- Interpretation: Poor refilling → ischemic limb

❖ Roos elevated arms test:

- Method: Abduct the shoulders to 90° + externally rotate fully → open and close the fist for 5 minutes
- Interpretation: Fatigue, pain, paresthesia in forearm or tingling and numbness in fingers → thoracic outlet syndrome

❖ Wright's hyperabduction test:

- Method: Examiner's hand on patient's radial pulse → arm passively hyperabducted
- Interpretation: Weakening or disappearance of pulse → pectoralis minor syndrome

❖ Halstead military position:

- Method: Examiner's hand on patient's radial pulse → patient throws shoulders backwards and downwards (like exaggerated attention position in military)
- Interpretation: Weakening or disappearance of pulse → costoclavicular syndrome

❖ Adson's (face turning) test:

- Method: Patient in sitting position → takes deep breath → turns face to affected side
- Interpretation: Weakening or disappearance of radial pulse → cervical rib or scalenus anticus syndrome

❖ Allen's test:

- Aim: To know the patency of radial artery, ulnar artery, and radio-ulnar anastomosis
- Method: Patient clenches fist tightly → examiner presses on radial and ulnar arteries to occlude them → wait for 1 minute → patient opens the fist → palm becomes pale → remove pressure on radial artery only → see color change

  Repeat the same procedure but remove pressure on ulnar artery.
- Interpretation: Palm becomes pink on removal of pressure → artery is patent

- Arteries:

  Pulse (Refer Chapter 2 in Section I for details)

Artery	Anatomical site (landmark)	Bone against which it is palpated
1. Superficial temporal	In front of tragus	Temporal bone
2. Facial	Antero-inferior angle of masseter muscle	Body of mandible
3. External carotid	Behind angle of mandible	Tubercle of C_2 vertebra
4. Internal carotid	Tonsillar fossa	No bone
5. Common carotid (by thumb, one at a time) First auscultate → then palpate	Just lateral to cricoid cartilage, medial to SCM muscle	Chassaignac's tubercle (anterior tubercle of C_6 vertebra)
6. Subclavian	Supraclavicular fossa	First rib
7. Axillary	Lateral wall of axilla	HEAD of humerus
8. Brachial	Medial to bicipital tendon in cubital fossa	Lower end of humerus
9. Radial (in semi-pronated and semi-flexed position)	Lower forearm lateral to flexor carpi radialis	Anterior surface of lower one-third of radius
	Anatomical snuff box	Scaphoid
10. Ulnar	Lower forearm lateral to flexor carpi ulnaris	Anterior surface of lower one-third of ulna
11. Abdominal aorta	Supraumbilical region (slightly to left) in supine position in expiration (not epigastrium)	Lumbar vertebrae
12. Femoral	1.25 cm (1/2 inch) below mid-inguinal point (NOT midpoint of inguinal ligament)	HEAD of femur
13. Popliteal: Four methods (Fig. 11.2)	A) Supine - knee flexed 135°, use both hands to palpate deep in popliteal fossa	Tibial condyles
	B) Supine - palpate by one hand and hyperextend the knee by elevating lower leg by other hand	Tibial condyles
	C) Prone - knee flexed 90°→ support legs by examiner's chest → active extension of knee against resistance to relax popliteal fascia	Femoral condyles
	D) Prone - extended knee	Tibial condyles

(Continued...)

Artery	Anatomical site (landmark)	Bone against which it is palpated
14. Anterior tibial	Midway between medial and lateral malleoli by tracing lateral side of extensor hallucis longus from toe upward	Lower part of tibia
15. Posterior tibial (in inverted and plantiflexed position)	Midway between medial malleolus and Achilles tendon insertion (PIMENTA'S POINT)	Medial surface of calcaneum
16. Dorsalis pedis	Proximal part of first intermetatarsal space lateral to extensor hallucis longus tendon	Intermediate cuneiform and navicular

Why to auscultate carotid before palpation → for identification of atherosclerosis by bruit → since inadvertent palpation may lead to dislodgment of plaque.

Abdominal aorta is palpated in supraumbilical region and not epigastrium → since lumbar lordosis at this site makes it most superficial.

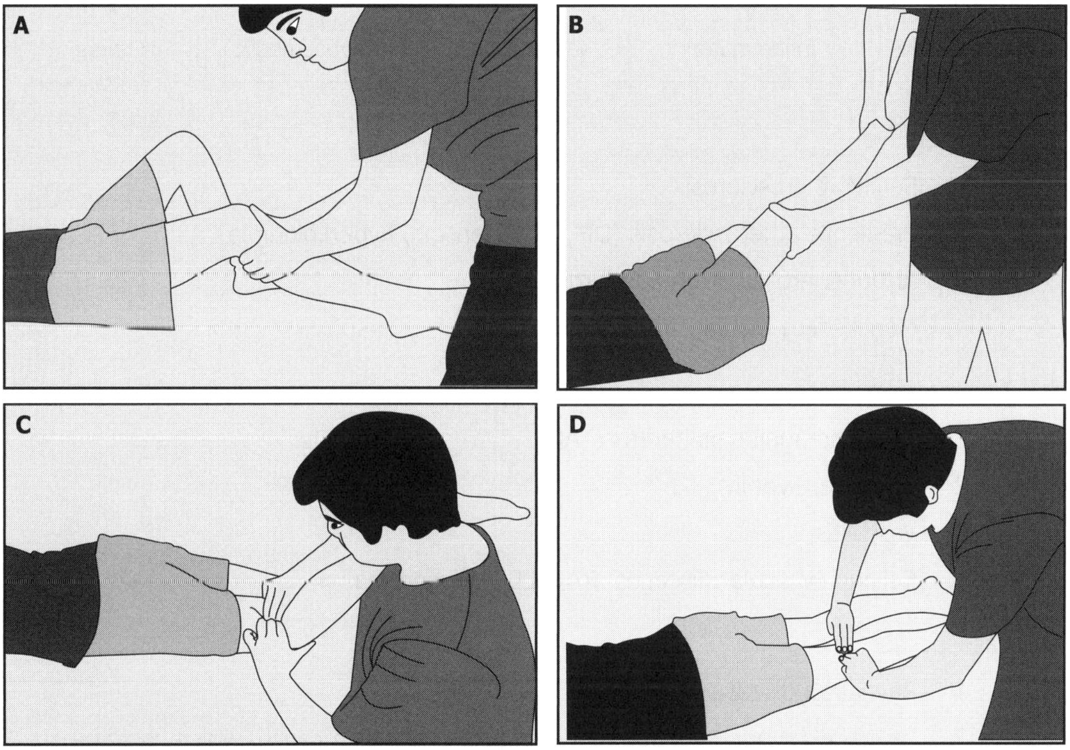

Fig. 11.2: Popliteal artery palpation

DIAGNOSIS

Sixty-five-year-old diabetic male/female is a case of peripheral vascular disease (do not use the abbreviation PVD) with dry gangrene of ____ (site) with chronic non-healing ulcer on___ (site) with level of block being _____(e.g. femoropopliteal) and amputation of _____ done, probable etiology being ____(e.g. generalized atherosclerosis)

DISCUSSION

- PVD (definition): Pathology of any artery of the body EXCEPT coronary and cerebral circulation
- Classification of PVD:

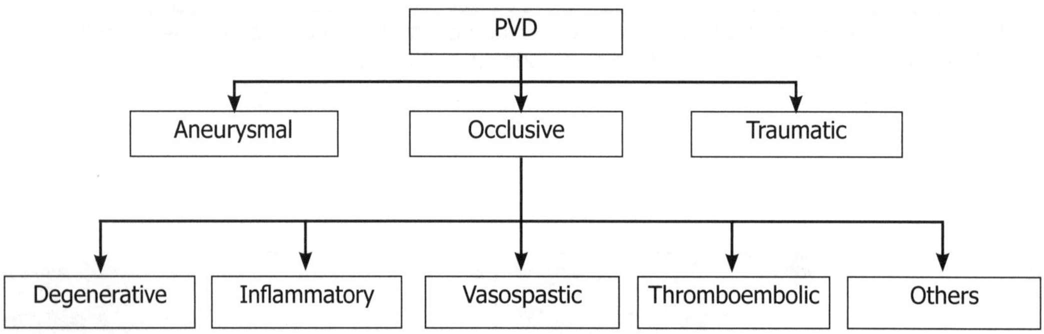

❖ Degenerative:

1. Senile atherosclerosis
2. Pre-senile atherosclerosis (DM, hypertension, hyperlipidemia)
3. Arteriosclerosis, arteriolosclerosis
4. Monckeberg medial calcific sclerosis

❖ Inflammatory:

1. Thrombo-angitis obliterans (TAO)
2. Infective: Syphilis, TB
3. Vasculitis
4. Collagen vascular diseases: RA, SLE, scleroderma

❖ Vasospastic:

1. Raynaud's disease (idiopathic)
2. Raynaud's syndrome (due to identifiable underlying cause, which could be any)

❖ Thromboembolic:

1. Thrombophilic states (inherited and acquired)

2. Embolism (cardiac intramural thrombi, atrial fibrillation, dislodged proximal vascular thrombi)

- Others:
  1. Compression (tight plaster, compartment syndrome)
  2. Connective tissue disease: Marfan's syndrome, Ehlers-Danlos syndrome
  3. AV fistula (causing reduced arterial flow distally)
  4. Steal phenomenon (e.g. subclavian steal phenomenon)

- In PVD, it is not good to have high Hb content → Hb of 9-10 g/dL is better

  (High Hb content → high viscosity)

- Signs of chronic ischemia:
  - Skin: Thinning of skin, shiny skin, ulcers, cold skin, loss of subcutaneous fat
  - Hair: Decreased hair, thinning of hair, easily pluckable
  - Nails: Brittle, opaque, thickened nails with transverse ridges
  - Wasting

- 6 Ps of acute limb ischemia:
  1. Pain
  2. Pallor
  3. Pulselessness
  4. Paralysis
  5. Paraesthesia
  6. Poikilothermia

- Mechanisms by which DM causes PVD:
  1. Accelerated atherosclerosis
  2. Sugar-related infections
  3. Peripheral neuropathy
  4. Arteritis

- Causes of night pain:
  1. Decrease in sympathetic tone while sleeping → vasodilation → but stealing of blood from collaterals → worsening of ischemia
  2. Abolishment of effect of gravity which helps blood flow

- In LL, most common site for ulcer formation is first web space (not tip of toes) → because mean arterial pressure is lowest at that point

- Skip lesions: Seen in wet gangrene due to spread of infection
- Pre-gangrenous changes: (CHOR)
    - Color change
    - Hyperesthesia
    - Oedema
    - Rest pain
- Gangrene:
    - Definition: Macroscopic death of tissue with superadded putrefaction (with or without underlying infection)
    - Causes:
        1. Secondary to arterial occlusion: **RESTED**
            - **i. R**aynaud's
            - **ii. E**mbolism
            - **iii. S**enile atherosclerosis
            - **iv. T**AO
            - **v. E**rgot (drugs)
            - **vi. D**M
        2. Physical causes: Burns, scalds, frostbite, electrical, chemical
        3. Infective:
            - i. Gas gangrene
            - ii. Fournier's gangrene
        4. Venous gangrene - phlegmasia cerulea dolens
    - Difference between dry and wet gangrene:

Dry gangrene	**Wet gangrene**
1. Pathology: SLOW occlusion of vessel	1. Pathology: FAST occlusion of vessel
2. Causes: Atherosclerosis, TAO, etc.	2. Causes: Embolism, trauma
3. Affected part is dry, shriveled and mummified	3. Affected part is edematous, putrified and foul smelling
4. Line of demarcation present	4. ABSENT (diffusely merges with adjacent normal area)
5. Skip areas ABSENT	5. Skip areas present
6. No infection	6. Infection present
7. Separates by aseptic ulceration	7. Separates by septic ulceration
8. Spreads slowly	8. Spreads rapidly
9. Treatment: Falls off on own (auto-amputation) or amputated electively	9. Treatment: Emergency amputation

ZONE of demarcation:

- Zone between living and dead tissue
- Living tissue keeps sending capillaries (so hyperaemic) and nerves (so hyperasthetic) across the junction

LINE of demarcation:

- Appears when granulation tissue fails to carry blood any further

- Differentiating features to be asked on history:
  1. Dry gangrene: Blackening associated with loss of sensations, non-edematous, non-foul smelling, not warm; if amputated - whether auto-amputation or elective amputation
  2. Wet gangrene: Blackening associated with loss of sensations, edematous, foul - smelling, can be associated with discharge; if amputated - emergency amputation
- Treatment of gangrene:
  1. Wet gangrene: Emergency amputation in ALL cases
  2. Dry gangrene:
     i. Forefoot (i.e. distal to tarso-metatarsal joint): Allowed to fall off on own (auto-amputation)
     ii. Proximal to forefoot: Elective amputation (since large amount of myonecrosis has high risk of AKI and ARDS)

• Claudication history:
  1. Arterial:
     - Cramp-like pain on walking and disappears at rest
     - Worsens on climbing UPHILL
  2. Venous:
     - Dull aching heaviness or discomfort maximum at the end of day relieved on lying down or lifting legs (varicose veins)
     - Bursting pain in DVT appears on walking and need not be relieved on rest, need not be in exercising muscle
  3. Nervous:
     - Sharp shooting pain, radiating, appears as soon as first step is taken
     - Worsens on climbing DOWNHILL

• Arterial claudication:
  - Claudius → limp (Roman emperor Claudius limped)

- Boyd's classification:

Grade	Presentation
I	Pain on walking → relieved after certain time (Due to vasodilation and washout of substance P)
II	Pain on walking → not relieved but patient can walk with bearable pain
III	Pain on walking → compels the patient to stop
(Note that rest pain is not included in Boyd's classification.)	

- Rest pain → cry of dying nerves

  Typical decubitus – hip flexed + knee flexed + heel on bed and holding the foot in both palms

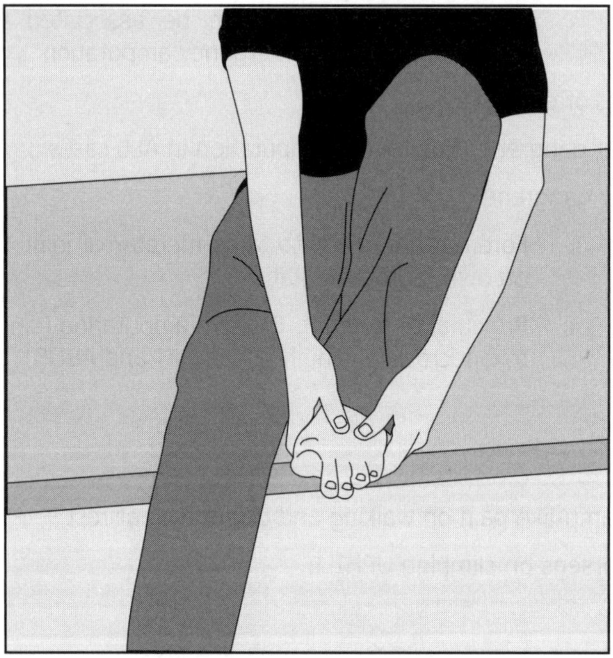

Fig. 11.3: Typical decubitus in PVD

- Method to test local rise of temperature:
  - Step 1 → check normal area (surrounding)

    Step 2 → check abnormal area

    Step3 → check normal area again (same area as in step 1)
  - Note that in PVD normal area means opposite limb and abnormal area means area adjacent to gangrene
  - Why to see adjacent area's temperature in PVD → because gangrenous area is always cold

- Veins:
  - Cord-like thickening + tenderness → thrombophlebitis
  - Varicose veins in PVD will appear as → guttered veins
  - Sometimes there can be dilated vein seen in leg but not tortuous → due to collaterals
  - Visible veins is a GOOD sign in PVD → indicates partial ischemia
- Nerves:
  - Test all sensations of dorsal column and spinothalamic tract
  - Test - affected area, surrounding area, and opposite limb
  - There will be area of hyperesthesia at line of demarcation between gangrene and normal area
  - First sensation to be affected in DM → vibration sense
- Ankle brachial index:
  - $ABI = \frac{\text{SBP at ankle}}{\text{SBP at upper arm}}$

    (SBP at ankle is taken as highest of the values amongst dorsalis pedis and posterior tibial artery

    SBP at upper arm is taken as highest of the values amongst right and left brachial arteries)
  - Measured by doppler ultrasound (CANNOT be measured clinically)
  - Interpretation according to values:

ABI value	Interpretation
>1.3	Indicates calcification of arteries
0.9-1.3	Normal
0.7-0.9	Mild PVD
0.4-0.7	Moderate PVD
<0.4	Critical limb ischemia

  - ABI > 1.3 indicates calcification of tunica media of arteries (mostly seen in DM) → in such cases toe systolic blood pressure or TBI (toe brachial index) is done (since it is not affected by calcification)

- Critical limb ischemia:
    - Clinically:
        1. Rest pain > 2 weeks
        2. Ulcer
        3. Gangrene
    - On investigations:
        1. ABI < 0.4
        2. Ankle SBP < 50 mmHg
        3. Toe SBP < 30 mmHg
- Characteristic features of common diseases:

Atherosclerosis	Buerger's disease	Raynaud's disease
Old (>50 years)	Young (<40 years)	Young (20-40 years)
M > F	M > F	F > M
Lower limbs > upper limbs	Lower limbs > upper limbs	Upper limbs > lower limbs
Distal > proximal	Proximal > distal	Distal > proximal
Unilateral to start with but ends as a bilateral disease	Generally bilateral	Generally bilateral

MANAGEMENT

- Management protocol:

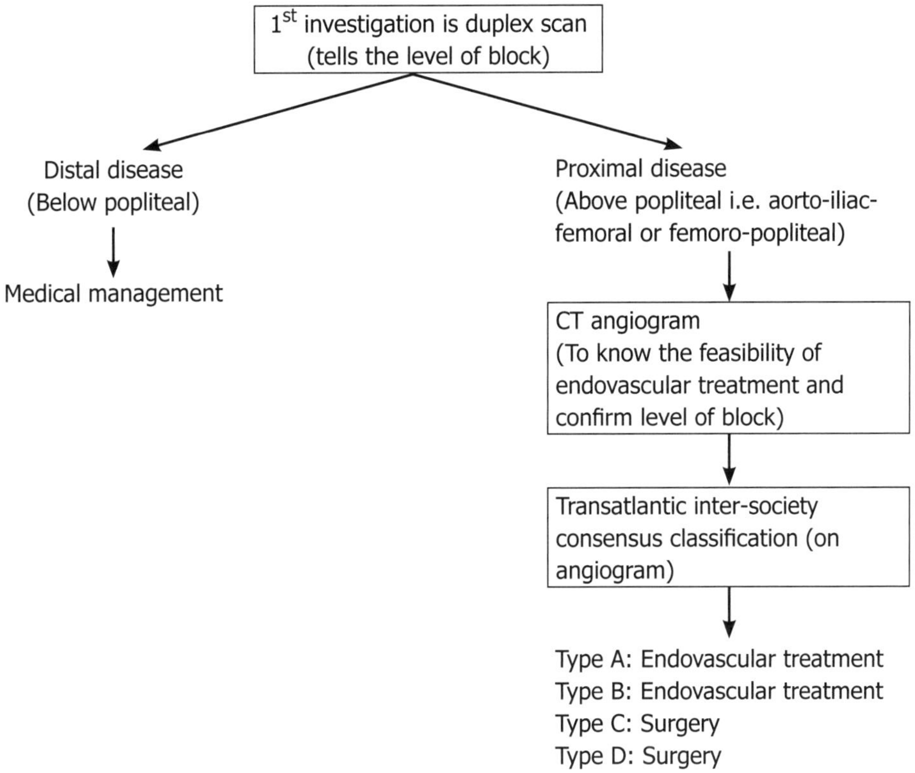

First line of management → LIFESTYLE CHANGES

- Investigations for etiology:
  - Blood glucose, urine glucose
  - Serum lipid profile
  - ECG
  - Pus for antibiotic sensitivity testing
- Duplex arterial USG:
  - First investigation done
  - Tells - site, extent, severity, collaterals, flow, ABI (ankle brachial index)
  - Flow - Normal: Triphasic

    Abnormal: Biphasic → monophasic → aphasic

- Angiography:
  - CT angiogram: Non-invasive (contrast through vein)
  - MR angiogram: Non-invasive (contrast through vein)
  - Conventional angiogram: Invasive (contrast through artery)
  - Indications:
    1. Conventional angiogram: Before surgical intervention
    2. CT/MR angiogram: For medical management
- Brown's vasomotor index:
  - Indicates degree of vasospasm
  - Method: Block the nerves with local anesthetic to determine the efficacy of sympathectomy
  - $$\text{BVMI} = \frac{\text{Rise in skin temperature} - \text{Rise in core temperature}}{\text{Rise in core temperature}}$$
  - Indication of sympathectomy: BVMI > 3.5
- Medical management:
  - Specific drugs:
    1. Aspirin - anti platelet agent (irreversible COX inhibitor)
    2. Pentoxyphylline - increases pliability of RBCs (non-selective phosphodiesterase inhibitor)
    3. Cilostazol - decreases viscosity of blood (selective PDE3 inhibitor)
    4. Xanthine nicotinate - decreases viscosity of blood
    5. Hypocholesterolemic agents - statins, fibrates, etc.
    6. CCBs - for Raynaud's phenomenon
  - Pain management: NSAIDS, opioids
  - General management: Buerger's exercises, Buerger's position

Buerger's exercises:
- Step 1 - elevate legs till they blanch (approximately 2 minutes)
- Step 2 - lower the legs below the level of body (for 5-10 minutes)
- Step 3 - bring the legs flat at the level of body (for 10 minutes)
- Done for 4 - 5 times/session and 3 sessions/day

Buerger's position: 15° head high position

- Endovascular treatment:
  1. Balloon angioplasty: High chance of recurrence
  2. Stenting (PTFE or metal)
  3. Laser atherectomy

Endovascular treatment CANNOT be done for:
1. Small vessels 2. Multiple blocks

- Surgical management:
  1. Bypass surgery:
     - Preferred for long segment or multiple blocks
     - Types:
       i. Autologous graft → GSV (least chance of thrombosis)
       ii. Synthetic graft → PTFE better than dacron
  2. Embolectomy
  3. Thromboendarterectomy
- Sympathectomy:
  - Indications:
    1. Non-healing ulcer
    2. Raynaud's
    3. Hyperhidrosis
  - Types:
    1. Depending on method:
       i. Chemical
       ii. Surgical
    2. Depending on location:
       I. Cervical : $T_2T_3T_4$
       ii. Lumbar: $L_1L_2L_3L_4$ (L_1 on one side spared if bilateral sympathectomy is to be done)
  - Incision given: Grid iron incision

Grid iron (McBurney's incision is used for:
1. Appendectomy 2. Sympathectomy 3. Middle one-third ureterotomy

12

Varicose Veins

HISTORY

[Only additional points on varicose veins history have been mentioned below. Refer Chapter 1 in Section I beforehand.]

- Personal profile:
  1. Age: More common in 45-70 years
  2. Sex: Females > Males → 10: 1
  3. Occupation:
     i. Prolonged standing - police, security guard, surgeon
     ii. Occupation involving excess muscular contractions - athletes, rickshaw pullers

        (Since more muscle contractions

        ↓

        More blood flow

        ↓

        More stress over valves

        ↓

        Perforator incompetence)
  4. Address: Not contributory
  5. Religion: Not contributory
- Chief complaints:
  1. Elongated and tortuous swelling in lower limb
  2. Pain
  3. Heaviness in lower limbs

- HOPI:
  - Symptoms
  - Etiology:

Etiology

- **Primary**
  - Congenital absence of valves
  - Inheritance (FOXC2 gene)
  - Klippel-Trenaunay syndrome
  - Parkes Weber syndrome
  - Occupational
- **Secondary**
  - Obstruction to outflow
    - Pregnancy
    - Abdominal lump
    - Pelvic cancer
    - Pelvic congestion syndrome
    - Portal hypertension
  - Destruction of valves
    - DVT
    - OC pills
    - Thrombophilic states
    - Trauma
    - Prolonged immobilization
  - High-pressure flow
    - AV fistula

- DVT: H/o acute cramp-like pain (bursting) in the calf associated with swelling and tightness in lower limb (requiring anticoagulation)
- Portal hypertension: H/o hematemesis or bleeding P/R associated with distention of abdomen

- Complications: Occur in following sequence

Varicose veins
↓
Stagnation
↓
Lysis of red blood cells (RBCs)
↓
Pigment deposition (skin discoloration)
↓
Itching (itching)
↓
Dermatitis
↓
Eczema
↓
Ulceration (wound)
↓
- Hemorrhage (Bleeding)
- Periostitis Osteomyelitis (pus discharge with fever)
- Tendoachilles equinus deformity (walking on toes)
- SCC (fungating growth)
- lipodermatosclerosis

- Thrombophlebitis: Attacks of redness and pain along the swelling associated with fever

- Past history: History of pelvic or hip surgery
- Personal history: Not contributory
- Family history: Inheritance (FOXC2 gene)

GENERAL EXAMINATION

[Only additional points on varicose veins general examination have been mentioned below. Refer Chapter 2 in Section I beforehand.]

- BMI: Obesity
- Edema: In DVT
- Lymphadenopathy (if any): Describe in local examination
- Port-wine stain: Klippel-Trenaunay syndrome (KTS)

LOCAL EXAMINATION

- Always say this first:
  1. Examined with due consent
  2. Under adequate illumination
  3. Exposed from umbilicus downwards
  4. In standing and supine positions
  5. In presence of female attendant (for female patients)
  6. **Opposite limb appears normal (in all limb cases**)
- Inspection:

Elongated tortuous swelling
(which system [GSV, SSV] is involved, if other system is normal or involved)
↓
Complications (ulcer, edema, deformity, etc.)
↓
Arteries
↓
Nerves
↓
Lymphatics and lymph nodes
↓
Joints

- Palpation:

  Say this first on palpation:

  1. Inspectory findings confirmed
  2. No local rise in temperature
  3. Tenderness - yes or no
  4. No cord-like thickening along course of veins

  Then comment on - veins (including special tests)
  ↓
  Arteries
  ↓
  Nerves
  ↓
  Lymphatics and lymph nodes
  ↓
  Joints

- Special tests:

  Say "Brodie-Trendelenburg test suggests ____(SFJ/perforator/both to be incompetent) as confirmed by Morrissey's cough impulse test, multiple tourniquet test denotes the incompetent perforators to be ___ (name of perforator); Fegan's test shows ____ (number and sites) pits in deep fascia.

  There is evidence/no evidence of DVT as concluded by ___ (name of the tests done)."

Method to empty the veins:

Patient in supine position
↓
Leg raised (keep that leg on examiner's shoulder)
↓
Milk the veins proximally

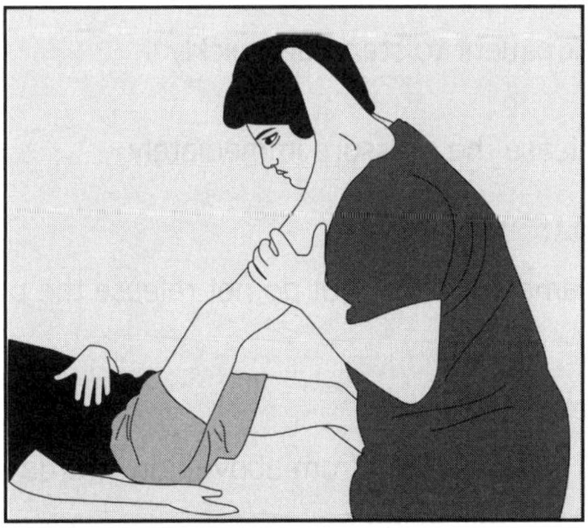

Fig. 12.1: Method to empty/ milk varicose veins

1. Tests for DVT (very important as presence of DVT changes management):
   i. Limb edema + tightness
   ii. Homan's sign: Passive forceful dorsiflexion of foot in extended knee causes pain in calf
   iii. Moses sign: Gentle rolling of calf muscles from side-to-side causes pain
   iv. Neuhof's sign: Thickening and tenderness on palpating deep in calf muscles
   v. Linton's test
   vi. Modified Perthe's test:
      - Aim: To check for DVT
      - Method:

        Empty the veins
        ↓
        Tourniquet at upper part of thigh
        ↓
        Ask the patient to walk

      - Interpretation: Veins becoming more prominent indicates DVT

2. Brodie-Trendelenburg test (has two parts):
   - Aim: Determine competency of SFJ or perforators or both
   - Method:

     Part I:

     Empty the veins
     ↓
     Occlude the SFJ with tourniquet or two thumbs
     ↓
     Ask patient to stand up quickly
     ↓
     Release the pressure immediately

     Part II:

     Same like part I but do not release the pressure till 1 minute

   - Interpretation:

     Part I → rapid filling from above downwards → SFJ incompetence

     Part II → slow filling from below upwards → perforator incompetence

3. Multiple tourniquet test:

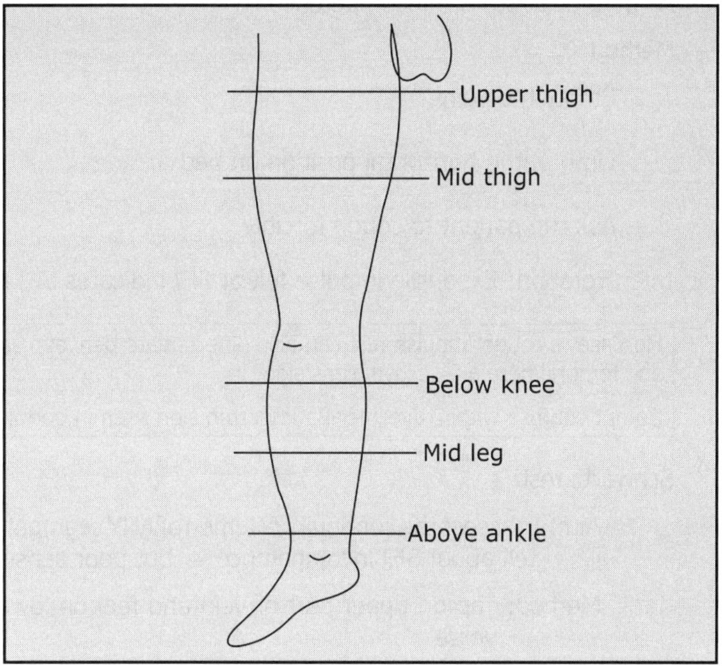

Fig. 12.2: Multiple tourniquet test (Oschner Mahorner test)

- Aim: To know which perforators are incompetent
- 3 tourniquet test (to be done in exam): Mid-leg, below knee, mid-thigh
- 5 tourniquet test (Oschner-Mahorner test): Above ankle, mid-leg, below knee, mid-thigh, upper thigh
- Method:

  Empty the veins

  ↓

  Tourniquets tied at various levels

  ↓

  Ask the patient to stand

- Interpretation: Filling of veins in between two tourniquets indicates site of incompetent perforator

Pathognomic sign of short saphenous varices: Application of tourniquet to upper thigh increases the strength of reflux in short saphenous system

4. Morrissey's cough impulse test:
   - Aim: To evaluate SFJ incompetence
   - Method:

     Empty the veins
     ↓
     Limb put in horizontal position on bed
     ↓
     Ask the patient to cough forcibly

   - Interpretation: Expansile impulse felt at SFJ indicates SFJ incompetence

> Morrissey's cough impulse test can also differentiate between saphena varix and femoral hernia → Cruveihier's sign.
>
> Do not confuse with Cruveilhier-Baumgarten sign seen in portal hypertension.

5. Schwartz test:
   - Aim: To assess the continuity of lumen of ANY segment of vein (can also tell about SFJ incompetence → but poor sensitivity)
   - Method: Tap on upper part of vein and feel on lower part and vice versa
   - Interpretation: Impulse felt → indicates continuity of lumen

6. Fegan's test:
   - Aim: To evaluate sites of perforators (does not show INCOMPETENT perforators specifically)
   - Method:

     Mark sites of excess bulges within the varicosities when patient is in standing position
     ↓
     Patient in supine position and empty the veins
     ↓
     Palpate along the line of marked varicosities

   - Interpretation: Gaps/pits in deep fascia → indicates sites of perforators

(Perthe's, Pratt's, and Linton's test need not be done in exam.)

[Abdominal examination can be done for lump in abdomen.]

[P/R examination can be done to check for hemorrhoids (only thrombosed piles can be felt)
Scrotal examination for varicocele]

DIAGNOSIS

Give CEAP score:

Case of right/left/bilateral lower limb primary/secondary (specify etiology if secondary) varicose veins involving GSV at ____ (sites e.g. calf and ankle) with incompetence of SFJ and/or perforators (specify which e.g. lower leg) with/without DVT with/without complications with CEAP score being _______ (e.g. $C_2 E_p A_{s,p} P_r$)

DISCUSSION

- Definition: Dilated, elongated, tortuous superficial veins (of lower limb) with reversal of flow/reflux with size being > 3 mm

- Types of dilated veins:
  - < 1 mm → telangiectasia (thread veins, spider veins), ankle flare
  - 1-3 mm → reticular veins
  - > 3 mm → varicose veins

- Venous pain:
  1. Varicose veins: Dull aching heaviness or discomfort maximum at the end of day relieved on lying down or lifting legs
  2. DVT: Bursting pain in DVT appears on walking and need not be relieved on rest, need not be in exercising muscle

- Prolonged immobilization means: ≥72 hours (3 days)
- Side involved: Left > right
- Klippel Trenauny syndrone (KTS):
  - Affects blood vessels or lymph vessels or both
  - Three main features:
    i. Nevus flammeus (port-wine stain)
    ii. Venous and lymphatic malformation
    iii. Soft-tissue hypertrophy of affected limb (local gigantism)

- Parkes Weber syndrome → KTS + AV fistula

- Importance of lymphadenopathy in varicose veins:
  1. Ulcer → infection → lymphadenopathy
  2. Pelvic tumours → lymphadenopathy

- Causes of bleeding in varicose veins:
    1. Trauma
    2. Spontaneous: Due to high pressure
    3. Ulceration
- Theories of varicose veins:
    1. Fibrin cuff theory
    2. White cell trapping theory
    3. Ambulatory venous hypertension
    4. Absence/destruction of valves

> Ambulatory venous hypertension: Venous pressure of > 80 mmHg at ankle while standing or walking or exercising (normally pressure should fall when calf muscles contract)

- Theories of varicose ulcers:
    1. Fibrin cuff theory
    2. White cell trapping theory
- Complications of varicose veins:
    1. Skin:
        - i. Pigmentation
        - ii. Lipodermatosclerosis (LDS) → woody feel → palpatory finding (NOT INSPECTORY)
        - iii. Eczema
        - iv. Ankle flare (red)
        - v. Atrophic blanche (whitish)
          (iv and v: Pre-ulcerative changes)
        - vi. Ulceration
        - vii. Trophic changes (Refer Chapter 11 in Section IV for details)
        - viii. Edema
    2. Veins:
        - i. Thrombophlebitis
        - ii. Calcification
    3. Hemorrhage

4. Bone:
   i. Periosteitis
   ii. Osteomyelitis
5. Adaptive changes:
   i. INVERTED CHAMPAGNE BOTTLE APPEARANCE - due to swelling of upper part of limb with thickening and constriction of lower part due to LDS
   ii. Talipes equino varus

- Gaiter's area:
  - Most common site of varicose ulcer → since more direct perforators present → since no muscle in that area
  - Site: Around medial malleolus
  - Derivation: From gitter (French) → piece of cloth used to cover ankle region by the bishops and horse riders
- Deep veins are 6 in number: Anterior tibial, posterior tibial, and peroneal (all are paired)
- Perforators: **MK-CBD-H**

Name	Site	Number
MK-May and Kuster	Ankle (inframalleolar)	Multiple
C-Cockett	Lower leg	3
B-Boyd	Below knee	2
D-Dodd	Above knee	1
H-Hunterian	Mid-thigh	

- SFJ:
  - Lies 4 cm below and lateral to pubic tubercle
  - How to locate: Adduct thigh against resistance → trace adductor longus upwards → identify pubic tubercle → trace 4 cm below and lateral
- Daflon: Herbal medicine for any venous problem (improves venous muscle tone)
- How will varicose veins present/look in concomitant PVD and varicose veins (i.e. both pathologies in same patient) → guttering of veins (empty veins)

Pudendal varicose veins are seen in pelvic congestion syndrome.

MANAGEMENT

- Management protocol:

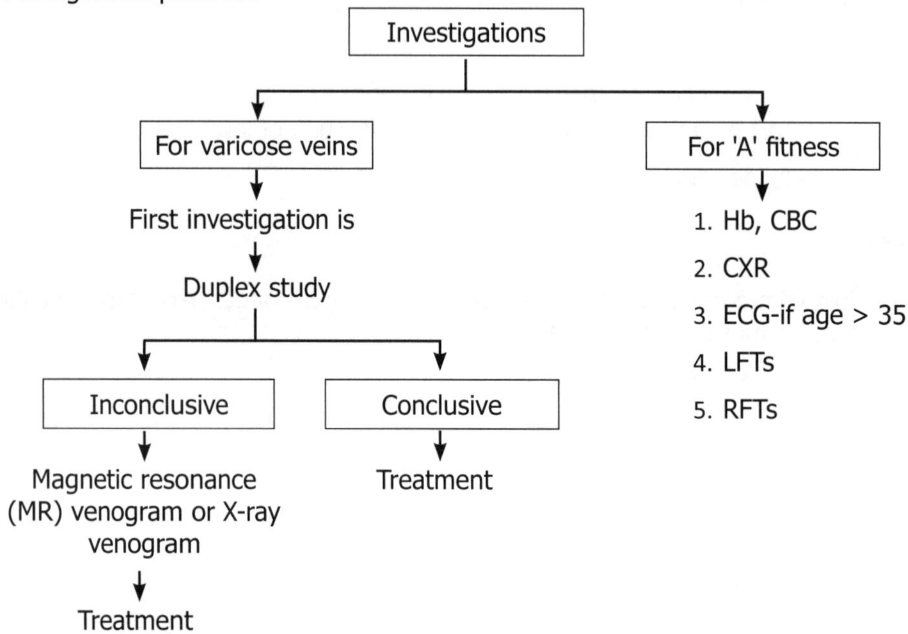

> In presence of DVT, NO surgery or intervention should be performed; because superficial venous system (although incompetent) is the only pathway for lower limb blood outflow; destruction of which will prove to be a disaster.

- Investigation modalities:
  1. USG: Has four modes
     i. A mode: Amplitude mode (gives graph) → used in ophthalmology
     ii. B mode: Brightness mode (gives anatomy in gray scale)
     iii. M mode
     iv. D mode: Doppler mode
  2. Doppler: Gives information about flow
     i. Flow velocity
     ii. Flow direction: Towards the probe → red, away from the probe → blue

3. Duplex scan: B + D modes
   - Patient's position: Standing position facing the examiner with leg in external rotation, heel on the ground and weight on the opposite limb

     Examiner's position: Kneeling down
   - Frequency of transducer: 7.5-13 MHz
   - Information obtained in varicose veins:
     a. Superficial veins: Site, size
     b. Perforators: Test for reflux → on pressing calf reflux should last >0.5 second
     c. Deep veins: DVT
     d. SFJ and SPJ: Saphenous eye, Mickey Mouse sign, test for reflux

- Tumescent anesthesia:
  - Given along the length of vein under USG guidance
  - Three components:

1. Sodium bicarbonate	→	5 mL, 8.3%	in 500 mL NS
2. Lignocaine	→	10 mL, 10%	
3. Adrenaline	→	1 mL	

  - Used in: Varicose vein treatment and liposuction
  - Principle: Same amount of local anesthetic can be used over larger area/length
  - Advantages:
    1. Decreased heat dissipation during endovenous laser ablation (EVLA) (so less tissue damage)
    2. Collapse of vein → so more contact with vein

> Maximum approved amount of local anaesthetic that can be used:
> - Lignocaine without adrenaline: 4.5 mg/kg
> - Lignocaine with adrenaline: 7 mg/kg
> - Tumescent aesthesia: 35 mg/kg

- Treatment of varicose veins:

> Uncomplicated varicose veins → conservative management
>
> Complicated varicose veins → surgery or interventional management

  - Indications of surgery/intervention in uncomplicated cases:
    1. Symptomatic patient
    2. For cosmesis
    3. Junctional incompetence

- Conservative management:
  1. Elevation of limb (above the level of heart)
  2. Calf muscle exercises, walk with heel first
  3. Calf massage
  4. Compression stockings:
     a. Wear throughout the day except bathing and sleeping
     b. British and European classification according to pressures:

Compression stockings			Indications
British standard	Class I	14-17 mmHg	DVT
	Class II	17-24 mmHg	Varicose veins
	Class III	24-35 mmHg	Venous ulcer
European standard	Class I	20-30 mmHg	DVT
	Class II	30-40 mmHg	Varicose veins
	Class III	40-50 mmHg	Venous ulcers
	Class IV	50-60 mmHg	Lymphedema

- Interventions (minimally invasive procedures):
  1. Sclerotherapy (foam sclerotherapy)-by Tessari method
  2. EVLA
  3. RFA

  (EVLA, RFA: Similar results like surgery, but minimally invasive. Hence preferred.)

  4. VENUS
  5. TRIVEX

- Surgeries:
  1. For SFJ incompetence:
     a. Trendelenburg operation (flush ligation of GSV at SFJ)
     b. Babcock surgery

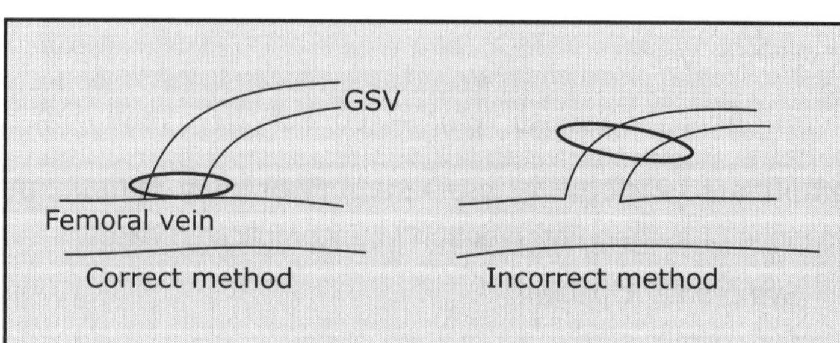

Fig. 12.3: Flush ligation

2. For perforator incompetence:
   a. Subfascial ligation of perforators - Dodd and Cockett procedure
   b. Extrafascial ligation of perforators - Linton's procedure
   c. Subfascial endoscopic perforator ligation surgery (SEPS)

- Management of varicose veins WITH DVT: After at least 6 months of anticoagulation, confirm recanalization of deep veins and then treat varicose veins

- Management of venous ulcer:

  Bisgaard regimen (conservative management)

  ↓

  Till granulation tissue appears (means ulcer becomes non-infective)

  ↓

  Definitive management of varicose veins

13

Amputation

(History taking and examination of amputation follows a different pattern from rest of the cases)

HISTORY

- Patient profile:
  Say "Name, age, sex, address, occupation, underwent _____ (emergency/elective) _______ (right/left) sided _______ (site e.g. below knee, above knee, etc.) __________ (type: Closed/open) amputation _____ months (duration) back in view of ________ (reason of amputation e.g. wet gangrene)

- H/O amputation and stump:
  1. Present symptoms:
     - Pain, discharge, bleeding, etc.
     - If no symptoms are present, say "Currently comfortable at rest"
  2. If it is closed or open stump
  3. Whether done for the first time or revision of earlier amputation?

     (All past amputations of same and/or opposite limb have to be mentioned IN DETAIL here)
  4. When is revision planned in future (only for open stumps)?

- H/O complications:
  1. Psychological: Depression
  2. Social and occupational effects:
     - Interaction with the society
     - Change in occupation?
  3. Limb complications: (See discussion part for details)
     i. Skin:
        - Douglas ulcer: H/o open wound

     ii. Scar:
        - Painful scar

iii. Subcutaneous tissue:
   - Abscess: H/o throbbing type of pain and warmth/fever associated with swelling and purulent discharge

iv. Muscle:
   - Contractures: H/o inability to perform full range of motion

v. Artery:
   - Hemorrhage: H/o spontaneous bleeding or excess soakage of dressing with blood

vi. Vein:
   - DVT: H/o acute cramp-like pain (bursting) in the calf associated with swelling and tightness in lower limb (requiring anticoagulation)

vii. Nerve:
   - Neuroma: H/o severe pain or paresthesia at distal end of the stump
   - Phantom limb: H/o sensation felt distal to the stump

viii. Bone:
   - Osteomyelitis: H/o discharge of bony pieces from stump

ix. Other limb:
   - Arthritis: H/o pain in joints of other limb

- H/O care of amputation stump:
  1. Taken care by whom?
  2. Dressing:
     - Type of dressing (soft, soft with splint, hard)
     - Frequency
  3. Regular exercises done or not as prescribed by physiotherapist?
- Past history/personal history/family history/menstrual history: To be commented upon only if it contributes to etiology or will affect further management
  (All addictions have to be mentioned.)

GENERAL EXAMINATION

[Only additional points on amputation general examination have been mentioned below. Refer Chapter 2 in Section I beforehand.]

- Non-cooperative patient: May indicate depression
- Tachycardia: Due to pain, sepsis
- Edema and lymphadenopathy (if not generalized) should be commented upon in local examination
- Gait: Amputee gait

- Signs of atherosclerosis: May indicate PVD

LOCAL EXAMINATION

- Always say this first:
    1. Examined with due consent
    2. Under adequate illumination
    3. Exposure from _____ downwards (expose the whole limb)
    4. In supine position
    5. In presence of female attendant (for female patients)
- Note that it may be a closed or open amputation stump, describe accordingly (details of ulcer should be mentioned in open stump)
- Examine in the following order:

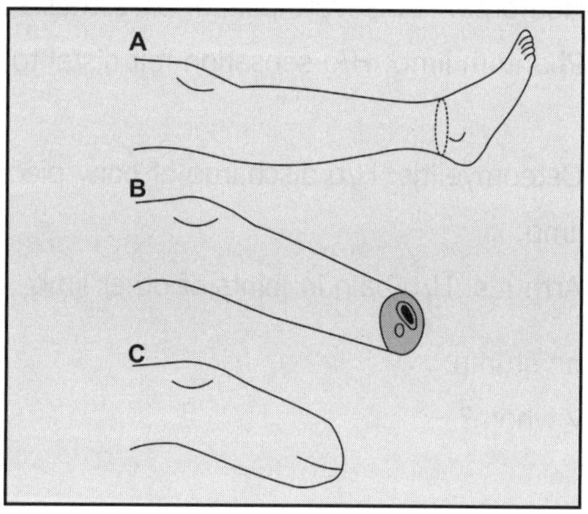

Fig. 13.1: Open stump (B) vs closed stump (C)

"opposite limb appears to be normal"

↓

affected limb-amputation stump (describe inside outwards)

↓

Arteries

↓

Veins

↓

Nerves

↓

Lymphatics

↓

Joints

(Arteries, Veins, Nerves, Lymphatics, Joints — Focal examination)

- Inspection:

INSPECTION OF CLOSED AMPUTATION STUMP

- Start by saying "Left limb appears to be normal, right limb shows a below knee closed amputation stump of _____ cm"
- Scar or suture line:
  1. Orientation (antero-posterior or transverse)
  2. Site (terminal, anteriorly placed, posteriorly placed)
  3. Length
  4. Any dog ears
  5. Signs of inflammation if any (redness, discharge, etc.)
- Surrounding skin:
  1. Color (erythematous if inflamed)
  2. Swelling if any (stretched shiny skin)
  3. Sinuses, dilated veins
- Stump:
  1. Length (from fixed bony point)
  2. Shape
  3. Drain (if any)
- Dressing:
  1. Type of dressing
  2. Discharge: Color, amount
- Proximal limb: Skip lesions or progress of disease

INSPECTION OF OPEN AMPUTATION STUMP

- Start by saying "Left limb appears to be normal, right limb shows a below knee open guillotine/flapped amputation stump of ____ cm"
- If guillotine stump: Say "Skin, subcutaneous tissue, muscle, and bone all are seen at the same level i.e. it is a guillotine amputation stump"

  If flaps seen: Say "Flaps are seen" and describe the flaps as anterior and posterior or medial and lateral; which is longer; which is broader; both contain muscle layer or one contains only skin and subcutaneous tissue
- Ulcer: Refer Chapter 10 in Section IV for details.

- Stump: Same as above
- Dressing: Same as above
- Proximal limb: Same as above

- Palpation:

  Always say this first on palpation:

  1. Inspectory findings confirmed
  2. No local rise of temperature
  3. Tenderness - yes or no

PALPATION OF CLOSED AMPUTATION STUMP

- Scar or suture line:
  1. Tender/non-tender
  2. Thin/thick (thick scar may indicate infection)
  3. Fixity: Can/cannot be pinched up

- Surrounding skin:
  1. Temperature
  2. Tenderness
  3. Swelling/edema
  4. Discharge from suture line on pressure

- Proximal limb:
  1. Temperature
  2. Tenderness
  3. Swelling/edema
  4. Progression of disease

PALPATION OF OPEN AMPUTATION STUMP

- Ulcer: Refer Chapter 10 in Section IV for details.

- Proximal limb: Same as above

DIAGNOSIS

_______ (right/left) sided ________ (site: e.g. below knee, above knee, etc.), non-end bearing, _______ (ideal/non-ideal) __________ (closed/open) amputation stump performed on _________ basis (elective/emergency) for ________ (cause e.g. wet gangrene because of PVD) with/without complications and is well taken care of.

DISCUSSION

- Definition (of amputation): Dismemberment of a limb or a part of limb along the circumference including bone, resulting in functional loss and disfigurement of limb
- Definition (of amputation stump): The terminal segment of limb which remains after amputation
- Etymology: Ambi = around, putare = to prune (amputare = to cut around)
- Types of amputation:
    1. Surgical
    2. Traumatic: Road traffic accident (RTA), wars, machinery injuries in factories
    3. Amputation due to medical illness: Gangrene, frostbite
    4. Congenital amputation: Amniotic band syndrome
- Indications of amputation: **3 Ds**
    1. Dead limb: (Means the limb is dead but not harmful)
        - Dry gangrene
    2. Deadly limb: (Means the limb has the potential to harm life irrespective of functionality)
        - Infections:
            i. Wet gangrene
            ii. Gas gangrene
            iii. Spreading osteomyelitis
            iv. Spreading cellulitis
        - Malignancy
        - Trauma: Severe crush injury
        - AV fistula
    3. Dead loss limb: (Means the limb is non-functional and decreases the quality of life)
        - Contractures
        - Severe rest pain
        - Severe deformity
        - Cerebral palsy
        - Paralysed limb
        - Severe elephantiasis
- Complications of amputations:
    1. Psychological: Depression

2. Social and occupational effects:
   - Change in occupation
   - Difficulty interacting with society
3. Limb complications:

   (OUTSIDE TO INSIDE)

   i. Skin:
      - Ulcer (DOUGLAS ulcer)
      - Pressure ulcer
      - Causalgia
   ii. Scar:
      - Scar dehiscence
      - Nerve entrapment
   iii. Subcutaneous tissue:
      - Infection (abscess)
   iv. Muscle:
      - Contracture
      - Jactitation (involuntary muscle twitching)
   v. Artery:
      - Hemorrhage (hematoma formation)
      - Flap necrosis
   vi. Vein:
      - DVT
   vii. Nerve:
      - Neuroma (neuroma is asymptomatic unless it is caught in scar, weight transmission, etc.)
      - Phantom limb
      - Phantom pain
   viii. Bone:
      - Bone spur
      - Osteomyelitis
      - Ring sequestrum
   ix. Other limb:
      - Arthritis (due to overuse)

> Phantom limb:
>
> - Explained by: Law of projection which states "no matter where along the nerve pathway one stimulates, the sensation will be felt at the site of receptor"
> - More common in upper limb
> - Prevention: By controlling pain before amputation
> - Treatment: Analgesia (gabapentin), mirror therapy

- Causes of pain in amputation stump:
    - Ulcer
    - Infection (abscess)
    - Poor blood supply or hematoma
    - Bony spur
    - Neuroma
    - Nerve entrapment in scar
    - Phantom pain
    - Causalgia
    - Adherent scar
    - Poor prosthetic fit (weight on scar)
- Classification of amputation:
    1. Based on the type of surgery:
        - Emergency
        - Elective
    2. Based on weight bearing:
        - End bearing
        - Non-end bearing
    3. Based on level of amputation: See below
    4. Based on stump:
        - Closed stump
        - Open stump: Guillotine, flaps
    5. Based on type of procedure:
        - Definitive: No further procedure required
        - Provisional: Requires further surgery
        - Revision: Refashioning of provisional stump

- Ideal amputation stump:
  1. Stump:
     - Adequate length
     - Broad based
     - Conical in shape
     - Smoothly rounded
  2. Skin:
     - Adequate tension
     - Mobile over deeper tissues
     - No puckering or dog ears
  3. Scar:
     - Thin
     - Painless
     - Mobile over deeper tissues
     - Non-terminal in lower limb
  4. Proximal joint:
     - Full range of movement
- Principles of amputation:
  - Once the decision to amputate has been made, efforts should be made to achieve the most distal level consistent with causal condition and a well-healed stump
  - Factors to be considered:
    1. Anatomy of the proposed level
    2. Surgery (tissue management)
    3. Available prosthetic replacement
    4. Personal factors: Age, occupation, etc.
  - Goals:
    1. Ablation: Removal of all that is necessary to eliminate the pathology and at the same time permit primary or secondary healing
    2. Reconstruction: Creation of best possible stump in terms of both motor and sensory function and provision of prosthetic substitution for restoration of function
  - Tourniquet is used in all cases except those operated for ischemia (for infective and tumor cases, tourniquet is used but the limb is not exsanguinated)

- Tissue management (sequential amputation of structures):
    1. Gentle handling of tissues during surgery (especially skin)
    2. Flaps should be mapped out to ensure as broad-based as possible
    3. Avoid tapering of skin to permit good abutment in wound closure (to achieve this blade should cut the skin at right angles to the surface)
    4. Nerve:
        - There is inevitable neuroma formation, but it's size can be reduced and entrapment in scar tissue can be avoided by the following:

          Pull down the nerve gently
          ↓
          Ligate it (prevents bleeding from small vessels)
          ↓
          Cut with blade (not scissors)
          ↓
          Allow to retract proximally into healthy muscle

    5. Blood vessels:
        - Effective hemostasis is the primary objective
        - Blood vessels to be securely ligated before division, use of cautery to be limited as far as possible
        - Troublesome bleeding from bone end is best controlled by sustained pressure (bone wax is rarely required)
    6. Muscles:
        - Length of muscle to be divided for amputation is based on judgment (but suture the muscles in slight tension)
        - Muscles are always cut distal to bone
        - Techniques of distal muscle stabilization:
            i. Myofascial closure (Burgess)
            ii. Myoplasty (Dederich)
            iii. Myodesis (Burgess)
            iv. Myopexy (Weiss)
            v. Tenodesis (Gottschalk)

Myodesis:

- Direct suturing of muscle to bone via drill holes
- Anchors muscle to bone
- Contraindicated in ischemic patients

Myoplasty:

- Opposing muscle groups are sutured to each other and then placed over the end of bone
- Done in PVD

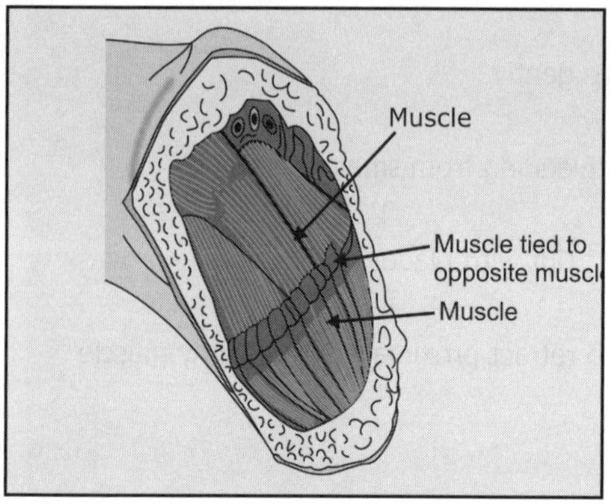

Fig. 13.2: Myodesis

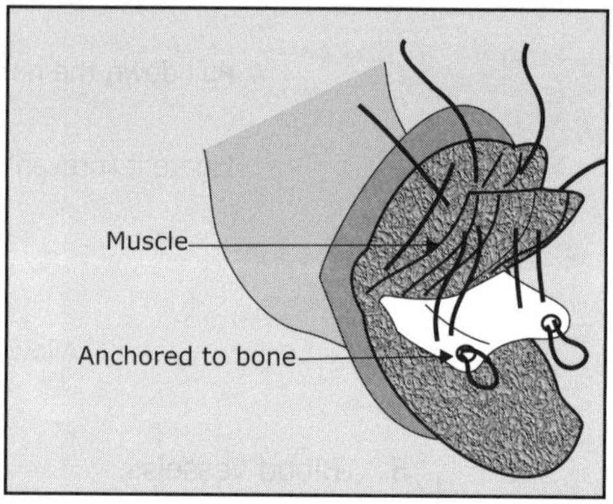

Fig. 13.3: Myoplasty

7. Bone:
   - Periosteum is cut distal to the cortex of bone or atleast at the same level (if periosteum is cut at a higher level, ring sequestrum is formed)
   - Bones are cut by electric saw or Gigli's saw
   - Cut edge of bone should be smoothly contoured (best achieved by a 30°- 45° bevelling cut)
   - How to check for smoothness of edges: Gently pull the skin of flap over the edge of bone and palpate (any irregularity however small will be immediately recognized)
   - Thinner bone is always cut first (e.g. fibula before tibia) because cutting of heavier bone first destabilizes the stump and thus leads to jagged cutting of the thinner bone and that too at a higher level
8. Wound closure:
   - Opposing tissues sutured under physiological tension
   - Dead spaces eliminated
   - Interrupted sutures preferred
   - Suction drain left deeper to the muscles

- Skin flaps:
    1. Types:
        i. Single
        ii. Double: Both equal, unequal
    2. Shorter flap should be broader than longer one for proper suturing of skin edges
    3. Longer flap is taken from that compartment (anterior or posterior) which has maximum bulk of muscle tissue e.g. long posterior flap in BK amputation
    4. Combined length of flaps = 1.5 × diameter of limb at the site of amputation

- Guillotine amputation:

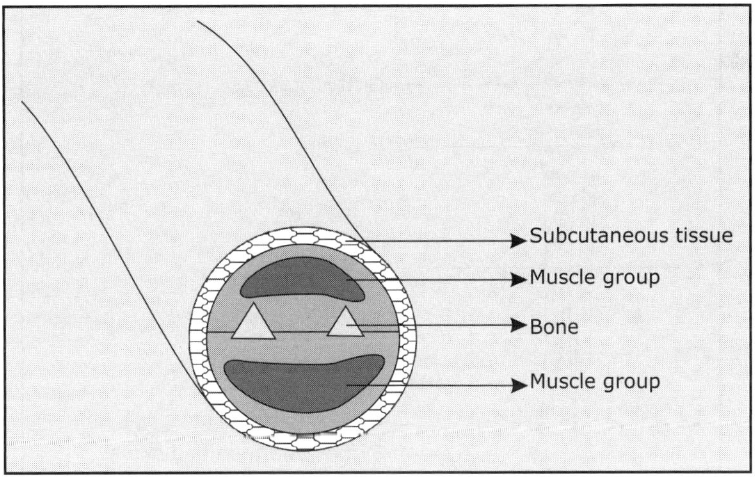

Fig. 13.4: Guillotine type of open amputation stump

- Explanation: All tissues cut at the same level
- Advantage: Easy and quick to perform
- Indication: Doubtful vascularity where likelihood of revision is more
- Disadvantage: Guillotine amputation is a problem since it will hyper-granulate (because bone end will always irritate it)

- Disarticulation:
    - Less preferred in adults (since it leads to end bearing stump)
    - Preferred in children (to preserve growing epiphysis)
    - Joint cartilage is always removed (to improve vascularity)

- Levels of amputation in lower limb:

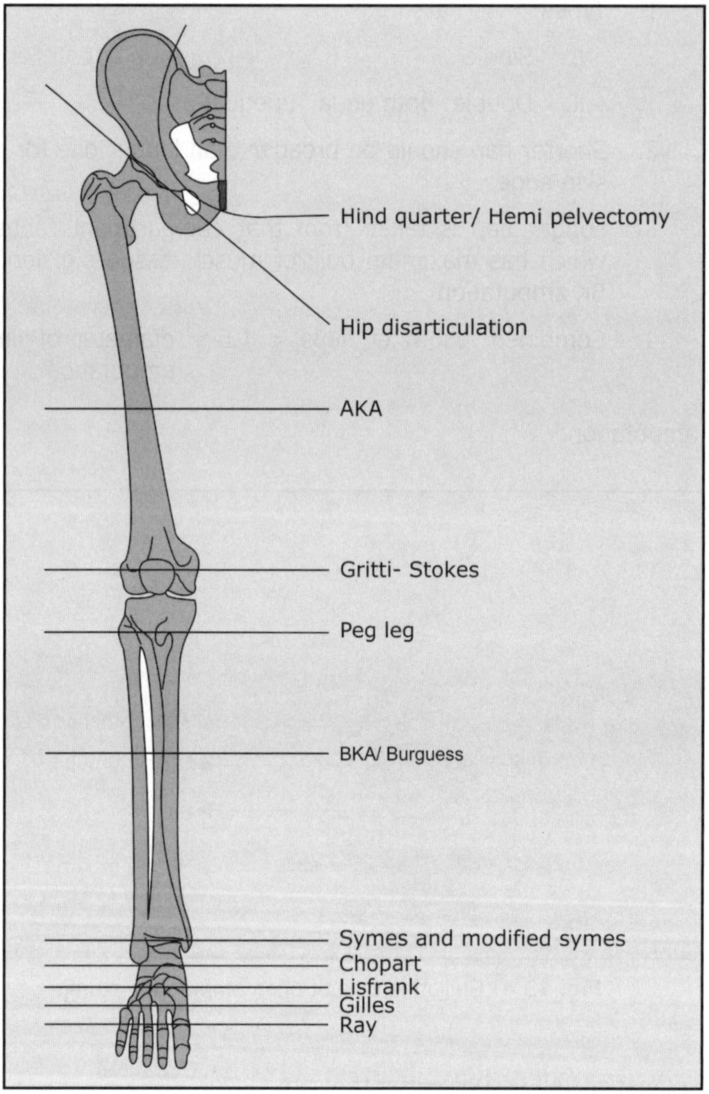

Fig. 13.5: Levels of amputation- lower limb

1. Toe amputation:
   - Means amputation through phalanges or disarticulation at metatarso-phalangeal joint
   - Amputation of distal phalanx in localized diseases (not at interphalangeal joints, since it leads to dorsiflexion contracture)
   - Amputation at interphalangeal joint can be done for great toe (and is in fact most valuable)
2. Metatarso-phalangeal (MTP) joint disarticulation

3. Ray amputation:
   - Means amputation of phalanges + some or all of corresponding metatarsus
   - Tennis racquet incision is taken (straight incision over the metatarsus + circumferential incision over the base of toe)
   - Through the head of metatarsus, since it has articular cartilage (articular cartilage being avascular, prevents healing)

> Articular cartilage is avascular, and thus hinders healing (Thus needs to be removed during amputation.)

4. Transmetatarsal (Gilles amputation):
   - Done through cancellous bone only (just distal to base)
   - Amputation through cortical bone (shaft) leads to bony resorption
5. Tarso-metatarsal dislocation: (Lisfranc procedure)
   - Obsolete procedure
6. Mid-tarsal disarticulation: (Chopart's disarticulation)
   - All tarsal bones removed except talus and calcaneum
7. Calcaneo-tibial fusion: (Pirogoff–Boyd technique)
   - Ankle joint sacrificed, calcaneum bisected vertically, rotated by 90° and fused to tibia
8. Ankle disarticulation: (Syme's disarticulation)
   - Classical Syme's method
   - Modified Syme's method → Sarmiento method
9. Below knee (BK)/ trans-tibial (TT): (Burguess procedure)
   - Commonest of all amputations done
   - Types:
     i. Short: 20% original length preserved
     ii. Mid: 20-50% original length preserved
     iii. Long: >50% original length preserved
   - Long posterior flap is preferred (since more bulk of muscles in posterior compartment of leg)
   - Skew flaps: If equal medial and lateral flaps are taken
10. Peg leg amputation: 3 cm BK amputation

11. Disarticulation of knee
12. Transcondylar: (Gritti-Stokes amputation)
    - Patella preserved
13. Above knee (AK) / Trans-femoral (TF):
    - Types:
        i. Short: <35 % original length preserved
        ii. Mid: 35-60% original length preserved
        iii. Long: >60% original length preserved
    - Long anterior flap or equal anterior and posterior flaps
14. Hip disarticulation
15. Hemipelvectomy/hindquarter amputation: (Sir Gordon Taylor's procedure)

- Levels of amputation in upper limb:

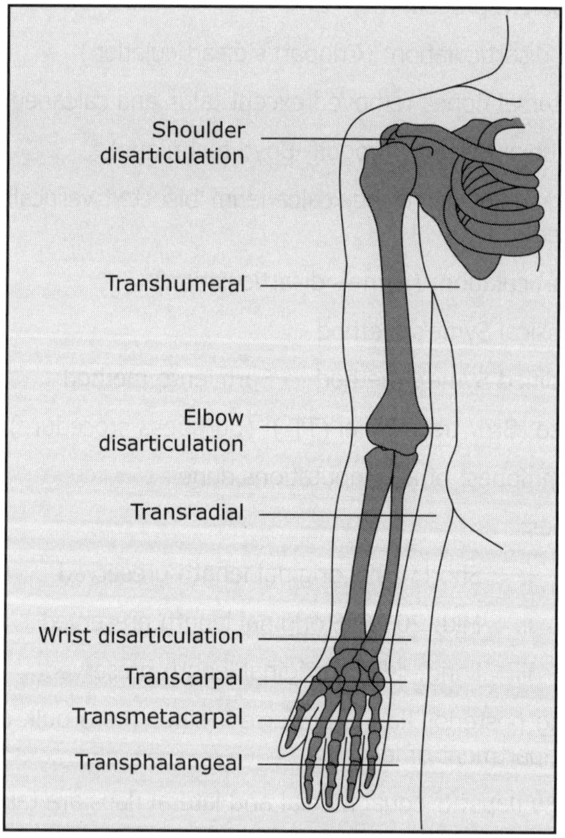

Fig. 13.6: Levels of amputation- upper limb

1. Thumb: Saved as much as possible (since thumb represents 40% functionality of hand)

   (100% impairment of thumb = 40% impairment of hand = 36% impairment of upper limb = 22% impairment of whole person)

2. Index finger:

   - Saved as much as possible except:

     i. Ray amputation: Metatarsal head removed to deepen web space for cosmetically better looking three finger hand

     ii. Labourers: Ray amputation not done. Oblique removal of metacarpal head is done to preserve deep transverse metacarpal ligament (to maintain strength and good grip).

3. Middle and ring finger: Amputation at all levels acceptable

4. Little finger: Saved as much as possible

5. Trans-carpal amputation:

   - Both flexion-extension and pronation-supination movements are preserved

6. Wrist joint disarticulation:

   - Done at radio-carpal joint
   - Flexion-extension movements lost but pronation-supination preserved

7. Forearm amputation (below elbow amputation) (Krukenberg procedure): Below elbow (BE) amputation with fork-like reconstruction of forearm stump to provide pincer-like grasp

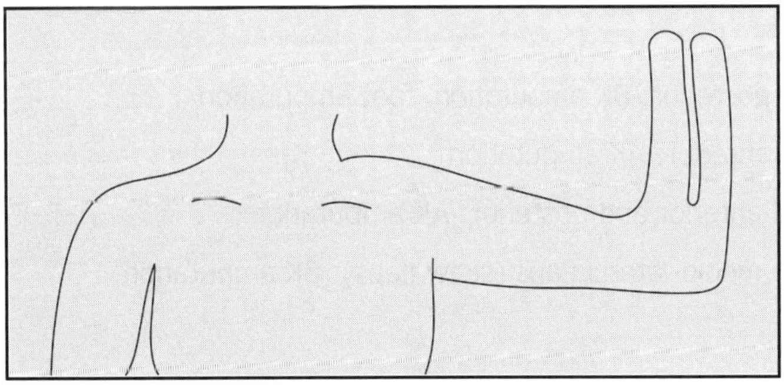

Fig. 13.7: Krukenberg amputation

8. Upper arm amputation (above elbow): Trans-humeral amputation

9. Shoulder disarticulation

10. Forequarter amputation (interscapulothoracic amputation)

- Two-stage amputation:
  - Initial procedure for provision of adequate drainage (provisional procedure)
  - Once infection is controlled, second procedure (revision procedure) either at same level or at a higher level
- Determination of level of amputation:
  - Emergency: Guillotine (based on level of lesion, injury, infection, etc.); later revised as elective procedure
  - Elective:
    1. Pre-operative:
       i. Level of disease (curative intent)
       ii. Infrared thermography
       iii. Skin blood flow measurement (^{125}I - 4 iodoantipyrine)
       iv. Doppler studies (viability)
       v. Palpable pulse (viability)
       vi. Functional use (for occupation)
       vii. Prosthetic fitting (ideal lengths)
    2. Intra-operative:
       i. Trial skin incision: If the skin bleeds at the proposed level of amputation, go ahead with that level
       ii. When punctate bleeding appears
       iii. When healthy tissues are seen
- Flaps:
  - Long posterior: BK amputation, foot amputation
  - Long anterior: AK amputation
  - Equal anterior and posterior: AK amputation
  - Equal medio-lateral flaps (skew flaps): BK amputation

- Incisions for amputation:

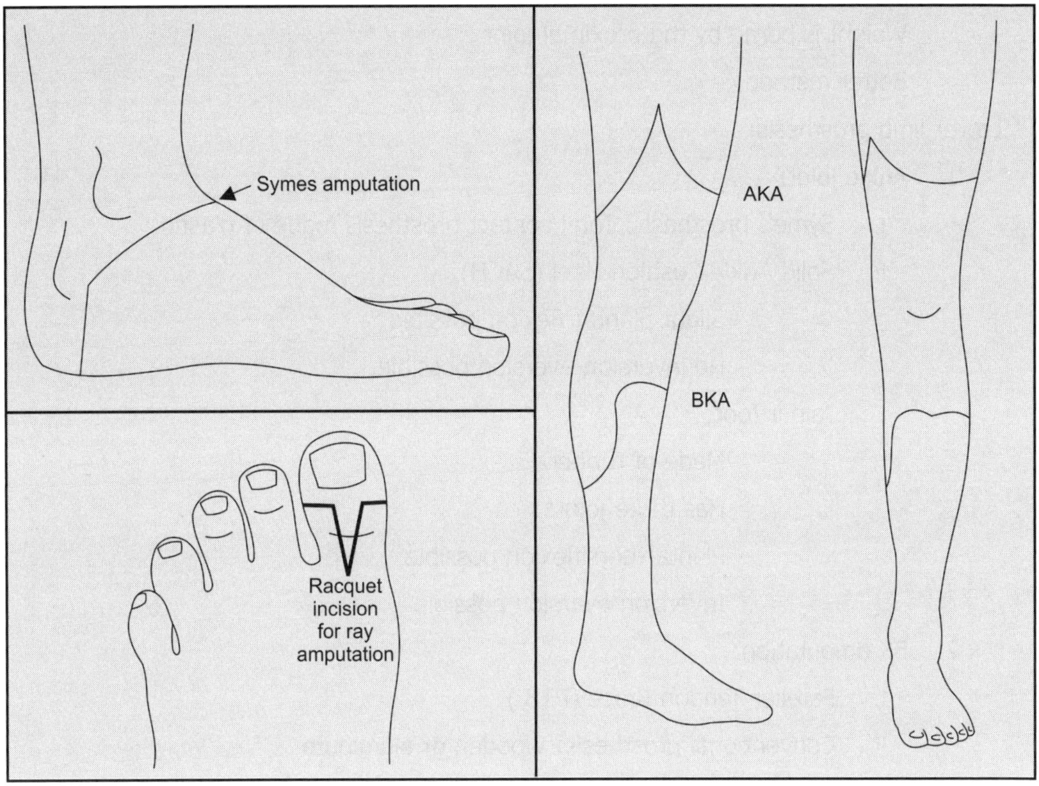

Fig. 13.8: Incisions for lower limb amputations

- Lengths of stumps:

Amputation level	Minimum length of stump	Ideal length of stump
Below knee	8 cm	8-12 cm from tibial tuberosity
Above knee	10 cm	24 cm from greater trochanter
Above elbow		20 cm
Below elbow		20 cm

- End bearing stump:
  - Amputation via joint
  - Weight is borne by the stump (so eventually it becomes necrosed)
  - Abandoned method

Non-end bearing stump:

- Amputation via bone (not joint)
- Weight is borne by the proximal joint
- Better method

- Lower limb prosthesis:
    1. Ankle joint:
        i. Syme's prosthesis: Total contact prosthesis made of plastic
        ii. Solid Ankle Cushion Heel (SACH):
            - Slight plantar flexion possible
            - No inversion-eversion possible
        iii. Jaipur foot:
            - Made of rubber
            - Has three joints
            - Plantar-dorsiflexion possible
            - Inversion-eversion possible
    2. BK amputation:
        i. Patellar Tendon Brace (PTB)
        ii. Conventional prosthesis: Wooden or aluminum
    3. AK amputation:
        i. Total contact socket
        ii. Conventional prosthesis
        iii. Suction socket prosthesis
    4. Hip joint disarticulation:
        i. Canadian hip disarticulation prosthesis

MANAGEMENT

- In limb trauma, salvage is determined by MESS scoring system (Mangled extremity severity score): MESS ≥ 7 are likely to require amputation
- Management of amputation stump includes:
    1. Immediate care
    2. Long-term management
    3. Management of complications

- ❖ Immediate care:
    - Analgesics
    - Antibiotics
    - IV fluids
    - Chart TPR-BP, input-output, urine output
    - Rest
    - Limb elevation
    - Dressing of stump
    - DVT prophylaxis
    - Drain removed in 48 hours
- ❖ Long term management:
    - Care of opposite limb
    - Control of systemic disease e.g. DM, PVD
    - Prosthesis
    - Rehabilitation:
        1. Physiotherapy: Positioning, passive stretch, active exercises
        2. Occupational therapy: Chairs, stairs, axillary crutches
- ❖ Management of complications:
    1. Ulcer: Refer Chapter 10 in Section IV for more details.
    2. Infection: Swab culture and antibiotic sensitivity testing followed by antibiotics and analgesics; Incision and Drainage if abscess has formed
    3. Contractures: Corrective surgeries

- Types of dressing:
    1. Soft dressing:
        - With gauze pieces as for ulcer
        - Easy inspection can be done, free movement, regular change of dressing possible
        - Has chances of joint contractures
    2. Soft dressing with splint:
        - Soft dressing + splint to prevent proximal joint contracture
    3. Rigid dressing:
        - With plaster cast
        - Best edema and pain control, prevents contractures

- Helps early fitting of prosthesis
- Dressing cannot be done regularly

- Common indications of revision surgery:
  1. Infection
  2. Protruding bone/bony spur
  3. Necrosis
  4. Fissuring and ulceration
  5. Neuroma
  6. Prosthetic unfitting
- Common revision surgeries:
  1. Wound debridement
  2. Skin grafting
  3. Wedge resection
  4. Re-amputation
  5. Excision of neuroma
- Intraoperative management of amputation:

Anesthesia ↓ Positioning of patient ↓ Exsanguination of limb ↓ Tourniquet ↓ Tissue management

❖ Exsanguination of limb:
  - Done by Esmarch's bandage
  - Contraindications: Infection (gangrene), tumor, ischemic limb

❖ Tourniquet:
  - Pneumatic tourniquet used
  - Contraindication: Ischemic limb (e.g. PVD)

❖ Tissue management:
  - Sequential amputation of structures
  - See above for details

- Post-operative phase:
  - First concern is pain control: Analgesics
  - Early mobilization done (patient should be out of bed, sitting with stump elevated as early as second post-operative day)
- Rehabilitation:

First give a tight cast (preparatory cast) to counter edema and mould the stump (stump maturation)

↓

Pylon prosthesis (for early mobilization)

↓

Definitive prosthesis after few weeks

- Definitions:
  1. Implant: Is an orthopedic rehabilitation device used internally to replace or in addition to a body part
  2. Prosthesis: Is an orthopedic rehabilitation device used internally or externally to replace normal body part
  3. Orthosis: Is an orthopedic rehabilitation device used externally to support normal body part
- Parts of prosthesis:

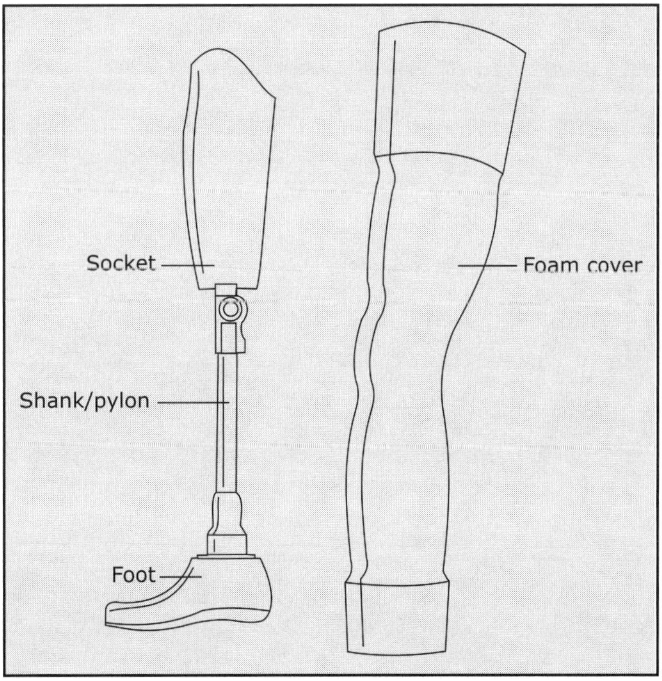

Fig. 13.9: Parts of prosthesis

1. Socket: For stump
2. Shank: Rod
3. Terminal device: Ankle-foot prosthesis

- Types of socket:
    1. Shuttle lock
    2. Suction
    3. Vacuum (best type)
- Care of prosthesis:

Remove every 6 hours
↓
Lubricate
↓
Wear socks
↓
Wear prosthesis back

14

Thyroid Swelling

HISTORY

[Only additional points on thyroid history have been mentioned below. Refer Chapter 1 in Section I beforehand.]

- Patient profile:
    1. Age:
        - Diffuse goiter: Growth spurts (adolescence, lactation, pregnancy) (due to high BMR)
        - Nodular goiter: Middle age
        - Hashimoto's thyroiditis: Middle age
        - Graves' disease: Middle age
        - Medullary carcinoma: Young age (15 - 50 years)
        - Papillary carcinoma: Young age (after radiation exposure) (3rd and 4th decades)
        - Follicular carcinoma: Middle age (4th and 5th decades)
        - Anaplastic carcinoma: Old age
    2. Sex: Female > Male (in all thyroid diseases)
    3. Occupation:
        - Radiation exposure: Scientists, medical professionals, X-ray technicians, etc.
    4. Religion: Not contributory
    5. Residence:
        - Important in all thyroid cases
        - Iodine deficiency goiter in hilly areas like Himalaya, Vindhya, and Satpura ranges, Ratnagiri, Nashik, and Dhule (in Maharashtra)

Note that iodine deficiency is more common in South India than in North India.

- Chief complaints:
    1. Swelling in neck
    2. Pain
    3. Warmth/fever

- HOPI:
  - ❖ Symptoms:
    1. Swelling:
       - Not much increase in size: Diffuse simple goiter, thyroid cysts
       - Slow growth: Diffuse simple goiter, nodular thyroid cysts
       - Rapid growth: Malignancy, nodular thyroid cyst (sometimes)
       - Sudden increase in size: Malignancy, hemorrhage within cyst
    2. Pain:
       - Inflammatory pathology (e.g. Hashimoto's thyroiditis - mild pain)
       - Late malignancy: Due to tumor invasion of nerves (early stages are painless)
    3. Warmth/fever:
       - Infective pathology
       - Inflammatory pathology
  - ❖ Etiology:

First rule out COMMON midline neck swellings

↓

Enquire for etiology of thyroid swelling

- COMMON midline neck swellings:
  1. TB lymphadenopathy: H/o low grade fever with cough/expectoration, TB contact
  2. Lymphoma: H/o similar swellings in groin or axilla
  3. Oropharyngeal infection or malignancy metastasizing in the neck: Any lesions/wounds/ulcers in oral cavity or tongue
  4. Larynx swellings: H/o change in voice or stridor
- Etiology of thyroid swelling:
  1. Endemic: H/o similar illness in locality
  2. Sporadic: H/o similar illness in the family
  3. Physiological: Onset of swelling associated with puberty, pregnancy, lactation, surgery, or stress
  4. Autoimmune: H/o any other autoimmune diseases
  5. Infective: Pain, warmth/fever
  6. Malignant: Rapid increase in size of swelling associated with anorexia, weight loss, fatigue (i.e. constitutional symptoms of malignancy)

- ❖ Hormonal and autoimmune status (ADDITIONAL HISTORY FOR EVERY THYROID CASE):
  - Hypothyroid: Weight gain DESPITE decreased appetite, constipation, lethargy, excess sleep
  - Hyperthyroid: Weight loss DESPITE increased appetite, intolerance to heat (all other symptoms like insomnia, palpitations, tremors, etc. are also seen in anxiety)
  - Autoimmune features of Graves' disease:
    1. Thyroid associated ophthalmopathy (OPHTHALMOPATHY)
    2. Pretibial myxedema (DERMOPATHY)
    3. Clubbing (ACROPACHY)
    4. Onycholysis
    5. Other coexistent autoimmune diseases
- ❖ Complications:
  - Compressive or infiltrative symptoms (in following order):
    1. Malignancy: Hoarseness → stridor/dyspnea → dysphagia
    2. Benign: Compressive features rarely seen even in large swellings
  - Retrosternal extension:
    1. Flushing of face
    2. Thoracic outlet obstruction: Upper limb PVD symptoms, syncopal attacks
- ❖ Treatment taken: Radiation (low dose) for acne

- Past history:
  - TB/TB contact: Midline neck swelling
  - LOW DOSE radiation exposure to neck in childhood (e.g. for treatment of acne): Papillary cancer of thyroid

  > High dose radiation causes thyroid atrophy (not cancer).

- Personal history:
  - Stress:
    1. Predisposes to autoimmune disorders
    2. Psychiatric complaints of hyperthyroidism
  - Diet history: For goitrogens

  > Do not ask/mention "use of iodised salts" since India banned the production of non-iodised salts in 2006.

	Hypothyroidism	Hyperthyroidism
Bowel	Constipation	Diarrhea
Sleep	Excess	Less/disturbed
Appetite	Decreased	Increased

- Family history:
  - Similar swelling in family/locality
  - Graves' disease, dyshormonogenesis: Sporadic goiter
  - Malignancy (papillary and follicular carcinoma): Specially MEN syndrome
- Menstrual and obstetric history:
  - Abnormal uterine bleeding: Both oligomenorrhea and menorrhagia can be seen in both hyperthyroid and hypothyroid patients; but commoner presentation is oligomenorrhea in hyperthyroidism while menorrhagia in hypothyroidism
  - Recent loss of pregnancy/abortion

GENERAL EXAMINATION

[Only additional points on thyroid general examination have been mentioned below. Refer Chapter 2 in Section I beforehand.]

- Conscious, co-operative, coherent:
  - Excited: Hyperthyroidism
  - Lethargic: Hypothyroidism
- Built, nourishment/BMI:
  - Lean: Hyperthyroidism
  - Obese: Hypothyroidism
- Temperature:
  - Raised: Hyperthyroidism (↑ BMR)
  - Decreased: Hypothyroidism (↓ BMR)
- Pulse:
  - Tachycardia, arrhythmias: Hyperthyroidism
  - Bradycardia (in spite poor health): Hypothyroidism

Nocturnal tachycardia/sleeping tachycardia: >90 bpm

- Characteristic for hyperthyroidism
- When to take: 2 hours before normal waking up time (i.e. in NREM sleep)
- Crile's grading:
  - Mild: 90 - 100 bpm
  - Moderate: 100 - 110 bpm
  - Severe: >110 bpm

- Respiration:
  - Tachypnea: Hyperthyroidism
  - Bradypnea: Hypothyroidism
- BP:
  - Increased in hyperthyroidism
  - Decreased in hypothyroidism
- JVP: Dilated veins may be seen due to compressive effects of swelling
- Edema:
  - Myxedema (non-pitting): Severe hypothyroidism
  - Pretibial myxedema: Characteristic of Grave's disease (due to deposition of mucopolysaccharides in the dermis)

  Pretibial MYXEDEMA is seen in HYPERthyroidism.
- Lymphadenopathy: Cervical lymphadenopathy in malignancy
- Clubbing: Graves' disease (thyroid acropachy)
- Skin:
  - Moist/warm: Hyperthyroidism
  - Dry/cold: Hypothyroidism
- Hormonal features:
  - Irritable, nervous: Hyperthyroidism

    Lethargic, slow, dull: Hypothyroidism
  - Deep tendon reflexes:

    Brisk: Hyperthyroidism

    Delayed relaxation: Hypothyroidism

Delayed relaxation of reflexes → Woltman sign

Characteristic reflex to be delayed in hypothyroidism → ANKLE JERK

- Fine tremors (check with paper on stretched hands): Hyperthyroidism

- Autoimmune features:
  - Ophthalmopathy (Refer discussion part for eye signs)
  - Dermopathy: Pretibial myxedema (swollen + red)
  - Acropachy: Clubbing
  - Onycholysis: Plummer's nail

Note that hormonal and autoimmune features have to be mentioned additionally in every case of thyroid.

LOCAL EXAMINATION

- Always say this first:
  1. Examined with due consent
  2. Under adequate illumination
  3. Exposure till sternum
  4. In sitting position
  5. In presence of female attendant (for female patients)

- Inspection: Done FROM FRONT (in slightly extended neck)
  1. Swelling:
     - Refer Chapter 9 in Section IV Surgery section for details
     - Additional points for thyroid swelling:
       i. Movement on deglutition
       ii. Movement on protrusion of tongue
       iii. Inferior margin of swelling can be appreciated or not (with and without deglutition)

Movement of swelling:

- Thyroid swelling moves with deglutition (due to ligament of Berry, condensation of pretracheal fascia) but not with protrusion of tongue
- Thyroglossal cyst moves with protrusion of tongue (due to connection with foramen cecum by fibrous tract) AS WELL AS with deglutition

Pizzillo's method of inspection:
- To be done ONLY for obese people with short neck (NOT in all cases)
- Method: Patient places hands on occiput with slight extension of neck

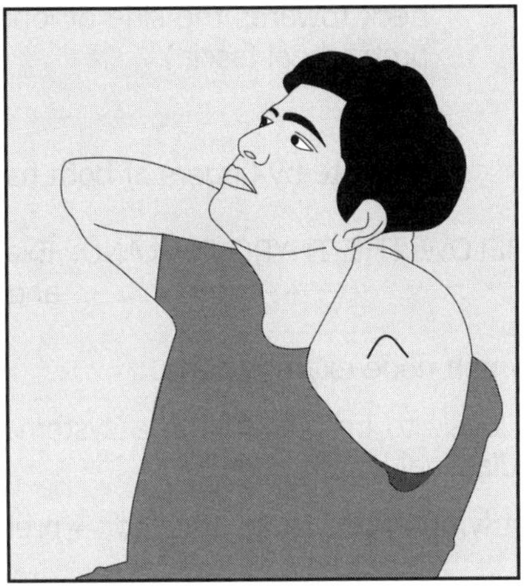

Fig. 14.1: Pizzillo's method

2. Pemberton's sign: Facial congestion on hyperabduction of both upper limbs till they touch sides of face for 1 minute → suggests retrosternal extension

3. Lymph node swelling (if any)

4. Tracheal deviation (Trail's sign): Prominence of sternal head of SCM muscle due to deviation of trachea to that side

- Palpation:
  - Always say this first on palpation:
    1. Inspectory findings confirmed
    2. No local rise of temperature
    3. Tenderness - yes or no

From back	From front
1. Usual palpation 2. Lymph node examination	1. Tracheal deviation 2. Lahey's method 3. Crile's method 4. Kocher's test 5. Berry's sign 6. Thrill 7. Fixity of swelling

- From back:
  1. Usual palpation:
     - Refer Chapter 9 in Section IV for details
     - Method: Thumbs on occiput (for slightly flexing and rotating the neck towards the side of lobe to be palpated to relax the pretracheal fascia)

       ↓

       palpate by fingers of both hands
  - TO GET BELOW THE THYROID GLAND: Examine for lower border (with and without deglutition)
  2. Cervical lymph node examination:
     - Six levels to be palpated in a systematic manner (seventh level is mediastinal lymph node)
     - First lymph node to be affected → pretracheal (Delphian node)

> Paget's paradox: Cystic swelling of thyroid is felt as a solid swelling (due to tense pretracheal fascia).

- From front:
  1. Tracheal deviation: Refer Chapter 5 in Section II for details (Two finger and three finger methods)
  2. Lahey's method:
     - Aim: For better palpation of lateral and posterior surface of lobe
     - Method: Push right lobe with left hand and palpate left lobe's posterior surface with right hand and vice versa

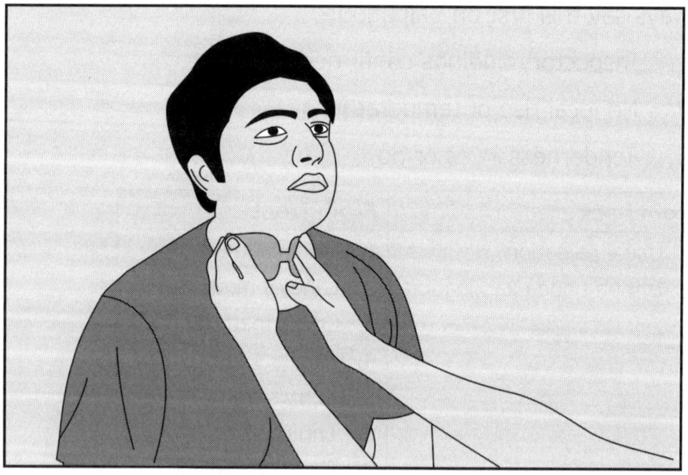

Fig. 14.2: Lahey's method

3. Crile's method:
   - Indication: To detect small nodules
   - Method: Place the thumb on suspected area of thyroid and ask the patient to swallow

4. Kocher's test:
   - Method: Gentle compression of thyroid gland on both lobes simultaneously
   - Interpretation: Stridor heard → SCABBARD trachea
   - Mechanism:

     LARGE thyroid causes lateral traction on trachea chronically (due to weight of thyroid gland)

     ↓

     Decrease in elasticity of trachea

     ↓

     Compression of both lobes causes loss of lateral pull

     ↓

     Narrowing of trachea

   - Seen in: ANY large long-standing thyroid swelling (need not be seen in malignancy)
   - Significance: Post-operative complication of tracheal collapse can be anticipated

5. Berry's sign:
   - Absence of carotid artery pulsations due to infiltration of carotid by thyroid malignancy (most commonly anaplastic carcinoma)
   - Note that displaced or absent pulsations due to benign lesions is NOT Berry's sign

6. Thrill: Upper pole (since superior thyroid artery is prominent, dominant, and tortuous)

7. Fixity to:
   i. SCM: By turning the neck to opposite side against resistance
   ii. Platysma: By contracting platysma

- Percussion: Bony percussion on manubrium (done directly on bone with plexor) → dull note in case of retrosternal thyroid/extension

  (normally the note is resonant.)

- Auscultation:
  - Done at SUPERIOR pole of thyroid → for bruit (same reason as for thrill)
  - Bruit: Seen in hypervascularity (malignancy, thyrotoxicosis)
  - Bronchial breathing (stridor for compressive effects)

DIAGNOSIS

_____ years, female/male is a case of uninodular/multinodular/diffuse goiter in hyper/eu/hypothyroid state with/without complications with most likely etiology being _________ with/without retrosternal extension

> Do not forget to mention retrosternal extension as it changes the management.

DISCUSSION

- Literal meaning of 'thyroid': Shield (name given by Thomas Wharton)
- Differentials of midline neck swellings:
  1. Thyroid swelling (DO NOT FORGET TO SAY THIS)
  2. Lymph node enlargement:
     - i. Lymphoma
     - ii. TB
     - iii. HFN infection
     - iv. HFN malignancy
  3. Thyroglossal cyst
  4. Subhyoid bursitis
  5. Laryngocele, larynx cancer
  6. Lipoma
  7. Sublingual dermoid
  8. Thymic enlargement
- Differentials of lateral neck swelling:
  1. Thyroid lobe swelling
  2. Lymph node enlargement:
     - i. Lymphoma
     - ii. TB
     - iii. HFN infection
     - iv. HFN malignancy

3. Salivary gland swelling
4. Cystic hygroma
5. Branchial cyst
6. Carotid body tumor
7. Plunging ranula
8. SCM tumor

- Recommended dietary allowance (RDA) for iodine:
  - Infants: 90 µg/day
  - Children up to 12 years: 100-120 µg/day
  - Adolescents and adults: 150 µg/day
  - Pregnant and lactating woman: 200 µg/day
- Goitrogens:
  1. Drugs:
     - Propylthiouracil (PTU): Inhibits thyroperoxidase
     - Carbimazole: Inhibits thyroperoxidase
     - Sulphonylurea
     - Paraminosalycylic acid (PAS)
     - Amiodarone
     - Lithium
     - Phenobarbitone
     - Phenytoin
     - Rifampin
     - KI (potassium iodide) (present in expectorants)
  2. Chemicals:
     - Thiocyanate: In smoke (smoking)
     - Perchlorate
     - Iopanoic acid
  3. Foodstuffs:
     - Flax, soya
     - Seafood (saltwater fishes are good sources but freshwater sources are iodine deficient)

- Brassica family:
    - i. **C**assava
    - ii. **C**abbage
    - iii. **C**auliflower
    - iv. **C**anola (rape seed)
    - v. Broccoli
    - vi. Brussel sprouts

- Goiter:
    - Definition: Enlargement of thyroid gland is called goiter
    - Classification:

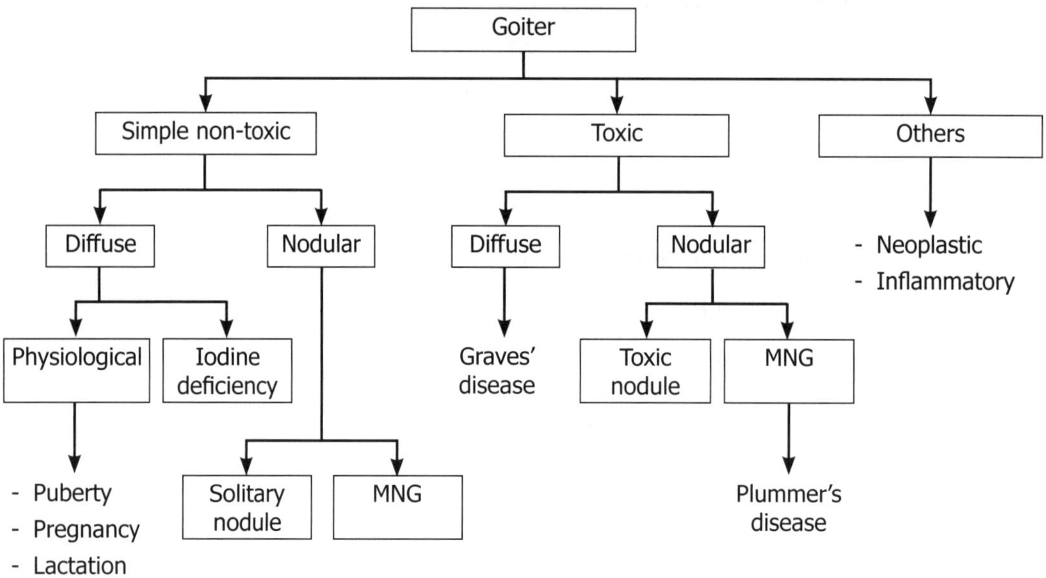

- WHO grading of goiter:

Grades	Visible swelling	Palpable swelling
0	×	×
1	×	✓
2	✓	✓

- Etiological classification of goiter:
    1. Congenital:
        - i. Congenital hypo/hyperthyroidism
        - ii. Thyroglossal cyst
        - iii. Aberrant thyroid

2. Inflammatory:
   i. Acute: Infective
   ii. Subacute: De Quervain's thyroiditis
   iii. Chronic: Hashimoto's thyroiditis, Graves' disease, Riedel's thyroiditis

3. Neoplastic:
   i. Benign: Follicular epithelial cell adenomas
      a. Macrofollicular (colloid)
      b. Normofollicular (simple)
      c. Microfollicular (fetal)
      d. Trabecular (embryonal)
      e. Hürthle cell (oncocytic)
   ii. Malignant:
      a. Follicular epithelial cell:
         1) Differentiated: PAPILLARY carcinoma, FOLLICULAR carcinoma, Hürthle cell carcinoma
         2) Undifferentiated: Anaplastic carcinoma
      b. C - cells: MEDULLARY carcinoma
      c. Others:
         1) Lymphoma
         2) Sarcoma
         3) Metastasis

4. Metabolic:
   i. Physiological: Pregnancy, lactation, puberty
   ii. Endemic: Iodine deficiency
   iii. Sporadic: Dyshormonogenesis, goitrogens

- Grades of retrosternal goiter:
  1. Substernal: Part of the goiter is palpable in neck
  2. Plunging: Totally intrathoracic in location, but part of the goiter can be palpated on coughing
  3. Intrathoracic: Totally intrathoracic in location, cannot be palpated even on coughing

> The term retrosternal 'goiter' is used when > 50% of the goitre is below the suprasternal notch; else use the term retrosternal 'extension.'

- Cause of nodularity: Cyclical fluctuations of TSH → abnormal involution and regeneration → formation of nodules

- Berry picking: Selective excision of grossly abnormal nodes to avoid unnecessary dissection of all nodes (it is now abandoned)

- Difference between primary and secondary thyrotoxicosis:

Primary thyrotoxicosis	**Secondary thyrotoxicosis**
Toxic features appear simultaneously with goiter	Toxic features appear after a time gap
Diffuse goiter	Nodular goiter
CNS more commonly affected	CVS more commonly affected

- Eye signs in thyrotoxicosis:
    1. Stellwag's sign
    2. Von Graefe's sign (lid lag sign)
    3. Mobius sign
    4. Gifford sign
    5. Dalrymple's sign
    6. Enroth sign
    7. Becker sign
    8. Joffroy's sign
    9. Rosenbach's sign
    10. Naffziger's sign

First sign to appear → Stellwag's sign

- Lateral aberrant thyroid: Is actually lymph node metastasis from differentiated thyroid carcinoma (note that it is not a congenital anomaly)

MANAGEMENT

- Investigations:
    1. Blood investigations:
        - Thyroid function tests (TFTs) → TSH, free T_3, free T_4
        - Antibodies:
            i. Anti-TPO: Hashimoto's thyroiditis
            ii. Anti-thyroglobulin: Hashimoto's thyroiditis

iii. Anti-TSH receptor:
   a. Blocking type - Hashimoto's thyroiditis
   b. Stimulating type (LATS) - Graves' disease

- Tumor markers:
  i. Thyroglobulin - differentiated thyroid carcinoma
  ii. Calcitonin - medullary carcinoma
  iii. Carcinoembryonic antigen (CEA) - medullary carcinoma

2. Imaging modalities:
   i. USG scan:
      - Differentiates cyst from nodule
      - Confirms multinodularity
      - Also used in USG - guided biopsy
      - Identification of neck nodes
      - Doppler mode calculates the resistivity index (RI) and pulsatility index (PI) which evaluates vascularity
   ii. Thyroid scan:
      - Structural + functional assessment of thyroid
      - Based on principle of SPECT (single positron emission computed tomography)
      - Indications:
        1. Solitary thyroid nodule (STN)
        2. Ectopic thyroid
        3. Post - surgery recurrence of carcinoma
      - Method:
        a. I^{123} ingested (1-2 mCi) → images taken by gamma camera after 24 hours
        b. I^{123} injected intravenously → images taken by gamma camera after 30 minutes
      - Interpretation: Hot, warm, or cold nodules
   iii. Thyroid update study:
      - ONLY functional assessment of thyroid (hence not done any more)
      - Method: I^{123} ingested → evaluated by Geiger-Muller counter at 6 and 24 hours
      - Gives only waves (not images) on Geiger-Muller counter

iv. CT/MRI scan:
  - For staging of cancer
  - For retrosternal extension

v. X-ray neck:
  - Only for detecting tracheal deviation to anticipate difficult airway intubation

3. Histopathology:
   i. Fine-needle aspiration cytology (FNAC): Method of choice for histopathology
   ii. Biopsy:
      - Only frozen section (on table) is done
      - Tru-cut and other types of biopsies are NOT done for thyroid swellings (because thyroid gland is extremely vascular)

4. Other investigations:
   i. Indirect laryngoscopy: (ALWAYS done)
      - To document vocal cord palsies (if any) in pre-operative cases for medicolegal purposes

- Management protocols:
  1. STN (solitary thyroid nodule)
  2. Diffuse goiter
  3. Multinodular goiter (MNG)
  4. Follicular disease
  5. Malignancies

1.

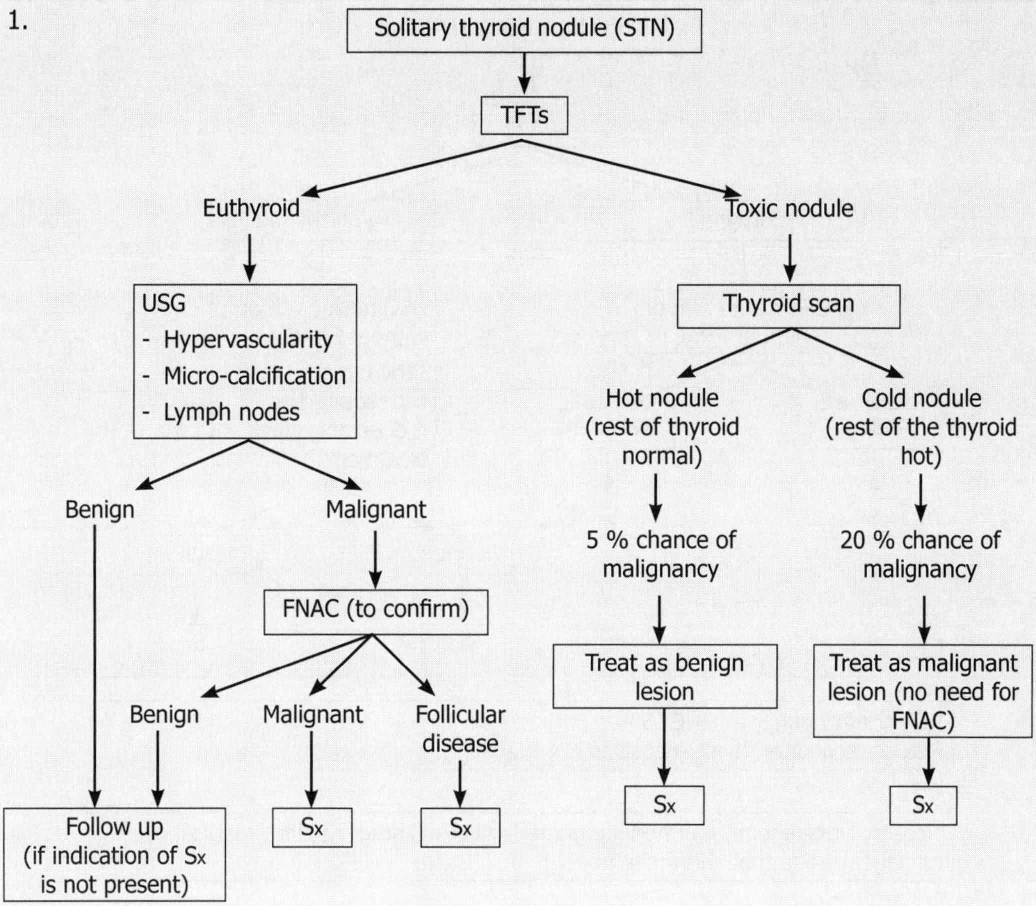
Solitary thyroid nodule (STN)
TFTs
Euthyroid
Toxic nodule
USG
- Hypervascularity
- Micro-calcification
- Lymph nodes
Thyroid scan
Hot nodule (rest of thyroid normal)
Cold nodule (rest of the thyroid hot)
Benign
Malignant
5 % chance of malignancy
20 % chance of malignancy
FNAC (to confirm)
Treat as benign lesion
Treat as malignant lesion (no need for FNAC)
Benign
Malignant
Follicular disease
Sx
Sx
Follow up (if indication of Sx is not present)
Sx
Sx

2.

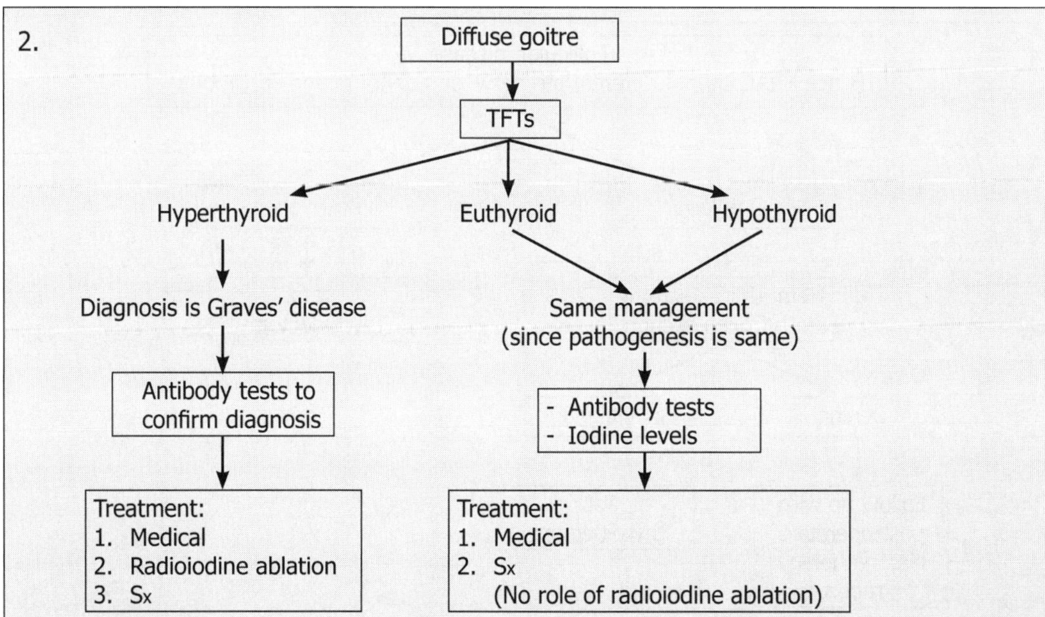
Diffuse goitre
TFTs
Hyperthyroid
Euthyroid
Hypothyroid
Diagnosis is Graves' disease
Same management (since pathogenesis is same)
Antibody tests to confirm diagnosis
- Antibody tests
- Iodine levels
Treatment:
1. Medical
2. Radioiodine ablation
3. Sx
Treatment:
1. Medical
2. Sx
(No role of radioiodine ablation)

3.

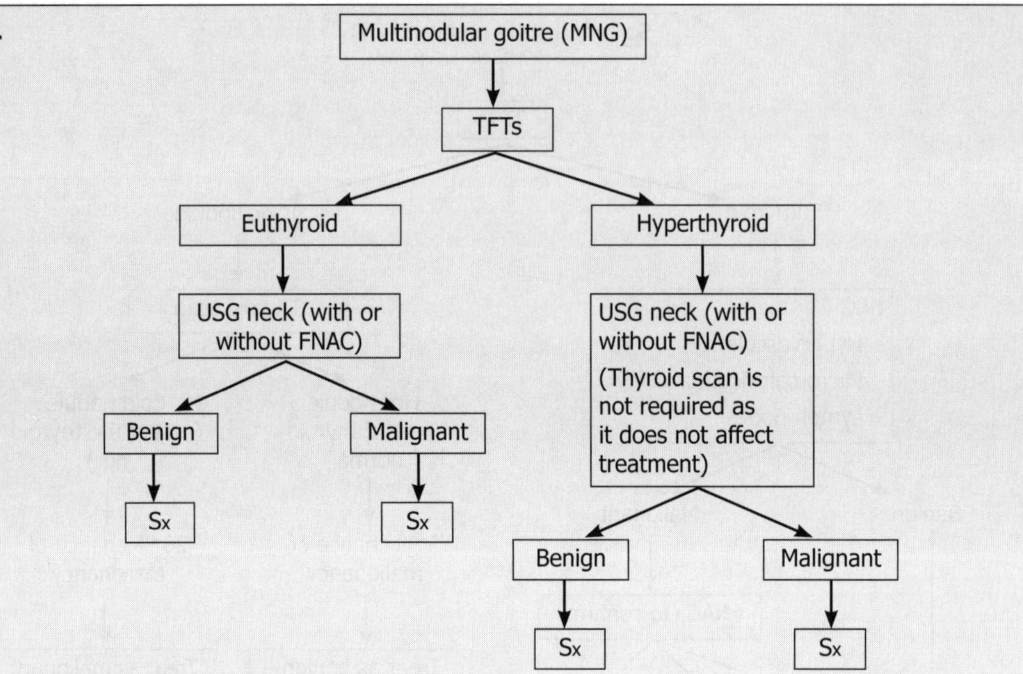

Risk of malignancy in MNG: 5%
Risk of secondary thyrotoxicosis in MNG: 20%

Note that management of nodular goitre is ALWAYS surgery, since medical management cannot shrink the nodule.

4.

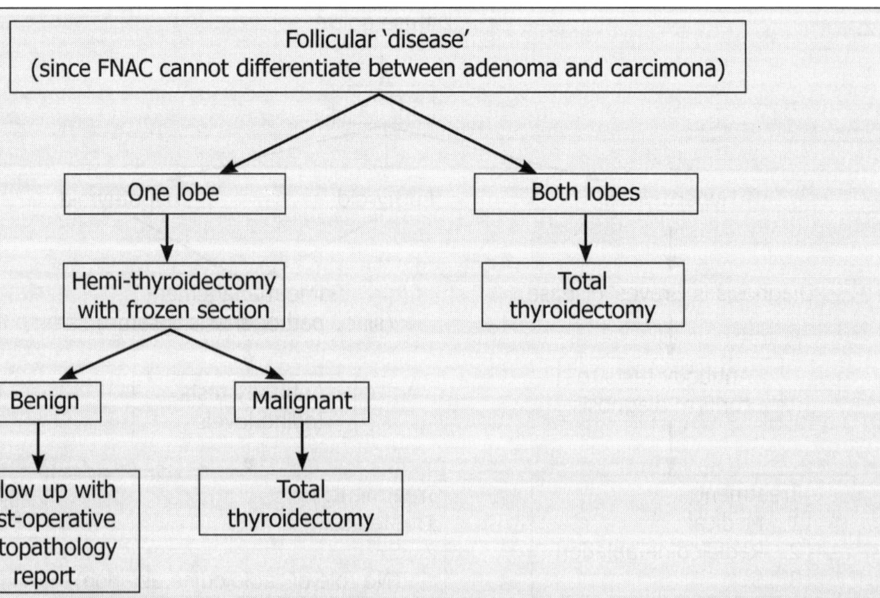

Malignancies:

1. Papillary cancer: Total thyroidectomy + level 6 node dissection
2. Follicular cancer: Total thyroidectomy
3. Medullary cancer: Total thyroidectomy + level 6 node dissection + bilateral modified neck dissection

Retrosternal extension mandates surgery.

- Treatment modalities:
  1. Medical treatment: Given in all cases (irrespective of other modalities)
  2. Radioiodine ablation
  3. Surgical treatment

  ❖ Medical treatment:
    1. PTU: In pregnancy
    2. Carbimazole
    3. Lugol's iodine: Started 2 weeks before surgery (Wolff - Chaikoff effect)
    4. Thyroxine:
       - In all hypothyroid patients
       - Post-thyroidectomy
       - Can suffice as the only modality of treatment in case of diffuse goiter of duration <6 months (irreversible changes start taking place after 6 months, which need surgery)

Wolff-Chaikoff effect: Iodine induced HYPOthyroidism (in hyperthyroid patients)

Jod-Basedow effect: Iodine induced HYPERthyroidism (in hypothyroid patients)

  ❖ Radioiodine ablation:
    - I^{131} at dose of 100 mCi
    - Indications:
      1. Graves' disease (treatment of choice)
      2. Post-thyroidectomy recurrent disease
    - Contraindications:
      1. Pregnancy
      2. Young patients (risk of leukemias)
      3. Nodular goiter (since uptake of iodine is not uniform)

❖ Surgical treatment:

Surgery	Description	Indications
Hemithyroidectomy	Removal of one lobe along with isthmus	1. Benign disease of one lobe 2. Thyroid cyst 3. Solitary nodule
Subtotal thyroidectomy	Removal of thyroid gland with preservation of strips of thyroid tissue in BOTH tracheo-esophageal grooves	NO INDICATION (since high rate of recurrence of disease)
Near total thyroidectomy (Dunhill operation)	Removal of thyroid gland with preservation of strip of thyroid tissue in ONLY ONE tracheo-esophageal groove	Benign diseases like diffuse goiter, Graves' disease, and MNG
Total thyroidectomy	Removal of all VISIBLE thyroid tissue	Malignancy

Thyroid tissue preserved in subtotal thyroidectomy:

- Strip in both tracheo-oesophageal grooves which is equivalent to 2 gm on each side, or thumb of surgeon, or walnut size
- Intent is to preserve the recurrent laryngeal nerve and parathyroid glands (and NOT thyroid tissue for it's function)

If parathyroid glands are accidentally removed during the operation, they should be reposed back or placed in the deltoid muscle (but never thrown away).

Isthmus is removed during ALL thyroidectomy procedures because it later gets fibrosed leading to tracheal compression.

- Post-operative management of cancer:
  - Tumor marker levels (thyroglobulin) → should be undetectable
  - Thyroid scan: After 6 weeks (by 6 weeks TSH level rises, thus any tissue of thyroid grows and can be detected)

    ↓

    If either tumor marker or thyroid scan shows residual disease

    ↓

    Radioiodine ablation
  - Thyroid supplements (thyroxine): Started after 6 weeks (after a thyroid scan is done, otherwise it will suppress TSH)

15

Breast Case

HISTORY

[Only additional points on breast case history have been mentioned below. Refer Chapter 1 in Section I beforehand.]

- Patient profile:
  1. Age:
     - Young age: Benign diseases (fibroadenoma in age group of 15-30 years)
     - Older age: Malignancy (breast cancer in age > 40 years)
     - Reproductive age: Mastitis
     - Any age: Fibroadenosis
  2. Sex: Breast cancer in females >> males = 150:1
  3. Occupation: Not contributory
  4. Address:
     - Barshi (village in Maharashtra): Low incidence of breast cancer
     - Delhi: High incidence of breast cancer
  5. Education and socioeconomic status:
     - Higher class: High incidence of breast cancer
  6. Religion: Not contributory
  7. Additionally mention (in EVERY breast case):
     i. married since
     ii. pre/peri/post-menopausal
- Chief complaints:
  1. Pain
  2. Lump in breast/distortion of breast
  3. Nipple discharge/deviation/retraction
  4. Skin changes (ulceration, color change, etc.)

- HOPI:
    - ❖ Symptoms:
        1. Painful → generally benign lesions

           Painless → generally malignant lesions

Painful breast lumps	Painless breast lumps
1. Breast abscess	1. Fibroadenoma
2. Fibroadenosis	2. Breast cancer
3. Fibrocystic disease	3. Phylloides tumor
4. Inflammatory carcinoma	4. Traumatic fat necrosis
5. Mastitis	5. Antibioma
6. Traumatic hematoma	

2. Lump in breast (Refer Chapter 9 in Section IV for details on lump / swelling)
3. Nipple discharge:
    - i. Milky: Lactation, endocrine disorders
    - ii. Serous: Duct ectasia
    - iii. Purulent: Breast abscess, mastitis
    - iv. Bloody: Breast cancer
    - v. Green colored: Duct ectasia

For nipple discharge ask:
- Color
- Nature
- Unilateral or bilateral
- Whether spontaneous
- Cyclical changes (whether associated with menstrual cycle)
- Amount

4. Nipple retraction:
    - Whether recent onset
    - Slit-like retraction → duct ectasia or periductal mastitis
    - Circumferential retraction → breast cancer

- ❖ Etiology:

First rule out other swellings
↓
Then proceed towards malignancy

  - Breast abscess: H/o pain, warmth/fever associated with lump
  - Fibroadenosis: Cyclical mastalgia
  - Traumatic fat hematoma and traumatic fat necrosis: H/o trauma to the breast followed by painful or painless lump (respectively)
  - Antibioma: H/o pain, warmth/fever, and lump in breast treated by antibiotics
  - Malignancy: H/o painless rapidly progressive lump with bloody nipple discharge (breast cancer rarely causes constitutional symptoms of malignancy → so do not ask for loss of weight/ appetite)
  - Fibroadenoma: No specific history except painless lump
- ❖ Complications:
  - i. Nipple displacement/deviation:
    - Pushed away from lump → benign lesion
    - Pulled toward lump → malignant lesion
  - ii. Ulceration
  - iii. Peau d'orange skin:
    - Occurs due to puckering of hair follicles in edematous skin (due to blockage of subdermal lymphatics)
- ❖ Treatment taken: Antibiotics (antibioma)

- Past history:
  - TB: Breast abscess
  - Previous breast/ovarian/endometrial cancer: Malignancy
- Personal history:
  - Alcoholism and smoking both are risk factors for breast cancer
  - Weight gain or obesity STARTING from peri-menopausal or post-menopausal age
- Family history:
  - Number of relatives affected and degree of relationship
  - Age when diagnosed → young age suggests poor outcome
  - Outcome → death (because familial tumors are very aggressive)

- H/O breast cancer screening:
  - Important because comparison of reports is very helpful in diagnosis
- Menstrual and obstetric history:
  - Early menarche, late menopause, late first pregnancy and nulliparity are risk factors for breast cancer

> Never miss menstrual/obstetric history in ANY breast lump.

GENERAL EXAMINATION

[Only additional points on breast case general examination have been mentioned below. Refer Chapter 2 in section I beforehand.]

- BMI: Obesity
- Edema: Of upper limb (breast cancer obstructing lymphatics or post-operative case)
- Lymphadenopathy: Lymphadenopathy in general examination refers to 'generalized' lymphadenopathy, so axillary nodes if palpable should be commented upon in local examination
- Spine: Check for bony tenderness (metastasis)
- Others (Refer Chapter 2 in Section I for more details.)

LOCAL EXAMINATION

- Always say this first:
  1. Examined with due consent
  2. Under adequate illumination
  3. Exposure till umbilicus
  4. In sitting and supine positions
  5. In presence of female attendant

- Follow the order (from inside outwards): For both inspection and palpation (Refer Chapter 9 in Section IV for details on swelling/lump.)

Opposite breast
↓
Nipple
↓
Areola
↓
Breast quadrants (with lump)
↓
Axilla
↓
Arm, thorax, shoulder joint
↓
Supraclavicular fossa

- Inspection: Done in SITTING posture only

  To be done in the following three positions:

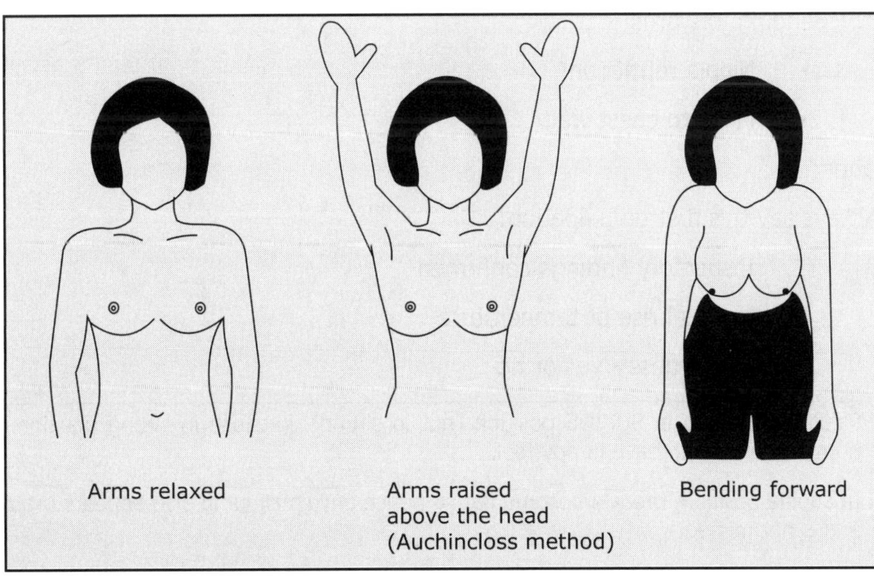

Fig. 15.1: Inspectory positions for breast examination

1. Hands by side:
   - Breast quadrants: If any obvious fullness
   - Nipple areola complex (NAC)
   - Dimpling and puckering cannot be seen in this position

2. Raising hands (Auchincloss maneuver):
   - Dimpling and puckering can be seen
   - Level of nipples (indicates asymmetry)
   - Axilla: Fullness if any

Dimpling	Tethering	Puckering
Phenomenon / sign which implies tethering	Infiltration of Cooper's ligaments	Involvement of skin
Demonstrated on maneuver like raising hands		Can be seen without any maneuver but better demonstrated on maneuver
On palpation, skin over the lump moves		On palpation, skin over the lump does not move

[Note that tethering is the pathology which manifests as dimpling.]

3. Bending forwards:
   - Nipple retraction
   - Fixity to chest wall

- Palpation:

  Always say this first on palpation:

  1. Inspectory findings confirmed
  2. No local rise of temperature
  3. Tenderness - yes or no

Palpation is done in SUPINE position (not in sitting), because in sitting position, even normal breasts can have lumpy feel.

In supine position, breasts become flat → hence any small lump also appears prominent and is not missed.

Palpation is done in semi-recumbent position INSTEAD OF supine ONLY in case of pendulous breasts.

- Done by flat of hand (palmar surface) → NOT by tips of fingers (because they are very sensitive, even normal nodules will be picked up as lumps)
- Lump: Refer Chapter 9 in Section IV for details on swelling/lump.

Fixity:

1. To skin:
   - Method: Pinch/slide the skin
   - Interpretation: Skin can be lifted up/glided over the lump → not fixed
2. To breast tissue:
   - Method: Move the lump
   - Interpretation: Lump can be moved inside the breast → not fixed
3. To pectoralis major muscle:
   - Method: FIRST CHECK FIXITY TO CHEST WALL → if not fixed to chest wall → ask the patient to press hands on waist (to contract the muscle) → check tautness of anterior axillary fold → move the lump in directions parallel and perpendicular to the muscle fibres
   - Interpretation: Lump can be moved perpendicular to the fibres but not parallel → fixed to muscle
4. To chest wall:
   - Method: Move the lump (without contracting pectoralis major muscle)
   - Interpretation: Lump cannot be moved in ANY direction → fixed to chest wall
5. To serratus anterior muscle:
   - ONLY for lumps in lower outer quadrant
   - Method: First check fixity to chest wall → if not fixed → ask the patient to push against a wall (to contract serratus anterior) → move the lump in directions parallel and perpendicular to the muscle fibres
   - Interpretation: Same as point number 3

- Lymph node examination:
  1. Axillary nodes
  2. Neck nodes: Levels 1 to 6 (palpated from behind)

Axillary lymph node palpation

While examining right axilla:

- Examiner's hand should be placed on patient's RIGHT shoulder (to support the shoulder when patient gives a jerk on touching the axilla)
- Patient's right hand should be kept on examiner's palpating hand (to relax the muscles and fascia)

Palpation of right axilla from FRONT is done for:

1. By left hand:
   i. Anterior group: At anterior axillary fold
   ii. Central group: Against the ribs (lateral chest wall) in between anterior and posterior axillary folds
   iii. Apical group (HALSTEAD'S nodes): Insinuate fingers deep in apex of axilla
2. By right hand :
   i. Lateral group: Upper part of medial border of humerus

Palpation of right axilla from BEHIND is done for:

i. Posterior group: Stabilise patient's right hand by examiner's left hand, palpate by right hand in posterior axillary fold
ii. Supraclavicular fossa

Internal mammary nodes are not clinically palpable.
Interpectoral lymph nodes (of Rotter) are not clinically palpable.

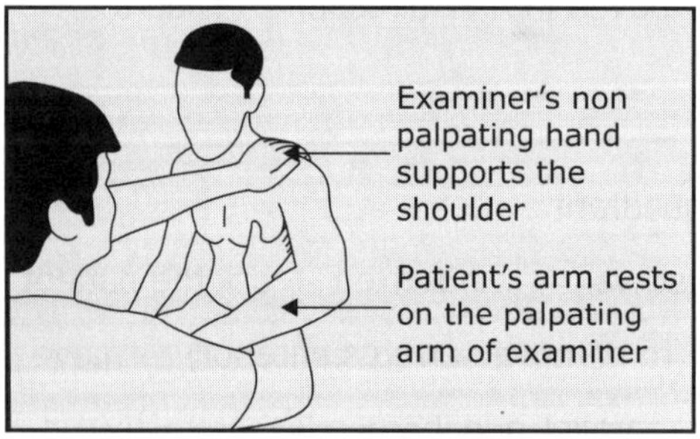

Fig. 15.2: Method to palpate axillary lymph nodes- anterior, central, apical groups

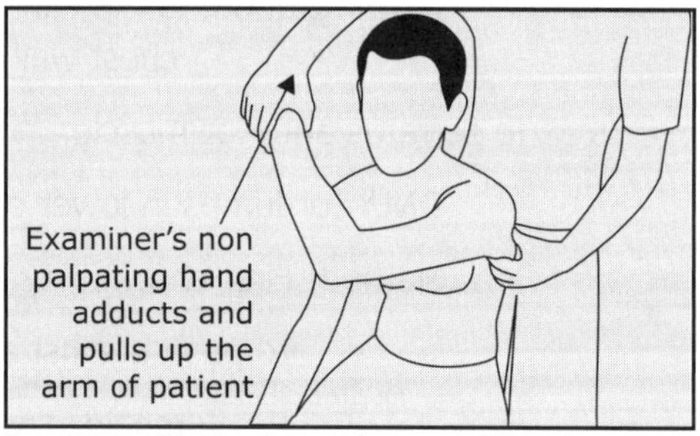

Fig. 15.3: Method to palpate axillary lymph nodes-posterior group

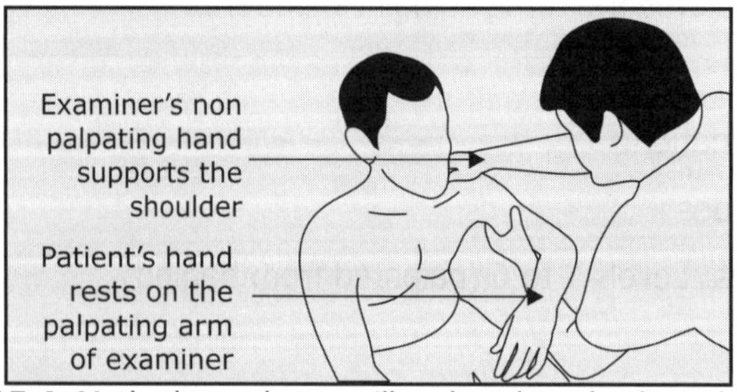

Fig. 15.4: Method to palpate axillary lymph nodes-lateral group

- Percussion: Not done in breast case
- Auscultation: Not done in breast case

Abdominal examination for metastasis
P/R or P/V examination for deposits in pouch of Douglas or Krukenberg tumor

DIAGNOSIS

50-year-old female is probably a case of carcinoma of breast of ______ (site, e.g. upper outer quadrant) with/without complications with/without metastasis with TNM stage being _____

[Manchester staging is obsolete and hence not to be mentioned. In spite of limitations of clinical methods, TNM staging should be done in exam.]

DISCUSSION

- Levels of axillary lymph nodes (BERG'S LEVELS):

  Based on PECTORALIS MINOR muscle as follows:

  - Level I: Below (lateral) to pectoralis minor muscle
  - Level II: Posterior (behind) to pectoralis minor muscle
  - Level III: Above (medial) to pectoralis minor muscle

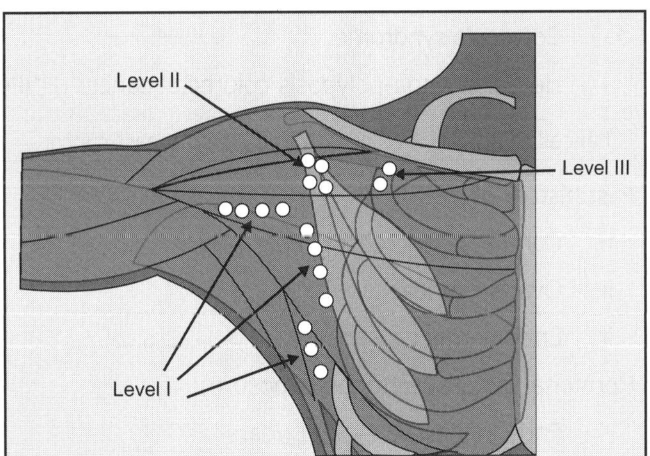

Fig. 15.5: Berg's levels of axillary lymph nodes

- Guidelines for screening:
  - Screening mammography: Once every year beginning at the age of 40 years
  - Clinical breast examination once in every 3 years for women in the age group of 20-40 years and once every year for women > 40 years
  - Breast self-examination starting at the age of 20 years

- Breast cancer:
  - Most common carcinoma in females
  - Incidence: 30% of all female cancers
    Bilateral → 2 - 4% cases
    Hereditary → 2 - 5% cases
    Median age → 47 years
  - Risk factors:
    1. Age: Most common age group is 40-60 years
    2. Sex: F:M = 150:1
    3. Race: West > east
    4. Family history of:
       i. Breast cancer: First degree relatives are at 2-3 times increased risk
       ii. Ovarian cancer
    5. Genetic factors:
       - BRCA 1 → chromosome 17 q (breast, ovaries)
       - BRCA 2 → chromosome 13 q (ovary, prostate, pancreas, larynx)
       - Li-Fraumeni syndrome → p53 gene
       - Cowden's syndrome
       - Hereditary non-polyposis colorectal cancer (HNPCC)

Chances of BRCA 1 +ve person to develop breast cancer → 80% to 100%

    6. Past history of:
       i. Contralateral breast cancer
       ii. Ovarian cancer
       iii. Endometrial cancer
    7. Hormonal factors (estrogen exposure):
       - Early menarche → <11 years
       - Late menopause → >52 years
       - Nulliparity
       - Obesity
       - High fat diet
       - Late first pregnancy → after 30 years

8. Alcoholism and smoking
9. Previous benign breast disease
10. Irradiation (before 30 years age)
11. HRT → with progesterone + estrogen (but no risk with OC pills)

   (Note that there is no increased risk with OC pills)

> Multiparity is protective against breast cancer (Number of children up to which it is protective is 2, no additional benefit is obtained after parity crosses 2.)
>
> Breast feeding is protective against breast cancer (Total number of months of breast feeding is more important than number of children fed.)

- Why is carcinoma commonest in upper outer quadrant: Because that quadrant has maximum amount of breast tissue (only mathematical relationship)
- Classification:

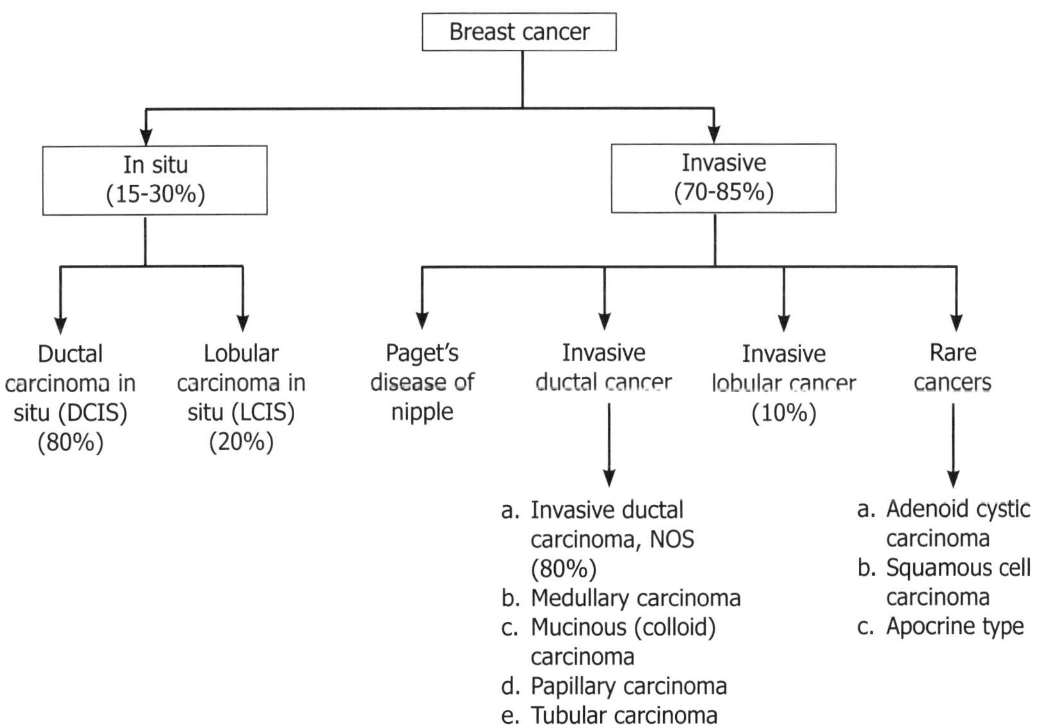

(Commonest → invasive ductal carcinoma, NOS

Worst prognosis → invasive ductal carcinoma, NOS

Best prognosis → tubular carcinoma)

(LCIS occurs bilaterally in → 50-70% cases

DCIS occurs bilaterally in → 10-20% cases

Therefore, management differs in both)

- Grading: Bloom-Richardson grading system
- Metastasis:

  Bone > lung > pleura > soft tissues > liver > brain

  ↓

  Lumbar vertebra > **F**emur > **T**horacic vertebra > rib > skull

  (L F T)
- Clinical staging: MANCHESTER STAGING

I	- Growth confined to breast - Does not involve pectoral or deeper plane - Skin involvement (if present) < size of tumor	AND	Ipsilateral axillary lymph nodes (LNs) not palpable
II	- Same as Stage I	AND	LNs palpable - mobile and discrete
III	Growth extends beyond parenchyma i.e. - Skin involvement > size of tumor - Underlying muscle involved	OR	LNs palpable - fixed or adherent
IV	- Tumor fixed to chest wall - Cancer-en-cuirasse - Metastasis - Inflammatory carcinoma	OR	Contralateral LNs palpable OR Supraclavicular nodes palpable

- TNM staging (salient features only):
  i. Skin involvement means either one of the following three only:
     a. Edema - Peau d' orange appearance
     b. Ulceration
     c. Satellite nodules

     (Puckering/dimpling/tethering is not considered as skin involvement)

  ii. Pectoralis major muscle involvement is NOT considered as chest wall involvement

  iii. Involvement of contralateral lymph nodes is considered as metastasis (M_1)

iv. Stages (simplified):

Stage 0	T_{is} N_0 M_0
Stage I	T_1 N_0 M_0
Stage II	- Remaining-
Stage III	T_3 N_1 M_0 Any T_4 Any N_2 or N_3
Stage IV	Any M_1

[Remember that stage III is T_3 N_1 or worse]

v. Early breast cancer **(EBC)** → Stages I, II

Locally advanced breast cancer **(LABC)** → Stage III

Metastatic breast cancer **(MBC)** → Stage IV

- ANDI (Aberration of Normal Development and Involution):
  - Involves variety of benign breast diseases affecting different stages in woman's life
  - Classification:

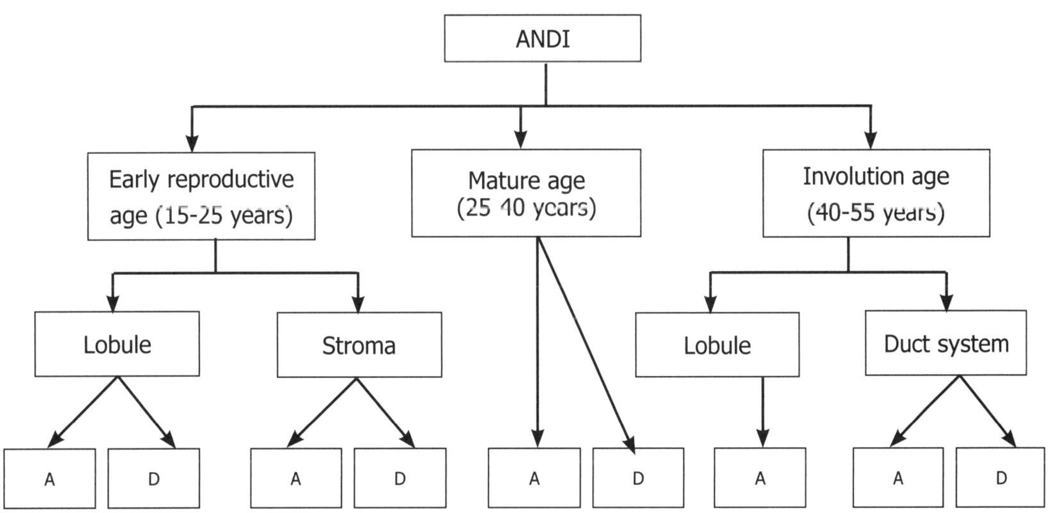

[A = aberration, D = disease]

❖ Early reproductive life lobule:
- Aberration: Fibroadenoma
- Disease: Giant fibroadenoma (>5 cm)

- ❖ Early reproductive life stroma:
    - Aberration: Juvenile hypertrophy of breast
    - Disease: Gigantomastia
- ❖ Mature age:
    - Aberration: Cyclical mastalgia with nodularity (fibrocystadenosis)
    - Disease: Incapacitating mastalgia
- ❖ Involution age lobule:
    - Aberration: Macrocysts, sclerosing lesions
- ❖ Involution age duct system:
    - Aberration: Ductal dilatation with nipple discharge (duct ectasia)
    - Disease: Periductal mastitis, duct fistula

- Fibroadenoma:
    - Most common benign tumor of breast
    - Age group: 15 - 25 years
    - Bilateral in 20% cases
    - Painless, movable lump (MOUSE IN BREAST)
    - Two types: Pericanalicular and intracanalicular
    - Giant fibroadenoma: Size > 5 cm

MANAGEMENT

MANAGEMENT OF BREAST CANCER

- Management protocol:

Step 1: History and general examination

↓

Step 2: Triple assessment

Clinical examination | Imaging | Histopathology

↓

Step 3: BIRADS score

↓

Step 4: Stage the disease

↓

Step 5: Metastatic work up

↓

Step 6: Treatment

- Imaging:
  1. Mammography - if age > 40 years
  2. Sonomammography - if age < 40 years (since denser breasts)

> Mammography:
> - Two views: Cranio-caudal, medio-lateral
> - Radiation dose: 0.8 mSv

> Safe limit of radiation exposure: 1 mSv/year for 5 years

- Histopathology techniques:
  1. Fine-needle aspiration cytology (FNAC)
  2. Core biopsy/trucut biopsy/ incisional biopsy (preferred)

3. Excisional biopsy - wide local excision
4. Mastectomy specimen

   (Advantage of biopsy over FNAC: Invasion of cancer, architectural distortion, grading of tumor and ER-PR status can be known)

- BIRADS score (on mammography):

  0 → Incomplete (cannot be evaluated)

  1 → Normal - 0% chance of malignancy

  2 → Benign - 0% chance of malignancy

  3 → Probably benign - <2% chance of malignancy

  4 → Suspicious abnormality - 2 to 95% chance of malignancy → consider biopsy

  5 → Highly suggestive of malignancy - ≥95% chance of malignancy

  6 → Biopsy proven cancer

- Investigations for staging:
  1. Bone scan
  2. USG abdomen
  3. Chest x-ray/CT chest

Treatment protocols:

1. Early breast cancer (EBC):

   Surgery (BCS ± axillary LN dissection, MRM)

   ↓

   Adjuvant therapy (chemo, radio, hormonal, combo)

2. Locally advanced breast cancer (LABC):

   Neoadjuvant chemotherapy (for downstaging)

   (Non-respondents are treated with radiotherapy)

   ↓

   Once downstaged, treat like EBC

3. Metastatic breast cancer (MBC):

   Palliative treatment

   (Chemo-radiotherapy ± toilet mastectomy)

   [Note that the term adjuvant means after surgery and neoadjuvant means before surgery.]

- Surgeries:
  1. Simple / total mastectomy:
     - Removal of:
       i. All breast tissue
       ii. Nipple areola complex (NAC)
       iii. Skin
  2. Extended simple mastectomy:
     - Simple mastectomy + level I axillary LNs
  3. MRM (modified radical mastectomy):
     - Simple mastectomy + Level I and II axillary LNs
     - Three modifications:
       i. Auchincloss - pectoralis minor only retracted
       ii. Scanlon - pectoralis minor divided and sutured back
       iii. Patey's - pectoralis minor removed (for level III node dissection)
     - Preserve: **ABCD** - **a**xillary vein, nerve of **B**ell, **c**ephalic vein, thoraco**d**orsal nerve
     - Limits till where flaps are raised in MRM:
       i. Medial: Midline of sternum
       ii. Lateral: Anterior margin of latissimus dorsi
       iii. Superior: Inferior border of clavicle (subclavius muscle)
       iv. Inferior: 2-3 cm inferior to inframammary fold (till rectus sheath appears)
  4. Halsted's radical mastectomy:
     - Simple mastectomy + pectoralis major and minor muscles + level I, II, III axillary LNs
- BCT - breast conservation THERAPY (different from breast conservation SURGERY):
  1. Wide local excision (i.e. BCS) - 1 cm clearance margin
  2. Sentinel LN biopsy (only when LNs are not palpable)
  3. Post-operative radiotherapy

  (When LNs are palpable, axillary dissection is performed instead of sentinel node biopsy.)

> NAC is removed in all surgeries (except BCT) because according to the OLD concept lymphatics of breast tissue converged to subareolar plexus of Sappy.

> Sentinel lymph node: First lymph node to drain the cancer site (literal meaning of the word 'sentinel' is 'guard')

- Chemotherapy:
  - Types: Adjuvant, neoadjuvant, palliative
  - Indications:
    1. Adjuvant chemotherapy:
       a. All node +ve cancers
       b. All node -ve cancers if >1 cm
       c. Node -ve cancers > 0.5 cm with adverse prognostic factors
    2. Neoadjuvant chemotherapy: LABC
  - Drugs: 3 weekly cycles × 6 months
    1. Cyclophosphamide, methotrexate, and 5-FU (CMF) regimen
    2. Cyclophosphamide, doxorubicin hydrochloride (Adriamycin), and 5-FU (CAF) regimen
    3. 5-FU, epidoxorubicin, and cyclophosphamide (FEC) regimen (better)
- Hormonal therapy:
  - ER positive:
    a. Premenopausal → tamoxifen 20 mg/day × 5 years
    b. Postmenopausal → aromatase inhibitors
  - HER-2/neu positive → trastuzumab (herceptin) × 1 year
- Radiotherapy:
  - Indications:
    1. BCT
    2. After toilet mastectomy
    3. ≥4 nodes +ve
    4. Inflammatory carcinoma
  - Given to breast, axilla, internal mammary, and supraclavicular nodes

- Total dose: 6000 cGY over 6 weeks
- Radiotherapy is always given after chemotherapy → since it thromboses the blood vessels

• Breast reconstruction:
    - Types: Immediate, delayed (3 - 9 months post-surgery)
    - Methods:
        1. Autogenous: TRAM flap, latissimus dorsi (LD) flap, Ruben's flap, gluteal flap
        2. Alloplastic: Silicone gel implant
        3. Combined

MANAGEMENT OF FIBROADENOMA

• Management protocol:

Clinical suspicion of fibroadenoma

↓

FNAC (tissue diagnosis)

↓

Explain to the patient the benign nature of lesion

(conservative management)

• Treatment options:
    1. Observation: First line of management
    2. Surgical excision:
        - Excision of lump along with capsule + small margin of breast tissue (for histopathology purpose)
        - Indications:
            1. Cosmesis/large size
            2. Suspicion of malignancy
        - Done under general anesthesia
        - Incisions: Circumareolar (Webster's), submammary (Gaillard Thomas)
    3. Percutaneous excision
    4. In situ cryoablation (under USG guidance)
    5. High-intensity focussed ultrasound (HIFU)

16

Hydrocele

HISTORY

[Only additional points on hydrocele history have been mentioned below. Refer Chapter 1 in Section I beforehand.]

- Personal profile:
    1. Age:
        - Primary hydrocele: Middle age
        - Secondary hydrocele: Any age
    2. Occupation: Not contributory
    3. Address: Uttar Pradesh and West Bengal have high prevalence of filariasis
    4. Religion: Not contributory

- Chief complaints:
    1. Swelling in the right/left side of scrotum
    2. Pain (in secondary hydrocele)

- HOPI:
    - ❖ Symptoms:
        1. Swelling: Growth of the swelling is from below upwards
        2. Pain: If painful, think of secondary hydrocele
    - ❖ Etiology:

Always ask history to rule out hernia after ODP (swelling does not ↑ on standing or straining, or ↓ on lying down or pressing it).

Epididymo-orchitis
↓
Filariasis
↓
TB
↓
Syphilis
↓
Trauma
↓
Tumor
↓
Others (liver, kidney, heart, hypoproteinemia)

- Epididymo-orchitis: H/o sudden onset pain in scrotum associated with fever, chills, and burning micturition
- Filariasis: H/o high grade cyclical fever associated with leg pain and swelling
- TB: H/o evening rise of fever associated with dysuria, pyuria, hematuria, or cough with expectoration
- Syphilis: H/o sexual exposure followed by sore on penis
- Tumor: H/o rapid loss of weight associated with lump in abdomen or supraclavicular fullness or low backache
- Hypoproteinemia: H/o recurrent infection associated with loss of weight, pedal edema or generalized distension of abdomen

❖ Complications:

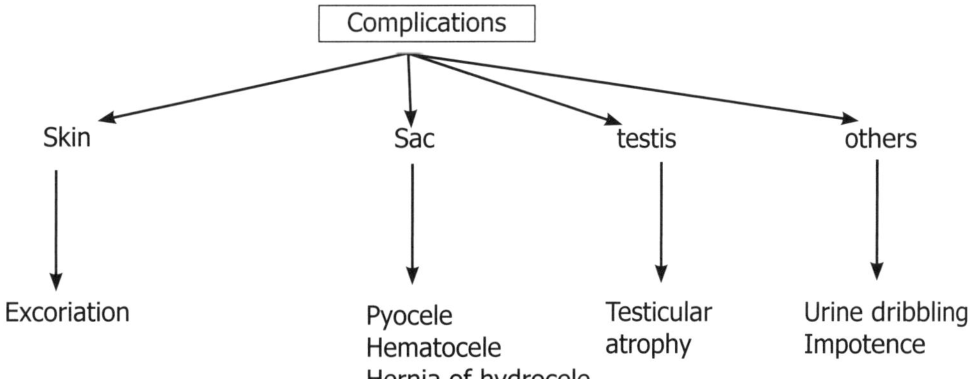

- Pyocele: H/o rapid ↑ in size of swelling associated with pain and high-grade fever with chills
- Hematocele: H/o trauma to the swelling followed by rapid ↑ in size and pain
- Hernia of hydrocele: H/o ↑ in size of swelling confined to one part only
- Testicular atrophy: H/o impotency, infertility, loss of secondary sexual characters

❖ Treatment taken:
  - Aspiration (if any)
  - Recurrence after surgery (if any)

- Past history: TB/TB contact, DM (for epididymo-orchitis)
- Personal history: Sexual exposure for syphilis
- Family history: Not contributory

GENERAL EXAMINATION

[Only additional points on hydrocele general examination have been mentioned below. Refer Chapter 2 in Section I beforehand.]

- Build and nourishment: May be poor in TB or testicular cancer
- Temperature: Fever in cases of TB, filariasis, chronic epididymo-orchitis
- Edema: Can point towards etiology
- Stigmata of TB
  Stigmata of syphilis

LOCAL EXAMINATION

- Always say this first:
  1. Examined with due consent
  2. Under adequate illumination
  3. Exposure from nipple to knees
  4. In standing as well as supine position

All inguino-scrotal swellings have to be examined in BOTH standing and supine positions.

[Refer Chapter 9 in Section IV for details on swelling/lump]

Follow the order in flow chart given below:

- Inspection:

Opposite side
↓
Swelling
↓
Scrotum → Smooth / Loss of rugosities / Tense
↓
Hernia
↓
Penis → Buried / Deviated
↓
Dribbling of urine (soiled undergarments)
↓
Inguinal, supraclavicular fullness

- Palpation:

Always say this first on palpation:

1. Inspectory findings confirmed
2. No local rise of temperature
3. Tenderness - yes or no

Opposite side → Testis / Spermatic cord
↓
Hernia (impulse on cough)
↓
Swelling → Get above the swelling / Fluctuation / Transillumination
↓
Testis
↓
Spermatic cord - at root of scrotum between the thumb and index finger (palpate simultaneously on both sides)
↓
Lymph nodes
↓
Abdomen + P/R examination

P/R examination for seminal vesicles and rectovesical pouch deposits.

- Percussion: Not applicable
- Auscultation: Not applicable

DIAGNOSIS

Left/right-sided uncomplicated, primary vaginal hydrocele

DISCUSSION

- Hydrocele (definition): Abnormal collection of fluid between layers of tunica vaginalis
- For consistency of hydrocele, always say → soft and tense (not firm) (since firm swellings cannot be fluctuant)
- Even slight swelling of scrotum is evident by loss of rugosities
- Edema of scrotal wall can be identified by pitting on pressure
- Peculiar method of fluctuation in hydrocele:

  1st fix by middle and ring fingers of both hands → make it tense → fluctuate by thumb and index fingers of both hands

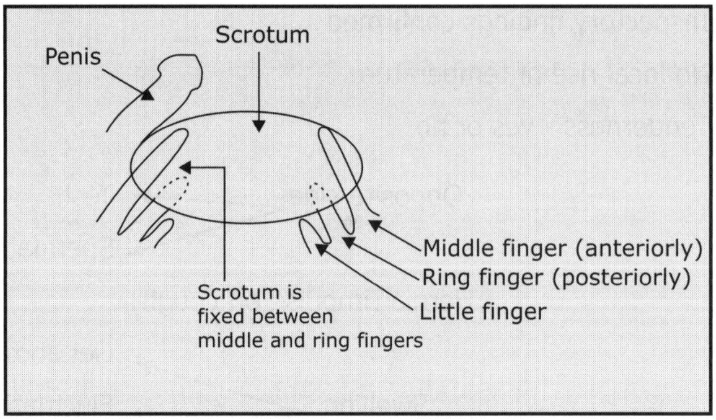

Fig. 16.1: Method to fix hydrocele for fluctuation

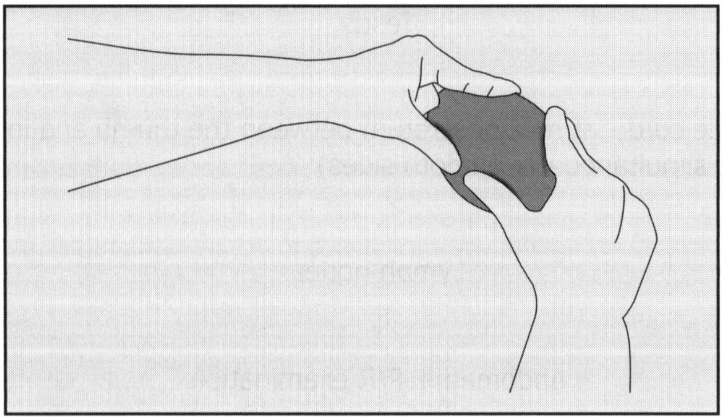

Fig. 16.2: Method to test fluctuation in a large swelling

- How to judge weight of testis → by balancing both testes on palm of hands
- Testicular sensation:
  - Sickening sensation felt by the patient when mild pressure is applied on testis
  - Lost in: Malignancy, syphilis, leprosy, atrophy, chronic hematocele, etc.
- Transillumination:
  - Never do anteroposterior → since testis comes in the way
  - Indicates CLEAR fluid
  - False negative transillumination:
    1. Wrong technique
    2. Thick wall: Thick skin, thick sac, skin with multiple sebaceous cysts
    3. Thick fluid: Pyocele, hematocele, chylocele
    4. Less fluid: Secondary hydrocele

    [Skin color does not affect transillumination.]
  - Other swellings which are transilluminant:
    1. Epididymal cyst (not spermatocele)
    2. Ranula
    3. Cystic hygroma
    4. Synovial cyst
    5. Meningocele with thin skin
- Hydrocele fluid:
  1. Amber colored
  2. Specific gravity: 1022 - 1024
  3. Contents: Water, inorganic salts, albumin (6%), cholesterol (gives iridescent effect), tyrosine, fibrinogen (if we put a drop of blood → it clots), occasionally microfilariae and spermatozoa

     (Other fluids with cholesterol crystals - branchial cyst, dentigerous cyst)
  4. Uses of hydrocele fluid: Culture medium for microfilaria and leishmania (obsolete)
- Feel of epididymis:
  1. TB - enlarged, firm, CRAGGY, slightly tender
  2. Filariasis - swollen, firm, slightly tender (but not craggy epididymis)

- Ulcer on scrotum:
    1. Anterior part: Syphilis (because it affects testis first)
    2. Posterior part: TB (because it affects epididymis first)
    3. Filariasis: Both testis and epididymis are affected simultaneously

- Filariasis:
    - Characteristics:
        1. Ram's Horn penis: Tremendously thickened skin and subcutaneous tissue of penis
        2. Lymph scrotum: Excess rugosities of scrotum with vesicles containing lymph (rupture cause lymphorrhagia)
        3. Thickening in elephantiasis: Starts at most dependent portion (max at bottom and min at root)
    - Clinical course: Asymptomatic microfilaremia → acute phase of adenolymphangitis → chronic irreversible lymphedema
    - Caused by: Culex mosquito → Wuchereria Bancrofti
    - Treatment: DEC 6 mg/kg × 12 days

- Stigmata of TB and syphilis (Refer Chapter 2 in Section I for details)

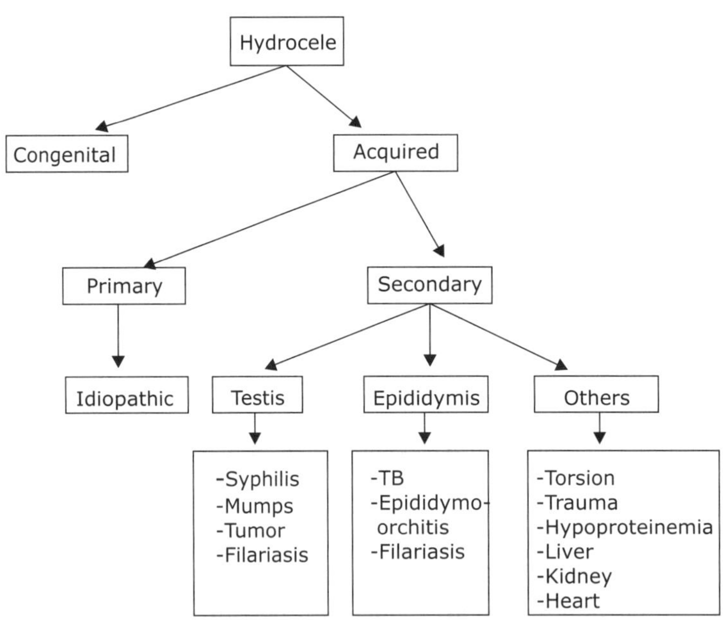

- Classification of hydrocele:

Primary hydrocele	Secondary hydrocele
1. Idiopathic	1. Always some cause
2. Tense hydrocele (because process/ pathology never stops)	2. Lax hydrocele (because little fluid)
3. Testes never felt	3. Always felt
4. Always transilluminant	4. Need not be always transilluminant
5. Transudate	5. Exudate
6. Painless	6. May be tender
7. Always surgery	7. Treat the cause

Hydrocele of hernia: Fluid collection in the hernial sac itself due to adhesion formation

Hernia of hydrocele: Herniation of a part of hydrocele sac through the dartos muscle appearing as another swelling below the skin of scrotum

Hydrocele-en-bissac: Presence of two inter-communicating sacs, one above and other below the neck of scrotum; thus showing cross fluctuation

[Other swellings with cross fluctuation - plunging ranula, psoas abscess, compound palmar ganglion]

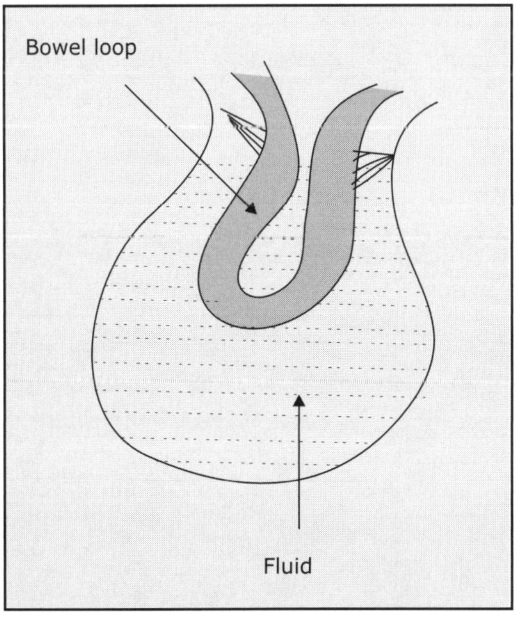

Fig. 16.3: Hydrocele of hernia

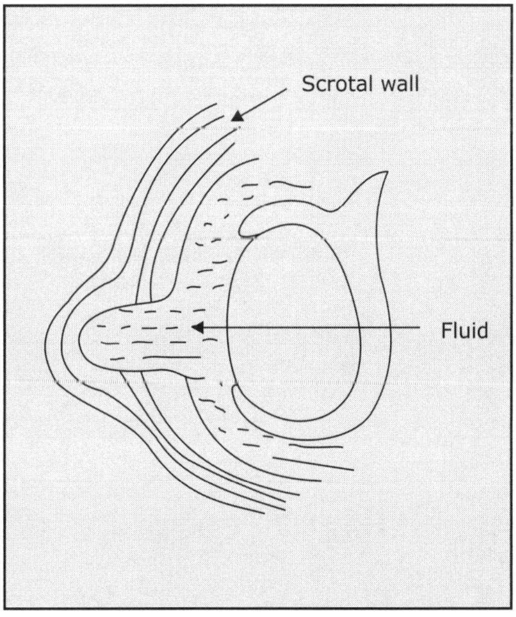

Fig. 16.4: Hernia of hydrocele

- Congenital hydrocele:
  - Occurs due to patent processus vaginalis (PPV)
  - Inverted ink - bottle phenomenon $\rightarrow$ swelling does not reduce when scrotum is lifted up by examiner, but reduces itself when child lies supine for a long time (overnight) (due to small opening)
  - Note that the pathology behind congenital hernia and hydrocele is same i.e. PPV, only difference being the size of neck (if neck is small, only fluid can enter leading to hydrocele), so treatment of both remains the same (only difference being the age at which they are operated)
  - Treatment: Herniotomy at 2 years of age (i.e. close PPV)

- Differential diagnoses of femoral swellings:
  1. Artery: Femoral artery aneurysm
  2. Vein: Saphena varix
  3. Lymphatics: Lymphadenopathy
  4. Bone: Osteomyelitis, tumors of upper end of femur
  5. Muscle: Psoas abscess
  6. Others: Femoral hernia, lipoma, ectopic testis

- Differential diagnoses of inguino-scrotal swellings:

Inguino - scrotal swellings

Spermatic cord

1. Encysted hydrocele of cord:
   - fluctation (+)
   - transillumination (+)
   - traction test (+)
   - no impulse on cough
2. Diffuse lipoma of cord:
   - soft, lobulated
   - impulse on cough (-)
3. Lymph varix (Lymphangiectasis):
   - filariasis
   - ↓ on lying down but slower than varicocele
   - impulse on cough is thrill-like
   - soft, cystic, doughy
4. Varicocele:
   - 'bag of worms' feel
   - impulse on cough is thrill-like
   - fast ↓on lying down
   - rapid onset on left side suggests renal carcinoma
5. Funiculitis (inflammation of spermatic cord)
6. Inflammatory thickening of cord extending upwards: TB

Testis

1. Malignant extension from testis:
   - hard and nodular cord
2. Undescended, ectopic, retractile testis:
   - theory of Lockwood
   - chair test
3. Torsion testis:
   - mimics strangulated hernia

Others

1. Hernia
2. Lymphadenopathy
3. Abscess in inguinal region
4. Aneurysm of external iliac artery

MANAGEMENT

- Management protocol:

Investigations to find out the etiology

↓

Relevant investigations as per history and examination:

1. TB - CXR, sputum examination, urine examination
2. Syphilis - VDRL test
3. Filariasis - peripheral smear for microfilariae
4. Tumor - USG, tumor markers, CT scan
5. Others - LFTs, RFTs, 2D-echocardiography

Primary hydrocele → Surgical management

Secondary hydrocele → Medical management → Treat the cause (e.g. AKT, penicillin, DEC, etc.)

Congenital hydrocele → herniotomy at 2 years of age

- Surgical management:
  - Principles:
    1. Reduce the secreting surface (visceral layer of tunica vaginalis)
    2. Bring the secreting surface in contact with a better absorbing surface (scrotal wall)
  - Techniques:
    1. Small size → Andrew's operation (simple eversion of sac)
    2. Medium size → Jaboulay's procedure (partial excision with eversion)
    3. Large size → Winkelman's procedure (subtotal excision)

    Lord's plication (crumpling of tunica vaginalis by radial stitches) → for small and medium-sized hydroceles

    Sharma and Jhawer's technique → keeping the testis in subdartos pouch

Anesthesia:

1. Spinal anesthesia: In adults
2. General anesthesia: In children (since non - cooperative)
3. Local anesthesia: In unfit patients

Note that hydrocele need not be operated in unfit patients

Site of local anesthesia: At root of scrotum + line of incision

17
Hernia

HISTORY

[Only additional points on hernia history have been mentioned below. Refer Chapter 1 in Section I beforehand.]

- Personal profile:
    1. Age:
        - Young age: Indirect hernia
        - Old age: Direct hernia
    2. Sex:
        - Hernias are more common in males
        - Most common type of hernia in males: Indirect inguinal hernia
        - Most common type of hernia in females: Indirect inguinal hernia (NOT femoral hernia)
    3. Occupation:
        - Occupations involving lifting heavy weights can cause hernia in post-operative cases i.e. incisional or recurrent hernias (but not in normal persons as was wrongly hypothesised previously)
    4. Address: Not contributory
    5. Religion: Not contributory
- Chief complaints:
    1. Swelling on the right/left side of groin
    2. Pain
- HOPI:
    - ❖ Symptoms:
        1. Swelling:
            - First site of appearance: Groin (hernia), scrotum (scrotal swelling), below groin crease (femoral hernia)

- Growth of the swelling is from above downwards in hernia (varicocele and lymph varix enlarge from below upwards)
- Confined to groin or extends to scrotum (direct hernia rarely extends to scrotum)
- Does it reduce by itself (on lying down or manually pushing it back)

2. Pain:
   - Dull aching or dragging type: Pull on mesentery (contents being intestine/omentum)
   - Acute pain in hernia:
     i. Inflamed contents
     ii. Strangulated hernia

❖ Etiology: (Refer Discussion part below for details)

1. Increased intra-abdominal pressure:
   - Respiratory system: H/o chronic cough, asthma, TB/TB contact or smoking
   - Urinary system: H/o frequency, hesitancy, precipitancy, nocturia or straining at micturition

     (Poor stream which improves on straining: Stricture urethra

     Poor stream which worsens on straining: BPH)
   - GI system: H/o chronic constipation (dry hard stools or straining at stools) or distension of abdomen
2. Weakness of abdominal muscles:
   - H/o surgery (appendicectomy)
   - H/o poliomyelitis
   - H/o drooping of eyelids associated with generalized muscle weakness (myasthenia gravis)

❖ Complications:

- Irreducibility: H/o irreducibility
- Obstruction: H/o vomiting and constipation associated with distension of abdomen
- Strangulation: H/o acute severe pain associated with fever/warmth and redness over the swelling

❖ Treatment taken:

- Scrotal support/Truss/conservative management for hernia (if any)
- Medications for pain

- Past history:
    - H/o surgery in past (if yes, type of surgery and when operated)
    - TB/TB contact, asthma
- Personal history:
    - Bowel: Chronic constipation
    - Bladder: Lower urinary tract symptoms (LUTS)
    - Addiction: Smoking (COPD)
- Family history: Positive family history is a risk factor for development of hernia

GENERAL EXAMINATION

[Only additional points on hernia general examination have been mentioned below. Refer Chapter 2 in Section I beforehand.]

- Built and nourishment: Obesity (risk factor for hernia)
- Temperature: Raised in strangulation

LOCAL EXAMINATION

- Always say this first:
    1. Examined with due consent
    2. Under adequate illumination
    3. Exposure from nipple to knees
    4. In standing as well as supine position
    5. In presence of female attendant (for female patients)

All inguino-scrotal swellings have to be examined in BOTH standing and supine positions.

[Refer Chapter 9 in Section IV for details on swelling/lump.]

[Refer Chapter 6 in Section II for abdominal examination.]

Follow the order in flow chart given below

- Inspection: (In standing as well as supine positions)

Opposite side

↓

Swelling

↓

Genitalia

↓

Abdominal examination

↓

Inguinal fullness, supraclavicular fullness,
renal angle fullness, other hernial sites

❖ Important features of hernia:
  - Impulse on cough is seen (inspected) at the site of hernia
  - Direct hernia rarely reaches scrotum
❖ Genitalia:
  - Penis will be deviated to the opposite side
❖ Abdominal examination:

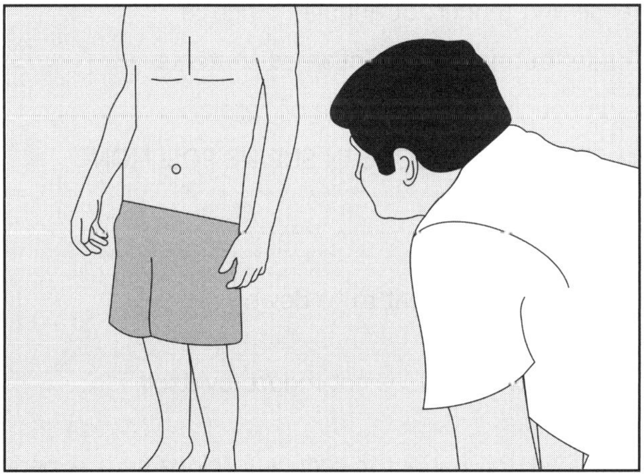

Fig. 17.1: Method to check for Malgaigne bulges

  - Malgaigne's bulge (is an inspectory finding): Seen from side in STANDING position in lower abdomen
  - Malgaigne's bulges indicate weakness of anterior abdominal wall

- Palpation:

  Always say this first on palpation:
  1. Inspectory findings confirmed
  2. No local rise of temperature
  3. Tenderness-yes or no

Opposite side
↓
Swelling
↓
Special tests
↓
Genitalia
↓
Abdominal examination

❖ Important examination of swelling:
  - Can get above the swelling:
    1. For scrotal swelling: To differentiate hydrocele from hernia
    2. For inguinal swelling: To differentiate hernia from hydrocele of canal of nuck
  - Consistency:
    1. Doughy: Omentocele
    2. Elastic: Enterocele
    3. Tense and tender: Strangulated hernia
    4. Tender but not tense: Inflamed contents
  - Impulse on cough: Felt at the site of hernia

❖ Special tests: ALL TESTS TO BE DONE IN SUPINE POSITION
  1. Reduction of hernia:
     - Method:

Ask the patient to lie down
↓
If swelling does not reduce by itself
↓
Ask the patient to reduce it (since he is experienced)
↓
If still does not reduce
↓
Do taxis manoeuvre

- Taxis manoeuvre:

  Flex, internally rotate and adduct the hip (to relax the fascia, inguinal ligament, and muscles)

  ↓

  Put one hand on fundus of sac and push inside

  ↓

  Put other hand on deep ring and pull

- Interpretation:
  i. Difficult to reduce initially (with gurgling sound) → enterocele (gas in the intestine gives resistance initially, later bowel collapses and reduces easily)
  ii. Difficult to reduce later → omentocele (due to adhesions at periphery/ neck)
  iii. Cannot be reduced: Irreducible hernia

2. Deep ring occlusion (DRO) test:

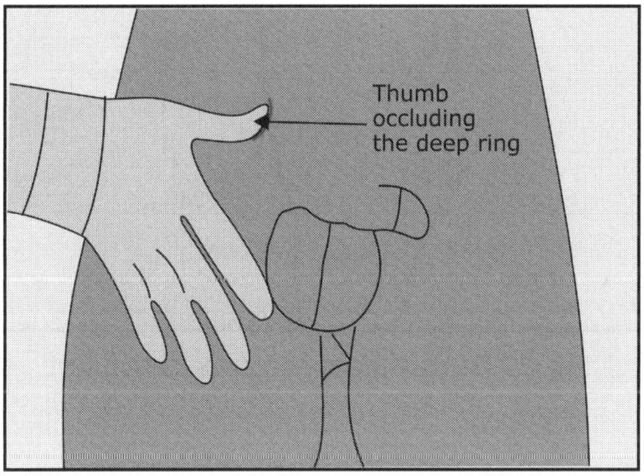

Fig. 17.2: Deep ring occlusion test

- Method:

  First reduce the hernia

  ↓

  Put pressure at 0.5 inch above mid-inguinal point

  ↓

  Ask the patient to cough

- Interpretation:
  i. Swelling visible (negative test): Direct hernia
  ii. Swelling not visible (positive test): Indirect hernia

- Fallacies of DRO test (false negatives):
  i. Pantaloon hernia
  ii. Big ring
  iii. Incorrect localization of deep ring

3. Superficial ring invagination test:

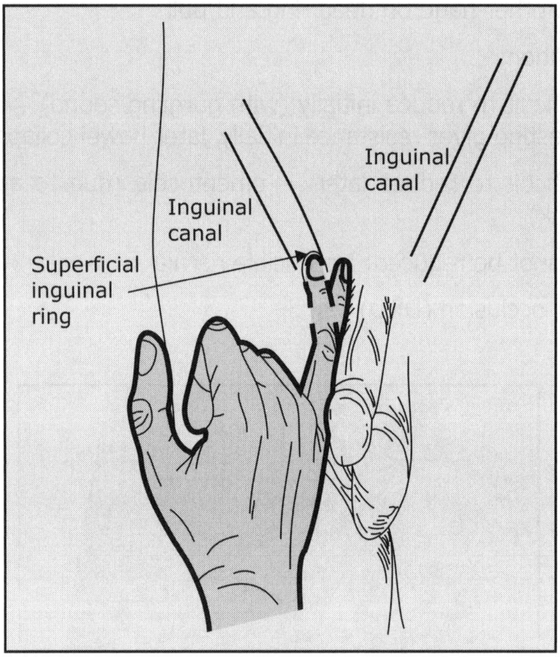

Fig. 17.3: Superficial ring invagination test

- Right hand to be used while examining right side
- Method:

First reduce the hernia

↓

Go via the root of scrotum by index or little finger

↓

Feel the pubic symphysis

↓

Go laterally and feel the pubic tubercle

↓

Invaginate above and lateral to pubic tubercle (superficial ring)

↓

Ask the patient to cough

- Interpretation:
  i. Size of ring: Ring should ideally admit just the tip of finger
  ii. Impulse felt where:
     a. Tip of finger: Indirect hernia
     b. Pulp of finger: Direct hernia
  iii. Pinch cock effect of muscle fibers (gripping by crural fibers)
  iv. Direction of finger:
     a. Goes directly backward (posteriorly): Direct hernia
     b. Goes obliquely: Indirect hernia

4. Zieman's test:

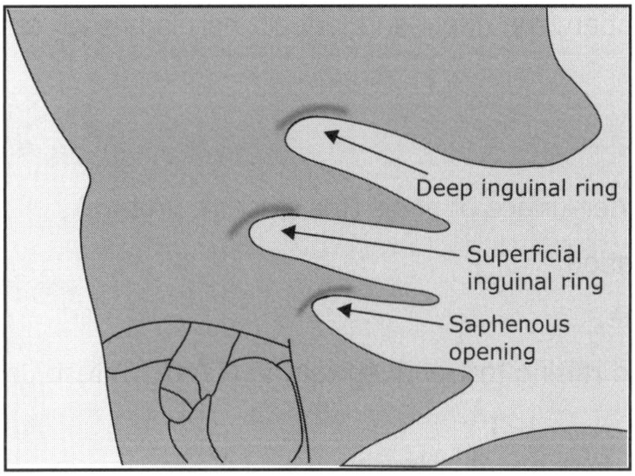

Fig. 17.4: Zieman's test

- Right hand to be used while examining right side
- Aim: To identify any missed hernias
- Method:

  First reduce the hernia
  ↓
  Keep index finger on deep ring, middle finger on superficial ring, and ring finger on saphenous opening
  ↓
  Ask the patient to cough

- Interpretation:
  i. Impulse hits the index finger: Indirect hernia
  ii. Impulse hits the middle finger: Direct hernia
  iii. Impulse hits the saphenous opening: Femoral hernia

Deep inguinal ring (internal ring):

- Half inch above the mid-inguinal point (not mid-point of inguinal ligament)
- U shaped
- Defect in transversalis fascia
- Medial to the ring are: Inferior epigastric vessels

Superficial inguinal ring (external ring):

- Just above and lateral to pubic tubercle
- Triangular in shape
- Defect in external oblique aponeurosis

Saphenous opening:

- 4 cm below and lateral to pubic tubercle

[Note that in case of irreducible hernias, special tests cannot be done. So clinically it is not possible to differentiate between direct and indirect hernia in such cases.]

❖ Genitalia:
  - Palpate undersurface of penis (for stricture urethra)

❖ Abdominal examination:
  - Muscle tone:
    1. Head raising test and leg raising (CARNIE) test

       ↓

       Feel the muscles

       ↓

       If fingers dip easily, it indicates poor tone
    2. Divarication of recti: Indicates poor abdominal muscle tone
    3. Palpate abdominal wall on Valsalva maneuver

       Do not forget to check abdominal muscle tone

- Percussion:
  - Dull note: Omentocele
  - Tympanic note: Enterocele
- Auscultation:
  - Peristaltic sounds: Enterocele
- Examine the chest (for etiological factors)

  P/R examination for BPH

DIAGNOSIS

________ sided (right/left/bilateral) _______ (direct/indirect), _______ (incomplete/complete) _________ (complicated/uncomplicated), inguinal hernia with content being _________ (omentum/intestine/bladder) with probable etiology being ______ (chronic cough, BPH, etc.) with _______ (good/poor) abdominal muscle tone

DISCUSSION

- Definition: ABNORMAL protrusion of a viscus or part of a viscus through a normal or abnormal opening in the cavity in which it is contained (do not forget to say the word 'abnormal', since tongue also protrudes through mouth, but is not a hernia)
- Etiology of hernia:
    1. Increased intra-abdominal pressure:
        - Respiratory system:
            i. Chronic cough
            ii. TB
            iii. COPD
            iv. Asthma
        - Urinary system:
            i. Stricture urethra
            ii. BEP
            iii. Bladder outlet obstruction (BOO)
        - GI system:
            i. Chronic constipation
            ii. Ascites
    2. Weakness of abdominal muscles:
        - Anterior horn cell problems: Poliomyelitis
        - Nerve is damaged: Incisions (surgery)
        - Problem in synaptic transmission: Myasthenia gravis
        - Myopathies
        - Hypoproteinemia (liver disease, nutritional)
    3. Patent processus vaginalis:
        - Russell's theory of patent processus vaginalis for congenital hernia
    4. Deficiency of collagen and mucopolysaccharides in muscles

- Congenital hydrocele → reduces overnight (inverted ink bottle phenomenon)
  Congenital hernia → reduces immediately
  (Refer to Chapter 16, Section IV for details)
- Nyhus classification (of inguinal hernias):
  - Type I : Indirect hernia with normal internal ring
  - Type II : Indirect hernia with enlarged internal ring
  - Type III A : Direct hernia
  - Type III B : Pantaloon hernia
  - Type III C : Femoral hernia
  - Type IV : Recurrent hernia
- Types of indirect inguinal hernia:
  1. Incomplete:
     i. Bubonocele: Sac is confined to inguinal canal
     ii. Funicular: Sac crosses the superficial inguinal ring but does not reach the bottom of scrotum
  2. Complete: Sac reaches the bottom of scrotum

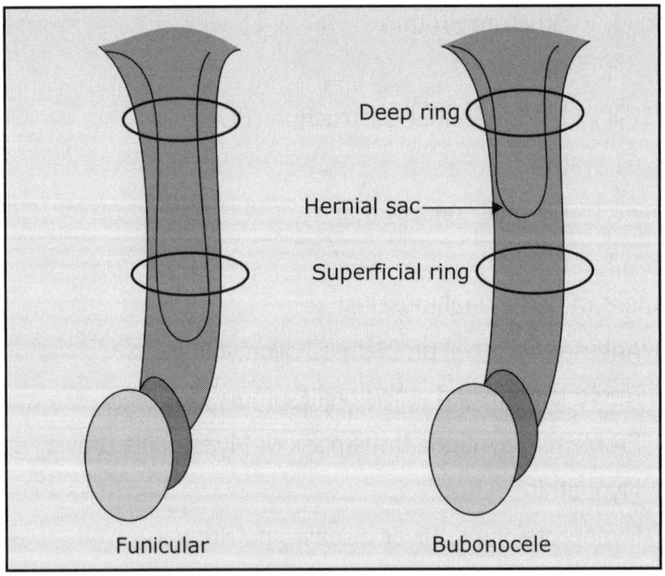

Fig. 17.5: Types of inguinal hernia

- Inguinal and femoral hernia can be differentiated based on pubic tubercle:
  - Neck of inguinal hernia lies: Above and medial to pubic tubercle
  - Neck of femoral hernia lies: Below and lateral to pubic tubercle

- Parts of hernia:
    1. Contents
    2. Sac (extension of peritoneum): Fundus, body, neck (narrowest part of sac)
    3. Coverings

  (Once the sac is formed, it does not go back; but contents can go back i.e. reduce.)
- Complications of hernia:
    - In sequence:

      Irreducibility
      ↓
      Obstruction/incarceration
      ↓
      Strangulation
      ↓
      Perforation
      ↓
      Septicemia
    - Differentiating features:

	Reducibility	**Lumen**	**Vascular supply**	**Cough impulse**
Reducible	✓	Patent	Patent	Present
Irreducible	×	Patent	Patent	Absent
Obstructed	×	Obstructed	Patent	Absent
Strangulated	×	Obstructed	Compromised	Absent

    - Causes of irreducibility:
        1. Adhesions between contents and sac, sac and sac, contents and contents
        2. Adhesions at the neck
        3. Large contents
    - All obstructed hernias should be considered strangulated unless proved otherwise (stresses the importance of immediate surgery)
    - Difference between inflamed hernia and strangulated hernia:

Strangulated hernia	**Inflamed hernia**
Clinically tense and tender	Clinically only tender (not tense)
Obstruction of lumen	No obstruction of lumen
Compromised blood supply	Normal blood supply

Difference between obstructed and incarcerated hernia:

- The term 'obstruction' is used when hernia is obstructed due to adhesions (i.e. cause outside lumen).
- The term 'incarceration' is used when hernia is obstructed due to fecolith (i.e. cause inside lumen).

- Highest risk of strangulation is with femoral hernia (since neck is very narrow)
- Appendicectomy can give rise to right DIRECT inguinal hernia: Nerve commonly injured during McBurney's incision is iliohypogastric nerve (causes weakness of conjoint tendon)
- Even if ilioinguinal nerve is cut in inguinal canal during surgery, hernia does not occur (because motor supply to muscles is given high up, and not in the inguinal canal)
- Method to identify the pubic tubercle:

Ask the patient to adduct the thigh against resistance

↓

Trace adductor longus upward till its origin (pubic tubercle)

- Omentocele = epiplocele
- Smoking (nicotine) → prevents conversion of proline to hydroxyl-proline → collagen III affected
- Direct vs. indirect hernia:

Direct hernia	**Indirect hernia**
	Commonest type of hernia
Usually bilateral	Usually unilateral (more common on right side) (bilateral in 12% cases)
Commoner in old	Commoner in young
Swelling is spherical or oval	Swelling is pyriform in shape
Easier to reduce	Difficult to reduce
Neck is wide (so obstruction is rare)	Neck is narrow (so obstruction is common)
Neck lies medial to inferior epigastric vessels	Neck lies lateral to inferior epigastric vessels
Sac is posteromedial to cord structures (since it comes from posterior wall of inguinal canal)	Sac is anterolateral to cord structures
Usually does not reach the scrotum	Can reach the scrotum

(Continued...)

Coverings: 1. Skin 2. Superficial fascia 3. External oblique aponeurosis 4. Conjoint tendon 5. Fascia transversalis 6. Peritoneum	Coverings: 1. Skin 2. Superficial fascia 3. External oblique aponeurosis in inguinal region and external spermatic fascia beyond external ring 4. Cremaster muscle 5. Internal spermatic fascia 6. Peritoneum

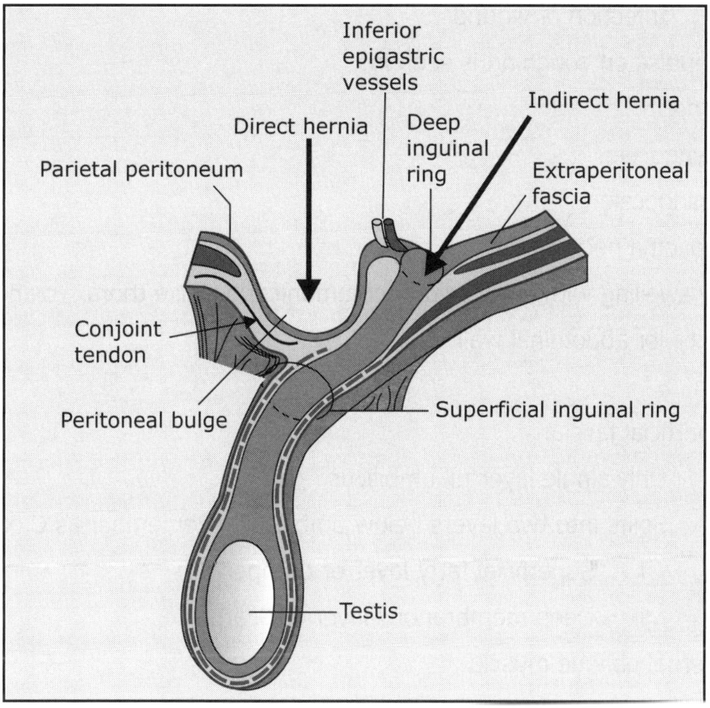

Fig. 17.6: Direct and indirect hernia

- Sliding hernia (hernia-en-glissade):
  - Hernia in which part of the sac is formed by contents
  - Significance: Viscera is liable to be injured if hernial sac is resected during surgery
  - Occurs almost exclusively in men
- Incisional hernia: Hernia created by incision where there was no potent space

  Recurrent hernia: Hernia which comes through existing potent space
- Causes of recurrence of hernia:
  1. Pre-operative causes:
     - Non-treatment of the precipitating factor (e.g. smoking, BPH, etc.)

2. Intra-operative causes:
    - Sac not ligated/transfixed at highest point
    - Inadequate hemostasis
    - Suture line under tension
    - Use of absorbable sutures
3. Post-operative causes:
    - Recurrence of cause of hernia (e.g. smoking)
    - Infection of wound

- Expansile impulse on coughing is seen in:
    - Hernia
    - Laryngocele
    - Meningocele
    - Empyema necessitans
    - Any swelling with intracavitary communications like thorax, cranium, abdomen
- Layers of anterior abdominal wall:
    1. Skin
    2. Superficial fascia:
        - Only single layer till umbilicus
        - Splits into two layers below umbilicus: (Remember as C comes before S)
            i. Superficial fatty layer of **C**amper
            ii. Deep membranous layer of **S**carpa
    3. External oblique muscle
    4. Internal oblique muscle
    5. Transversus abdominis
    6. Fascia transversalis
    7. Preperitoneal (extraperitoneal) pad of fat
    8. Peritoneum
- Inguinal canal:
    - 4 cm long oblique space in inguinal region, half inch above and parallel to medial two-thirds of inguinal ligament
    - Boundaries:
        1. Anteriorly: External oblique aponeurosis throughout the entire length, lacunar ligament on medial part, conjoint muscle on lateral part

2. Superiorly: Conjoint muscle (arching fibers)
3. Inferiorly: Upturned part of inguinal ligament
4. Posteriorly: Transversalis fascia throughout the entire length, conjoint tendon medially

- Contents of inguinal canal:
  1. Ilioinguinal nerve (L_1)
  2. Spermatic cord in males
  3. Round ligament in females
- The ilioinguinal nerve enters the inguinal canal by piercing the posterior wall (and not through the deep inguinal ring)

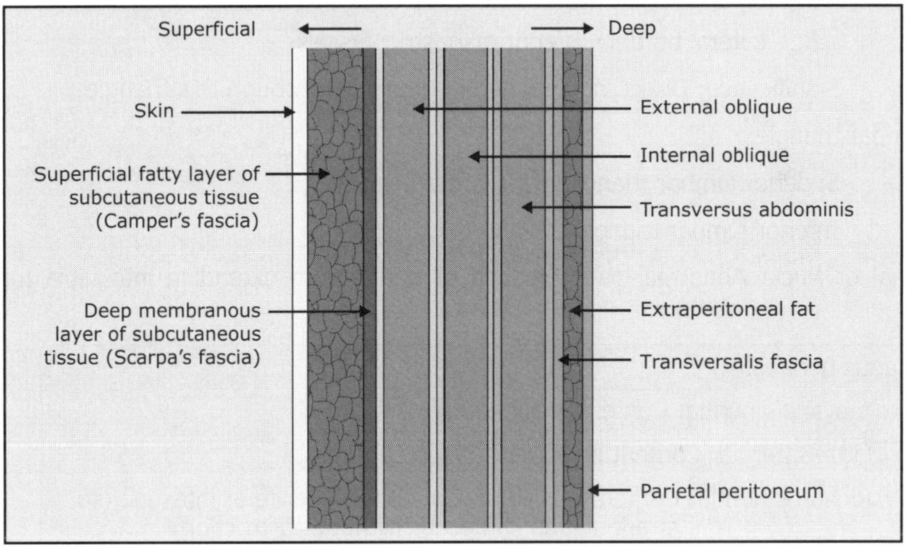

Fig. 17.7: Layers of abdominal wall

- Mid-inguinal point: Mid-point of ASIS and pubic SYMPHYSIS

  Mid-point of inguinal ligament: Mid-point of ASIS and pubic TUBERCLE
- Spermatic cord:
  - Coverings of spermatic cord:
    1. Internal spermatic fascia: From fascia transversalis
    2. Cremasteric fascia: From internal oblique muscle
    3. External spermatic fascia: From external oblique aponeurosis
  - Contents of spermatic cord:
    1. Vas deferens
    2. Artery to vas deferens

3. Testicular artery
4. Cremasteric artery
5. Pampiniform plexus of veins
6. Lymphatics of testis
7. Nerves (sympathetic)
8. Genital branch of genitofemoral nerve

- Hesselbach's triangle:
  - Boundaries:
    1. Inferior border: Inguinal ligament
    2. Medial border: Lateral border of rectus sheath (linea semilunaris)
    3. Lateral border: Inferior epigastric vessels
  - Significance: Direct inguinal hernia protrudes through this triangle
- Lumbar triangle:
  - Superior lumbar triangle of Grynfeltt-Lesshaft
  - Inferior lumbar triangle of Petit
- Canal of Nuck: Abnormal patent pouch of peritoneum extending into labia majora in woman

Eponymous hernias:

- Amyand's hernia: Content is appendix
- Littre's hernia: Content is Meckel's diverticulum
- Richter's hernia: Content is only part of circumference of intestine (so strangulation can occur without obstruction)
- Maydl hernia: Two loops of intestine herniate in a manner of 'W'
- Pantaloon hernia: Inguinal hernia with both direct and indirect components
- Gibbon's hernia: Hernia with hydrocele
- Blandin hernia: Internal hernia through foramen of Winslow

MANAGEMENT

- Management protocol: Hernia is a CLINICAL DIAGNOSIS

Clinical diagnosis/suspicion of hernia
→ Complicated hernia → Emergency investigations and surgery
→ Uncomplicated hernia → Investigations → First treat the cause of hernia → Elective surgery at a later date

> Note that treatment of hernia is ALWAYS surgery (to avoid complications which eventually lead to resection).
>
> NO ROLE OF CONSERVATIVE MANAGEMENT (Exceptions: Very old unfit patient having hernia with large defect)

- Emergency investigations:
  1. For 'A' fitness
  2. USG scan
  3. Doppler scan/contrast CT scan: To know the vascularity of obstructed hernia
- Investigations for uncomplicated hernia:
  1. For 'A' fitness
  2. USG scan
  3. To diagnose the cause (as per the symptoms):
     - i. Chest X-ray: For RS system causes
     - ii. Urinary flow rate/USG prostate: For urinary system causes
  4. There is no role of CT/MRI scan in hernia
- Principles of hernia surgeries:
  1. Herniotomy:
     - Excision of the sac of hernia
  2. Herniorrhaphy:
     - Strengthening the posterior wall of inguinal canal by APPROXIMATION of local tissues
     - Causes tension on sutures (recurrence is higher)

3. Hernioplasty:
   - Strengthening the weakness or bridging the gap of posterior wall by synthetic material
   - Tension-free repair (recurrence is lower)

❖ Herniotomy:
- Technique:

  Identify, dissect, and isolate the sac

  ↓

  Open the fundus and reduce contents

  ↓

  High transfixation/ligation of the sac (at neck/deep inguinal ring)

  ↓

  Cut the redundant sac
- Indication: Patient below 18 years with INDIRECT hernia

❖ Herniorrhaphy:
- Indications:
  1. Strangulated hernia
  2. Infection
  3. Inflammation
- Techniques:
  1. Bassini's repair: Strengthening the posterior wall by suturing the conjoined tendon to inguinal ligament
  2. Lytle repair: Narrowing down the internal ring (i.e. reducing its size) by 'figure of 8' stitches
  3. Shouldice repair: Double breasting of fascia transversalis (4 or 6 layers strengthening can also be done)
  4. Tanner's release incision with Bassini's repair: To decrease the tension on sutures in Bassini's repair, release incision is taken on rectus sheath

❖ Hernioplasty:
- Indications:
  1. Patient >18 years with indirect hernia
  2. All direct hernias (ANY AGE)
- Techniques:
  1. LTFM (Lichtenstein's tension-free meshplasty)

2. GPRVS (Giant Prosthetic Reinforcement of Visceral Sac):
    - Also called as Stoppa's repair
    - Open preperitoneal approach
    - Large size mesh placed between peritoneum and anterior + inferior + lateral abdominal wall
    - Indications:
        i. Multiple lower abdominal wall hernias
        ii. Recurrent hernias
        iii. Large defect/bilateral defect

Treatment of inguinal hernias:

- Any direct hernia (any age): LTFM
- For indirect hernia:
    - Up to 18 years: herniotomy ONLY
    - > 18 years: TFLM

- Principle of mesh:
    - Mesh is a foreign body which stimulates fibroblasts and causes fibrous tissue formation, which in turn strengthens the wall
    - Types of mesh:
        1. Prolene
        2. PTFE
        3. Dacron
        4. Gortex
    - Hernia repair needs non-absorbable type of mesh
    - Size of mesh: Tailored according to the defect to have overlap of 5 cm with the margins
    - Types of mesh repair: (Refer Fig. 17.8)
        1. Onlay repair: Mesh placed anterior to fascia
        2. Inlay repair: Mesh placed in the hernial defect and secured circumferentially to the edges of fascia
        3. Sublay repair: Retro-rectus or pre-peritoneal mesh placement
        4. Underlay repair: Mesh placed in intraperitoneal position
    - Contraindications:
        1. Infection
        2. Inflammation

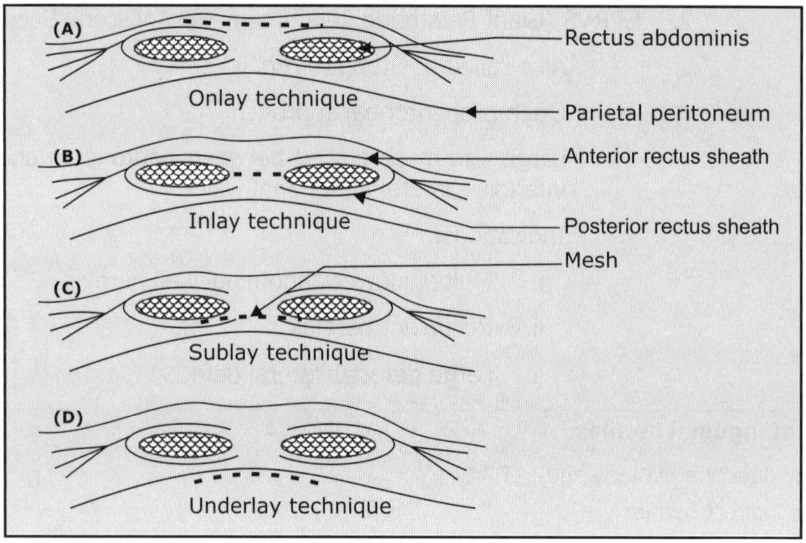

Fig. 17.8: Types of mesh repair

- Laparoscopic repair:
  - Types:
    1. TAPP: Transabdominal preperitoneal repair
    2. TEP: Totally extraperitoneal repair
  - Principle: As the names suggest
    1. TAPP: Peritoneal space is entered by laparoscopy (meaning transabdominal), peritoneum incised and dissected away as flap to enter the preperitoneal space (meaning preperitoneal)
    2. TEP: Preperitoneal space is approached without entering the peritoneal cavity (meaning totally extraperitoneal)
  - Indications:
    1. Indirect/direct inguinal hernias
    2. Recurrent hernia
    3. Bilateral hernia
  - Contraindications:
    1. Obstructed/strangulated hernias
    2. Previous lower abdominal surgeries (like appendicectomy) rendering space inaccessible
    3. General contraindications to laparoscopic surgery: Ascites, TB, etc.

Note that the mesh is put in pre-peritoneal space in BOTH types of laparoscopic repairs, only difference being the method of approaching that space.

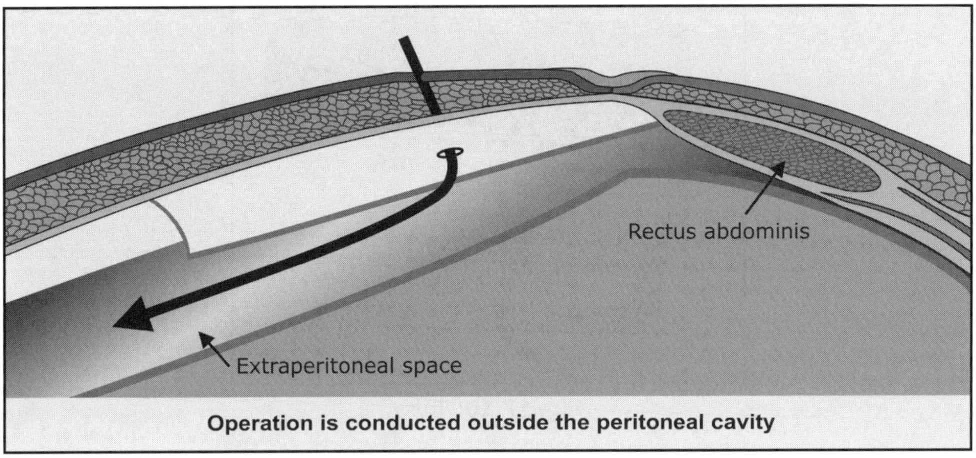

Fig. 17.9: Totally extraperitoneal hernia repair (TEP)

- Anesthesia during hernia repair:
    - Spinal anesthesia and local anesthesia (inguinal block) is preferred for open repair
    - General anesthesia is used for laparoscopic repair
- During surgery:
    - How to identify the deep inguinal ring: Visualization of preperitoneal pad of fat indicates the plane of deep inguinal ring
    - Management of hernial sac during surgery:
        1. Indirect hernia: Sac is dissected, transfixed/ligated and cut (i.e. herniotomy done ALWAYS)
        2. Direct hernia: Sacs are usually not opened/cut, instead just inverted into peritoneal cavity (since they are too broad based for ligation)
    - Any indirect hernia: First part of surgery is herniotomy (prior to both herniorrhaphy and hernioplasty)
- Bilateral hernia repair: Operate at the SAME time

  Hernia and hydrocele on same side: Operate at the SAME time

  Hernia and hydrocele on opposite sides: Operate at the SAME time
- Truss:
    - Conservative management of hernia
    - Abandoned modality of treatment (has high chance of obstruction)
    - Can be used for old, unfit patients with direct hernia having wide neck (never for indirect hernia)

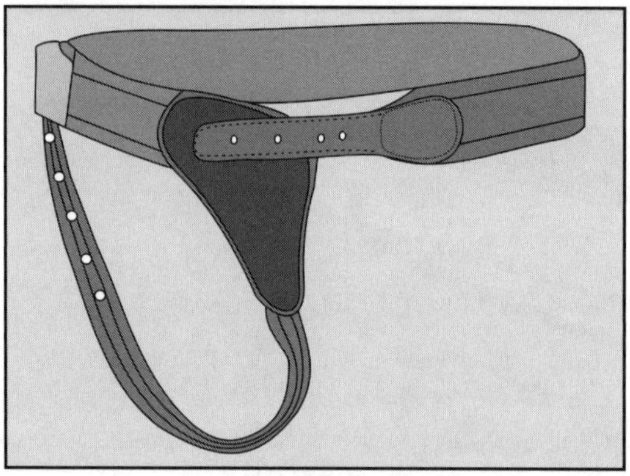

Fig. 17.10: Truss

- Recurrent hernias:
  - Previous laparoscopic repair: Do open repair
  - Previous open repair: Do laparoscopic repair
- Umbilical hernia:
  - Small asymptomatic hernias do not need surgery
  - Indications of surgical treatment:
    1. Symptomatic hernia
    2. Increasing size
    3. Complications
- Incisional hernias: Laparoscopic/open mesh repair

18

Obstructive Jaundice

HISTORY

[Only additional points on OJ history have been mentioned below. Refer Chapter 1 in Section I beforehand.]

- Personal profile:
  1. Age:
     - Choledochal cyst: Childhood and young adults
     - Gallstones: Adults (middle age onwards)
     - Periampullary cancer: Elderly (>40 years)
  2. Sex:
     - Choledochal cyst: F > M (4:1)
     - Gallstones: F > M
     - Periampullary carcinoma: M > F (only slightly higher incidence)
  3. Occupation: Not contributory
  4. Address:
     - Gall bladder diseases are common in North and East India (particularly in West Bengal, Uttar Pradesh, Bihar, Punjab)
  5. Religion: not contributory

- Chief complaints :
  1. Jaundice
  2. High colored urine
  3. Clay colored stools
  4. Pruritus

4 cardinal symptoms of OJ

- HOPI:
  - ❖ Symptoms:
    1. Jaundice:
       i. Waxing - waning:
          - Seen in periampullary carcinoma
          - Jaundice is ALWAYS present but increases and decreases in intensity (since necrotic tissue falls off, but never completely)
          - Never has jaundice free intervals

       ii. Intermittent:
          - Seen in CBD stones
          - Jaundice free intervals present (stones may slip and pass into duodenum, thus relieving the obstruction completely)

       iii. Progression:
          - Rapid → stone in CBD (sudden severe jaundice)
          - Slow → malignancy (gradually increasing jaundice)

       iv. Pain (in RHC or epigastrium)
          - Painless → malignancy
          - Painful → benign

Aim is to differentiate between benign and malignant etiologies of jaundice on history. (So proceed with history accordingly.)

    2. Urine: Dark colored - due to direct bilirubin (conjugated bilirubin is water soluble → hence passes in urine)

    3. Stools:
       i. Clay colored stools: Due to absence of stercobilinogen in stools (bilirubin cannot enter GI tract because of obstruction → urobilinogen not formed → stercobilinogen not formed)
       ii. Melena:
          a. Stomach cancer with metastasis to porta hepatis
          b. Periampullary carcinoma
       iii. Hematochezia:
          a. Colon cancer with metastasis to porta hepatis
       iv. Aluminum-stained stools/silvery stools

Aluminum-stained stools/silvery stools are seen in periampullary carcinoma (due to shedding of tumor in duodenum).

4. Pruritus:
   - It is generalized in nature
   - Due to bile salt deposition in skin

❖ Etiology: (No need to rule out medical causes of jaundice if cardinal symptoms of OJ are present)

- Hepatitis: H/o pain in RHC or epigastrium with fever, anorexia, nausea-vomiting, h/o blood transfusion or high-risk behavior
- Benign causes:
  1. Gallstone disease: H/o biliary colic, flatulent dyspepsia with recurrent episodes of jaundice
  2. Biliary stricture: H/o cholecystectomy or ERCP
  3. Cholangitis: H/o pain and fever associated with jaundice (Charcot's triad)
  4. Choledochal cyst: H/o pain and mass associated with jaundice
- Malignant causes:
  1. Periampullary carcinoma: H/o waxing - waning jaundice or silvery stools, mass in abdomen, constipation/diarrhea associated with weight loss and anorexia
  2. Porta hepatis lymphadenopathy: Swelling at other sites associated with night sweats, fever and bone pain (lymphoma) or TB/TB contact
  3. Metastasis to porta hepatis: H/o hematemesis, melena, or hematochezia

Biliary colic: Sharp shooting intermittent pain in RHC or epigastrium which may be referred to right shoulder which may be brought about by fatty meal and associated with nausea.

❖ Complications:

1. Cholangitis: H/o pain and fever associated with jaundice (Charcot's triad)
2. Bleeding tendencies: H/o easy bruisability or bleed from any natural orifice (due to vitamin K deficiency or cholangitis causing sepsis)

   [Note that it is not due to cirrhosis (because cirrhosis is a very late complication).]
3. Pancreatitis: H/o nausea and vomiting associated with abdominal pain radiating to the back which gets relieved on bending forwards
4. Metastasis:
   i. Peritoneum: H/o ascites
5. Liver status: Need not be enquired in case of OJ (as liver failure is rare)

- ❖ Treatment history: Instrumentation (ERCP) if any

- Past history:
    - h/o biliary colic or gall stone disease in the past
    - h/o surgery for post-operative biliary stricture (most commonly after cholecystectomy and ERCP)

- Personal history:
    - Bowel: Steatorrhea in etiologies causing pancreatic exocrine failure e.g. carcinoma head of pancreas
    - Sleep: Altered sleep pattern (liver cell failure)
    - Addiction:
        1. Smoking causes pancreatic cancer
        2. Alcoholic cirrhosis leads to pigment stones
    - Appetite: Reduced in malignancy

- Family history: Not contributory

- Menstrual and obstetric history:
    - Fat, FERTILE, flatulent female of forty is at high risk for gallstone disease

GENERAL EXAMINATION

[Only additional points on OJ general examination have been mentioned below. Refer Chapter 2 in Section I beforehand.]

- Confused and disoriented: In cholangitis (Reynold's pentad)
- Built and nourishment/BMI:
    - Obese in gallstone disease
    - Poorly nourished in malignancy (weight loss)
- Temperature: Fever in cholangitis and cholecystitis
- Pulse: BRADYCARDIA in OJ (due to bile salt deposition in SA node)
- BP: Hypotension in cholangitis
- Pallor: In liver cell failure
- Edema: In liver cell failure
- Lymphadenopathy: Generalized lymphadenopathy + OJ → lymphoma (due to compression by porta hepatis nodes)

- Icterus: Refer to jaundice in Chapter 2 in Section I for more details
- Clubbing: In primary biliary cirrhosis
- Skin:
  - SCRATCH marks (to confirm pruritus)
  - Petechiae/purpura (due to deficiency of vitamin K)
- Others:
  - Signs of liver cell failure (Refer Chapter 6 in Section II for details.)
  - Dark color of urine in urinary bag (if catheter is inserted)

LOCAL EXAMINATION

- Always say this first:
  1. Examined with due consent
  2. Under adequate illumination
  3. Exposure from nipple to knees
  4. In standing as well as supine position
  5. In presence of female attendant (for female patients)

  [Refer Chapter 9 in Section IV for details on swelling/lump.]

- Inspection:

  Upper GI tract

  ↓

  Inspection of swelling and abdomen

  ↓

  1. External genitalia
  2. Hernial orifices
  3. Supraclavicular fullness
  4. Renal angle fullness

- Palpation:
  - Always say this first on palpation:
    1. Inspectory findings confirmed
    2. No local rise of temperature
    3. Tenderness - yes or no

- Lump in RHC :

Liver mass	Gall bladder mass
	Pear shaped
No mobility form side to side	Side to side mobility present
Continuous with liver margin	Protrudes from inferior margin of liver (felt as an indentation)
Generally firm in consistency (except hydatid cyst)	Generally soft in consistency (hard in Ca. GB)
Moves with respiration	Moves with respiration

How to describe GB lump: Single, pear-shaped lump of size __ × ___ cm in RHC (specify if it extends to other quadrant), soft in consistency, smooth texture, moves with respiration with presence of side-to-side mobility and distinct indentation felt from liver surface.

- Liver: Not palpable normally in adults (palpable physiologically only till 3 years of age)
- Other organs (as in standard abdominal examination)

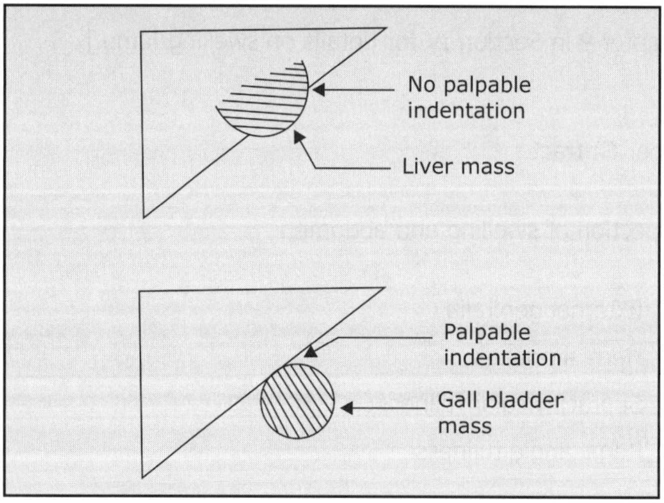

Fig. 18.1: Liver vs. gall bladder mass

- Percussion:
  1. To note the liver span (for hepatomegaly)
  2. For free fluid in abdomen
- Auscultation: Bruit heard in hepatocellular carcinoma

- PR examination in OJ:
    - i. To check for stools - clay colored/melena/hematochezia
    - ii. To check for palpable metastatic nodules

Blumer's shelf:
Metastatic tumor cells from intra-abdominal malignancy that can be detected as nodules in rectovesical or rectouterine pouch on P/R or P/V examination.

DIAGNOSIS

_____ year-old male/female is a case of obstructive jaundice and in accordance to Courvoisier's law, it has benign/malignant etiology with most probable cause being _____ with likely level of block being _____ (CBD/proximal to CBD) with/without complications. However due to exceptions to the law, I would like to keep the following differentials in mind ______.

DISCUSSION

- Clarification of terms:
    - 'Chole' means bile
      'Cholecysto' means GB (gallbladder)
      'Choledocho' means CBD (common bile duct)
      'lith' means stone
    - Cholelithiasis: Stones in GB
      Choledocholithiasis: Stones in CBD
    - Cholecystectomy: Removal of GB
      Choledochotomy: Opening of CBD
- OJ vs. surgical jaundice:

OJ	Surgical jaundice
Involves obstruction to bile flow	Involves obstruction to bile flow
May or may not be amenable to surgery	Amenable to surgery
Obstruction at level of EITHER intrahepatic or extrahepatic biliary tree or both	Obstruction at the level of extrahepatic biliary tree only

> Concept of biliary colic:
> - Occurs due to stone impacted at GB neck (cholelithiasis) and not per se due to CBD stone (choledocholithiasis).
> - This is because GB has smooth muscle while CBD lacks smooth muscle (unlike ureter).
>
> Concept of gallstones and jaundice:
> - Jaundice occurs only when there is obstruction to the flow of bile FROM LIVER (not to be confused with gallbladder).
> - So cholelithiasis and cholecystitis per se never give rise to jaundice but choledocholithiasis and cholangitis do.

- Normal capacity of GB: 50 mL
- CBD:
    - Length: 7 - 11 cm (10 cm)
    - Diameter: 4 - 8 mm
    - Parts:
        1. Supraduodenal part
        2. Retroduodenal part
        3. Infraduodenal part
        4. Intraduodenal part
- Gall stones:
    - Types:
        1. Cholesterol stones: 10%
        2. Pigment stones: 15%
            i. Black pigment stones
            ii. Brown pigment stones (infection)
        3. Mixed stones: 70 - 90%
    - Gallstones are formed in GB (which slip into CBD)
    - Etiology of gallstones:
        1. Cholesterol stones:
            i. Supersaturated bile: OC pills, impaired enterohepatic circulation (ileal disease or resection), obesity
            ii. Nucleation of cholesterol: Infections
            iii. GB hypomotility: Prolonged TPN, fasting, pregnancy, OC pills, surgery

2. Pigment stones:
    i. Chronic hemolysis
    ii. Pernicious anemia
    iii. Alcoholic cirrhosis
    iv. Infection

- Stones in CBD are of two types:
    1. Secondary: Formed in GB (very common)
    2. Primary: Formed in CBD (rare)

Criteria of primary CBD stones: Stones formed 2 years after cholecystectomy

- Admirand and Small theory (micellar theory) of cholesterol stone formation:
    1. Normally bile salt: Cholesterol ratio is 25:1
    2. Critical ratio is 13:1

- Causes of OJ:
    1. Alimentary tract:
        i. Stomach:
            a. Carcinoma stomach with metastasis to porta hepatis nodes
            b. Carcinoma of pylorus infiltrating the CBD
        ii. Periampullary carcinoma
        iii. Carcinoma of colon with metastasis to porta hepatis nodes
    2. Biliary tree:
        i. Congenital causes:
            a. Congenital biliary atresia
            b. Choledochal cyst
        ii. Acquired causes:
            a. Traumatic: Surgery or instrumentation
            b. Inflammatory: Cholangitis
            c. Neoplastic: Ca. GB, cholangiocarcinoma
            d. Miscellaneous: Choledocholithiasis, Mirizzi's syndrome
    3. Pancreas:
        i. Congenital causes:
            a. Pancreatic duct atresia
            b. Annular pancreas

   ii. Acquired causes:
      a. Traumatic
      b. Inflammatory: Acute and chronic pancreatitis
      c. Neoplastic: Carcinoma pancreas
      d. Miscellaneous: Pancreatic stones

4. Liver:
   i. Hepatoma with metastasis to porta hepatis nodes
   ii. Large hydatid cyst in anteroinferior lobe causing direct compression
5. Miscellaneous:
   i. Ovarian tumor with metastasis to porta hepatis nodes
   ii. Cirrhosis and portal hypertension (due to formation of collaterals which compress porta hepatis) (very rare)

Most common cause of OJ: Choledocholithiasis

- Wadsworth syndrome:
  - Chronic pancreatitis causing OJ (due to fibrosis of intraduodenal part of CBD)
  - Very rare
- Periampullary carcinoma:
  - The term 'periampullary' carcinoma includes:
    1. Duodenal cancer
    2. Cancer of ampulla of Vater
    3. Pancreatic head cancer (most common)
    4. Cholangiocarcinoma
  - Factors in favor of periampullary carcinoma:
    1. Jaundice (waxing - waning type)
    2. Melena/silvery stools/aluminum stained stools
    3. Hematemesis
    4. H/o smoking
    5. Constitutional symptoms of malignancy (anorexia, weight loss)

- Pain (due to infiltration of retroperitoneal nerves) and lump in abdomen are very late features of carcinoma of pancreas, most common symptoms are weight loss, anorexia, nausea, abdominal discomfort.

- KLATSKIN TUMOR (hilar cholangiocarcinoma): Cholangiocarcinoma occurring at the level of confluence of hepatic ducts (proximal to insertion of cystic duct).

- Courvoisier's law:
    - Original statement: "If in a jaundiced patient, the gallbladder is palpably enlarged, it is not a case of stone impacted in CBD because previous cholecystitis may have rendered the gallbladder fibrotic"
    - Explanation:

        Jaundice with nonpalpable GB → gallstone disease

        Jaundice with palpable GB → other etiologies

        (This is because chronic irritation due to gallstones causes fibrosis of the gallbladder)
    - Holds true in how much percent of cases: Only 30%
    - Exceptions:
        1. GB is palpable even in the presence of stone:
            i. Early CBD stone (may be 1st attack)
            ii. Mirizzi's syndrome
            iii. Double impaction of stones (GB neck and CBD)
        2. Gall bladder is not palpable, but there is no stone: (Anything obstructing proximal to insertion of cystic duct)
            i. Klatskin tumor
            ii. Lymph nodes at porta hepatis

Causes of porta hepatis lymphadenopathy are (in decreasing order of frequency):

1. Carcinoma of GB (most common cause)
2. Hepatoma
3. GI tract malignancy
4. TB, lymphoma

- Mirizzi's syndrome:
  - Extrinsic compression of common hepatic duct or CBD due to stone impacted in cystic duct or Hartmann's pouch
  - Types: Without fistula (type I), with fistula (types II, III, IV)
  - Exception to Courvoisier's law

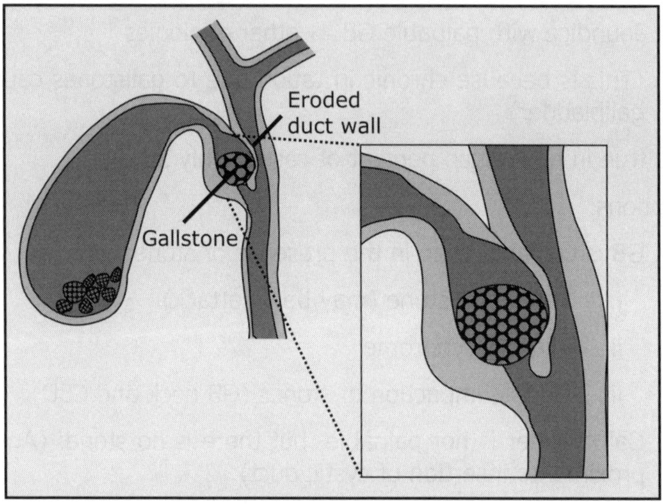

Fig. 18.2: Mirizzi's syndrome

- Charcot's triad (P/F/J):
  - Pain (Intermittent biliary colic), fever (with chills/rigors), jaundice (intermittent)
  - Seen in: Cholangitis
- Reynold's pentad (P/F/J/H/C):
  - Pain, fever, jaundice, hypotension (due to shock), confusion (due to altered mental status)
  - Seen in: Cholangitis
- Choledochal triad (P/M/J):
  - Pain, mass, jaundice
  - Seen in: Choledochal cyst
- Sandblom's triad:
  - Biliary colic, OJ, melena
  - Seen in: Hemobilia
- Saint's triad:
  - Cholelithiasis, hiatal hernia, diverticulosis of colon

- Rigler's triad (on X-ray):
  - Small bowel obstruction (multiple air fluid levels), pneumobilia (air in biliary tree), stones on X-ray
  - Seen in: Gallstone ileus

- Boa's sign:
  - Hyperesthesia over the 9th and 10th ICS posterolaterally (below the scapula)
  - Seen in: Acute cholecystitis

- Murphy's sign:
  - Method: Ask the patient to breathe out

    ↓

    Place palpating hand below the costal margin on the right side at MCL

    ↓

    Ask the patient to breathe in deeply

    ↓

    Patient winces with a 'catch' in breath
  - Seen in: Acute cholecystitis

- Stricture of CBD (due to cholecystectomy) occurs due to:
  1. Damage to blood supply (ischemic damage) of CBD (during dissection or wrong clipping of artery)
  2. Direct injury due to wrong clipping (causes high injuries)

- Gallstone ileus: Small bowel obstruction due to impaction of stone (most commonly 60 cm proximal to ileocecal valve) arising from cholecysto-enteric fistula

  Bouveret's syndrome: Gastric outlet obstruction due to impaction of stone in 1st part of duodenum from cholecysto-gastric fistula

- Bile acids (degradation products of cholesterol):
  1. Primary bile acids:
     - Synthesized by liver
     - Cholic acid and chenodeoxycholic acid
  2. Secondary bile acids:
     - Due to bacterial actions in colon
     - Deoxycholic acid and lithocholic acid

> Conjugated bile acids: Glycine and taurine conjugates of bile acids
>
> Bile salts: Sodium and potassium salts of bile acids
>
> Bile pigments:
>
> - Degradation products of hemoglobin
> - Bilirubin (yellow) and biliverdin (green)

- Calot's triangle:
  - Boundaries: Cystic duct (inferiorly), common hepatic duct (medially), cystic artery (superiorly)
  - Contents: Lymph node of Lund
- Hepatocystic triangle:
  - Boundaries: Cystic duct (inferiorly), common hepatic duct (medially), inferior surface of liver (superiorly)
  - Contents: Cystic artery and lymph node of Lund

MANAGEMENT

- Management protocol of OJ:

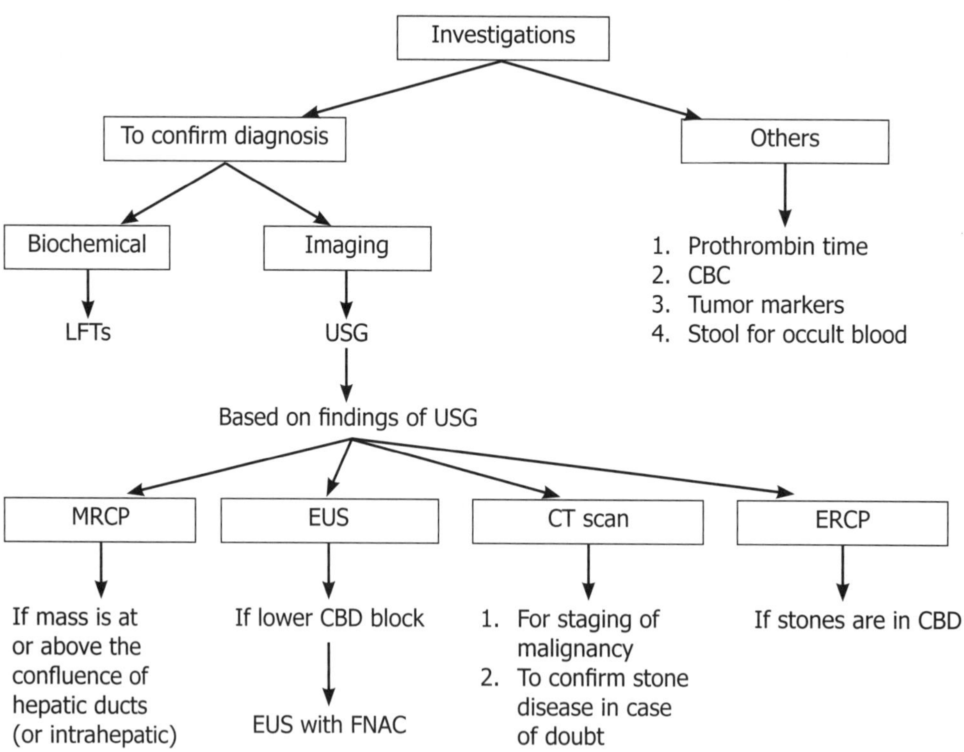

- Investigations:
  1. LFTs: To rule out hepatic etiology
  2. Prothrombin time: For evaluation of bleeding tendency (due to vitamin K deficiency)
  3. Tumor markers (CEA and CA 19 - 9):
     - If malignancy of GB is suspected
     - Done to know prognosis (not diagnosis)
  4. Stool examination: For occult blood loss (malignancy)
  5. USG scan:
     - Site of block
     - Extent of block
     - Dilatations:
       i. IHBRD: Intrahepatic biliary radicles dilatation
       ii. CBD dilatation (with size)
     - Enlarged lymph nodes
     - Liver/gall bladder mass
     - Ascites
  6. EUS: Enables to take tissue biopsy for confirmation of diagnosis
- Medical management:
  - Dissolution therapy:
    1. Given concurrently with surgical management (cannot cure gallstone disease by itself)
    2. Indications:
       i. Single stone <1.5 cm
       ii. Radiolucent stone
       iii. Functioning GB with cholesterol stone
       iv. Patient unfit for surgery
    3. Drugs used:
       i. Ursodeoxycholic acid (UDCA):
          a. Preferred drug
          b. Followed up by USG every 6 months and therapy is stopped after 3 months of successful dissolution
       ii. Chenodeoxycholic acid (CDCA): For 2 years
  - Vitamin K: 10 mg intramuscular once daily × 5 days

- Treatment protocol of CBD stones:

ERCP with papillotomy with CBD clearance and stenting

↓

Cholecystectomy (laparoscopic or open)

↓

Intraoperative confirmation of CBD clearance by:

1. Manual palpation of CBD
2. Intraoperative cholangiogram
3. Intraoperative USG scan
4. Intraoperative choledochoscopy

→ CBD cleared

→ CBD not cleared

↓

Choledochotomy and CBD clearance by:

1. Cholangioscope
2. Desjardin's choledochotomy forceps and Bake's dilator

→ Sure CBD clearance → Primary closure of CBD

→ Not sure about CBD clearance →

1. T tube insertion
2. Open sphincteroplasty
3. Choledochoduodenostomy (not choledochojejunostomy)

Note that cholecystectomy is to be done irrespective of presence or absence of stones in GB (since GB is the source of stones).

- Treatment protocol of periampullary carcinoma:

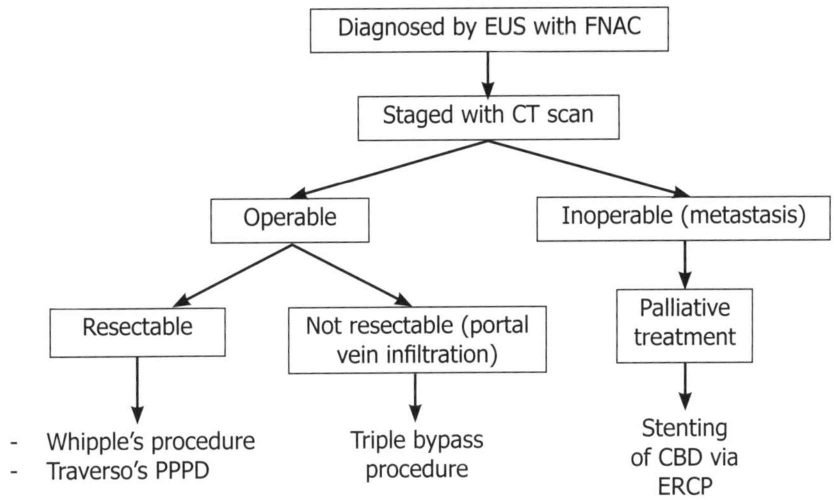

❖ ERCP (endoscopic retrograde cholangiopancreatography):

- Procedure: As the name suggests, 'endoscopic' means via an endoscope; 'retrograde' means opposite the bile flow (i.e. duodenum → CBD); 'cholangiopancreato' means biliary tree and pancreatic duct systems; and 'graphy' means imaging

  Side viewing endoscope passed till ampulla of vater
  ↓
  Cannula (not endoscope) passed into the biliary tree via ampulla
  ↓
  Dye injected
  ↓
  Images taken

- It is both diagnostic as well as therapeutic modality
- Stones not removed by ERCP:
  1. Stones >1.5 cm size
  2. Stones high up in the biliary tree
  3. Multiple stones

❖ Concept of T-tube:

- A T-tube is put in CBD when there is doubt about CBD clearance after choledochotomy

↓

A cholangiogram is taken after 10 days

↓

If cholangiogram shows clear CBD, T-tube is removed

↓

But if cholangiogram shows residual stones, either:

1. ERCP is done (preferred)
2. T-tube is left in place for 4 - 6 weeks for the tract to mature and stones are then removed via the tract (BURHENNE TECHNIQUE) (obsolete)

- Method of removal: Simply pull out the T-tube (fistula closes by itself as the normal passage opens)

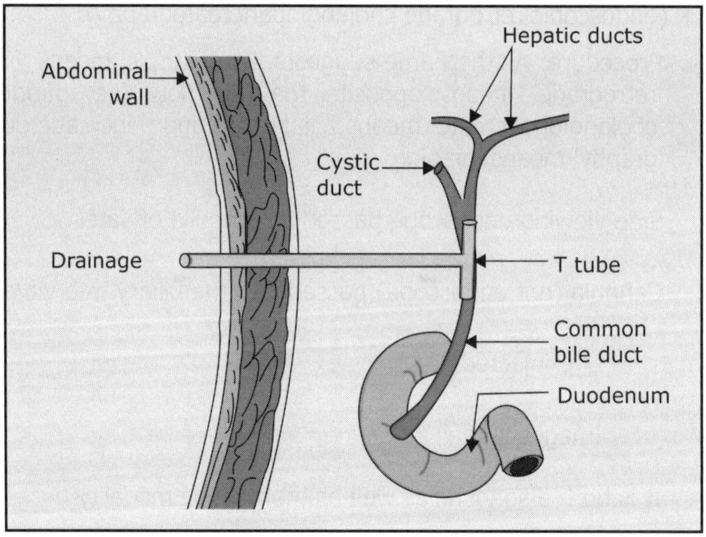

Fig. 18.3: T-tube (in situ)

- Whipple's procedure (pancreaticoduodenectomy):
  - Indication: Periampullary carcinoma
  - Resection of:
    1. Distal stomach
    2. Duodenum
    3. Proximal jejunum (till mobile part of jejunum)
    4. Head of pancreas
    5. CBD
    6. GB
    7. Lymph nodes and lymphatics
  - With following anastomosis:
    1. Pancreatico-jejunostomy (PJ)
    2. Choledocho-jejunostomy (CJ)
    3. Gastro-jejunostomy (GJ)
  - Reason for removal of duodenum in carcinoma of pancreas: Both duodenum and head of pancreas share COMMON blood supply from pancreaticoduodenal arteries → removal of either one can lead to gangrene of other structure
  - Reasons for removal of GB:
    1. GB functions because of sphincter of Oddi (which is removed in Whipple's procedure)
    2. No CCK hormone (due to duodenectomy) → no contractions of GB → stasis → predisposes to gallstones

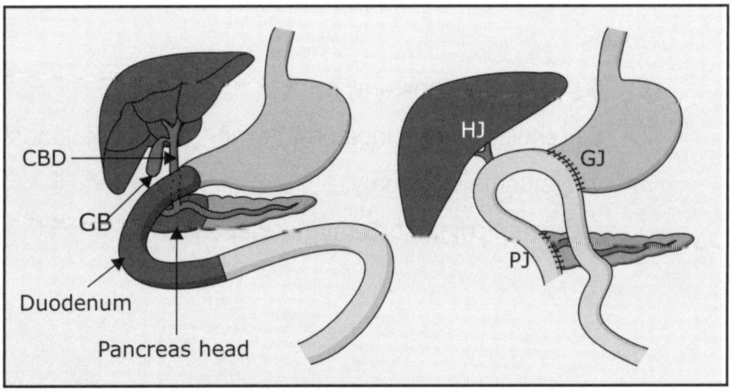

Fig. 18.4: Whipple's surgery

❖ Traverso's pylorus preserving pancreaticoduodenectomy (PPPD):

- Indication: Periampullary carcinoma
- Similar to Whipple's procedure but with sparing of pylorus (by transecting duodenum 2 cm distal to pylorus)

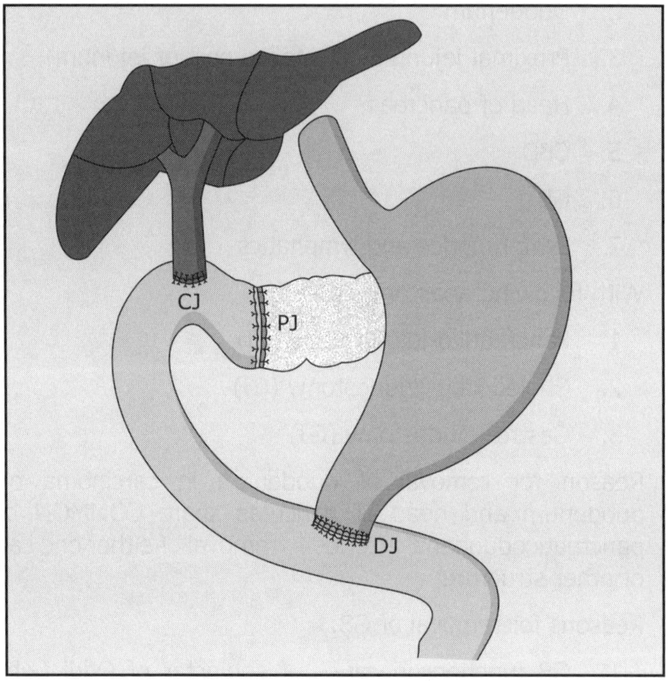

Fig. 18.5: Traverso's PPPD

❖ Triple bypass procedure:

- Indication: Unresectable periampullary carcinoma
- Involves:
  1. GJ (gastrojejunostomy)
  2. CJ (choledochojejunostomy) or HJ (hepaticojejunostomy)
  3. JJ (jejunojejunostomy)

  (pancreaticojejunostomy not needed)

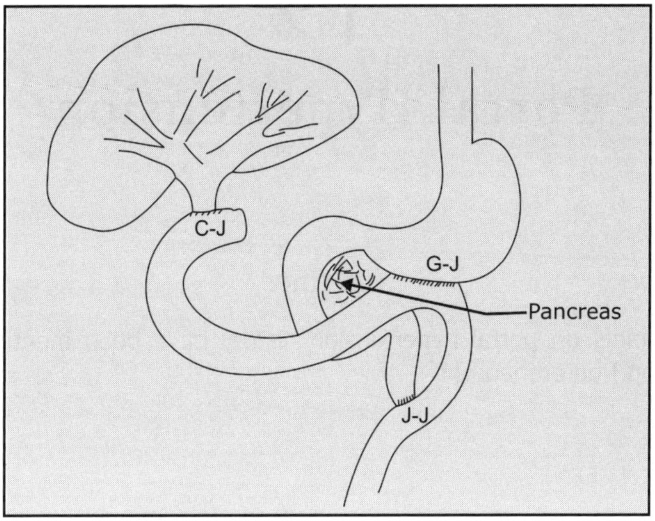

Fig. 18.6: Triple bypass procedure

19

Portal Hypertension

HISTORY

[Only additional points on portal hypertension history have been mentioned below. Refer Chapter 1 in Section I beforehand.]

- Patient profile:
    1. Age:
        - Children and adolescents: EHPVO
        - Adults (20 - 40 years): NCPF
        - Adults (>40 years): Cirrhosis, cardiac failure
    2. Sex: M > F
    3. Occupation: Not contributory
    4. Residence: Not contributory
    5. Religion: Not contributory
- Chief complaints:
    1. Hematemesis (most common complaint)
    2. Distension of abdomen
    3. Melena
    4. Bleeding P/R (i.e. hematochezia)
    5. Lump in abdomen
- HOPI:
    - ❖ Symptoms:
        1. Hematemesis:
            - Painless/painful
            - Number of episodes

- Color:
  i. Bright red: Indicates acute bleeding
  ii. Coffee brown: It is due to production of acid hematin from hemoglobin by action of gastric acid. Indicates that bleeding is not acute.
  iii. Duodenal causes of hematemesis have associated bilious vomiting (green color)
- Quantity
- Projectile/non-projectile
- Whether mixed with food particles

> Projectile vomiting indicates contents below the lower esophageal sphincter (since force is required to overcome its resistance) or raised ICT.
>
> Non-projectile vomiting is seen if the contents are above the LES and in CNS causes of vomiting.

2. Distension of abdomen:
   - Gradual or sudden
   - Whether associated with abdominal pain, vomiting, constipation (to rule out intestinal obstruction)
3. Melena: (Refer Chapter 9 in Section IV for details.)
   - Black, tarry, foul smelling, sticky stools
4. Bleeding P/R: (Refer Chapter 9 in Section IV for details.)
   - Painful/painless (painless bleeding is present in anorectal varices)
   - With or without passage of stools
   - Bright red blood/altered color
5. Lump in abdomen:
   - It is due to splenomegaly
   - Refer Chapter 9 in Section IV for details on lump/swelling.

> Generally melena occurs 2 days after hematemesis (transit time of blood), simultaneous occurrence suggests that initially bleeding was too little to cause hematemesis.

- ❖ Etiology:

First rule out other common causes of hematemesis
↓
Then rule out hepatic, pre-hepatic and post-hepatic causes of portal hypertension

- Common causes of hematemesis:
    1. Acid peptic disease: H/o burning pain in abdomen relieved by antacids or h/o ingestion of NSAIDS
    2. Mallory Weiss tear: H/o repeated episodes of vomiting and retching prior to hematemesis
    3. Gastric cancer: H/o anorexia, loss of weight associated with melena, asthenia, or fatigue (5 As of stomach cancer)
- Common hepatic causes of portal hypertension:
    1. Alcoholic cirrhosis: H/o jaundice and alcohol consumption
    2. Infective hepatitis: H/o blood transfusion, high-risk behavior or jaundice associated with pain in abdomen, fever, and malaise
    3. Drug induced hepatitis: H/o ingestion of drugs for any disease
- Common pre-hepatic causes of portal hypertension:
    1. Portal vein thrombosis: H/o stroke, heart attack, PVD, DVT, OC pills consumption (for hypercoagulable states)
    2. Neonatal umbilical sepsis: H/o umbilical catheterization or gastroenteritis in neonates
    3. Pancreatitis: H/o epigastric pain radiating to the back, relieved on bending forwards
    4. Portal pyemia: H/o high-grade fever with chills associated with recent pain in abdomen (appendicitis, enteritis, etc.)
- Common post-hepatic causes of portal hypertension:
    1. Cardiac failure: H/o chest pain associated with breathlessness and pedal edema
    2. Budd-Chiari syndrome: H/o sudden distension of abdomen associated with abdominal pain

- ❖ Complications:
    1. Spontaneous bacterial peritonitis (SBP): H/o fever and pain associated with generalized distension of abdomen
    2. Hypotension: H/o fainting or dizziness

3. Hypersplenism: H/o fatigue, pedal edema or bleeding from any site
4. Failure to thrive (for EHPVO)
5. Liver cell failure: History for liver status should be taken separately

❖ Treatment taken:
  - Blood transfusion for hematemesis
  - Sclerotherapy/band ligation of esophageal varices
  - Treatment for liver disease (if any)
  - Tapping of ascites

- History for liver status:
  - Jaundice, abdominal distension
  - Easy bruisability, petechiae, bleeding from any natural orifice
  - Malaise, edema feet, foul breath
  - Loss of axillary/pubic hair
  - Inversion of sleep rhythm associated with impaired consciousness or confusion (do not forget to ask this for hepatic encephalopathy)
- Past history: As usual + similar illness in past
- Personal history:
  - Bowel: Altered bowel habits, bleeding P/R, melena
  - Sleep: Inversion of sleep rhythm (hepatic encephalopathy)
  - Addictions: Need to be mentioned in h/o etiology
  - Appetite: Reduced
- Family history:
  - h/o similar illness in the family (Wilson's disease)

GENERAL EXAMINATION

[Only additional points on portal hypertension case general examination have been mentioned below. Refer Chapter 2 in Section I beforehand.]

- Consciousness: Affected in hepatic encephalopathy, hypotension (due to third space loss)
- Built and nourishment: Wasting is seen in liver disease
- Temperature: High-grade fever in SBP
- Pulse: May be bradycardia (if the patient is on beta blocker prophylaxis for varices)

- BP: May be hypotensive (third space loss)
- JVP: Elevated in cardiac cirrhosis
- Pallor: Seen in liver disease
- Edema: Seen in liver disease, cardiac cirrhosis
- Icterus: Refer Chapter 2 in Section I for details
- Cyanosis: May be seen in hepatopulmonary syndrome
- Skin: Petechiae (liver cell failure)
- Others: SIGNS OF LIVER CELL FAILURE (refer to chapter 6, Section II for details)
- Treatment taken: Tap mark (tapping of ascites)

LOCAL EXAMINATION

- Always say this first:
    1. Examined with due consent
    2. Under adequate illumination
    3. Exposure from nipple to knees
    4. In supine and standing positions
    5. In presence of female attendant (for female patients)
- Inspection: (Refer Chapter 6 in Section II for proforma and details.)
    1. Shape/contour: Distended abdomen
    2. Symmetry
    3. Umbilicus: Flat or everted, smiling (transversely stretched), distance from umbilicus to xiphoid is more than distance from umbilicus to pubic symphysis (due to ascites)
    4. Movements: Absent movements (still abdomen) suggests SBP
    5. Pulsations
    6. Peristalsis
    7. Skin: Tense shiny skin due to distension
    8. Scars
    9. Sinuses

10. Dilated veins:
    - Caput medusae, SVC/IVC obstruction
    - Have to be examined in STANDING position
11. Hernial orifices + divarication of recti

    External genitalia: Testicular atrophy in liver cell failure

    Renal angle fullness

    Supraclavicular fossa

    [These four points are to be examined in all abdominal cases.]

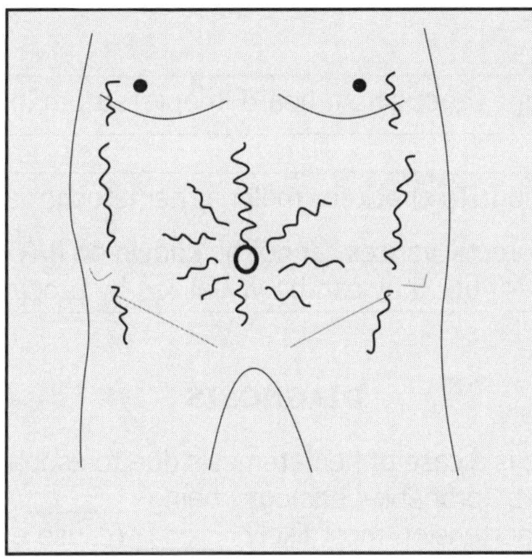

Fig. 19.1: Dilated veins over abdominal wall

- Palpation: (Refer Chapter 6 in Section II for proforma and details.)

  Always say this first on palpation:
  1. Inspectory findings confirmed
  2. No local rise of temperature
  3. Tenderness - yes or no

  - Superficial palpation: Local rise of temperature, tenderness, and guarding/rigidity suggests SBP
  - Deep palpation: Splenomegaly may be present (Refer Chapter 9 in Section IV for details.)
  - Measurements
- Percussion: (Refer Chapter 6 in Section II for proforma and details.)
  - Of free fluid
  - Of organs

More you go from right to left according to causes of portal hypertension, more is splenomegaly (i.e. sinistral portal hypertension will have maximum splenomegaly). More you go from left to right according to causes of portal hypertension, more is ascites (i.e. post-hepatic causes will present with ascites rather than splenomegaly).

- Auscultation:
  - Peristalsis
  - Venous hum

Canaway's sign: Venous hum heard in epigastrium in splenic vein thrombosis

P/R examination: To check for melena, hematochezia (Note that anorectal varices cannot be known on P/R examination unless they are thrombosed, but they can be visualized by proctoscopy.)

DIAGNOSIS

_____ year old male/female is a case of hematemesis due to esophageal varices and _______ (ascites/splenomegaly/both), probable etiology being ______ (pre-hepatic/hepatic/post-hepatic) cause of portal hypertension most likely ______ (cause e.g. cirrhosis) with no other complications and no signs of liver cell failure with approximate Child–Pugh score being class ___ (A, B, C)

(Refer discussion part below for Child-Pugh score.)

DISCUSSION

- Portal hypertension: Portal pressure >10 mmHg (25 cm of saline)

  (Normal portal pressure: 5 - 10 mmHg)

Variceal formation occurs when portal pressure is >10 mmHg. Variceal bleeding occurs when portal pressure is >12 mmHg.

HVPG (hepatic venous pressure gradient) represents the pressure in the hepatic sinusoids and portal vein and is a measure of portal venous pressure.

- Anatomy:
  - Portal venous system does not have valves
  - Portal vein supplies 75% of blood and 72% of oxygen supply to liver
  - Formation of portal vein: Union of SMV and splenic vein

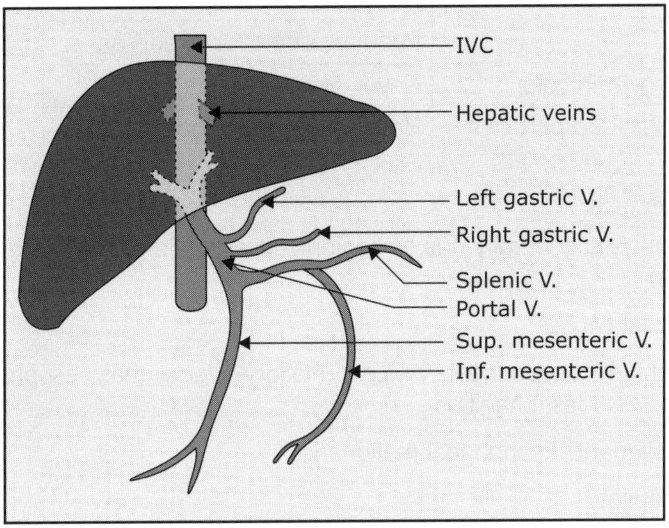

Fig. 19.2: Portal venous system

- Sites of porto-systemic anastomosis:

Location	Portal component	Systemic component
Esophageal varices	Left gastric vein (mainly by anterior branch i.e. coronary vein)	Azygous and accessory hemiazygous vein
Anorectal varices	Superior rectal vein	Middle and inferior rectal veins
Umbilicus (caput medusae)	Left branch of portal vein (paraumbilical veins)	Superficial epigastric veins (veins of anterior abdominal wall)
Retroperitoneum	Colic and omental veins	Retroperitoneal veins
Bare area of liver	Hepatic venules (right branch of portal vein)	Phrenic and intercostal veins
Liver	Patent ductus venosus	IVC
Stoma site	Tributaries of superior and inferior mesenteric veins	Veins of anterior abdominal wall

(Approximately 30% of patients with compensated cirrhosis and 60% of patients with decompensated cirrhosis have esophageal varices. One third of all patients with varices will experience variceal bleeding.)

- Infection of portal vein is called PYLEPHLEBITIS
- Difference between hematemesis and hemoptysis:

Hematemesis	Hemoptysis
Profuse	Not profuse
	Requires effort for expulsion
Usually coffee brown in color	Never coffee brown in color
Can be mixed with food particles	Never mixed with food particles

- Causes of hematemesis:
  (Painful hematemesis is generally due to benign causes while painless is generally due to malignant causes)
  1. Esophageal causes:
     i. Benign: Esophageal varices, Mallory–Weiss tear, esophageal rupture, esophagitis
     ii. Malignant: Esophageal malignancy
  2. Gastric causes:
     i. Benign: Gastric ulcer, erosive gastritis, Dieulafoy's lesion, GAVE
     ii. Malignant: Gastric malignancy
  3. Duodenal causes:
     i. Benign: Duodenal ulcer, erosions
     ii. Malignant: Duodenal malignancy
  4. Others:
     - Blood dyscrasias
     - Anticoagulant therapy
     - Uremia
     - Vasculitis
     - Spurious hematemesis (swallowed nose bleed)

     (most common cause is peptic ulcer)
- Etiology of portal hypertension:
  - Pre-sinusoidal causes:
    1. Pre-hepatic causes (sinistral portal hypertension):
       a. Portal vein/splenic vein thrombosis:
          - Neonatal sepsis
          - Umbilical vein catheterization

        - Appendicitis (causes pylephlebitis)
        - Necrotizing enterocolitis (causes pylephlebitis)
        - Hypercoagulable states
        - Chronic dehydration
      b. Splenic AV fistula
      c. Pancreatitis
      d. Pancreatic malignancy
    2. Intrahepatic causes:
      a. Congenital hepatic fibrosis
      b. Idiopathic portal fibrosis
      c. Myeloproliferative disorder
      d. Sarcoidosis
      e. Schistosomiasis
      f. Nodular reactive hyperplasia
- Sinusoidal causes (intrahepatic causes only): Cirrhosis
      a. Alcoholism
      b. Post-infectious
      c. PBC
      d. Autoimmune hepatitis
      e. PSC
- Post-sinusoidal causes:
      1. Intrahepatic causes:
        a. Vascular occlusive disease
      2. Post-hepatic causes:
        a. Budd-Chiari syndrome
        b. Cardiac failure
        c. IVC web

Left-sided portal hypertension (extrahepatic pre-sinusoidal etiology) is called as SINISTRAL portal hypertension.

- Complications of portal hypertension:
  1. Ascites:
     - SBP
     - Hypotension (third space loss)

2. Congestive splenomegaly
3. Secondary hypersplenism: Pancytopenia
4. Opening up of portosystemic shunts: GI bleed
   - Esophageal varices
   - Anorectal varices
5. Failure to thrive (in EHPVO)
6. Hepatocellular failure (in post-hepatic cause)
7. Hepatic encephalopathy: Refer Chapter 6 in Section II for details.

Portal hypertension can rarely cause OJ called as 'portal biliopathy.'

- Spleen might shrink in size after a bout of hematemesis (due to decrease in portal pressure which reduces congestion).

Triad of portal hypertension: Splenomegaly, ascites, varices Triad of Budd-Chiari syndrome: Abdominal pain, ascites, hepatomegaly

- Budd-Chiari syndrome:
  - Obstruction of hepatic venous outflow
  - Most important feature of Budd-Chiari syndrome: Acute onset ascites
  - Most effective therapy: Side to side porto-caval shunt surgery

  (Note that in veno-occlusive disease, hepatic venous outflow obstruction occurs from diffuse involvement of hepatic venules; whereas in Budd–Chiari syndrome, outflow obstruction is due to involvement of major hepatic veins or hepatic portion of IVC.)

- Cruveilhier–Baumgarten syndrome: Distension of umbilical or paraumbilical veins with abdominal wall bruit and palpable thrill in a case of portal hypertension with splenomegaly, hypersplenism, and varices with normal or small liver

- Scores to assess liver status (mainly used in reference to liver transplantation):
  1. Child-Pugh score (Child-Turcotte-Pugh score)
  2. MELD score (Model for End Stage Liver Disease)
  3. PELD score (Pediatric End-stage Liver Disease)

- Child-Pugh score:

Criteria	Points		
	1	2	3
Hepatic encephalopathy	Absent	Moderate	Advanced
Ascites	Absent	Slight or controlled	Severe or refractory
Albumin (g/dL)	>3.5	2.8-3.5	<2.8
Bilirubin (mg/dL)	<2	2-3	>3
Prothrombin time (prolonged) (sec)	<4	4-6	>6

APPROXIMATE Child–Pugh score can also be known CLINICALLY:

Criteria	Points		
	1	2	3
Hepatic encephalopathy	Absent	Grade 1 or 2	Grade 3 or 4
Ascites	Absent	Shifting dullness/ horse shoe dullness +ve and controlled	Fluid thrill +ve or refractory
Albumin (g/dL)	No edema	–	Anasarca
Bilirubin (mg/dL)	No jaundice	Only yellowing of sclera	Yellowing of other sites too
Prothrombin time (prolonged) (sec)	No bleeding	–	Bleeding from natural orifices/ petechiae

Classification according to Child–Pugh score:

1. Class A: 5-6 points (well compensated liver disease)
2. Class B: 7-9 points (significant functional impairment)
3. Class C: 10-15 points (decompensated liver disease)

(note that minimum score is 5)

- Theories of variceal bleed:
  1. Erosion by acid
  2. Explosion

- Theories of ascites:
    1. Overfill theory: Portal pooling of blood causes renal hypoperfusion leading to activation of RAAS
    2. Underfill theory: Increased sodium retention causes volume overload
    3. Hypoalbuminemia
    4. Weeping liver (lymphatic ooze from liver surface)
    5. Hyperaldosteronism

MANAGEMENT

MANAGEMENT OF ACUTE VARICEAL BLEEDING

- Management protocol of acute variceal bleed:

Stabilize the patient

↓

ABCDE

Secure 2 large bore i.v. lines with RL as the resuscitation fluid of choice

↓

Put Ryle's tube (for conforming hematemesis and to give saline washes)

↓

Urgent blood investigations:

1. Hb/CBC with hematocrit (pancytopenia)
2. LFTs (liver status)
3. RFTs (for prerenal failure)
4. Blood grouping and cross matching (for blood transfusion if required)

↓

Put central line to measure CVP if required

↓

Start pharmacotherapy for controlling bleed (cause splanchnic vasoconstriction to decrease portal pressure)

1. Terlipressin (1 mg 8 hourly) is better than vasopressin (4 mg bolus followed by 1 - 2 mg every 6 hourly)
2. Somatostatin (250 μg/h drip)
3. Octreotide (50 μg bolus followed by 50 μg/h)

↓

Antacid drip (PPI drip)

↓

↓

UGI scopy (diagnostic + therapeutic)

1. Band ligation
2. Sclerotherapy
3. Cyanoacrylate glue

→ **Bleeding stopped**

↓

Watch for 48 hours and continue pharmacotherapy

↓

Beta blockers prophylaxis on discharge

→ **Bleeding not stopped**

↓

Balloon tamponade by SB tube or Minnesota tube

↓

Remove tube

↓

If rebleeds

↓

Interventions:

1. TIPS
2. Surgical devascularization
3. Shunt surgery

↓

If TIPS is the first procedure

→ **TIPS successful**

- → **Child score is A or early B** → Chronic endotherapy
- → **Child score is late B or C** → Liver transplant

→ **TIPS fails**

↓

Surgical devascularization (if expertise is available, shunt surgery can be done in the same setting)

- ❖ Secondary prophylaxis (to prevent rebleed) is given by propranolol (dose is titrated to achieve SBP around 100–110 mmHg and pulse 60–65 bpm, usually 40–60 mg/day)
- ❖ UGI scopy for variceal bleed:
  - Diagnostic as well as therapeutic

- Features of impending variceal bleed:
    1. Cherry red spot
    2. Varix on varix appearance
    3. Large varix
- Feature of already bled varix: Platelet plug (platelet nipple)
- Aim: To eradicate the varices so as to prevent morbidity/mortality from UGI bleed
- Therapeutic techniques:
    1. Sclerotherapy/EST (endoscopic sclerotherapy):
        - Principle: Causes aseptic inflammation and thrombosis of veins
        - Sclerosants used: Polidocanol, ethanolamine, sodium tetradecyl sulphate
        - Types:
            a. Intra-variceal: In acute bleeding
            b. Peri-variceal: In follow-up cases
            c. Combined
        - Disadvantage: Sclerotherapy cannot be done all around the circumference (causes stricture)
        - Indication: Massively bleeding varices
    2. Band ligation/EVL (endoscopic variceal ligation):
        - Technique: Placement of elastic O-ring ligatures, causing strangulation of the varix. Ligation should begin at most distal variceal columns in the esophagus just above the esophago-gastric junction.
        - Indication: Varices with no active bleed/little bleed
    3. Cyanoacrylate glue: For gastric and junctional varices

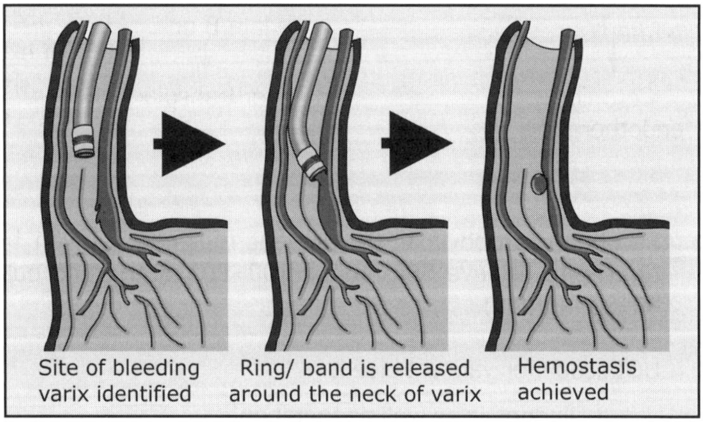

Fig. 19.3: Endoscopic variceal band ligation

❖ SB tube (Sengstaken–Blakemore tube):

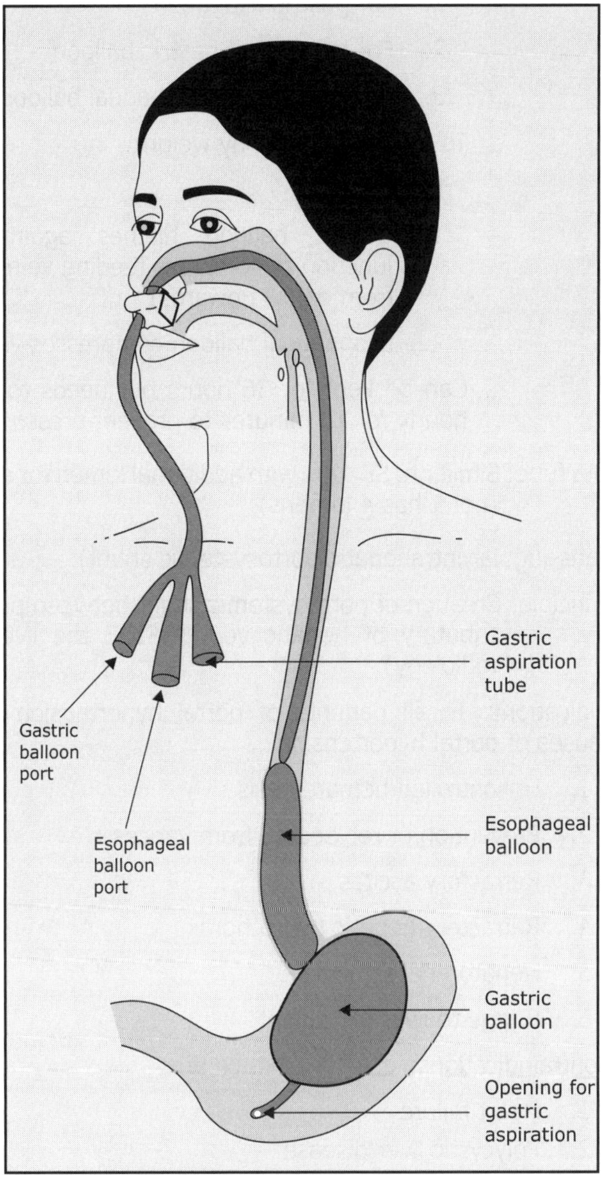

Fig. 19.4: Sengstaken-Blakemore tube

- Two balloons:
    1. Gastric balloon: To be inflated before esophageal balloon by saline (250-300 cc)
    2. Esophageal balloon: To be inflated by air (50 cc) only if gastric balloon fails to stop bleeding

- Three lumens:
    1. For gastric aspiration
    2. For inflation of gastric balloon
    3. For inflation of esophageal balloon
- To be kept hitched by weight
- Principle:
    1. Gastric balloon hitches against esophago-gastric junction to compress feeding veins (since blood flow is from below upwards)
    2. Esophageal balloon compresses varices directly
- Can be kept for 36 hours but needs to be deflated every 6 hourly for 15 minutes to prevent pressure necrosis

❖ Minnesota tube: Similar to SB tube with additional lumen for esophageal aspiration (i.e. it has 4 lumens)

❖ TIPS (trans-jugular intrahepatic portosystemic shunt):

- Principle: Creation of portosystemic shunt between portal vein branch and tributary of hepatic vein INSIDE the liver (by interventional radiology)
- Indications: In all patients of portal hypertension EXCEPT pre-hepatic causes of portal hypertension
    1. Uncontrolled hematemesis
    2. Prevention of rebleeding from varices
    3. Refractory ascites
    4. Refractory hepatic hydrothorax
    5. Hepatorenal syndrome
    6. Bridge to liver transplant
- Contraindications:
    1. Heart failure
    2. Polycystic liver disease
    3. Uncontrolled septicemia
    4. Hepatopulmonary syndrome
    5. Hepatic encephalopathy
    6. Pre-hepatic portal hypertension
- Disadvantages:
    1. Restenosis: Short life span of stent (generally one year)
    2. Hepatic encephalopathy is worsened (due to shunting of ammonia directly in systemic circulation)

- Surgical devascularization:
  - Does not decrease portal pressure (so shunt surgery is essential)
  - Types:
    1. TAGEO (trans-abdominal gastroesophageal devascularization) + EGS (esophageal gastric stapling): Supply of upper two-thirds of stomach and 7 cm of lower esophagus is hampered, preferred method
    2. Esophageal transection: Distal esophagus is transected (to break the continuity of blood column) and sutured/stapled back together after ligation of varices
    3. Borema and Crile's procedure
    4. Milne Walker's esophageal mucosal transection
    5. GE junction devascularization: Sugiura procedure

- Shunt surgery:
  - Decreases portal pressure
  - Indications:
    1. MELD score <15
    2. Contraindications to liver transplant
    3. Limited access to TIPS therapy
  - Types:
    1. Non-selective shunts:
       a. Side-to-side portocaval shunt: Preferred in Budd–Chiari syndrome
       b. End-to-side portocaval shunt: High risk of hepatic encephalopathy
       c. Mesocaval shunt
       d. Proximal splenorenal shunt (Linton's shunt): Preferred in EHPVO
    2. Selective shunts:
       a. Distal splenorenal shunts (Warren's shunt)
       b. Inokuchi shunt

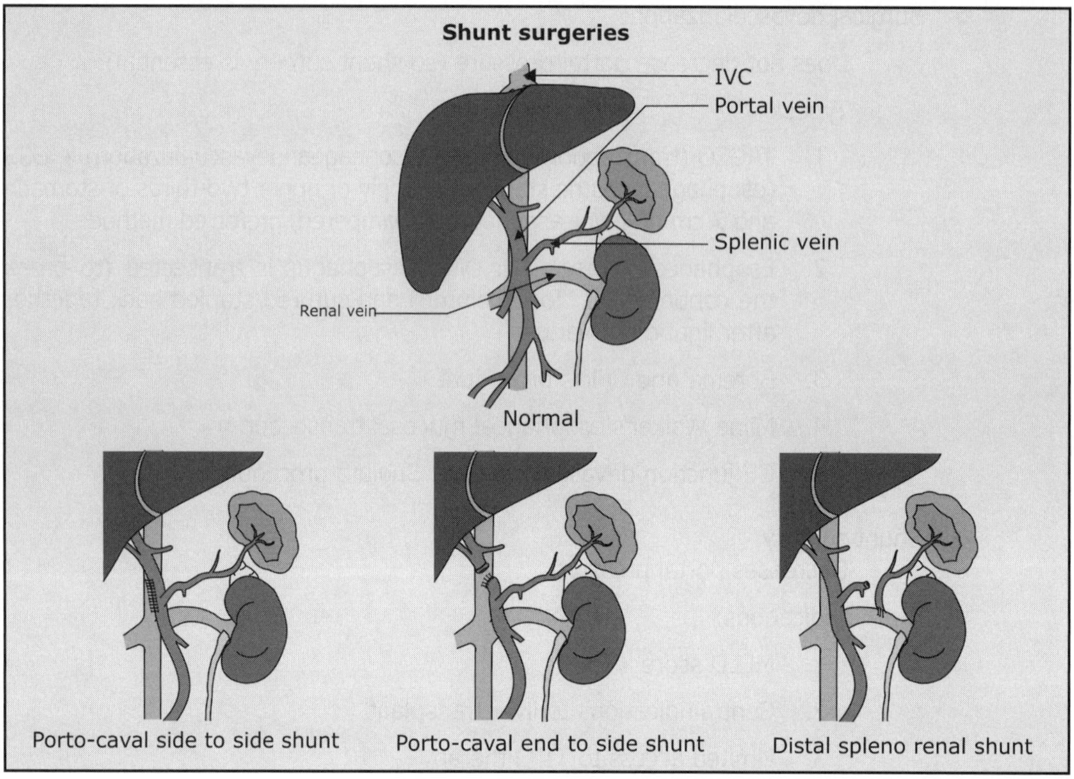

Fig. 19.5: Shunt surgeries

MANAGEMENT OF
PORTAL HYPERTENSION (without active variceal bleeding)

- Investigations:
  1. Blood investigations:
     a. Hb/CBC: Anemia due to hemorrhage, pancytopenia in hypersplenism
     b. LFTs: For liver status
     c. RFTs
  2. For source of bleeding:
     a. UGI scopy
     b. Proctoscopy
  3. For etiology of portal hypertension:
     a. Doppler/duplex scan
     b. USG abdomen
     c. CT abdomen (triple phase): Arterial phase, venous phase, portal phase
  4. For ascites: Ascitic tap (cell count, SAAG)

- Treatment:
  - General care:
    1. Adequate nutrition
    2. Vitamin K 10 mg i.m. for 5 days
  - Management of esophageal varices: Refer earlier management part
  - Management of ascites:
    1. Salt restriction
    2. Spironolactone, furosemide
    3. Therapeutic tapping (with albumin infusion)
  - Management of hepatic encephalopathy:
    1. Acute encephalopathy:
       a. Oral cleansing of clots (via RT)
       b. Rectal cleansing of clots (enema)
       c. Lactulose
       d. Oral neomycin/rifaximin
       e. Flumazenil
    2. Chronic encephalopathy:
       a. Low-protein diet
       b. Lactulose
       c. Neomycin/rifaximin
       d. Ion exchange resins
  - Management of etiology:
    1. Pre-hepatic cause:
       a. Conservative management: If patient can follow for chronic endoscopic therapy
       b. Shunt surgery: If patient cannot follow-up for chronic endoscopic therapy
    2. Hepatic cause (cirrhosis):
       a. Child score A or early B: Chronic endotherapy/shunt surgery
       b. Child score late B or C: Liver transplant
    3. Post-hepatic cause:
       a. Conservative management
       b. For IVC thrombus: Anticoagulation

20

Stoma

(History taking and examination of stoma follows a different pattern from rest of the cases)

HISTORY

- Patient profile:

  Say "Name, age, sex, address, occupation, underwent _____ (emergency/elective) stoma creation _____ months (duration) back due to _____ (reason) [e.g. left hemicolectomy with most likely etiology being carcinoma of the colon]

  If patient does not know the reason for stoma creation → say "for symptoms being _______ suggestive of _______(etiology)"

  Always keep brief history about primary disease ready to answer leading questions from examiner, for example:

  - Ileocecal tuberculosis (TB): H/o TB
  - Intussusception: H/o recurrent right lower abdominal pain
  - Left-sided carcinoma of colon: Bleeding per rectum
  - Right-sided carcinoma of colon: Features of intestinal obstruction
  - Inflammatory bowel disease (UC and Crohn's disease): Abdominal pain, vomiting, diarrhea associated with bleeding PR or tenesmus

- H/O stoma:

  1. Site
  2. Closure planned or not (if yes, when)

- H/O stools:

  1. Volume
  2. Frequency
  3. Color
  4. Consistency

- H/O appliance:
  1. One piece or two piece
  2. Disposable/non-disposable

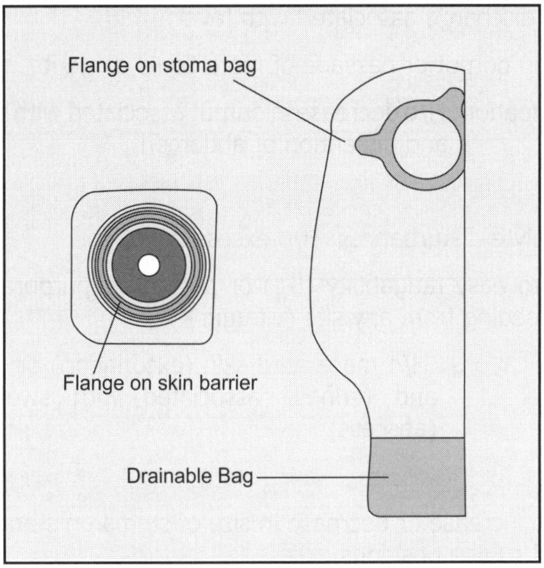

Fig. 20.1: Two-piece stoma bag

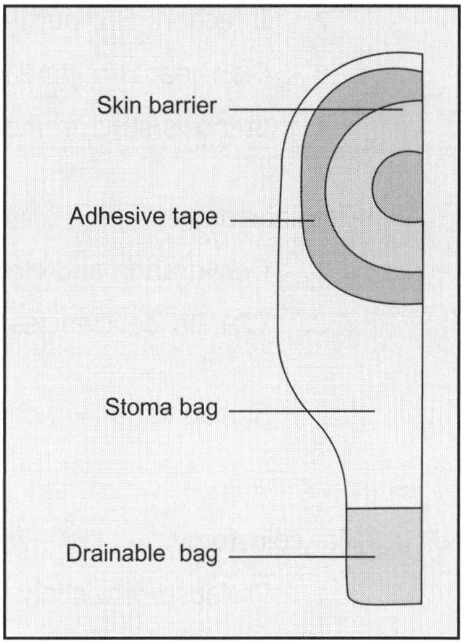

Fig. 20.2: One-piece stoma bag

- H/O care:
  1. Appliance:
     i. How often do you change?
     ii. Who changes it?
     iii. Whether diary maintained or not?
  2. Skin:
     i. Any excoriation?
     ii. Ointments/jellies used?
  3. Colostomy irrigation (if done):
     i. Time of day when done?
     ii. When was it started (after stoma creation)?
     iii. Time gap after which stools are passed?
  4. Attended any stoma clinics?
  5. Social (psychological): (To enquire about depression)
     i. How do you go to work?
     ii. How do you feel about interacting in society?
  6. Diet

- H/O complications:
  - Common complications:
    1. Mucosal dryness and ulceration: H/o bleeding
    2. Infection: H/o purulent discharge associated with fever
    3. Diarrhea: H/o increase in output or passage of more liquid contents
    4. Stenosis/stricture/constipation: H/o decrease in output associated with pain and distention of abdomen
  - For ileostomy:
    1. Dehydration and electrolyte disturbances: H/o excess thirst
    2. Vitamin deficiencies: H/o easy fatigability (B_{12}) or petechiae, purpura, or bleeding from any site (vitamin K)
    3. Surrounding skin complications: H/o macerated skin (excoriation) or pain and redness associated with swelling (abscess)
  - For colostomy:
    1. Prolapse/retraction: H/o increase or decrease in size of stoma on standing and supine positions
- Past history/personal history/family history/menstrual history: To be commented upon only if it contributes to etiology or will affect further management

  (All addictions have to be mentioned)

GENERAL EXAMINATION

(Only additional points on stoma case general examination have been mentioned below. Refer Chapter 2 in Section I beforehand.)

- Non-cooperative patient: May indicate depression
- Built and nourishment: Malnutrition (can be due to effect or cause of stoma e.g. TB, malignancy, etc.)
- Temperature: Fever in case of infection or abscess
- Pallor: Anemia in vitamin B_{12} deficiency following ileostomy
- Clubbing: Ulcerative colitis and Crohn's disease
- Signs of fluid and electrolyte imbalance (dehydration)

LOCAL EXAMINATION

- Always say this first:
    1. Examined with due consent
    2. Under adequate illumination
    3. Exposure from nipple to knees
    4. In standing as well as supine position
    5. In presence of female attendant (for female patients)

  Follow the sequence for both inspection and palpation:
  (either inside out or outside inwards)

Stoma
↓
Mucosa
↓
Wall of stoma
↓
Anastomosis with skin (edge)
↓
Surrounding skin
↓
Abdominal examination (separately)

- Inspection:
    - ❖ Stoma:
        1. Type:
            - i. Loop/end/double barrel/spectacle
            - ii. Colostomy/ileostomy (justify this by describing the following points)
        2. Flushed or pouting
        3. Site: RIF/LIF/LHC/RHC, etc.
        4. Distance from umbilicus, ASIS, or other bony point
        5. Opening(s) → 1 or 2
    - ❖ Mucosa:
        1. Color: Pink/pale/dusky (ischemic)/black (gangrene)
        2. Signs of inflammation/dry
        3. Bleeding, discharge (type, color)

- ❖ Wall of stoma:
  1. Visible impulse on cough: Normally present
  2. Protrusion/retraction of stoma on standing or supine position
- ❖ Anastomosis with skin:
  1. Discharge (if any)
  2. Signs of inflammation
- ❖ Surrounding skin:
  1. Signs of inflammation
  2. Sinuses
  3. Excoriation (occurs due to irritation by contents of stoma)

- Palpation: (Per-stomal examination should be carried out by gloved and well lubricated finger)

  Always say this first on palpation:
  1. Inspectory findings confirmed
  2. No local rise of temperature
  3. Tenderness - yes or no

  - ❖ Stoma:
    1. End/loop stoma
    2. Viability: Checked by TUBE TEST (see Discussion part below)
  - ❖ Mucosa:
    1. Dry (sticks to the finger)/edematous
    2. Bleeding
  - ❖ Wall of stoma:
    1. Palpable impulse on cough
    2. Stenosis/stricture
    3. Impaction
  - ❖ Anastomosis with skin:
    1. Warmth
    2. Tenderness
  - ❖ Surrounding skin:
    1. Warmth
    2. Tenderness
    3. Swelling (for abscess)

- Bag/appliance:
  1. Type:
     i. One piece/two piece
     ii. Disposable/non-disposable
     iii. Transparent/opaque
  2. Contents: Empty or filled (color, consistency, quantity)

  > Do not forget to examine the appliance.

- Abdominal examination: (Refer Chapter 9 in Section IV for more details.)
  - Distension
  - Scar (of previous surgery): Gives an idea about the etiology of stoma creation
  - Guarding/rigidity
  - Tenderness
  - Hernial orifices, external genitalia, renal angle fullness, supraclavicular fullness
  - Tympanic/dull note

  > Do not forget to mention the laparotomy scar and drains.

- P/R examination:
  1. Absence/presence of anal opening
  2. Scars in anal region (of previous surgery)
  3. Discharge of mucus
  4. Impacted feces

  > Anal opening is absent in cases of APR (done for rectal carcinoma).

DIAGNOSIS

________ (temporary/permanent), _______ (loop/end), __________ (ileostomy/colostomy), complicated/non-complicated done due to______ (cause) and is well taken care of

DISCUSSION

(Only relevant stomas, i.e. ileostomy and colostomy are discussed here)

- Definition: Temporary or permanent surgical exteriorization of a hollow organ to serve part or total of its function
- Person having stoma is called as 'ostomate'

- Tube test (to check viability of stoma): Insert test tube in stoma and project light → note the color of mucosa (pink, dusky, black)

> Normal output of
> - Early postoperative ileostomy: 1000-1800 mL
> - Fully adapted ileostomy: 800-1000 mL
> - Colostomy: 300-700 mL

- According to the organ, stoma can be classified as:
  1. GI tract: Esophagostomy, gastrostomy, jejunostomy, etc.
  2. Biliary tract: Cholecystostomy
  3. Urinary tract: Nephrostomy, ureterostomy, cystostomy, urethrostomy
- Incidence of stoma: (According to western data)
  - Ileostomy > colostomy
  - Ileostomy: Most commonly done for UC and Crohn's disease (20-40 years age group)
  - Colostomy: Most commonly done for colorectal cancer (60-80 years age group)
- Incidence of surgery (revision) to correct stoma complications:
  - Ileostomy: 10% (most commonly done for Crohn's disease)
  - Sigmoid colostomy: 7%
- Classification of stomas:
  1. According to duration:
     a. Temporary
     b. Permanent
  2. According to type of surgery:
     a. Elective
     b. Emergency
  3. According to function:
     a. Diverting
     b. Decompressing
  4. According to morphology:
     a. End stomas
     b. Loop stomas
     c. Double barrel stomas
     d. Spectacle stomas

5. According to level with skin:
    a. Pouting stomas
    b. Flush stomas
6. According to organ involved:
    a. Sigmoidostomy
    b. Colostomy
    c. Ileostomy
    d. Jejunostomy, etc.

❖ Diversion means only redirection of feces by a route other than its normal path.

  Decompression involves depressurising the intestine as well as diversion.

❖ For complete diversion, end stomas are best (but since they are permanent, loop stomas are preferred).

Concept of stoma:

- In LOOP STOMA, the bowel is incompletely separated and brought out through a single opening on anterior abdominal wall.
- In END STOMA, the bowel is completely separated and brought out separately (such that the cut surface of bowel attaches on the abdominal surface) on the abdominal wall. Sometimes, the distal segment is completely excised (e.g. APR for rectal cancers), here there is no distal segment, and only the proximal bowel has end stoma. When the distal bowel is brought out separately (e.g. after resection of an ischemic bowel segment) it is referred to as MUCOUS FISTULA.
- If a narrow patch of skin exists in between the two openings it is called SPECTACLE stoma.
- If both the separated bowel are brought out through same opening on the abdominal wall, it is called DOUBLE BARREL stoma.
- If the distal bowel exists, but it is closed and placed within the abdomen (due to short mesentery), it is called HARTMANN'S POUCH, and the procedure is HARTMANN'S procedure.
- Since we maintain the continuity of bowel in loop stomas, it is employed as a TEMPORARY stoma that Is reversed when indicated.
- END stoma can be either temporary or permanent, although they are more commonly employed as permanent stomas.

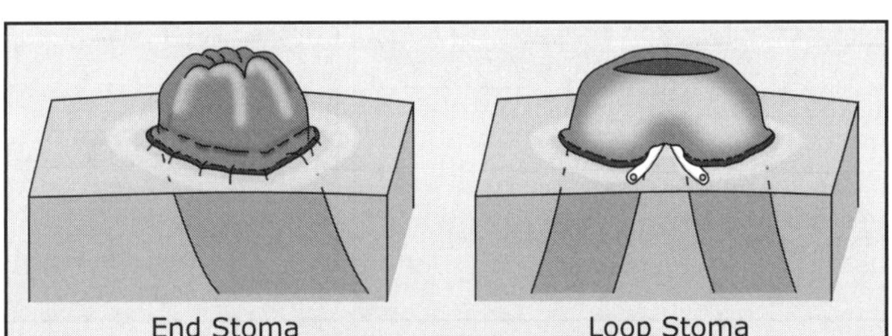

Fig. 20.3: End stoma and loop stoma

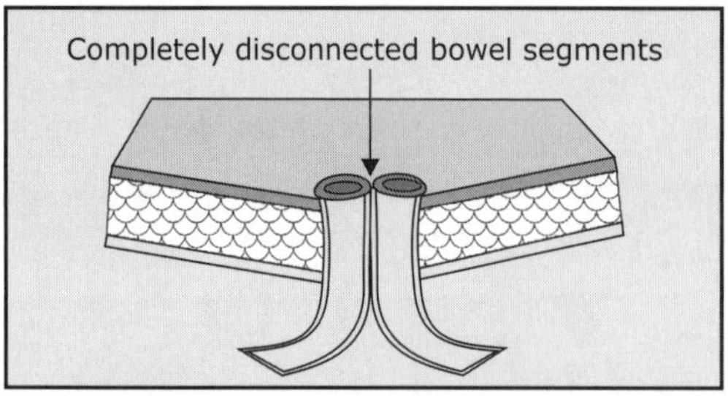

Fig. 20.4: Double barrel stoma

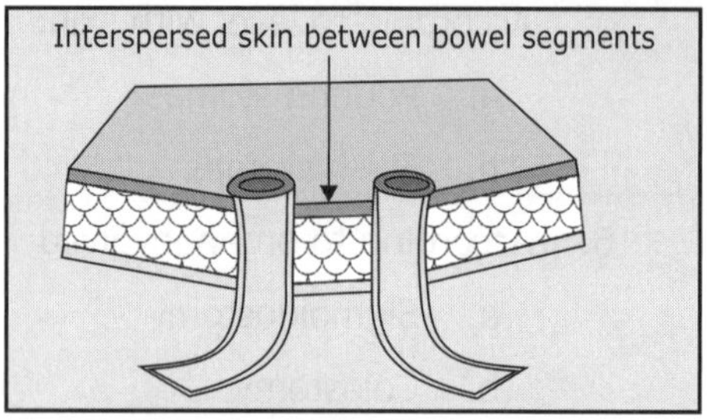

Fig. 20.5: Spectacle stoma

- Pouting : Means everting the edges 1 cm from the skin surface before suturing (this is done to minimize the seepage of liquids in subcutaneous planes and also to prevent maceration of surrounding skin)

  Flush: Means suturing the edges in-line with the skin surface

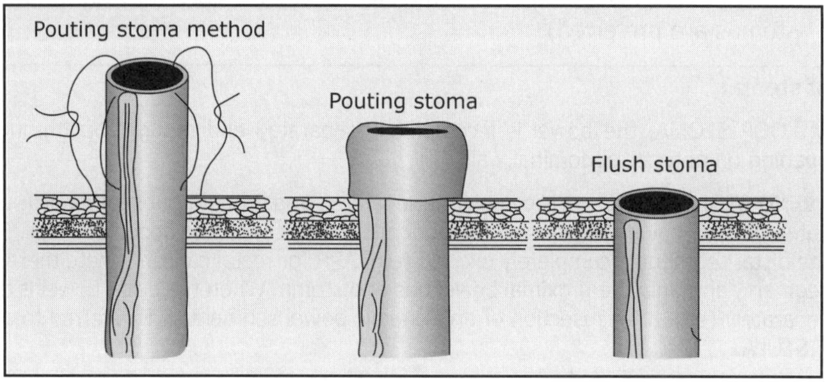

Fig. 20.6: Pouting vs. flush stoma

Loop-end stoma: It is like an end stoma where instead of bringing the blind end out, loop is opened on the skin. This is done in cases of short mesentery e.g., infection, radiation.

End-loop stoma (Rodless stoma): It is a like a loop stoma with the distal opening closed partially in the subfascial plane giving two openings on the skin such that opening of distal loop is
very small. Advantage over double barrel stoma is that it ensures complete diversion (due to narrow opening of distal bowel loop).

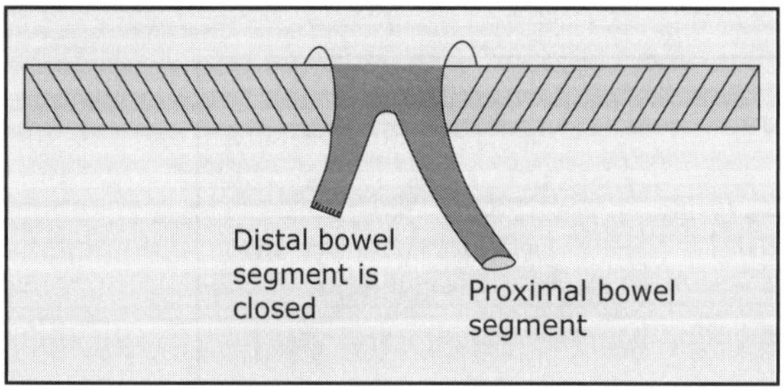

Fig. 20.7: Loop end stoma

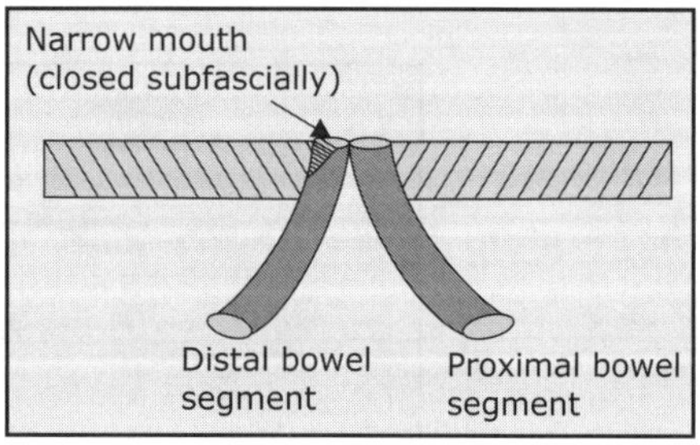

Fig. 20.8: End loop stoma

- Complications of stoma:
    1. Common to both:
        a. Mucosa:
            - Dryness
            - edema
            - Bleeding
            - Infection: Diarrhea
        b. Wall of stoma:
            - Stenosis/stricture
            - Constipation
            - Gangrene
            - Prolapse
            - Retraction
            - Herniation
            - Perforation
        c. Anastomosis with skin:
            - Stitch infection
            - Stitch abscess
        d. Surrounding skin:
            - Excoriation
            - Parastomal abscess formation
            - Fistulae adjacent to stoma site (due to recurrence of Crohn's disease)
            - Pseudoepitheliomatous hyperplasia at mucocutaneous borders (due to chronic malfitting appliance)
            - Varices in patient with portal hypertension (stoma is a site of portosystemic shunt)
    2. Commoner to ileostomy:
        a. Electrolyte disturbances
        b. Dehydration
        c. Subcutaneous abscess (liquid contents easily seep through subcutaneous planes and get infected)
        d. Skin excoriation/chemical dermatitis (due to liquid nature of contents)

e. Deficiencies:

- Vitamin B_{12} (since it is absorbed in terminal ileum)
- Fat-soluble vitamins (since enterohepatic circulation of bile is affected)
- Iron

3. Commoner to colostomy:
   a. Parastomal hernias
   b. Prolapse
   c. Gangrene
   d. Stricture

> More PROXIMAL is the stoma, more is the LIQUID nature of its contents, more are the chances of electrolyte imbalances, dehydration, skin excoriation, and subcutaneous abscess.

❖ According to output, enterocutaneous fistulas are classified as (note that these terminologies are not applicable for stoma):

- Low-output fistulas: Output < 200 mL/day
- Medium-output fistulas: Output of 200-500 mL/day
- High-output fistulas: Output > 500 mL/day

❖ Prolapse:

- Bowel protrudes through the stomal opening at abnormal lengths
- More common in loop colostomies

❖ Retraction:

- Stoma lies flush with or below the skin surface in supine (or even standing) position
- Can occur due to inappropriate site selection or improper suturing of stoma to rectus sheath
- More common with ileostomies

❖ Parastomal hernias:

- Definition: Incisional hernia at the site of stoma
- More common in end colostomies
- Are of four types (Devlin's classification):
  1. Subcutaneous
  2. Interstitial
  3. Perstomal
  4. Intrastomal

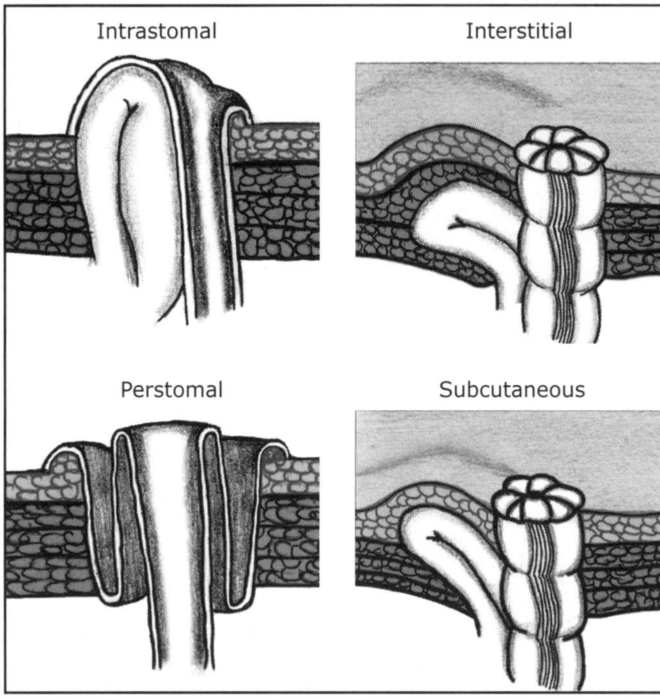

Fig. 20.9: Devlin's types of parastomal hernia

- Colostomy:
  - Most common indication: Carcinoma of the rectum
  - Why not opened in perineum: Difficult to take care of stoma
  - Types:

Colostomy
- By anatomic location
  1. Sigmoid colostomy
  2. Descending colostomy
  3. Transverse colostomy
  4. Cecostomy
- By function
  - Decompressing
    1. Blow hole cecostomy
    2. Tube cecostomy
    3. Loop transverse colostomy
  - Diverting
    - Complete diversion → End stomas
    - Near complete diversion → Loop stomas

- Physiology of colon:

Right colon	Left colon
Absorbs water	Acts as a conduit and reservoir of feces
Has irregular peristaltic contractions	Has few mass peristaltic motions
So has more liquid contents in stoma bag	So has more solid contents in stoma bag + output can be regulated by stomal irrigation

- Indications of colostomy:
  1. Decompressing (to overcome distal obstruction):
     a. Carcinoma of the rectum/colon
     b. Hirschsprung's disease
     c. Trauma
     d. Stricture
  2. Diverting:
     a. To protect distal anastomosis:
        - Anterior resection (for carcinoma rectum)
        - Colonic injury
     b. To provide rest to bowel:
        - Diverticulitis
        - Ischemic colitis
     c. To serve the function of incontinent anus:
        - APR (for carcinoma of the rectum)
        - Post-anal surgeries
        - Post-trauma

• Ileostomy:
  - Indications of ileostomy:
    1. Decompressing (to overcome distal obstruction):
       a. Distal carcinoma
       b. Stricture
    2. Diverting:
       a. To protect distal anastomosis:
          - Right hemicolectomy

b. To provide rest to bowel:
   - Ulcerative colitis
   - Crohn's disease
   - Diverticulitis
   - Ischemic colitis

c. To serve the function of incontinent anus:
   - Total proctocolectomy (TPC) for intractable UC or familial adenoma polyposis

- Loop ileostomy is generally done 30 cm proximal to ileocecal valve (to prevent the effect of reverse flow of contents in colon if ileocecal valve is incompetent)
- End ileostomy is called as BROOKE'S ILEOSTOMY

• Difference between ileostomy and colostomy:

	Ileostomy	**Colostomy**
Common site(s)	RIF	LIF, LHC, RHC
	Less common	More common
Mucosa	Pink and circular mucosal folds (valves of Kerckring)	Pale and featureless
Contents	Liquid Greenish	Semisolid to solid Yellowish
Frequency	More	Less
Common complications	Skin excoriation, dehydration, vitamin deficiencies	Prolapse and parastomal hernias

Types of cecostomy:
- Blow hole cecostomy: Done in colonic pseudo-obstruction
- Tube cecostomy: Done in recurrent ileocecal volvulus

MANAGEMENT

• Management of stoma includes:
1. Immediate care
2. Long-term management
3. Management of complications

- Immediate care:
  - Nil per oral
  - Analgesics
  - Antibiotics
  - IV fluids
  - Chart TPR-BP, input-output, urine output
  - RT output (if nasogastric tube is put)
  - When peristalsis return and flatus is passed, start sips of water, gradually soft diet
  - Keep a watch on stoma (color and output)

- Long-term management:
  - Diet: High-fibre diet with avoidance of gas-forming foods
  - Colostomy irrigation for training of bowel
  - Charcoal filter in appliance for absorbing gas
  - Glycerine application on mucosa, if edematous
    Vaseline application on mucosa, if dry
  - Skin protectives
  - Avoid lifting heavy weights
  - Rehabilitation: Physical, social, occupational

- Management of complications:
  1. Skin excoriations:
     - Change in the pouching system
     - Skin protectives
  2. Diarrhea:
     - Adequate diet
     - Diphenoxylate, loperamide
     - Antibiotics (if infective)
  3. Parastomal hernia:
     - Asymptomatic: Observe
     - Symptomatic: Relocation or repair
  4. Stomal stricture:
     - At skin level: Local repair
     - If involves longer segment: Revision of stoma

5. Stomal necrosis:
   - Limited to area of stoma anterior to fascia: Observe (stoma revision electively at a later date)
   - If extends into peritoneal cavity: Immediate exploration and recreation of stoma
6. Stomal prolapse:
   - If possible, treat primary disease and restore intestinal continuity
   - If not possible → convert loop stoma to end stoma
7. Retraction:
   - Convex barriers, ostomy belt
   - Refashioning
8. Stoma perforation:
   - Surgical emergency → emergency laparotomy with reconstruction of stoma

- Management of high-output stoma:
  - For output > 1 L/day, appropriate IV fluids have to be started
  - Restricting the patient's oral hypotonic fluids (e.g., water, tea, etc.) to 500 mL/day and replacing further fluid needs with ORS helps to decrease stomal ouptut
  - Use of low-fibre diet
  - Proton-pump inhibitors (PPIs)
  - Antimotility drugs like loperamide can be used

- Location of stoma:
  - Ideally to be marked PREOPERATIVELY
  - Depends on the following factors:
    1. Ability of the patient to take care of stoma (should be easily visualized by and accessible to the patient)
    2. Anatomic location of the organ
  - Avoid deep folds of fat, scars, bony prominences
  - Site chosen by evaluating the patient in standing + sitting + supine positions
  - Stoma faceplate is applied to abdominal wall (and stoma site marked)
  - Preferred sites:
    1. Sigmoid or descending colostomy:
       i. Average person: Left-lower quadrant
       ii. Obese person: Left-upper quadrant

2. Distal transverse colostomy: Left-upper quadrant
3. Ileostomy: Right-lower quadrant

> Stoma is generally taken out through rectus muscle because it is easy to suture the walls of stoma to rectus sheath for support (to prevent retraction) and NOT because muscle acts as sphincter.

- Colostomy irrigation:
  - Principle: Distal colon exhibits FEW MASS peristaltic motions each day, which can be stimulated by distension of intestine
    ↓
    Colon can be trained to evacuate daily at the same time
  - Procedure:
    Started before 30 days post-operatively (generally 10th day)
    ↓
    Done in morning (at same time every day)
    ↓
    Cone tip instrument that snugly fits into stoma
    ↓
    Instillation of 500-1000 mL water
    ↓
    Stoma bag applied again
    ↓
    Colon evacuates after 30-60 minutes
  - It takes around 6 weeks for the colon to get adapted
  - Advantages:
    1. Absence of need for wearing of appliance at all times
    2. Decrease in uncontrolled passage of stools and gas
    3. Regulated lifestyle
  - Disadvantages:
    1. Time consuming
    2. Sometimes discomfortable due to distension of colon
    3. Theoretical risk of perforation
    4. Absorption of water might be significant
  - Contraindications:
    1. Irritable bowel syndrome
    2. Proximal colostomies

- Steps of stoma creation: Loop ileostomy

Possible stomal site marked preoperatively

↓

Laparotomy done and pathology tackled

↓

Island of skin and subcutaneous tissue of approximate size of loop is cut

↓

Cruciate incision (X) on rectus sheath is made to create four flaps

↓

Muscle is split and peritoneum opened

↓

Loop of intestine to be brought out as stoma is identified

↓

Small window in the mesentery is made to pass a glass rod or infant feeding tube (to suspend the loop out of peritoneal cavity as a sling)

↓

Loop of intestine brought out

↓

Seromuscular stitches taken to fix the loop to four flaps (prevents prolapse, retraction and parastomal hernias)

↓

Enterotomy done (small incision should be perpendicular to the length of bowel while large incision can be parallel or perpendicular; this eases pouting)

↓

Pouting done (edges everted) (if done correctly, posterior wall should bulge)

↓

Edges sutured to skin (maturation of stoma)

Note that enterotomy is a small incision to be done only on anterior wall of loop (i.e. one facing the surgeon or the antimesenteric border) and not circumferential.

Distal bowel loop has to be placed ABOVE the proximal bowel loop (to avoid passage of contents from proximal to distal bowel).

MATURATION of stoma means suturing of stoma to skin (It has nothing to do with the duration of stoma or amount or type of contents passed.)

- Closure of stoma:
  - When to do: After the pathology for which stoma was done is eliminated (can be as early as 10 weeks)
  - Prerequisites:
    1. Disease for which stoma was made should be resolved
    2. Anal sphincter should be competent (if incompetent, stoma cannot be closed), checked by:
       i. Manometric studies
       ii. Electromyographic studies
       iii. Enema method
    3. Distal bowel should be patent, checked by:
       i. Distal loopogram: Barium examination
       ii. Colonoscopy from anus or stomal opening
  - Methods:
    1. Intraperitoneal
    2. Extraperitoneal (no longer done)
  - Steps (of intraperitoneal technique):

All prerequisites fulfilled

↓

Circumferential incision taken all around stoma including small rim of skin

↓

Incision deepened till peritoneal cavity is entered

↓

Bowel loops brought out through the incision

↓

Serosal surface freshened (cleared of skin and fibrofatty tissue rim)

↓

Bowel examined thoroughly

↓

If perfectly healthy, loops are anastomosed
If compromised, resection and anastomosis is done

↓

Bowel returned to peritoneal cavity

↓

Abdomen closed

21
Trauma

- Always say/write this first:

  As per Advanced Trauma Life Support (ATLS) guidelines by American College of Surgeons (ACS), management of trauma consists of:

  Primary survey → secondary survey → definitive care

PRIMARY SURVEY

- Primary survey consists of following steps:
  - A → Airway with cervical spine immobilization
  - B → Breathing
  - C → Circulation
  - D → Disability (neurological)
  - E → Exposure
  - F → FAST
- Airway assessment and management protocol:

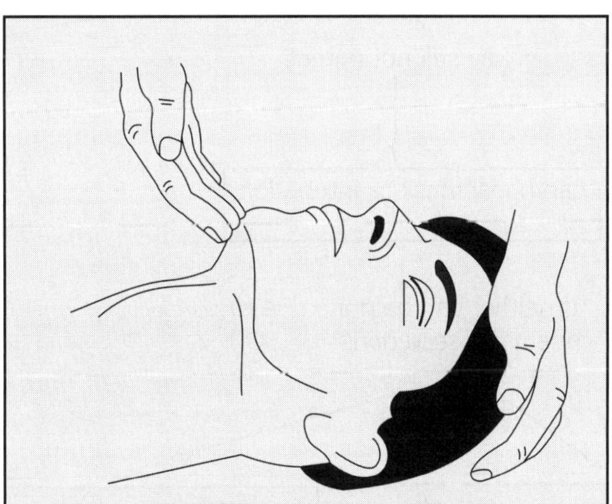

Fig. 21.1: Head tilt-chin lift maneuver

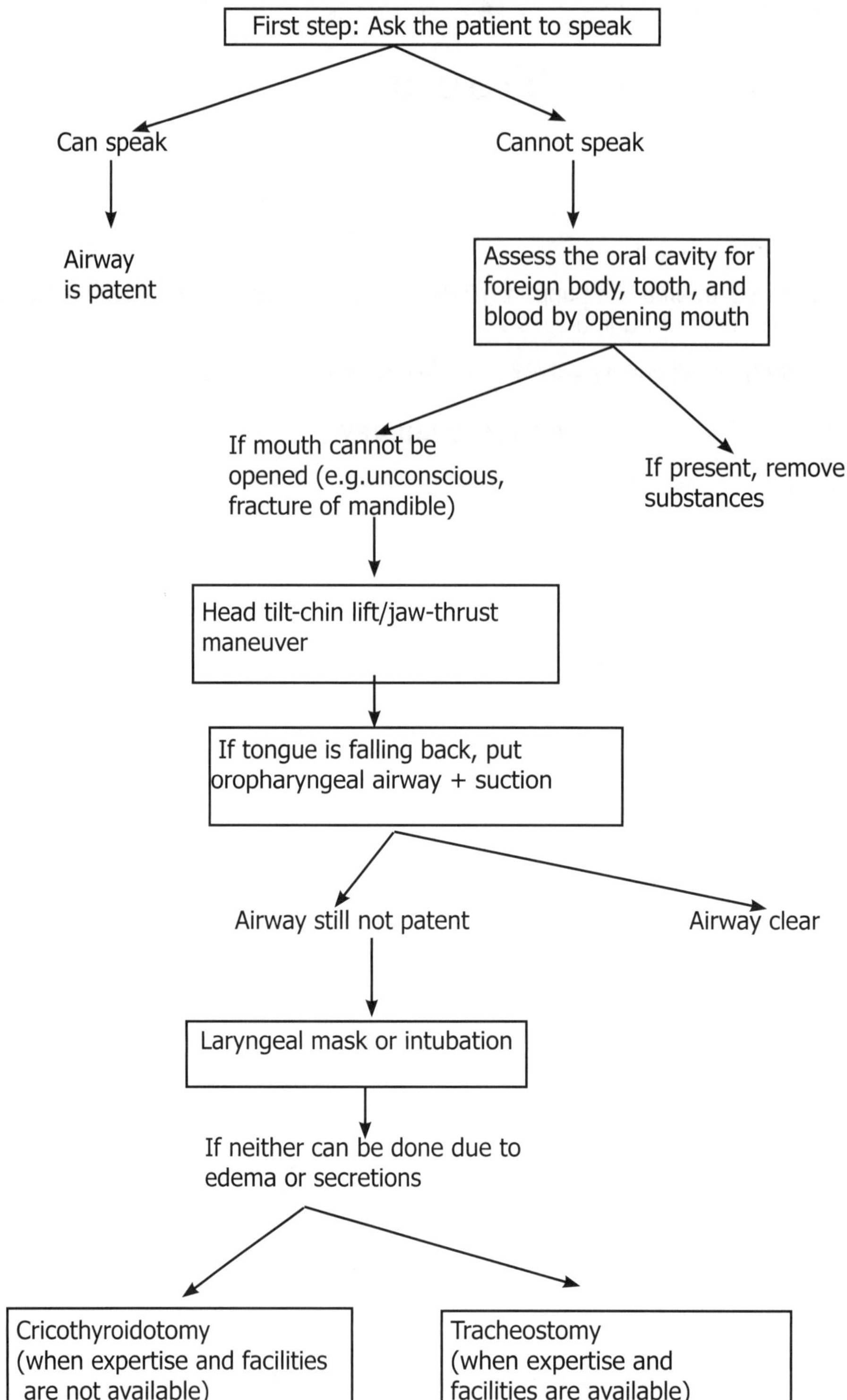
First step: Ask the patient to speak
Can speak
Cannot speak
Airway is patent
Assess the oral cavity for foreign body, tooth, and blood by opening mouth
If mouth cannot be opened (e.g.unconscious, fracture of mandible)
If present, remove substances
Head tilt-chin lift/jaw-thrust maneuver
If tongue is falling back, put oropharyngeal airway + suction
Airway still not patent
Airway clear
Laryngeal mask or intubation
If neither can be done due to edema or secretions
Cricothyroidotomy (when expertise and facilities are not available)
Tracheostomy (when expertise and facilities are available)

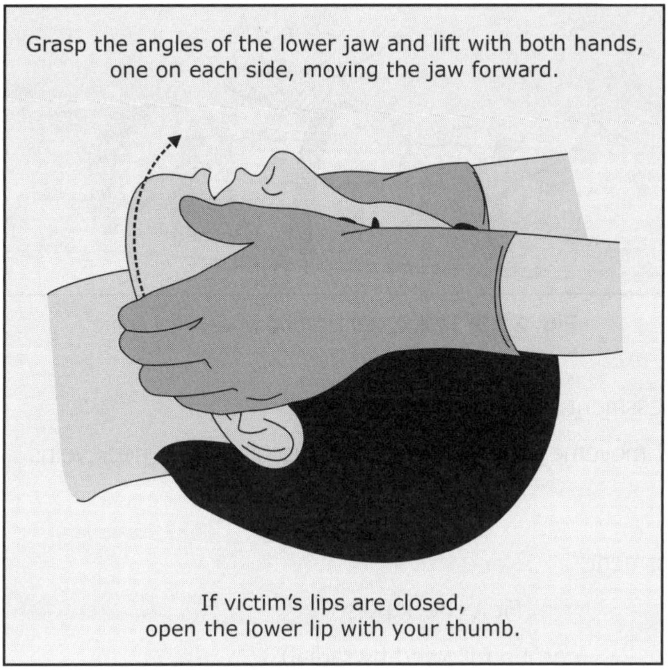

Fig. 21.2: Jaw thrust maneuver

- If cervical spine injury is evident/suspected, do not perform head tilt-chin lift maneuver; instead, do a jaw-thrust maneuver
- Cricothyroidotomy:
    1. Easy bedside procedure, less risk of other injuries
    2. Can be either needle or tube cricothyroidotomy
    3. Less preferred than tracheostomy due to risk of subglottic stenosis if kept for long term
- Cervical spine immobilization:

By cervical collar (hard)

↓

If not available

↓

In-line stabilization of cervical spine

(Keep patient on hard board and strap shoulders and head to it.)

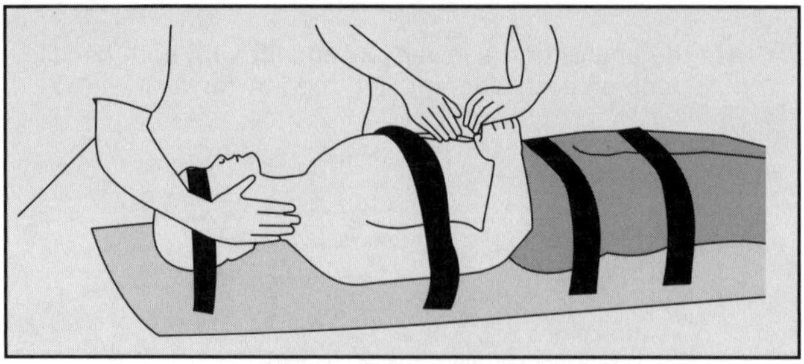

Fig. 21.3: In line stabilisation of cervical spine

- Breathing assessment:

  Observe chest movements + percussion + auscultation + neck veins

- Circulation:
  - Assessment:

    First check pulse

    (carotid followed by radial)

    ↓

    then JVP

  - Rough estimate of blood pressure from pulse:
    1. Carotid palpable: SBP is at least 40-60 mm of Hg
    2. Femoral palpable: SBP is at least 60-80 mm Hg
    3. Radial palpable: SBP is at least 80-100 mm Hg
  - Management:

    First secure two large bore i.v. lines

    ↓

    Start i.v. fluids (crystalloids)

    (RESUSCITATION FLUID OF CHOICE is Ringer's lactate [RL], since it closely resembles plasma.)

- Disability (neurological):
  - Assessed by Glasgow coma scale (GCS) score (Refer to 'consciousness' in Chapter 2 in Section I for details)
  - Score < 8: Intubate

- Exposure:
  - Undress whole body and examine for
    1. Any ongoing hemorrhage: Stop by catch, clamp, crush, ligate, cautery, pack, pressure, pray
    2. Obvious fractures: Assessed by swelling, crepitus, tenderness or restricted movements (If fractured: Splint it in same position)
    3. Contusions over dangerous sites: Head, chest, abdomen, urethra
    4. P/R examination: For injuries and blood per rectum
  - All above things should be looked for both anteriorly and posteriorly (for examining posterior parts, patient should be put in prone position by log-roll maneuver)

- FAST (Focussed assessment by sonography in trauma):
  - Immediate USG scan done to assess abdominal trauma
  - It visualizes four sites:
    1. Epigastrium: Cardiac tamponade
    2. Left hypochondrium: Blood, splenic injury
    3. Right hypochondrium: Blood, hepatic injury
    4. Pelvis: Free fluid in pelvis

SECONDARY SURVEY

- Elicit history from patients and/or relatives: **AMPLE** history in trauma

  A : Allergy

  M : Medications

  P : Past history

  L : Last meal

  E : Events leading to trauma

- Head to toe examination

DEFINITIVE CARE

- Definitive care is according to the trauma incurred (e.g. head injury with SDH, chest injury with hemothorax, abdominal trauma with injuries to visceral organs, etc.)